FEELINGS MATERIALIZED

SPEKTRUM: Publications of the German Studies Association
Series editor: David M. Luebke, University of Oregon

Published under the auspices of the German Studies Association, *Spektrum* offers current perspectives on culture, society, and political life in the German-speaking lands of central Europe—Austria, Switzerland, and the Federal Republic—from the late Middle Ages to the present day. Its titles and themes reflect the composition of the GSA and the work of its members within and across the disciplines to which they belong—literary criticism, history, cultural studies, political science, and anthropology.

Recent volumes:

Volume 21
Feelings Materialized
Emotions, Bodies, and Things in Germany, 1500–1950
Edited by Derek Hillard, Heikki Lempa, and Russell Spinney

Volume 20
Names and Naming in Early Modern Germany
Edited by Marjorie Elizabeth Plummer and Joel F. Harrington

Volume 19
Views of Violence
Representing the Second World War in German and European Museums and Memorials
Edited by Jörg Echternkamp and Stephan Jaeger

Volume 18
Dreams of Germany
Musical Imaginaries from the Concert Hall to the Dance Floor
Edited by Neil Gregor and Thomas Irvine

Volume 17
Money in the German-Speaking Lands
Edited by Mary Lindemann and Jared Poley

Volume 16
Archeologies of Confession
Writing the German Reformation, 1517–2017
Edited by Carina L. Johnson, David M. Luebke, Marjorie Elizabeth Plummer, and Jesse Spohnholz

Volume 15
Ruptures in the Everyday
Views of Modern Germany from the Ground
Andrew Stuart Bergerson, Leonard Schmieding, et al.

Volume 14
Reluctant Skeptic
Siegfried Kracauer and the Crises of Weimar Culture
Harry T. Craver

Volume 13
Migrations in the German Lands, 1500–2000
Edited by Jason Coy, Jared Poley, and Alexander Schunka

Volume 12
The Total Work of Art
Foundations, Articulations, Inspirations
Edited by David Imhoof, Margaret Eleanor Menninger, and Anthony J. Steinhoff

For a full volume listing, please see the series page on our website:
http://berghahnbooks.com/series/spektrum

Feelings Materialized

Emotions, Bodies, and Things in Germany, 1500–1950

Edited by Derek Hillard, Heikki Lempa, and Russell Spinney

First published in 2020 by
Berghahn Books
www.berghahnbooks.com

© 2020, 2025 Derek Hillard, Heikki Lempa, and Russell Spinney
First paperback edition published in 2025

All rights reserved. Except for the quotation of short passages
for the purposes of criticism and review, no part of this book
may be reproduced in any form or by any means, electronic or
mechanical, including photocopying, recording, or any information
storage and retrieval system now known or to be invented,
without written permission of the publisher.

Library of Congress Cataloging-in-Publication Data
Names: Hillard, Derek, 1965- editor.
Title: Feelings materialized : emotions, bodies, and things in Germany,
　1500-1950 / edited by Derek Hillard, Heikki Lempa, and Russell Spinney.
Description: New York : Berghahn Books, 2020. | Series: Spektrum:
　publications of the German Studies Association ; volume 21 | Includes
　bibliographical references and index.
Identifiers: LCCN 2019042447 (print) | LCCN 2019042448 (ebook) | ISBN
　9781789205510 (hardback) | ISBN 9781789205527 (ebook)
Subjects: LCSH: Emotions--History. | Social psychology--Germany--History.
Classification: LCC BF511 .F44 2020 (print) | LCC BF511 (ebook) | DDC
　152.40943/0903--dc23
LC record available at https://lccn.loc.gov/2019042447
LC ebook record available at https://lccn.loc.gov/2019042448

British Library Cataloguing in Publication Data
A catalogue record for this book is available from the British Library

EU GPSR Authorized Representative
LOGOS EUROPE, 9 rue Nicolas Poussin, 17000, LA ROCHELLE, France
Email: Contact@logoseurope.eu

ISBN 978-1-78920-551-0 hardback
ISBN 978-1-83695-067-7 paperback
ISBN 978-1-83695-212-1 epub
ISBN 978-1-78920-552-7 web pdf

https://doi.org/10.3167/9781789205510

CONTENTS

List of Illustrations — vii

Acknowledgments — ix

Introduction — 1
    Derek Hillard, Heikki Lempa, and Russell Spinney

Part I. Emotions and Bodies

Chapter 1. Mesmerizing Encounters: Affect and Animal Magnetism — 25
    Sara Luly

Chapter 2. Emotional Contagions: Franz Liszt and the Materiality of Celebrity Culture in the 1830s and 1840s — 41
    Hannu Salmi

Chapter 3. Reading Embodied Emotions in Rilke's *Die Aufzeichnungen des Malte Laurids Brigge* — 62
    Derek Hillard

Chapter 4. Embodied Emotions: On the Communist Habitus of Agitprop — 77
    Sabine Hake

Chapter 5. A Skin of Hatred: How Bodies Are Involved in the Memory of Emotions and Anti-Semitic Practice of the Weimar Republic — 95
    Russell Spinney

Part II. Emotions, Spaces, and Material Interests

Chapter 6. Early Modern Embodiments of Laughter: The Journal of Felix Platter — 115
    Joy Wiltenburg

Chapter 7. Beyond Interiority: Shame and Empathy in Karl Philipp Moritz's *Anton Reiser* — 127
    Christian Sieg

Chapter 8. Gambling and Emotion 142
   Jared Poley

Chapter 9. Emotions and Material Interests in the Sales Talk of
   German Spa Guides, 1830–1900 155
   Heikki Lempa

Part III. Emotions and Things

Chapter 10. The Paper Bird: Emotions and Things in the Pedagogy of
   Johann Heinrich Pestalozzi and Friedrich Fröbel 171
   Ann Taylor Allen

Chapter 11. Reading Early German Photographs for Histories of
   Emotion 187
   Sarah L. Leonard

Chapter 12. The Emotional Language of Flowers 202
   Ute Frevert

Chapter 13. Banners and Flags, Mottoes, *Lieder*: German Choral
   Societies and Material Culture, 1871–1918 222
   Ruth Dewhurst

Chapter 14. Corporeality, Materiality, and Unnamed Emotions in
   Rilke's *Dinggedichte* 235
   Lorna Martens

Chapter 15. Inscribing Grief: Private Practices of Bereavement in
   Wartime Germany 252
   Erika Quinn

Index 269

ILLUSTRATIONS

Figure 2.1. Liszt playing the *Grand galop chromatique* (1843). Image: Bibliothèque nationale et universitaire de Strasbourg, NIM35493, http://catalogue.bnf.fr/ark:/12148/cb41932328g. Public domain.   45

Figure 2.2. The sites of Franz Liszt's concerts, 1839–1847. The size of the ballot refers to the frequency of concerts during the time span. Image: Hannu Salmi.   47

Figure 2.3. Franz Liszt at the Singakademie in Berlin (1847). Image: Lebrecht Music & Arts/Alamy Stock Photo.   48

Figure 4.1. Conrad Felixmüller, *Der Agitator: Otto Rühle spricht/ The Agitator: Otto Rühle Speaks* (1920), oil on canvas, Nationalgalerie Berlin, 1946 reproduction. Copyright 2017 Artists Rights Society (ARS), New York/VG Bild-Kunst Bonn.   81

Figure 4.2. Curt Querner, *Agitator* (1930), oil on canvas, Nationalgalerie Berlin. Copyright 2017 Artists Rights Society (ARS), New York/VG Bild-Kunst Bonn.   82

Figure 4.3. Magnus Zeller, *Agitator/Volksredner* (1920), oil on canvas, Los Angeles County Museum of Art (LACMA). Copyright 2017 Artists Rights Society (ARS), New York/VG Bild-Kunst Bonn.   84

Figure 4.4. Jean Weidt, *Der Arbeiter/The Worker* (1925), Sammlung Weidt. With permission of Universitätsbibliothek Leipzig, Tanzarchiv, Slg. Weidt.   86

Figure 4.5. Jo Mihaly, *Arbeiter/Worker* from *Feierliche Tänze*, c. 1926. Photo: Atelier Stone. With permission of Deutsches Tanzarchiv Köln.   87

Figure 11.1. Portrait of government administrator Otto Weise by Bertha Beckmann, Daguerreotype, 1843. From the collection of the Stadtgeschichtliches Museum Leipzig.   188

Figure 11.2. Portrait of singer and actress Auguste Götze by Bertha Wehnert-Beckmann, Daguerreotype, c. 1856–65. From the collection of the Stadtgeschichtliches Museum Leipzig.   193

Figure 11.3. Portrait of an unknown family by Bertha Wehnert-Beckmann, Daguerreotype, c. 1845–50. From the collection of the Stadtgeschichtliches Museum Leipzig. 196

Figure 11.4. Portrait of six men, a boy, and a small child by Bertha Wehnert-Beckmann, albumen print, c. 1855. From the collection of the Stadtgeschichtliches Museum Leipzig. 197

ACKNOWLEDGMENTS

This book has a long history that is intimately intertwined with the history of emotion studies at the German Studies Association (GSA). As we argue in this book, the history of the study of emotions in German culture is much older than usually assumed. It did not start with this book or with the projects that eventually became this book. When Russell Spinney convened a roundtable on Emotions in Modern Germany at the GSA meeting in Louisville 2011, emotion studies took a leap forward in the GSA. It is here that the history of this book starts. Inspired by the success of the roundtable, we—Russell Spinney, Derek Hillard, and Heikki Lempa—organized a series of panels at the following GSA meeting in Milwaukee. The crucial logistical and intellectual support came from Andrew Bergerson, who as a codirector of the Alltag Network offered his support. The roots of this project are thereby—at least for the two historians among the editors, Spinney and Lempa—in the German *Alltagsgeschichte* (the history of everyday life). These roots were clearly visible at the GSA meeting in Denver 2013 when the editors convened a seminar on the study of emotions. Among its thirty-one participants, there was a significant presence of *Alltagsgeschichte*. Especially notable was the participation of Alf Lüdtke, a leading historian of everyday life. Alongside historians, the seminar included literary scholars and philosophers whose fields of expertise spanned from the sixteenth into the twenty-first centuries. This interdisciplinary and *longue durée* approach became an integral part of Emotion Studies Network, which saw daylight at the GSA meeting in Kansas City 2014. A roundtable on "The Body and Emotions, 1500–1999" was another clear expression of this approach. In 2015, the Emotion Studies Network continued this approach by organizing a series of panels entitled "The Corporeality and Materiality of Emotions." The need for the study of corporeal and material aspects of emotions in German culture thus became clear, especially at the roundtable discussion. Many of the participants of that roundtable as well as panels and seminars throughout these years are also contributors to this volume. In the spring of 2016, the editors of this volume sent out a call for papers for a new GSA seminar, "The Materiality and Corporeality of Emotions in German Culture since 1500." Many of the contributors to this volume participated in that seminar in San Diego in 2016. Although this volume is not a product of a conference or even a series of conferences, we are thankful to the GSA for providing such a stimulating environment to incubate our project.

As we were preparing the book for publication, several colleagues provided tremendous help. As the editor of the Spektrum series, David Luebke guided the book project with wisdom and patience. From Berghahn Books, Chris Chappell and, especially in the last phase, Mykelin Higham and Caroline Kuhtz were kind, patient, efficient, and professional to bring this project to its conclusion. Finally, we would like to thank all our contributors for their work on this project in many different settings.

Derek Hillard
Heikki Lempa
Russell Spinney

~: INTRODUCTION :~

DEREK HILLARD, HEIKKI LEMPA, AND RUSSELL SPINNEY

The scholarship on emotions has focused on how emotions are produced—in and through words or neurological processes—but only rarely asked how they can be perceived. The studies in this book focus on both the production and the perception of emotions, and by doing so they investigate the materiality and corporeality of emotions, be it in our bodily behavior and gestures, the objects that endear us, or the material conditions that impose on us certain social relationships with emotional valence. This approach deviates from the dominant understanding and study of emotions, which has long based itself on the concept of interiority.

In the eighteenth century, the concept of interiority changed the ways in which emotions were performed and experienced. In the Germanic world, this emerging culture, *Innerlichkeit* (interiority), placed emotions, affects, and passions in the interior of the self and prior to actions, behavior, and expressions. As Rüdiger Campe and Julia Weber have recently shown, the concept of *Innerlichkeit* was a long time in the making. Present already in the Stoics, Medieval Jewish religion, and Christian mysticism, and shaped by Luther in his idea of an inner man in the early sixteenth century, it gained crucial momentum in Christian piety in the late seventeenth century and broke into broadly defined cultural and social patterns in the late eighteenth century. This model of emotions has firmly retained its normative and compelling power into the late twentieth century.[1] It is difficult, perhaps impossible, to give a definitive explanation of the power of *Innerlichkeit* for the understanding and performance of emotions in the Germanic world and beyond. But it undoubtedly made possible conceptual solutions that aimed at bridging what was perceived as the gap between internally experienced emotions and their external expressions. At the same time, interiority functioned as the privileged, noble, and potentially free space compared with the messy world of bodies and things. This model has continued to inform investigations centered on words and languages of emotions, and it also can be seen in cultural studies inspired by neuroscience that try to locate the place where emotions emerge firmly in the interior of the human body and psyche.

There is an increasing body of scholarship, informed by modern psychology and neuroscience, focusing on what goes on inside the naturally hardwired human brain, and specific parts of the brain like the amygdala, most clearly expressed in human facial expressions. Although this "bio-revolution" can be helpful in understanding neurological, physiological, and endocrinal aspects of emotions, even in different historical contexts, it also has its limitations.[2] As Barbara Rosenwein has argued, neuroscience has been able to demonstrate that our physiological system has *affective potential*. But it cannot delineate the meanings of emotions, present or past.[3] And that is the main focus of historical and cultural studies—to reconstruct the meaning of historical experiences, expressions, and their changes. At its best, historical studies of the rise of scientific knowledge show how such knowledge has influenced individuals, societies, and nations to understand their feelings, resulting actions, and their employment in practices of everyday life. Late nineteenth-century knowledge about the nervous system, for example, could influence how people attempted to shape how they should feel. To conceive of feelings in terms of nerves—be it in diaries or public arenas—and if possible show that one was calm, cool, and collected with nerves of steel could be a major focus.[4] But the horizon that purely scientific approaches yield is too narrow to capture the broader societal—and personal—meanings of emotions.

This book does not limit itself to scientific frameworks. It understands the "bodiliness" and "thingliness" of emotions not in terms of an isolated interiority but as relational and embedded in social spaces and embodied practices. Inspired by a range of historical emotions that is broader than what interiority or traditional, cognitive understandings permit, it aims to rethink the ways in which bodies and things give rise to and shape emotions. To understand and accept the variety of disciplinary definitions of emotions, we want to reach back to the intellectual traditions that gave rise to that very variety. Although in the current parlance, "affect" is a term frequently used in literary studies and "theory" (and those working on the eighteenth century often use "sentiments" or "passions"), whereas historians prefer words such as "emotion" and "feeling," historically these concepts share common roots.[5] With regards to our characterization of "emotion," our approach is, to borrow a distinction from linguistics, descriptive, or observational, rather than definitional or prescriptive. All these words refer to those habits and perceptions of the mind and the body that drive or situate us rather than we controlling them.

Emotions, sentiments, passions, and affects have a long-lasting presence in German cultural and historical studies. The *locus communis* of the emotion discourse has been rhetoric. Not only the art of persuasion in forensic speech but also the realms of artistic expression derive their infatuation with emotions from rhetoric. In their classical configurations, painting, poetry, theater, dance, and even music—a German composer and theorist Johann Mattheson (1681–1764) called it *Klangrede*—were seen as rhetorical techniques of evoking and expressing emotions.[6] Even the study of textual meaning, hermeneutics, went through a rhetorical turn in the beginning of the eighteenth century when, among others, the German pietist theologian August Herrmann Francke claimed that the understanding of the Bible was based on the understanding of the affects (emotions) of its author.[7] From here a line extends to Friedrich Schleiermacher and the hermeneutics of Wilhelm Dilthey, who in his mature thinking saw emotions as essential for the methodical understanding of human expressions (*Ausdrücke*), but, at the same time, posited language as the highest form of these expressions.[8] In Dilthey's hermeneutics, the old, linguistic understanding of emotions reached its high point. This emphasis on language is important to keep in mind given Dilthey's seminal role in shaping the methodologies of the Humanities in the German-speaking world and beyond.

Dilthey's contemporary, art historian Aby Warburg, emphasized a cultural feature that transcended the expression of an individual's lived experience and opened up new ways to think about objects in relation to emotions. In his view, works of art are not only defined by individual subjectivity but also something that he called *Pathosformel*, or pathos formula, which is the foundation of "the historical psychology of human expression."[9] Warburg's conceptual tools opened up objects—in this case works of art—and gestures as spaces for their own subjectivity and thereby agents of emotion. It is this capacity of objects to move and mobilize emotions that has recently received renewed attention. For instance, Caroline van Eck has forcefully argued for the living presence of the objects of art. At the same time, the Marxist notion of commodity fetishism has been rediscovered and newly employed in studies on material culture.[10] Both of these concepts—living presence and commodity fetishism—frame objects as vehicles or even as perceived agents of emotional intentionality. As Stephanie Downes, Sally Holloway, and Sarah Randles show in their recent volume on the materiality of early modern European emotions, a work of art or any material object can exhibit agency because it can be claimed to emotionally influence us.[11]

Besides art history and the study of material culture, the materiality of emotions was an important theme in early emotion research stemming from family history. Hans Medick and David Sabean, leading historians of the Göttingen School, argued in their 1984 volume on *Interest and Emotion* that emotions were embedded in material interests and social networks. To contest the prevalent interpretation in family history that emotions and (material) interests were mutually exclusive and that they constituted a social and civilizational hierarchy—middle class families became increasingly emotionalized whereas peasant and working class families resorted to the language of property and material needs—these scholars argued that emotions and material interests, be it in terms of property or material survival, were firmly intertwined.[12] By the time Medick and Sabean's piece came out, Peter and Carol Stearns were working on an article that set the direction for the history of emotions for the next twenty years. With their concept of emotionology, the Stearnses underlined the primacy of language for historical understanding of emotions and especially their change.[13] In the wake of this focus on the history of emotions as a history of concepts, terms, discursive shifts, and so on, the materiality and embodiment of emotions disappeared from the mainstream.

The work of Sabean and Medick notwithstanding, it is clear that in the 1990s, the history of emotions was caught in the linguistic turn that set the agendas for many fields of historical and literary scholarship.[14] The materiality of emotions was an early victim.[15] It is also of great significance for the current state of research that when the critique against the linguistic turn and linguistic understanding of emotions emerged in the mid 1990s, its point of departure in finding the counterpoint to the constructionist theory of emotions was not their materiality but their physicality, their bodiliness. Bodies became the counterweight to language in the understanding of emotions. Yet, as this book aims to argue, there is even more work to be done not only on mapping the words, phrases, and metaphors of how the body is involved in both perceiving and producing emotions, but also on how the feeling body is embedded within a web of material conditions, objects, and things.[16]

Since the late 1990s, a renewed interest in material culture has emerged. As Bill Brown, one of its early advocates, suggests, the "history in things might be understood as the crystallization of the anxieties and aspirations that linger there in the material object."[17] Leora Auslander, a material culture historian, has argued that the difference between words and texts on one hand and the objects on the other is the capacity of objects to convey emotions in different ways since they served several functions whereas words have a directed and focused intentionality.[18] Monique Scheer's influential concept of emotions as practices also suggests an uneasiness with the distinctions between the interior and exterior dimensions of emotions.[19] More specifically, the lives of things are often to be found in their mode of circulation; things are commodities and, as Marx and later Benjamin argued, in modern capitalism they are often animated, become fetishized, and are perceived as having the capacity to affect us.[20] Predating capitalism, the animation of things is a profound feature of civilizations. It stretches from art works to everyday objects, such as money, banners, diaries, photographs, or flowers—things that manifest emotions, emotions that would not exist without them.[21]

As we have discussed, important debates have led to the creation of a lively historical subfield, the "history of emotions." Yet a comparable momentum seems delayed or less asserted in literary studies. This is in part because a concern with literary emotions, a lingering association with roots in the classical world, has in the post-World War II era been considered naive, unmediated, and affirmative. To put it differently, a specific literary study of emotions was considered unnecessary because emotions were assumed to have long been a major focus of literature and traditional literary study into the early twentieth century. Consensus emerged that emotions in literature required no further discussion or that to do so was subjective or mystification. It was precisely this concern that theories of literature aimed to move beyond or demystify. Thus, in the second half of the twentieth century, German literary studies paid increasingly less and less attention to emotions. In what we might call the "heyday of theory," scholars were drawn to studies informed by interests in fields such as psychoanalysis, sexuality, feminism, deconstruction, semiotics, discourse analysis, and anthropology.[22] This seemed fitting in a humanities landscape that identified discourse, signification, class consciousness, and the politics of representation as the urgent questions and provocations of the day (in some but not all cases, these issues were also at the core of the distinctiveness purportedly characterizing literary and artistic artifacts). Consensus prevailed that exposing rhetoric, representation, and structures formed the seemingly never-ending task of literary study. If mentioned at all, emotions were considered just rhetorical figures that revealed the impossibility of stable structures.[23] That there was once broad agreement that emotions were central to the humanities was not considered significant for their further development.

That the literary studies have neglected the emotions and especially their corporeality and materiality is surprising given the history of the humanities in the last 150 years. Two key disciplines that emerged in the second half of the nineteenth century, psychological aesthetics and hermeneutics, built their projects largely on emotions, bodies, and the physical world. With regards to recent efforts to take the cultural study of emotions to the next stage by paying attention to corporeality and materiality, these two forerunners deserve mention.

From its beginnings in the 1860s, *Einfühlungsästhetik* (empathy aesthetics), the dominant school of psychological aesthetics, placed bodies and things and our emotions relative to them unabashedly at the core its project. Today, we might conceive of the project of *Einfühlungsästhetik* as a dual attempt both to widen the range of specific emotions adhering in aesthetic events beyond the limitations of the duality of pleasure/displeasure promulgated by formalists working in a Kantian framework, and at the same time to recognize the presence of the body and the particularities of material worlds. The path-breaking thinker of *Einfühlungsästhetik*, Friedrich Theodor Vischer, observed how, per the act of empathy described by the new aesthetics, our sense of self, "with its physical feeling and bodily perception, extends its forms and movements into the object."²⁴ Both the activities of an artist and those of a viewer can only be possible on the basis of such relationships as the "intrinsic connection between seeing and touching," which is in play in the perception of phenomena such as mountain ranges.²⁵ In things, per *Einfühlungsästhetiker*, we recognize our emotions—the cloudy sky reminds us of our facial expressions of concern—because we have already symbolically projected our emotions into things and their movements. Hence, in this view, what we would today call material culture exists because of emotional projection wherein people attempt to mimic themselves through object making.²⁶

While empathy thinkers such as Vischer emphasized empirically framed processes of emotional projection into natural objects, the creator of the *Geisteswissenschaften*, Wilhelm Dilthey, sought to build his new discipline on the reader's emotionally informed intervention into the objective expression of historical, emotionally tinged, lived experience. At the same time, Dilthey asserted a basic human need for enhancing and intensifying "lived experience," which is also to say an intensification of feeling. Elucidating various spheres of feeling, which he associated with formal features of literary works, he linked, for instance, the rhythmic features organizing poetry to those organizing bodies and their movements, such as walking, breathing, and regular alternations of waking and sleeping.²⁷

Emotional interiority remained a component of Dilthey's thought. Yet scholars have been slow to appreciate how Dilthey's new discipline conceded from its beginnings the embodied nature of emotional life: "Life always consists in the interaction of a living body [*beseelter Körper*] and external world which constitutes its milieu."²⁸ The modern historical emphasis on language and literature as largely mental rather than fully lived, that is embodied, has no doubt contributed to this often one-sided reading of Dilthey. Out of this interaction, contended Dilthey, emerge specific changes to our emotional states (*Gefühlslage*), which then guide and inform our actions, basic drives, and further emotions: "The most powerful are those that are permanently embedded in bodily states."²⁹ While it has been pointed out that Dilthey, particularly in his later works, emphasized the expression or objectifications of lived experience, critics have yet to devote much effort to discussing the role of materiality or corporeality in Dilthey's writings.³⁰ At the same time that he identified in emotion the source of understanding, he identified objects, gestures, historical narratives, literary works, and musical scores as the medium for accessing the psychic-emotional and historical worlds of people in and behind these objects and actions. It is significant that this foundational figure in the history of German literary theory attributed such importance to the material dimensions of texts. Indeed, he emphasized how a range of expression includes "gestures and facial expressions," "every room in which chairs are arranged," "the swing of a hammer," a staged drama, or a musical score. To take the example of music: "The object of the historical study of music is not some mental or psychic process behind the composition, but something objective, namely the tonal nexus that appears in the imagination as expression."[31] Thus material culture, spatial practices, and the body were integral concerns at the dawn of literary and historical criticism in the German-speaking traditions.[32]

Phenomenology also indicates productive directions for contemporary research in literary and cultural studies.[33] A certain lineage stretches from Dilthey's emphasis on the question of life, specifically its threefold articulation (*Erlebnis-Ausdruck-Verstehen*), to phenomenology, at least through an early adherent, Martin Heidegger.[34] In *Sein und Zeit* (*Being and Time*, 1927), for instance, Heidegger discussed phenomena such as *Furcht* and *Angst*, which he chose not to characterize as emotions (per tradition) but as manifestations of *Befindlichkeit* (attunement), or, in their most familiar understanding, *Stimmungen* (moods).[35] For Heidegger, such emotional phenomena do not relate to psychological states, nor do they operate according to distinctions of interiority/exteriority.[36] We do not cognitively or observationally assess situations and judge them to be fearful.[37] Instead, fear is a way to "sense out" the world. His discussion is clearly influenced by Edmund Husserl's reflections on feeling, which is caught up in our "lived experience of value," that is, how we in incline toward or away from something. For Heidegger, affect (*Affektion*), or being sensuously moved, as well as something mattering to us, are only possible because we can be attuned to the world in particular ways: "In attunement lies existentially a disclosive submission to world out of which things that matter to us can be encountered."[38] What are traditionally referred to as emotions become, in Heidegger's work, modes (*Befindlichkeit*) through which the world can manifest itself and matter for us. Husserl's affectivity and Heidegger's moods are a far cry from the discussions of historically and culturally situated emotions undertaken in this book. Yet the emphasis, which can also be found in Dilthey, on feeling, one that is related to a first-person approach, one that is situated and that serves as a basis for determining what is good and bad for us, offers to enrich current discussions in emotion studies.

Current and recent literary research on emotions in the German context reveals both innovative and traditional approaches.[39] While the representations of melancholy in early modernity, or terror in the gothic novel, or love in modernist novels have occasionally been the subject of study in a traditional vein—focusing on themes or subjective expression—recent work that problematizes models of feeling points in new directions.[40] Other scholars have studied the history of literary emotions as features of texts and literary genres or the modalities and operations of emotions in readers as they encounter fictional depictions.[41] While recent years have seen scholars in German literary studies rediscovering emotions, the assumption that what is at stake, so to speak, centers on discourse, rhetoric, and representation still dominates.

Affect Theory, associated with studies by Gilles Deleuze, Brian Massumi, Eve Kosofsky Sedgwick, and Lawrence Grossberg, has at times attempted to complicate, to some extent, this trend.[42] Of course, a lack of consensus prevails among affect theorists concerning just what affect is and what it is to do.[43] Depending on the theorist, it means something different and has a different provenance.[44] The most prominent mode of affect theory assumes an unconvincing distinction between "emotion" as secondary, subjective, ideological, or representational, and "affect" (per affect theory) as unqualified and subversive intensity.[45] The emphasis on intensity remains nevertheless indebted to the concept of representation by privileging the purported disrupting power of affect. The discussion of embodiment, for instance in Massumi, is not only idealized but is vigilantly controlled by the opposition of intensity versus content leaving embodiment feeling generalized, unsituated, dehistoricized, and flat.[46] What links most work under the name "affect theory" is the notion that what supremely holds our attention as critics is the "virtual" and the unsignifiable with its excess of acceleration. By contrast, the authors of the present volume are interested in just those moments of emotion materialized and embodied where things are emerging from absolute indeterminacy or flux and begin to impact observers. At the same time, research on bodies, embodiment, presence, material culture, materiality, neuroscience, and pleasures continue apace and have led to waves of perturbations and provocations across the humanities. We might speak then of twin recent developments: the challenges that studies of embodiment and "thingliness," or corporeality and materiality, pose on the one hand, and the rediscovery of emotions in literary studies on the other. The study of emotions in literature and the visual arts has yet to come to terms with the contention that bodies and things are essential factors in the cultural appearance of emotions. This volume attempts to do just that.

* * *

With these considerations of corporeality and materiality in mind, this book examines the long history of emotions in the German-speaking world since the sixteenth century through a range of different disciplinary approaches. To do this, it presents three closely intertwined approaches to understand and study the culture and history of emotions: emotions and bodies, emotions as practices of space and material interests, and emotions and things.

The first part of the book centers on the embodied nature of emotions by both tracing medical languages, gestures, and artistic tropes that have influenced the understanding of bodies in the practices of emotions, and unpacking the tangibility of emotions and their memories on the human body itself, namely through the skin. Sara Luly's essay probes magnetism, a late eighteenth century medical movement that runs parallel and often against the concept of *Innerlichkeit*. The medical doctor Franz Anton Mesmer wanted to overcome

Cartesian dualism by positing the universal fluids as the metaphysical foundation of all living and nonliving beings. Animal magnetists thus believed they could direct the fluids and thereby heal their patients. Magnetism, argues Luly, recognized "the interconnectivity of objects and bodies as well as the way in which those interconnectivities are manifested physically in embodied affective responses," which provided a mechanism to challenge gender hierarchies within the family. As a popular discourse that recognized the bodiliness of emotions, it continues to influence our thinking about emotions through terms such as "mesmerized" and "animal" attraction. In the course of the nineteenth century, for example, this popular medical discourse made it for the composer and pianist Franz Liszt, as Hannu Salmi shows in his study, to emerge as an instigator of what Salmi calls emotional contagion. An early designer of celebrity culture, Liszt was not only known as a virtuoso of his instrument but also as a performer who captivated his audience. He did this, Salmi argues, by using his staged body and amplifying its emotional impact with modern communication and transportation technology.

In the end of the nineteenth century, the migration of the body to the figure of the *Ausdrucksbewegung* allowed, as Derek Hillard argues in his chapter, the development of an approach to the bodiliness of emotions that was as equally powerful as magnetism and other popular medical discourses. Rainer Maria Rilke's novel of 1910, *Die Aufzeichnungen des Malte Laurids Brigge*, considers emotions not as hidden, inner events expressed in conventional gestures, such as facial movements, as many scientists and theorists did at the turn of the century. Instead, emotions are created through kinetic bodies as people attempt to make sense of their social and material environments. In her study on the communist agitprop groups in the 1920s, Sabine Hake discovers this same functionality of the body in making emotional statements—for instance, taking a stand by crafting a certain bodily and highly gendered habitus. "The communist habitus," Hake argues, "relied heavily on the spectacle of masculinity both to distinguish the militant culture of the KPD from the communitarian culture of the SPD and to align the project of class struggle explicitly with the emotional regimes of self-discipline and self-control." It is this regime that gripped participants at their performances, quite the opposite of the mania provoked by Liszt some eighty years earlier.

The importance of the body for the understanding and experience of emotions in the Weimar Republic and especially in the politically charged environments of the everyday, is further confirmed by Russell Spinney in his study of the affective practices of anti-Semitism. In this case, persecution was literally preserved through a memory of goose bumps on one's body discovered in an oral history interview. The individual's memory of her skin's reaction to her teacher's anti-Semitic efforts in the classroom, however, did not just simply reveal a feeling of fear from the exclusionary practices of one's peers, but rather a more complex interplay of interiority and exteriority, including an individual's physical sensations, personal goals, and stubbornness, along with the increasingly widespread practices of harassment from teachers and peers, which continued to shape more specific feelings later in life. The growing anti-Semitic threat to Jewish children and their families was thus made very clear. Yet the expression of fear was not necessarily so direct if even visible at all; and as Spinney shows, Jewish children and their parents creatively responded to the growing threat of anti-Semitism in a wide variety of ways.

The second part of the book takes a step beyond the thesis of interiority of emotions and explores emotions as relational practices of space and material interests. Joy Wiltenburg examines the meaning of social space in defining emotions, in particular laughter, in early sixteenth-century Switzerland. Her case study on the famous medical doctor and memoirist Felix Platter makes a clear distinction between reproducible and commodified jokes widely traded and available in jestbooks and forms of laughter embedded in social relations and spaces, in both public and private spaces involving courtship, friendships, and relationships of power across different generations and gender. Although scholars have yet to unearth sufficient case studies, it seems that the interiority doctrine and commodification—as found in the jestbooks—were contemporaries. Christian Sieg traces the notion of interiority to Luther's idea of inner man and then follows its development and maturation into a widespread cultural pattern toward the end of the eighteenth century. Contrary to what we might expect, interiority does not fully explain such emotions as shame and empathy. At the end of the eighteenth century, as Sieg suggests in his analysis of Karl Philipp Moritz's *Anton Reiser*, shame and empathy were still understood in social and spatial terms. Spaces lend themselves to commodification, which deploy emotions, as Jared Poley's study in gambling and especially the role casinos and gaming tables shows. In the nineteenth century, German casinos experienced intense growth when gambling became illegal in France after the 1830 Revolution. In this era that saw the rise of the modern casino in the Rhineland, casinos "weaponized" the emotions of the gamblers against them, Poley suggests, by using the gambling halls and tables as tools of intensification and deadening of affects. The casinos were a clear example of the capitalist commodification of emotions that Hannu Salmi described in his contribution on Liszt. The commodification process can be seen in another area as well. In the course of the nineteenth century, German spas were transformed, as Heikki Lempa argues, from sites of tranquility and serenity to places of excitement and joy. Emotions were an important part of traditional medicine and its therapeutic tools. To restore one's health, a doctor often prescribed a spa visit, which helped rebuild emotional balance and tranquility. This was reflected in common sales talk for German spas in the beginning of the nineteenth century. As a result of the changing medical conceptualizations and the increasing commercial pressures, the emotional sales talk emphasizing serenity and tranquility was replaced with sales pitches for adventures and excitement, be it in casinos, theaters, restaurants, or sporting opportunities at spas.

In the third part of this volume, the attention shifts to the relationships between things and emotions. As we mentioned, spaces and even social relationships could be harnessed to material interests by "weaponizing" emotions for financial gain, sales talk, and political suppression. At the same time, spatialized and socialized emotions could also resist the forces of commodification, as Hake shows. But how did the status of things change? The political meaning of emotionalized objects becomes obvious when we look at the ways in which German educators discovered things, natural objects, and playthings as instruments of their pedagogical agenda. In her investigation of Johann Heinrich Pestalozzi and Friedrich Fröbel, two of the most influential figures of early childhood education in the nineteenth century, Ann Taylor Allen traces their use of objects to instill maternal love as an educational strategy. Although playthings of all kinds became important to Fröbel, the commodification of reproducible toys was yet to come. In the 1840s, however, a new technique and technology expanded to allow potentially unlimited reproducibility of images, the daguerreotype. But, as Sarah Leonard suggests, the photographs produced were "static, colorless, and two dimensional." The intention of these images was not individuation but capturing the sitters' "particular emotional style" in highly conventionalized spaces and gestures that conveyed discipline and reserve for women and often a more expressive repertoire of emotions for men. In her study of the work by the photographer Bertha Wehnert-Beckmann, Leonard shows how such emotionally charged objects as rings and daguerreotype photographs themselves were used to produce these styles. In a way, photography therefore became an educational tool in self-fashioning of men and women and families that could afford them.

Since the late eighteenth century, a particular object assumed a central role in the new emotional language, the flower. In her study on emotional language of flowers, Ute Frevert investigates their rise as symbols and agents of gendered emotions since 1800. The flowers, she suggests, were used to express political meanings and personal intimacy because they gave an objective conceptual form to emotions attached to those meanings. Flowers became popular symbols of political leaders and political parties, while they underlined gender distinctions by expressing personal relationships. In the course of the nineteenth century, a codified language of emotions attached to flowers emerged. The "use of flowers in private and public communication since around 1800," Frevert argues, "testifies to a growing emotionalization that set foot in European and other Westernized societies." But objects were also given a more active role in evoking emotions as Frevert's study shows, for flowers could be perceived as emotional agents.

Objects also served civil society in enforcing emotional communities, as Ruth Dewhurst's study on choral societies in Imperial Germany shows. Songs, banners, flags, architectural structures, and other "objects," she argues, "elicited enthusiasm, joy, excitement, or national pride" to create emotional communities. This question of agency became acute to Rainer Maria Rilke who in his poetry explored the ways in which objects impressed themselves on us. In her study of Rilke's *Neue Gedichte*, Lorna Martens discovers the poet's attention to how objects provoked radical, emotional appeals in us, thereby displaying themselves as agents of emotions. As Erika Quinn's detailed analysis of the practices of bereavement in wartime Germany shows, objects could turn into emotional icons that exhibited a living presence in their user's everyday life. The wartime diary of Vera Conrad became a placeholder for her husband in the Second World War as she awaited his return from the Eastern Front. The diary entries reveal her attempts to make sense of their relationship and maintain communication. But as in the daguerreotype photographs analyzed by Sarah Leonard, it was not only what the diary contained but what it was. For Vera, it became an object that carried special emotional valence; it became a "totemic object for its author as well as her children."

The studies of this volume suggest four separate but closely intertwined trends that defined the culture of emotions in the Germanic world between 1500 and 1950. First, a culture of emotional interiority emerged in theology and philosophy, which then put its stamp on religious practices, poetry, literature, music, and also on forms of personal interaction. Yet, even during the time of its hegemony, in the early nineteenth century, the culture of interiority was contested. The modern Germanic world and its models of the self were clearly not understood to be shaped exclusively by feelings from within. The second trend plays out against the background of the *longue durée* of exteriority, the manifestation of emotions in the body persisting from early modern precursors. Yet since the early nineteenth century, these underwent changes that reflected the social and cultural transformations of the era. When medical knowledge and practices changed, for instance, so did the understanding of the body and its emotions; when music changed, so did its relationship to emotions and the body; when theater changed, so did its understanding of the body and its emotional agency. The question is, then, what was the nature of these changes? This brings us to the third trend. Our studies have discovered a duality of strategies that indicate, since the middle of the nineteenth century, a commodification of emotions ranging from their educational usage, commercial manipulations with flowers, concerts, spa visits, and photographs to outright "weaponization" for profit mongering with gambling. Yet, and this is particularly pronounced in our studies on the twentieth-century, emotions, especially as they were manifested in the body and objects, also provided forms and resources of resistance to commodification and repressive politics, be it the actor's pose in socialist theater, a child's response to anti-Semitism, a motto of a choral society, or a family icon. Finally, emotions were gendered. The question is not about the ownership of emotions and affects, but the strategies and forces that employed these emotions to enforce gender hierarchies, undermine them, and find new ways of emotional agency. In an early modern family setting, a joke and laughter could serve as a tool of enforcing masculine hegemony; and around 1800, the affective language of magnetism could enforce standards of heteronormative sexuality. Yet there are increasing signs and expressions of women's emotional intimacy and agency, be it in the reserved emotional style in daguerreotypes, flowers, or the adornment of a diary. More importantly emotions became tools of political symbolism as we see in the use of flowers in the emerging women's movement since the late nineteenth century and the masculine pose in the Communist agitprop performances in the 1920s.

Derek Hillard is Professor of German at Kansas State University. His research concerns German modernism. In particular, he has investigated the languages of emotion and pain, the representation of violence and sacrifice, and discourses of the mind. He is the author of *Poetry as Individuality: The Discourse of Observation in Paul Celan* (2010), as well as recent essays on Alfred Döblin and Ernst Jünger.

Heikki Lempa is a Professor of Modern European and German History at Moravian College. His interests are in German cultural and social history, the history of emotions, the body, education, masculinity, and honor. He is the author of *Beyond the Gymnasium: Educating the Middle-Class Bodies in Classical Germany* (2007) and *Bildung der Triebe: Der deutsche Philanthropismus (1768–1788)* (1993).

Russell Spinney is an independent historian and instructor at the Thacher School in Ojai, California, and he is a coorganizer of the Emotions Studies network for the German Studies Association. His research interests include emotions, particularly fear and courage, in the political practices of the Weimar Republic and the US. He has coauthored and edited a special journal issue on the history of emotions in twentieth-century European social movements, political protests and revolutions for the Cambridge journal, *Contemporary European History* (Fall 2014). Additional publications include "Through the Sons of the Old Chiefs: Surveying Space, Identity and European-American Relationships in the 'New Purchase' Territory (Centre County, Pennsylvania 1769–1778)," in *Pennsylvania's Revolution*, ed. William Pencak (University Park, PA: Penn State Press, 2010); and "Fear, Courage and Civic Behavior in the Weimar Republic," *Revue Suisse d'Histoire* (Swiss Historical Review) 61 (2011): 74–89.

Notes

1. See Rüdiger Campe and Julia Weber, eds. *Rethinking Emotion: Interiority and Exteriority in Premodern, Modern, and Contemporary Thought* (Berlin: De Gruyter, 2014), and especially the editors' "Rethinking Emotion: Moving beyond Interiority. An Introduction." See also Christian Sieg's contribution in this volume.
2. For further discussion of this "bio-revolution," see Jan Plamper, *History of Emotions: An Introduction* (Oxford: Oxford University Press, 2017), 60–67, 137, 302, 206–50.
3. Nicole Eustace, Eugenia Lean, Julie Livingston, Jan Plamper, William M. Reddy, and Barbara H. Rosenwein, "AHR Conversation: The Historical Study of Emotions," *The American Historical Review* 117 (2012): 1505.
4. Uffa Jensen and Daniel Morat, eds., *Rationalisierungen des Gefühls: Zum Verhältnis von Wissenschaft und Emotionen, 1880–1930* (Munich: Wilhelm Fink, 2008); Joachim Radtkau, *Das Zeitalter der Nervosität: Deutschland zwischen Bismarck und Hitler* (Munich: Hanser, 1998); Cf. Martina Kessel, *Langeweile: Zum Umgang mit der Zeit und Gefühlen in Deutschland vom späten 18. bis zum frühen 20. Jahrhundert* (Göttingen: Wallstein Verlag, 2001); and Peter N. Stearns, *American Cool: Constructing a Twentieth-Century Emotional Style* (New York: New York University Press, 1994).
5. On emotion words, see, for instance, Barbara H. Rosenwein, *Emotional Communities in the Early Middle Ages* (Ithaca: Cornell University Press, 2006), 32–56.
6. As Rüdiger Campe has shown in his *Affekt und Ausdruck: zur Umwandlung der literarischen Rede im 17. und 18. Jahrhundert* (Tübingen: M. Niemeyer, 1990), in the German-speaking world the rhetorical discourse of "affect" was the dominant conceptualization of emotions until the late eighteenth century.
7. Markus Matthias, "Die Grundlegung der pietistischen Hermeneutik bei August Hermann Francke," in *Hermeneutik, Methodenlehre, Exegese: zur Theorie der Interpretation in der frühen Neuzeit*, ed. Günter Frank and Stephan Meier-Oeser (Stuttgart: Fromann-Holzboog, 2011), 194–98.
8. Wilhelm Dilthey, *Der Aufbau der geschichtlichen Welt in den Geisteswissenschaften* (Frankfurt am Main: Suhrkamp, 1981), 267. See also Daniel Morat, "Verstehen als Gefühlsmethode: Zu Wilhelm Diltheys hermeneutischer Grundlegung der Geisteswissenschaften," in *Rationalisierungen des Gefühls: Zum Verhältnis von Wissenschaft und Emotionen, 1880–1930*, ed. Uffa Jensen and Daniel Morat (Munich: Wilhelm Fink, 2008), 113–14.
9. Aby Warburg, "Italian Art and International Astrology in the Palazzo Schifanoia, Ferrara (1912)," in *The Renewal of Pagan Antiquity: Contributions to the Cultural History of the European Renaissance* (Los Angeles: The Getty Research Institute for the History of Art and the Humanities, 1999), 585. According to Caroline van Eck, Warburg's pathos formula tried to capture "facial expressions, gestures and figures, in particular drapery, that result from the impact of extreme emotions," *Art, Agency and Living Presence: From the Animated Image to the Excessive Object* (Boston: De Gruyter, 2015), 179.

10. See, for instance, Hartmut Böhme's encyclopedic *Fetishism and Culture: A Different Theory of Modernity* (Boston: de Gryuter, 2014).
11. Stephanie Downes, Sally Holloway, and Sarah Randles, "A Feeling for Things, Past and Present," in *Feeling Things. Objects and Emotions through History* (Oxford: Oxford University Press, 2018), 10–12, draw especially on the work of the anthropologist Alfred Gell and the literary critic Bill Brown.
12. Hans Medick and David Warren Sabean, eds., *Interest and Emotion: Essays on the Study of Family and Kinship* (Cambridge: Cambridge University Press, 1984), see especially the editors' "Interest and Emotion in Family and Kinship Studies: A Critique of Social History and Anthropology."
13. Peter N. Stearns and Carol Z. Stearns, "Emotionology: Clarifying the History of Emotions and Emotional Standards," *The American Historical Review* 90 (1985): 813–36.
14. Besides Stearns, the work of William Reddy is of crucial importance for the linguistic turn in the history of emotions. See especially William M. Reddy, "Against Constructionism: The Historical Ethnography of Emotions," *Current Anthropology* 38 (1997): 327–51; and William M. Reddy, *The Navigation of Feeling: A Framework for the History of Emotions* (Cambridge, UK: Cambridge University Press, 2001).
15. Not even the gender and feminist studies could change this trajectory. In fact, in the early literature on gender and women, emotions were hardly a subject of systematic investigation. A great exception is the work of Anne-Charlott Trepp who, especially in her "The Emotional Side of Men in Late Eighteenth-Century Germany (Theory and Example)," *Central European History* 27 (1994): 127–52, argued that around 1800, German educated middle class developed peculiar emotional behavior that amounted to what she calls sensitive masculinity. See also her "Liebe als erlebte Emotion und gesellschaftliche Wertsetzung im 18. und beginnenden 19. Jahrhundert," *Sowi: Sozialwissenschaftliche Informationen* 3 (2001): 14–21; and "Code contra Gefühl? Emotionen in der Geschichte," *Sowi: Sozialwissenschaftliche Informationen* 3 (2001): 44–52. More recently, the gendered bodily and material nature of emotions has become a mark of emotion studies. See, for instance, Deborah B. Gould, *Moving Politics: Emotion and ACT UP's Fight against AIDS* (Chicago: The University of Chicago Press, 2009); Ute Frevert, *Emotions in History—Lost and Found* (Budapest: Central European University Press, 2011), chapter 2, "Gendering Emotions," 87–147, and the literature there; and Katie Barclay, "Performing Emotion and Reading the Male Body in the Irish Court, C. 1800–1845," *Journal of Social History* 51 (2017): 293–312.
16. On mapping the body and words and phrases that link the body and feelings to emotions, see, for example, the extensive work by Ute Frevert and others in their *Emotional Lexicons* on terms like the heart. Ute Frevert, et al., *Emotional Lexicons: Continuity and Change in the Vocabulary of Feeling 1700–2000* (Oxford: Oxford University Press, 2014). They suggest an increasing "somatization" of emotions that may have replaced the spirit or soul as "emotional points for navigation" with the rise of modern science, but there is still much room for further exploration of this shift and mapping of other parts of the body involved in emotions (e.g., the stomach or skin). On the body and emotions across different cultures, see also Plamper's *History of Emotions*, 29–32 and 268–70.
17. Bill Brown, "How to Do Things with Things (A Toy Story)," *Critical Inquiry* 24 (1998): 935.

18. Leora Auslander, Amy Bentley, Leor Halevi, H. Otto Sibum, and Christopher Witmore, "AHR Conversation: Historians and the Study of Material Culture," *The American Historical Review* 114 (2009): 1356.
19. Monique Scheer, "Are Emotions a Kind of Practice (and Is That What Makes Them Have a History)? A Bourdieuan Approach to Understanding Emotion," *History and Theory* 51, no. 2 (2012): 193–220.
20. Karl Marx, *Capital: A Critique of Political Economy* (London: Penguin Books, 1990), esp. chapter "The Fetishism of the Commodity and Its Secret"; Walter Benjamin, "The Paris of the Second Empire in Baudelaire," in *Selected Writings* (Cambridge, MA: Belknap Press, 2006), 31.
21. On fetishism and its relationship to emotions, see Caroline van Eck, *Art, Agency and Living Presence*; Caroline van Eck, "Living Statues: Alfred Gell's Art and Agency, Living Presence Response and the Sublime," *Art History* 33 (2010): 642–59; and Böhme, *Fetishism and Culture*, 190–93. A stimulating methodological intervention is found in Oliver J. T. Harris and Tim Flohr Sørensen, "Rethinking Emotion and Material Culture," *Archaeological Dialogues* 17 (2010): 145–63; and Oliver J. T. Harris and Tim Flohr Sørensen, "Talk About the Passion," *Archaeological Dialogues* 17 (2010): 186–98. For the development of a theory of accumulation and circulation of affects in a Marxist sense, see Sara Ahmed, *The Cultural Politics of Emotion* (New York: Routledge, 2004).
22. David E. Wellbery, *Positionen der Literaturwissenschaft: acht Modellanalysen am Beispiel von Kleists Das Erdbeben in Chili* (Munich: C. H. Beck, 1993).
23. Paul De Man, *Allegories of Reading: Figural Language in Rousseau, Nietzsche, Rilke, and Proust* (New Haven: Yale University Press, 1979), 169.
24. Friedrich Theodor Vischer, "The Symbol," *Art in Translation* 7 (2015): 434.
25. Vischer, "The Symbol," 435.
26. Vischer, "The Symbol," 444.
27. Wilhelm Dilthey, *Poetry and Experience* (Princeton: Princeton University Press), 1985, 80.
28. Dilthey, *Poetry and Experience*, 96.
29. Dilthey, *Poetry and Experience*, 97.
30. Peter N. Miller, *Cultural Histories of the Material World* (University of Michigan Press, 2013). Hans Ulrich Gumbrecht, by contrast, suggests a potential in Dilthey's attempt at "bridging the distance between the material surfaces of cultural objects and a sphere of original *Erleben*,"—*The Powers of Philology: Dynamics of Textual Scholarship* (Urbana, IL: University of Illinois Press, 2003), 77.
31. Wilhelm Dilthey, *The Formation of the Historical World in the Human Sciences* (Princeton: Princeton University Press, 2010), 229–30, 241–42.
32. It is the central, mediating term in the title for the first section of his *Plan for the Continuation of the Formation of the Historical World in the Human Sciences*: "Lived Experience, Expression, and Understanding," Dilthey, *The Formation of the Historical World*, 191.
33. In philosophy, phenomenology has brought emotions to the foreground. See Andreas Elpidorou and Lauren Freeman, "The Phenomenology and Science of Emotions: An Introduction," *Phenomenology and the Cognitive Sciences* 13 (2014): 507–11. See also Giovanna Colombetti, *The Feeling Body: Affective Science Meets the Enactive Mind* (Cambridge, MA: MIT Press, 2014).

34. Dilthey's influence on Heidegger is evident in *Sein und Zeit*. See Sebastian Luft, "Kant, Neo-Kantianism, and Phenomenology," in *The Oxford Handbook of the History of Phenomenology*, ed. Dan Zahavi (Oxford: Oxford University Press, 2018), 57.
35. Martin Heidegger, *Being and Time* (Albany: State University Press of New York, 1996), 126–31.
36. Heidegger, *Being and Time*, 128–29.
37. Heidegger, *Being and Time*, 132.
38. Heidegger, *Being and Time*, 130.
39. For volumes with both innovative and very traditional studies, see, for instance, Anne Fuchs and Sabine Strümper-Krobb, eds., *Sentimente, Gefühle, Empfindungen: zur Geschichte und Literatur des Affektiven von 1770 bis heute; Tagung zum 60. Geburtstag von Hugh Ridley im Juli 2001* (Würzburg: Königshausen & Neumann, 2003); and Lars Saetre, Patrizia Lombardo, and Julian Zanetta, eds., *Exploring Text and Emotions* (Aarhus: Aarhus University Press, 2014).
40. See, for instance, Martin von Koppenfels and Cornelia Zumbusch, eds., *Handbuch Literatur & Emotionen* (Berlin: De Gruyter, 2016). In a historical context see also Ute Frevert, Pascal Eitler, Stephanie Olsen, eds., *Learning How to Feel: Children's Literature and Emotional Socialization, 1870–1970* (Oxford: Oxford University Press, 2014).
41. Burkhard Meyer-Sickendiek, *Affektpoetik: eine Kulturgeschichte literarischer Emotionen* (Würzburg: Königshausen & Neumann, 2005); and Sandra Poppe, *Emotionen in Literatur und Film* (Würzburg: Königshausen & Neumann, 2012).
42. For a view of the current discussion on affect, see Melissa Gregg and Gregory J. Seigworth, *The Affect Theory Reader* (Durham, NC: Duke University Press, 2010).
43. The use of the term "affect" (instead of emotion, feeling, sentiment) does not make the work at hand a case of "affect theory." Contributors in the present volume who engage with "affect theory," such as Sara Luly and Hannu Salmi, find it lacking, and offer their own implied or explicit uses of the term "affect."
44. Because of its form and content, what Sedgwick terms "affect" would be considered emotion by Massumi. Deriving her "affect" from the psychology of Silvan Tomkins, Sedgwick critiques prevailing notions of affect as "reified substance," a "unitary category" without an interest in particular feelings: Eve Kosofsky Sedgwick, and Adam Frank, "Shame in the Cybernetic Fold: Reading Silvan Tomkins," in *Shame and Its Sisters: A Silvan Tomkins Reader*, ed. Eve Kosofsky Sedgwick, Adam Frank, and Irving E. Alexander (Durham, NC: Duke University Press, 1995), 17. Lawrence Grossberg, on the other hand, draws explicitly on Freud (and Raymond Williams) for his notion of identify investment, *We Gotta Get Out of This Place: Popular Conservatism and Postmodern Culture* (New York: Routledge, 2014), 79.
45. "Emotion" and "affect," per Massumi, "pertain to different orders": Brian Massumi, *Parables for the Virtual: Movement, Affect, Sensation* (Durham, NC: Duke University Press, 2002), 27.
46. Massumi, *Parables for the Virtual*, 25.

Bibliography

Ahmed, Sara. *The Cultural Politics of Emotion*. New York: Routledge, 2004.
Auslander, Leora, Amy Bentley, Leor Halevi, H. Otto Sibum, and Christopher Witmore. "AHR Conversation: Historians and the Study of Material Culture." *The American Historical Review* 114 (2009): 1354–1404.
Barclay, Katie. "Performing Emotion and Reading the Male Body in the Irish Court, C. 1800–1845." *Journal of Social History* 51 (2017): 293–312.
Barclay, Katie. "New Materialism and the New History of Emotions." *Emotions: History, Culture, Society* 1, no. 1 (2017): 161–83.
Benjamin, Walter. "The Paris of the Second Empire in Baudelaire." In *Selected Writings*, 3–92. Cambridge, MA: Belknap Press, 2006.
Böhme, Hartmut. *Fetishism and Culture: A Different Theory of Modernity*. Boston: De Gryuter, 2014.
Brown, Bill. "How to Do Things with Things (A Toy Story)." *Critical Inquiry* 24 (1998): 935–64.
Campe, Rüdiger. *Affekt und Ausdruck: zur Umwandlung der literarischen Rede im 17. und 18. Jahrhundert*. Tübingen: M. Niemeyer, 1990.
Campe, Rüdiger, and Julia Weber, eds. *Rethinking Emotion: Interiority and Exteriority in Premodern, Modern, and Contemporary Thought*. Berlin: De Gruyter, 2014.
——— "Rethinking Emotion: Moving beyond Interiority. An Introduction." In *Rethinking Emotion: Interiority and Exteriority in Premodern, Modern, and Contemporary Thought*, edited by Rüdiger Campe and Julia Weber. Berlin: De Gruyter, 2014.
Colombetti, Giovanna. *The Feeling Body: Affective Science Meets the Enactive Mind*. Cambridge, MA: MIT Press, 2014.
De Man, Paul. *Allegories of Reading: Figural Language in Rousseau, Nietzsche, Rilke, and Proust*. New Haven: Yale University Press, 1979.
Dilthey, Wilhelm. *Der Aufbau der geschichtlichen Welt in den Geisteswissenschaften*. Frankfurt am Main: Suhrkamp, 1981.
——— *The Formation of the Historical World in the Human Sciences*. Princeton: Princeton University Press, 2010.
——— *Poetry and Experience*. Princeton: Princeton University Press, 1985.
Downes, Stephanie, Sally Holloway, and Sarah Randles. "A Feeling for Things, Past and Present." In *Feeling Things: Objects and Emotions through History*, edited by Stephanie Downes, Sally Holloway, and Sarah Randles, 8–26. Oxford: Oxford University Press, 2018.
Elpidorou, Andreas, and Lauren Freeman. "The Phenomenology and Science of Emotions: An Introduction." *Phenomenology and the Cognitive Sciences* 13 (2014): 507–11.

Eustace, Nicole, Eugenia Lean, Julie Livingston, Jan Plamper, William M. Reddy, and Barbara H. Rosenwein. "AHR Conversation: The Historical Study of Emotions." *The American Historical Review* 117 (2012): 1486–1531.
Frevert, Ute. *Emotions in History—Lost and Found*. Budapest: Central European University Press, 2011.
Frevert, Ute, et al. *Emotional Lexicons: Continuity and Change in the Vocabulary of Feeling 1700–2000*. Oxford: Oxford University Press, 2014.
Frevert, Ute, Pascal Eitler, and Stephanie Olsen, eds. *Learning How to Feel: Children's Literature and Emotional Socialization, 1870–1970*. Oxford: Oxford University Press, 2014.
Fuchs, Anne, and Sabine Strümper-Krobb, eds. *Sentimente, Gefühle, Empfindungen: zur Geschichte und Literatur des Affektiven von 1770 bis heute; Tagung zum 60. Geburtstag von Hugh Ridley im Juli 2001*. Würzburg: Königshausen & Neumann, 2003.
Gallagher, Shaun. *How the Body Shapes the Mind*. Oxford: Oxford University Press, 2005.
Gould, Deborah B. *Moving Politics: Emotion and ACT UP's Fight against AIDS*. Chicago: The University of Chicago Press, 2009.
Gregg, Melissa, and Gregory J. Seigworth, eds. *The Affect Theory Reader*. Durham, NC: Duke University Press, 2010.
Grossberg, Lawrence. *We Gotta Get Out of This Place: Popular Conservatism and Postmodern Culture*. New York: Routledge, 2014.
Gumbrecht, Hans Ulrich. *The Powers of Philology: Dynamics of Textual Scholarship*. Urbana, IL: University of Illinois Press, 2003.
Harris, Oliver J. T., and Tim Flohr Sørensen. "Rethinking Emotion and Material Culture." *Archaeological Dialogues* 17 (2010): 145–63.
——— "Talk About the Passion." *Archaeological Dialogues* 17 (2010): 186–98.
Heidegger, Martin. *Being and Time*. Albany: State University Press of New York, 1996.
——— *Nietzsche*. Vols. I–II. San Francisco: HarperCollins, 1991.
Jensen, Uffa, and Daniel Morat, eds. *Rationalisierungen des Gefühls: Zum Verhältnis von Wissenschaft und Emotionen, 1880–1930*. Munich: Wilhelm Fink, 2008.
Kessel, Martina. *Langeweile: Zum Umgang mit der Zeit und Gefühlen in Deutschland vom späten 18. bis zum frühen 20. Jahrhundert*. Göttingen: Wallstein Verlag, 2001.
Luft, Sebastian. "Kant, Neo-Kantianism, and Phenomenology." In *The Oxford Handbook of the History of Phenomenology*, edited by Dan Zahavi, 45–68. Oxford: Oxford University Press, 2018.
Marx, Karl. *Capital: A Critique of Political Economy*. London: Penguin Books, 1990.
Massumi, Brian. *Parables for the Virtual: Movement, Affect, Sensation*. Durham, NC: Duke University Press, 2002.
Matthias, Markus. "Die Grundlegung der pietistischen Hermeneutik bei August Hermann Francke." In *Hermeneutik, Methodenlehre, Exegese: zur Theorie der*

Interpretation in der frühen Neuzeit, edited by Günter Frank and Stephan Meier-Oeser, 189–202. Stuttgart: Fromann-Holzboog, 2011.

Medick, Hans, and David Warren Sabean, eds. *Interest and Emotion: Essays on the Study of Family and Kinship*. Cambridge: Cambridge University Press, 1984.

——— "Interest and Emotion in Family and Kinship Studies: A Critique of Social History and Anthropology." In *Interest and Emotion: Essays on the Study of Family and Kinship*, edited by Hans Medick and David Warren Sabean, 9–27. Cambridge: Cambridge University Press, 1984.

Meyer-Sickendiek, Burkhard. *Affektpoetik: eine Kulturgeschichte literarischer Emotionen*. Würzburg: Königshausen & Neumann, 2005.

Miller, Peter N. *Cultural Histories of the Material World*. University of Michigan Press, 2013.

Morat, Daniel. "Verstehen als Gefühlmethode: Zu Wilhelm Diltheys hermeneutischer Grundlegung der Geisteswissenschaften." In *Rationalisierungen des Gefühls: Zum Verhältnis von Wissenschaft und Emotionen, 1880–1930*, edited by Uffa Jensen and Daniel Morat, 101–17. Munich: Wilhelm Fink, 2008.

Plamper, Jan. *History of Emotions: An Introduction*. Oxford: Oxford University Press, 2017.

Poppe, Sandra. *Emotionen in Literatur und Film*. Würzburg: Königshausen & Neumann, 2012.

Radtkau, Joachim. *Das Zeitalter der Nervosität: Deutschland zwischen Bismarck und Hitler*. Munich: Hanser, 1998.

Reddy, William M. "Against Constructionism: The Historical Ethnography of Emotions." *Current Anthropology* 38 (1997): 327–51.

——— *The Navigation of Feeling: A Framework for the History of Emotions*. Cambridge, UK: Cambridge University Press, 2001.

Rosenwein, Barbara H. *Emotional Communities in the Early Middle Ages*. Ithaca: Cornell University Press, 2006.

Saetre, Lars, Patrizia Lombardo, and Julian Zanetta, eds. *Exploring Text and Emotions*. Aarhus: Aarhus University Press, 2014.

Scheer, Monique. "Are Emotions a Kind of Practice (and Is That What Makes Them Have a History)? A Bourdieuan Approach to Understanding Emotion." *History and Theory* 51, no. 2 (2012): 193–220.

Sedgwick, Eve Kosofsky, and Adam Frank. "Shame in the Cybernetic Fold: Reading Silvan Tomkins." In *Shame and Its Sisters: A Silvan Tomkins Reader*, edited by Eve Kosofsky Sedgwick, Adam Frank, and Irving E. Alexander, 1–28. Durham, NC: Duke University Press, 1995.

Stearns, Peter N. *American Cool: Constructing a Twentieth-Century Emotional Style*. New York: New York University Press, 1994.

Stearns, Peter N., and Carol Z. Stearns. "Emotionology: Clarifying the History of Emotions and Emotional Standards." *The American Historical Review* 90 (1985): 813–36.

Trepp, Anne-Charlott. "Code contra Gefühl? Emotionen in der Geschichte." *Sowi: Sozialwissenschaftliche Informationen* 3 (2001): 44–52.

——— "The Emotional Side of Men in Late Eighteenth-Century Germany (Theory and Example)." *Central European History* 27 (1994): 127–52.

——— "Liebe als erlebte Emotion und gesellschaftliche Wertsetzung im 18. und beginnenden 19. Jahrhundert." *Sowi: Sozialwissenschaftliche Informationen* 3 (2001): 14–21.

van Eck, Caroline. *Art, Agency and Living Presence: From the Animated Image to the Excessive Object*. Boston: De Gruyter, 2015.

——— "Living Statues: Alfred Gell's Art and Agency, Living Presence Response and the Sublime." *Art History* 33 (2010): 642–59.

Vischer, Friedrich Theodor. "The Symbol." *Art in Translation* 7 (2015): 417–48.

von Koppenfels, Martin, and Cornelia Zumbusch, eds. *Handbuch Literatur & Emotionen*. Berlin: De Gruyter, 2016.

Warburg, Aby. "Italian Art and International Astrology in the Palazzo Schifanoia, Ferrara (1912)." In *The Renewal of Pagan Antiquity: Contributions to the Cultural History of the European Renaissance*. Los Angeles: The Getty Research Institute for the History of Art and the Humanities, 1999.

Wellbery, David E. *Positionen der Literaturwissenschaft: acht Modellanalysen am Beispiel von Kleists Das Erdbeben in Chili*. Munich: C. H. Beck, 1993.

PART I

Emotions and Bodies

CHAPTER 1

Mesmerizing Encounters
Affect and Animal Magnetism

SARA LULY

Animal magnetic case studies tell the stories of bodies: bodies in pain, bodies experiencing relief, bodies reacting to objects, as well as bodies experiencing physiological and psychological connections across time and space. A healing technique created by Franz Anton Mesmer at the end of the eighteenth century, animal magnetism sought to undermine Cartesian dualism by theorizing a connection between mind and body as well as self and environment. Mesmer proposed that universal fluids (*All-Flut*) connected all living and nonliving things, and argued that certain types of illness were caused by obstructions in a patient's body that prevented the correct flow of universal fluid. Such patients could be healed by an animal magnetist (often shortened to "magnetist")—a practitioner of sorts who redirected these fluids, thus removing the blockage and restoring health. What began with Mesmer's practice in Vienna—and later Paris—spread quickly throughout Western Europe and the United States, leading to medical treatises, literary depictions of magnetism, and plenty of scandals. In the case studies and treatises of animal magnetists, we see many of the same themes that are addressed in this edited volume, namely the interconnectivity of objects and bodies as well as the way in which those interconnectivities are manifested physically in embodied affective responses.[1]

In this chapter, I propose that animal magnetism is an eighteenth-century attempt to conceptualize affect and affective relationships between people and things, one that emphasizes the embodied qualities of affect. When we look at the case studies of animal magnetists, affect is apparent in multiple ways, three of which will be the focus of the chapter. First, affect appears as *rapport*, which is the positive connection between patient and doctor believed to be the prerequisite to successful magnetism. Second, affect establishes the authenticity of the magnetism (and thus of the magnetist) through the patient's ability to feel certain sensations considered abnormal in a healthy state. Third, affect provides language with which patients could control emotional interfamily relationships and gender hierarchies within the family. To address these three affective aspects, I will analyze Eberhard Gmelin's case study of Herr Reichardt from *Materialien für die Anthropologie*, a collection of animal magnetic and psychological case studies published in 1791.[2] Through a close reading of this case study, I will illustrate how animal magnetism provides a discourse to conceptualize and describe affective relationships between the patient, other people, objects, and their surroundings.

Although the relationship of animal magnetism to modern notions of affect has not been addressed in the secondary literature, several scholars have examined a related line of inquiry, namely the role of animal magnetism and somnambulism in expressing socially taboo emotions and desires. When in a magnetic state, patients were not believed to have the same degree of control over their actions and words as when they were awake. For this reason, any behavior that would be viewed as inappropriate in the waking state was excused while magnetized. Several scholars have discussed the subversive potential of this position, analyzing the way in which female patients used their role as somnambulist to articulate feelings and desires that were socially unacceptable.[3] Jürgen Barkhoff identifies how animal magnetism enabled female patients to act out "feelings and attitudes that were strongly tabooed by society," using Gmelin's case study of Lisette who, while magnetized, would recommend treatment techniques with erotic overtones.[4] In her work on Justus Kerner's *Seherin von Prevorst*, Bettina Gruber recognizes the potential of animal magnetism to invert traditional structures of power between doctor and patient.[5] She points to the relative passivity of the doctor during magnetism, and the active role that the female patient played in diagnosing and treating her body as well as shaping magnetic theory.[6] Other scholars have examined how literary depictions of magnetism construct or undermine heteronormative gender roles.[7]

This secondary literature has several shortcomings with regard to discussions of affect. First, current scholarship focuses on the sociocultural construction of gender in magnetism and does not sufficiently address the embodied, affective elements.[8] This results in readings in which parts of the body become visible to the extent that they are sexualized, but the body as a whole remains largely invisible. Second, there is a tendency in secondary literature to focus on female patients, thus overlooking the male embodied experience. The case studies of male patients allow for an examination of multiple masculinities, including the experiences of male bodies whose masculinity challenged heteronormative gendered expectations.

Affect and Animal Magnetism

Both "affect" and "animal magnetism" are terms with contested definitions, in part because of their contradictory usages in different times and contexts. For this reason, each warrants a brief definition here. I am using the term "affect" to refer to an embodied sensation closely related to emotion, similar to Brian Massumi's usage.[9] However, I differ from Massumi's strict separation between affect and emotion. He defines affect as preconscious intensity felt in/on the body[10] and distinguishes it from emotion, which he defines as "qualified intensity," the "sociolinguistic fixing of the quality of an experience."[11] For Massumi, affect is notoriously difficult to discuss, as it cannot be "qualified" and therefore "is not ownable or recognizable and is thus resistant to critique."[12] Many theorists have rejected the strict division between affect and emotion on the basis of cognition. Ruth Leys, for example, argues that Massumi's theories are based on an idealized, and ultimately incorrect, separation of body and mind, so that body can experience something completely independent from the mind.[13] My use of the term departs from Massumi's strict separation in a similar way.

Since animal magnetism challenged the body/mind division by theorizing in spatial and embodied terms the connection between object, body, mind, and sensation, any strict separation of body and mind is ahistorical and cannot be applied to animal magnetism. In addition, the cognitive/noncognitive distinction Massumi makes is not in keeping with the way that magnetists theorized cognition and consciousness. By virtue of describing their sensations, somnambulists would have, according to Massumi, already moved from precognitive affect to "nameable" emotion. Given, however, that animal magnetic theory viewed somnambulism as a state separate from normal cognition, one in which the patient had unmediated access to nature including the workings of their body and mind, then it does not make sense to speak of their utterances as either precognitive or cognitive. In the end, I use the term "affect" here to refer to an embodied sensation and reject an affect/emotion dichotomy based in cognition, recognizing that magnetists sought the connection of mind and body.

The terminology of animal magnetism poses its own problems due to its inconsistency, both in the late eighteenth/early nineteenth centuries and in modern discussions. Franz Anton Mesmer refers to his theory of healing as "animal magnetism" (*tierisches Magnetismus*), differentiating it from "mineral magnetism" (magnetism between metals). The term "mesmerism" quickly emerged, however, emphasizing the role that Mesmer's personality played in spreading animal magnetism. While the term for one who practices animal magnetism is almost always "magnetist" (in later periods, "mesmerist" enters fashion), the person who is magnetized has several names, including somnambulist and magnetic sleep-talker (*magnetischer Schlafredner*). In the texts under investigation, all these terms are used interchangeably, and I will be using "animal magnetism" (often shortened to "magnetism").

Case Study: Herr Reichardt

One of Gmelin's case studies in *Materialien* is that of Herr Reichardt, a twenty-four-year-old man of delicate constitution who presents with attacks of severe cramping in his throat, chest, and lower abdomen, as well as episodes of lameness.[14] His constitution is weak, Gmelin suggests, because of the material and emotional conditions in which he was raised—namely, that he was coddled as a child, protected against "every little breeze," and "had free choice to enjoy every tasty delicacy."[15] Herr Reichardt is feminized here and throughout the text, in part to explain his receptivity to animal magnetism. Many magnetists believed that women were most easily magnetized because of their natural passivity, a characteristic that is extended to sickly, weak men (such as Reichardt) as well as children.

Reichardt describes the experience of being magnetized in positive affective terms: "whenever I [Gmelin] manipulate [Reichardt], he vividly feels that something flows out of the tips of my fingers and into him, something that calms his nerves, animates and warms his entire body."[16] Here, the verb "to manipulate" names the process of magnetizing. The unnamed "something" (*etwas*) stands in for the animal magnetic force moving into and through his body. This warm, calming, and also animating force moves from one body to the other, forming a connection between the men that is perceived to be physiological and characterized by positive affect. Embodied sensations of warmth verify the presence of magnetic fluids, and the fact that Reichardt "feels" something flowing into him, instead of merely seeing it, emphasizes the sensory, unmediated nature of the experience. The barriers between internal and external world are clear and emphasized by the fingertips. At the same time, at the moment of magnetism, the two men's bodies and spirits are linked through an invisible fluid, suggesting the temporary fluidity of these barriers. In this way, we see an example of how animal magnetism both challenges the strict division between inside and outside, which was characteristic of *Innerlichkeit*, while relying on inside/outside barriers such as the skin to conceptualize the flow of animal magnetism.[17]

Oftentimes, objects were used to forge affective magnetic connections. Magnetists employed at times a variety of "magnetized objects" in their practice, including glasses of water, pieces of glass, and *baquets*,[18] while at other times, only passes of their hand were used to create the desired effect. The ability of animal magnetic fluids to "stick" to certain objects and circulate with those objects highlights a moment of intersection between animal magnetism and affect theory. While animal magnetic fluids were conceptualized in more material terms than affect, both theories are interested in the circulation of objects and their relationship to the affect that people experience when interacting with these objects.

For example, Gmelin studies Herr Reichardt's reactions to metals, a common animal magnetic experiment. These experiments occur in the text after Gmelin asks Herr Reichardt if there is any way to differentiate between true magnetism and faked magnetism, suggesting that the purpose of this experiment was to establish the validity of Herr Reichardt's magnetized condition. Gmelin writes, "I placed silver in his hand; he could not hold it long due to the disagreeable (*widerlich*) impression it made, copper made an even more disagreeable impression, so that he complained of pain in his entire arm, and asked me to magnetize him from his armpit to his fingers."[19] "Widerlich" describes an affect, an embodied sensation that is negative and connected to emotion. This can be illustrated when one tries to translate it into English and must pick from a variety of synonyms that connect body and emotion, including "abhorrent," "nauseating," and "disgusting." While magnetized, Reichardt is unable to hold the metal, thus driving his hand away from the object. The metal leaves traces of pain in his arm, which in turn drives him toward his magnetist in search of relief. This experiment is repeated numerous times with various metals, summarized by the phrase, "I tried it with multiple watches with the same results."[20] Gmelin emphasizes that Reichardt could not name the metals, "as no somnambulist can,"[21] and only knew the name after the patient had vocalized the impression it made. The patient's inability to name the metal based on contact indicates that he is not "seeing" the object, but rather "sensing it" through the impression is makes on his skin. Identifying metals by sensation rather than visual input was thought to indicate a phenomenological orientation unique to animal magnetists, a way of experiencing that is depicted as more "direct" than sight.

Although Gmelin claims that the results of this experiment are consistent, he also records Reichardt's responses to objects that did not evoke the same unpleasant reaction, such as a gold watch chain made of a "fine grade of Gold."[22] Gmelin is accounting for this inconsistency indirectly, suggesting that the purity of the gold corresponded with the intensity of feeling. Reichardt, however, is more direct in accounting for perceived inconsistencies. He explains to the doctor that such experiments were "not a reliable means of physically recognizing [magnetism] because the metal would bring about different impressions on different magnetized persons."[23] By accounting for the subjective nature of the sensation, Reichardt undermines the doctors attempt to standardize the experience. This is one moment in which Reichardt claims the right to define his affective experience on his own terms, rejecting the consistency and repeatability that is the goal of a scientific experiment. He does so despite the doctor's attempt to control his experience through the language of science. Many such moments of tension are present in this and other magnetic experiments using objects.

In his comments on this case study, Gmelin explains the physiological relationships between object and subject in an attempt to explain the reactions to objects he witnessed during Reichardt's treatment. Embedded in nerve theory, Gmelin's explanation is founded on the belief that objects impress on nerves in a physiological way:[24]

> A fiber that many years ago had an impression made on it by some object—an impression that is no longer perceivable for the soul in its normal condition—and that hardly has a traces of this motion inflicted [that had been inflicted] by the object or the corresponding sensation,—[this fiber] in the state of heightened agility, if it is either again affected by neighboring or otherwise connected fibers or struck by any other impulse, comes into such a lively motion that the lively sensation that corresponds to the motion is reproduced in the soul.[25]

An object impresses upon the nerves, setting them into motion in a specific direction. Gmelin perceives this impression as a physical interaction and throughout the description focuses on physical contact. The terminology used underscores the physical contact between material objects; the fibers are impressed (*einprägen*) by the object and the striking (*anschlagen*) of the nerve fibers against one another. The soul is in turn shaped by the movements of the fibers, and thus by the very object itself. The "other impulse" that moves to strike the fibers, causing them to move in a new way, can be any number of things, including animal magnetism. For this reason, patients in a magnetic state can exhibit different reactions to objects.

During magnetic sleep, the patient is more strongly effected by objects, because "during magnetic sleep the action of the object and the reaction of the soul are increased and multiplied."[26] This increased reaction of the soul, coupled with an intensity of focus, accounts for "the increased clarity of sensation and imagination [*Vorstellungen*], and the higher functioning of all operations of the soul."[27] In other words, magnetic sleep enables new object/body affective relationships, which in turn results in seemingly supernatural senses and clarity of thought. To apply this to one of the experiments discussed earlier, the metal has an increased influence on Richardt's nerves, which in turn makes him able to distinguish between metals based on the sensation he feels. The *widerlich* sensation that is caused by contact with the silver, for example, is only possible in this heightened state. To the unmagnetized person, this silver would not have had an extraordinary effect.

The patient's heightened sensibility and resulting ability to form abnormal affective relationships were used by many magnetists as diagnostic tools to treat other patients. In these instances, the patient became an instrument in the doctor's medical practice.[28] Their heightened state enabled patients to extend their senses across time, space, and into objects, enabling access to their own bodies and the bodies of others. They could also recognize traces of people on objects. The somnambulist's ability to feel what others couldn't, to be sensitive to characteristics of people and objects that others couldn't, and to collect information through affective responses made somnambulists a valuable part of animal magnetism. They legitimated the "science" by validating their magnetist's animal magnetic power and verifying their own skills through feeling—or at least performing the feeling—of specific affects.

During his treatment, Reichardt is asked several times to diagnose the illness of another patient. In one such instance, Reichardt is given a glass that had been touched by an ill person and was asked what impression it made on him. Presumably, Gmelin's hope was that Reichardt would be able to diagnosis the unnamed person's illness based on the impressions left on the glass. Reichardt answers, "I feel something odd in my hand, it makes an unpleasant impression on me, an adverse sensation in my nerves, but I cannot clearly specify it."[29] Reichardt perceives himself to be passive in this interaction, with the objects making the impression on him and producing the sensation in him. Although he is unable to glean any information about the sick person who once held the glass, the illness of the sick owner lingers on/in the glass, manifesting itself as a negative feeling on and in Reichardt. The sensation at the moment of contact with the glass is depicted as the echo of the sensations of the ill person.

In a second instance, Reichardt is asked to diagnose a young woman, Miss Kornacher. Gmelin puts the two people in contact by asking Reichardt to touch the young woman, and comments that "[Reichardt] could tolerate her touch well."[30] Gmelin asks if he "feels a disorder in her body,"[31] with the choice of verb emphasizing Reichardt's role as an affective instrument of diagnosis.[32] Reichardt goes on to misdiagnose the illness and suggest a cure. In this way, he is positioned as both an object of diagnosis himself and an agent of Miss Kornacher's objectification.

Rapport

Given the potential usefulness of a somnambulist, magnetists sought the most effective techniques to magnetize. Time and again, theorists identified that a positive affective bond between magnetist and patient was a prerequisite for a successful magnetic healing. This relationship was called "rapport," and was perceived as an affective relationship, I argue, in so much as it described an embodied sensation intertwined with emotion. Armand-Marie-Jacques de

Chastenent, Marquis de Puysegur, was the first to identify rapport and subsequent magnetists attributed greater or lesser importance to it.[33] For Mesmer, rapport was the key to the patient's unmediated access to things and people. Mesmer writes that in rapport, the movements of the thoughts "in the mind and within the substance of the nerves, being at the same time in communication with the series of a subtle fluid with which this nervous substance is in continuity, can independently extend, without the help of air or ether, to unlimited distances and can 'immediately' relate to the internal sense of another individual."[34] As a result, "the will of two persons can communicate with each other through their internal sense organs"; this "reciprocity between two wills" is called "being in rapport."[35] Mesmer describes rapport here as precognitive, working independently of language and conscious thought, the ability of one person to directly access the senses of the other in a state of immediate, perfect communication. Grounded in nerve-theory, Mesmer's concept of rapport offers an embodied affective connection between magnetizer and magnetized, which is made possible by the animal magnetic fluid. Ultimately, Mesmer was more interested in magnetic fluid than in rapport.

Other magnetists theorized rapport in terms of sympathy, the term itself emphasizing its affective character. When Gotthilf Heinrich von Schubert describes rapport, he calls it a "deep sympathy" (*tiefe Sympathie*).[36] In *Über Sympathie*, Friedrich Hufeland describes the affective bond between magnetist and somnambulist in terms of universal *Sympathie*—a force he believed connected all living things.[37] According to Hufeland, the tie of sympathy is so strong between magnetist and magnetized that they form "one individual," able to share thoughts and feelings.[38] Typically, such sharing was thought to be unidirectional, moving from magnetist to somnambulist only, as the former was believed to have the stronger will. C. A. von Eschenmayer likewise defines rapport as a connection forged from sympathy creating a positive affective connection to magnetizer and a negative affect toward others.[39] Despite the variety of terms, one consistent element remains, namely that positive affect is necessary for magnetism.

Reichardt uses the language of rapport and sympathy to assert authority over his father and define the parameters of their relationship, if only briefly in the context of his treatment. The tension in the text between father and son is not commented upon by Gmelin in the observations section, but over the course of his notes it emerges as an unintended subplot of the treatment. Herr Reichardt asserts multiple times during the treatment that Gmelin is the best possible magnetist for him, positioning Gmelin in the role Reichardt's father wanted to assume. Reichardt grounds these claims in physiological arguments. When asked if anyone else could magnetize him, Reichardt admits that others might have a magnetic effect, but he knew of no one who "would have had such a positive affect on him as I [Gmelin]" ("*so gut auf ihn wirkte, als ich*").[40] The verb choice and adverb "gut" emphasizes both the level of effectiveness and the affective quality of the magnetism.

During his first magnetic session on May 7, Reichardt brings up the issue of his father magnetizing him. Gmelin writes, "He said that his gentleman father could not magnetize him, why not? He said that he did not know why at this time."[41] Richardt's comments seem strangely out of place, as there has been no indication that his father was going to magnetize him. The assertion that he cannot appears unprompted and begins what will become a preoccupation of the son and father throughout the text. The son repeatedly complains that his father's presence is counter-productive for his treatment, while the father, in turn, becomes strangely insistent that he be given the opportunity to magnetize his son.

On May 8, Reichardt goes into more detail regarding his father as potential magnetizer: "His [Reichardt's] gentleman father could not magnetize him, his father would have affected him so negatively, that he [the son] would have an attack; his lady mother would have a better effect on him, still not as good as I [Gmelin]."[42] The patient's insistence on Gmelin magnetizing him is indicative of the strong affective relationship. Here, Herr Reichardt communicates a hierarchy of affective magnetic relationships by identifying the person with whom he would have a positive affective experience. His father has the most adverse effect, his mother less so, and his magnetist the most positive. If, in the logic of animal magnetism, men were the best magnetizers because they had the strongest will, then identifying his father as the one least likely to magnetize him is a challenge to his father's masculinity.

Reichardt's father tries repeatedly to interfere in the healing, and the patient repeatedly employs the language of animal magnetism to articulate the negative affect that characterizes their relationship. On May 9, Gmelin records the following: "His gentlemen father did not have a beneficial effect on him, but rather a negative one, because his nerves had a completely opposing mood than his [the patient's] own."[43] When Gmelin asks Reichardt directly "if his gentleman father might not be allowed to touch him?" Reichardt gives an uncharacteristically short answer: "No."[44] Echoing ideas of sympathy at the core of Gmelin's magnetic theories, the patient characterizes a potential affective relationship with his father as adverse. From the patient's perspective, the two men are physiologically and emotionally hostile to one another. Through this statement, Reichardt exerts power over his father by denying him the ability to control his body and mind.

The patient continues to reject the possibility of an affective connection with his father and exclude him from his healing. On May 14, Gmelin magnetises Herr Reichardt in a room with multiple family members and friends. Each take turns speaking to Reichardt, and Gmelin records his responses. Gmelin claims that Herr Reichardt can hear everyone speak except his father:

"he did not hear his gentleman father at all."[45] Patients often reported only being able to hear or see those people with whom they were in rapport during a magnetic session.[46] According to Gmelin, Reichardt can hear and understand his magnetist, while he can only partially understand the others in the room and cannot hear his father at all. By not hearing his father, Reichardt has again established a hierarchy based on sensation. Father and magnetist symbolize two poles of male affective relationships.

Reichardt's father attempts again to participate in the magnetization later that day. Gmelin conducts another experiment in which visitors take turns touching Reichardt's hand, and he records the sensation that each hand makes. In general, the visitors' hands have a positive or neutral effect, but the patient always indicates that Gmelin's hand is the most pleasant (*angenehmer*). And then comes his father: "When his gentleman father touched him, without his knowledge, he complained of a very painful sensation in his arm."[47] Not only is the touch painful, but counterproductive to his magnetism. His father appears to have a kind of "anti-rapport," juxtaposing him with the beneficial figure of the magnetist.

On July 18, Reichardt's father makes one last attempt to magnetize his son: "His gentlemen father asked him, if perhaps he wouldn't be able to magnetism him once? . . . He answered: no, you cannot and would not be able to magnetize me; there must be a harmony of nerves and nerve aether between the magnetized and magnetist, and the magnetist's own nerve-current can't be too strong or too weak in relationship to the magnetized."[48] The way in which the question is formulated has an almost pleading tone. Using the terminology of magnetism, the son describes once again why he and his father cannot achieve rapport. In this quote, *Harmonie* describes the ideal state between magnetist and magnetized, one that is achieved through balance of *Nervenaether* flowing between the two parties. The son's use of the modals *können* and *dürfen* eliminates any chance that Reichardt and his father could have the harmonious affective relationship required for magnetism.

In the end, Reichardt's treatment is successful. Gmelin's magnetic influence on him decreases in proportion to the patient's improving health. The end of Gmelin's magnetic influence indicates that Reichardt is once again a healthy man and therefore, according to magnetic theory, unable to be magnetized. Gmelin does not comment on the relationship between father and son, and the reader never learns why the former wanted so desperately to magnetize the latter.

Conclusion

When we approach magnetism through the lens of affect, it enriches our discussion of animal magnetism in several ways. For example, this approach accounts for the popularity of metaphors of animal magnetism in modern discussions of affect. The word "mesmerize," for instance, is derived from the name of the founder of animal magnetism, Franz Anton Mesmer, and is popularly used today to describe the affective power of people and objects over other people. In addition, an affective approach to magnetism shifts the perspective from the physician to the patient, focusing on their embodied perspective, even if it is heavily mediated through the physician-narrator. Since most patients of magnetists were either women or "feminized" men, a focus on the patient's embodied experience could potentially problematize, if not subvert, the official patriarchal narrative that shapes the case study. Finally, approaching magnetism with an emphasis on affect can lead to new productive areas of inquiry, such as the study of affective relationships in other medical case studies around 1800.

Approaching this case study through affect enables us to examine how the language of animal magnetism was used to conceptualize affective relationships between patient, magnetist, and family members. Reichardt uses the language of animal magnetism to assert his own embodied affective experience. He is able to control relationships and validate through "science" affects that could have otherwise challenged traditional familial hierarchies. While much work has been done examining the, albeit limited, power that animal magnetism afforded female patients to control their families and their surroundings, instances of male somnambulism are often overlooked. A reading attentive to affect, however, reveals this element of Reichardt's case that is otherwise relegated to the periphery. What we see is the story of male body, whose expression of gender in the text is feminized and therefore does not align with heteronormative ideals. This man uses animal magnetism to tell his story of his body and articulate its affective connections with the people around him.

Sara Luly is Associate Professor of German at Kansas State University. Her research interests are late eighteenth and early nineteenth century literature and culture, with an emphasis on German Romanticism and Gender Studies. Currently, her research examines German Gothic literature and questions of masculinity in the works of German Romanticism.

Notes

1. For an overview of the historical development of Mesmer's theories, their subgroups, and their relationship to contemporary and modern psychology, see Alan Gauld, *A History of Hypnotism* (Cambridge, UK: Cambridge University Press, 1995); Adam Crabtree, *From Mesmer to Freud: Magnetic Sleep and the Roots of Psychological Healing* (New Haven: Yale University Press, 1993), especially chapter 7; Gereon Wolters and Walter Bongartz, eds., *Franz Anton Mesmer und der Mesmerismus: Wissenschaft, Scharlatanerie, Poesie* (Konstanz: Universitätsverlag Konstanz, 1988); Heinz Schott, "Über den 'thierischen Magnetismus' und sein Legitimationsproblem," *Medizinhistorisches Journal* 21, (1986): 104–21; Ernst Benz, "Franz Anton Mesmer und die philosophischen Grundlagen des 'animalischen Magnetismus,'" *Akademie der Wissenschaften und der Literatur* 4 (1977) 5–45; and Robert Darnton, *Mesmerism and the End of the Enlightenment in France* (Cambridge, MA: Harvard University Press, 1968).
2. Eberhard Gmelin, *Materialien für die Anthropologie. Band 1*, (Tübingen: J. G. Cottische Buchhandlung, 1791). I will focus on three theoretical texts on animal magnetism: Gmelin, *Materialien*, mentioned above; Franz Anton Mesmer, *Mesmerismus: oder, System der Wechselwirkungen, Theorie und Anwendung des Thierischen Magnetismus als die Allgemeine Heilkunde zur Erhaltung des Menschen* (Amsterdam: E. J. Bonset, 1966); and Franz Anton Mesmer, "Dissertation by F. A. Mesmer, Doctor of Medicine, on His Discoveries," in *Mesmerism: A Translation of the Original Scientific and Medical Writings of F. A. Mesmer*, ed. George Bloch, 43–80 (Los Altos, CA: William Kaufmann, 1980). The genesis of Wolfart's text is convoluted, claiming to be work of Mesmer and listing Karl Christian Wolfart as the editor and translator. In his foreword, Wolfart claims the text is a direct translation of conversations he had with Mesmer in French in 1812. While we cannot take *Mesmerismus* as the direct words of Mesmer, the theories put forth are in line with other texts written by Mesmer himself, such as "Dissertation," and therefore represent his approach to animal magnetism. Mesmer wrote relatively little on the topic of animal magnetism and therefore Wolfart's text is the most extensive work on Mesmer's theories. All translations are my own unless otherwise indicated. I would like to thank Jan Jost-Fritz for editing my translations, as well as Benjamin McCloskey, Necia Chronister, and the members of K-State's GWSS intellectual circle for their feedback and editing.
3. A somnambulist was a patient (typically female) who, while magnetized, exhibited supernatural abilities including clairvoyance, reading sealed letters, and "seeing" into the bodies of others.
4. Jürgen Barkhoff, "Darstellungsformen von Leib und Seele in Fallgeschichten des Animalischen Magnetismus," in *Der ganze Mensch: Anthropologie und Literatur im 18. Jahrhundert: DFG-Symposion*, ed. Hans-Jürgen Schings, 214–41 (Stuttgart: Metzler, 1994), 232.
5. Bettina Gruber, *Die Seherin von Prevorst: Romantischer Okkultismus als Religion, Wissenschaft und Literatur* (Paderborn: Ferdinand Schöningh, 2000).
6. Gruber, *Die Seherin von Prevorst*, 85–97.
7. See Maria Tatar, *Spellbound: Studies on Mesmerism and Literature* (Princeton: Princeton University Press, 1978); Jürgen Barkhoff, *Magnetische Fiktionen*:

Literarisierung des Mesmerismus in der Romantik (Stuttgart: Verlag J. B. Metzler, 1995); Jürgen Barkhoff, "Geschlechteranthropologie und Mesmerismus: Literarische Magnetiseurinnen bei und um E. T. A. Hoffmann," in *"Hoffmanneske Geschichte" Zu einer Literaturwissenschaft als Kulturwissenschaft*, ed. Gehard Neumann, 15–42 (Bonn: Königshausen & Neumann, 2005); Silke Arnold-de Simine, *Leichen im Keller: Zu Fragen des Gender in Angstinszenierungen der Schauer- und Kriminalliteratur 1790–1830* (St. Ingbert: Röhrig Universitätsverlag, 2000); Katharine Weder, *Kleists Magnetische Poesie: Experimente des Mesmerismus* (Götingen: Wallstein, 2008); and Sara Luly, "Magnetism and Masculinity in E. T. A. Hoffmann's Der Magnetiseur," *The Germanic Review: Literature, Culture and Theory* 88, no. 3 (2013): 418–34.
8. Barkhoff, "Darstellungsformen," touches on how magnetic fluids had embodied effect, constituting for the patient an "unmediated, psycho-physical reality" (219). In this way, animal magnetism provided a mode for understanding, shaping, and relating their embodied experience. Barkhoff discusses the depiction of Romantik literature as "mesmerizing" around 1800 in "Mesmerismus zwischen Wissenschaft und Narration: Pathogenes und curatives Erzählen bei E.T.A. Hoffmann," In *Von Schillers Räubern zu Shellys Frankenstein: Wissenschaft und Literatur im Dialog um 1800*, ed. Dietrich von Engelhardt and Hans Wißkirchen, (Stuttgart: Schattauer, 2006), 83–96. While it does not address affect directly, it does indicate the psychological influence of objects (in this case, books) on people and the use of mesmeric terminology to describe that influence.
9. Brian Massumi, *Parables for the Virtual: Movement, Affect, Sensation* (Durham, NC: Duke University Press, 2002).
10. Massumi, *Parables for the Virtual*, 27.
11. Massumi, *Parables for the Virtual*, 28.
12. Massumi, *Parables for the Virtual*, 28.
13. Ruth Leys, "The Turn to Affect: A Critique," *Critical Inquiry* 37, (2011): 458.
14. Each case begins with a brief patient history; gives a detailed, dated account of each day's symptoms and treatments; ends with a sentence or two indicating how the patient's health continued after the treatment was over; and is followed by a section titled "Observations" in which Gmelin explains the case in the context of contemporary medical theories. For a discussion of this collection's contribution to the case study genre, see Barkhoff "Darstellungsformen," 214–15. The case study is written from Gmelin's point of view, including both direct and indirect quotes from the patient. Herr Reichardt is first identified as "the son of Herr Reichardt," but referred to as Herr Reichardt throughout the text. To avoid confusion, I refer to the patient as "Herr Reichardt" and the father as "his gentleman father."
15. Gmelin, *Materialien*, 93–4.
16. Gmelin, *Materialien*, 107.
17. Rüdiger Campe and Julia Weber, "Rethinking Emotion: Moving beyond Interiority; An Introduction," in *Rethinking Emotion: Interiority and Exteriority in Premodern, Modern, and Contemporary Thought* (Berlin: De Gruyter, 2014), 1–18. Jörn Steigerwald discusses Mesmerism and its relationship to contemporary medical mapping of the body in "Die Normalisierung des Menschen: Eine Anthropologische Problemskizze am Beispiel der Mesmerismusdiskussion des Jahres 1784," in *Reiz, Imagination, Aufmerksamkeit; Erregung und Steuerung von Einbildungskraft im klassischen Zeitalter, 1680–1830*, ed. Jörn Steigerwald and Daniela Watzke (Würzburg: Königshausen und Neuman, 2003): 13–40.

18. *Baquets* were tubs filled with objects magnetized by the magnetist and then sealed shut, with ropes and metal rods protruding from the top. Patients would touch the rods or attach the ropes to the ailing parts of their body, causing the animal magnetic energy to pass into their bodies and heal them. See Mesmer, *Mesmerismus*, 116.
19. Gmelin, *Materialien*, 135.
20. Gmelin, *Materialien*, 135.
21. Gmelin, *Materialien*, 135–36.
22. Gmelin, *Materialien*, 135.
23. Gmelin, *Materialien*, 136.
24. Barkhoff, "Darstellungsformen," 220–21, discusses Gmelin's theories in the context of nerve theory.
25. Gmelin, *Materialien*, 273–74.
26. Gmelin, *Materialien*, 274–75.
27. Gmelin, *Materialien*, 275.
28. Mesmer, *Mesmerismus*, 124, likens a somnambulist to a telescope.
29. Gmelin, *Materialien*, 140.
30. Gmelin, *Materialien*, 140.
31. Gmelin, *Materialien*, 140.
32. Gmelin, *Materialien*, 140–41.
33. Crabtree, *From Mesmer to Freud*, 41. Adam Crabtree, *Animal Magnetism, Early Hypnotism, and Psychical Research, 1766–1925: An Annotated Bibliography* (White Plains, NY: Kraus International Publications, 1988), 26, cites Armand-Marie-Jacques de Chastenet, Marquis de Puysegur, *Suite des mémoires pour servir à l'histoire et à l'établissement du magnétisme animal* (Paris and London: n.p., 1785), as the first time the term "rapport" refers to the connection between magnetizer and somnambulist.
34. Mesmer, "Dissertation," 121.
35. Mesmer, "Dissertation," 121.
36. Gotthilf Heinrich von Schubert, "Dreizehnte Vorlesung: Von dem thierischen Magnetismus und einigen ihm verwandten Erscheinungen," in *Ansichten von der Nachtseite der Naturwissenschaft* (Dreseden and Leipzig: Arnoldischen Buchhandlung, 1840), 214.
37. Friedrich Hufeland, *Über Sympathie* (Weimar: Verlage des Landes- Industrie-Comptoirs, 1811).
38. Hufeland, *Über Sympathie*, 117.
39. C. A. von Eschenmayer, *Versuch die scheinbare Magie des thierischen Magnetismus aus physiologischen und psychischen Gesetzen zu erklären* (Stuttgart: J. G. Cotta'schen Verlag, 1816), 37.
40. Gmelin, *Materialien*, 101.
41. Gmelin, *Materialien*, 99.
42. Gmelin, *Materialien*, 101.
43. Gmelin, *Materialien*, 107.
44. Gmelin, *Materialien*, 144.
45. Gmelin, *Materialien*, 139.
46. Friedrich Fischer, "Einige Beobachtungen über thierischen Magnetismus und Somnambulismus von F. Fischer" *Archiv für die Physiologie* 6 (1805): 268.
47. Gmelin, *Materialien*, 145.
48. Gmelin, *Materialien*, 243–44.

Bibliography

Arnold-de Simine, Silke. *Leichen im Keller: Zu Fragen des Gender in Angstinszenierung der Schauer- und Kriminalliteratur.* St. Ingbert: Röhrig Universitätsverlag, 2000.

Barkhoff, Jürgen. "Darstellungsformen von Leib und Seele in Fallgeschichten des Animalischen Magnetismus." In *Der ganze Mensch: Anthropologie und Literatur im 18. Jahrhundert; DFG-Symposion,* edited by Hans-Jürgen Schings, 214–41. Stuttgart: Metzler, 1994.

———. "Geschlechteranthropologie und Mesmerismus: Literarische Magnetiseurinnen bei und um E. T. A. Hoffmann." In *"Hoffmanneske Geschichte" Zu einer Literaturwissenschaft als Kulturwissenschaft,* edited by Gehard Neumann, 15–42. Bonn: Königshausen & Neumann, 2005.

———. *Magnetische Fiktionen: Literarisierung des Mesmerismus in der Romantik.* Stuttgart: Verlag J. B. Metzler, 1995.

———. "Mesmerismus zwischen Wissenschaft und Narration: Pathogenes und curatives Erzählen bei E. T. A. Hoffmann." In *Von Schillers Räubern zu Shellys Frankenstein: Wissenschaft und Literatur im Dialog um 1800,* edited by Dietrich von Engelhardt and Hans Wißkirchen, 83–96. Stuttgart: Schattauer, 2006.

Benz, Ernst. "Franz Anton Mesmer und die philosophischen Grundlagen des 'animalischen Magnetismus.'" *Akademie der Wissenschaften und der Literatur* 4 (1977): 5–45.

Campe, Rüdiger, and Julia Weber. "Rethinking Emotion: Moving beyond Interiority; An Introduction." In *Rethinking Emotion: Interiority and Exteriority in Premodern, Modern, and Contemporary Thought,* edited by Rüdiger Campe and Julia Weber, 1–18. Berlin: De Gruyter, 2014.

Crabtree, Adam. *Animal Magnetism, Early Hypnotism, and Psychical Research, 1766–1925: An Annotated Bibliography.* White Plains, NY: Kraus International Publications, 1988.

———. *From Mesmer to Freud: Magnetic Sleep and the Roots of Psychological Healing.* New Haven: Yale University Press, 1993.

Darnton, Robert. *Mesmerism and the End of the Enlightenment in France.* Cambridge, MA: Harvard University Press, 1968.

de Chastenet, Armand-Marie-Jacques, Marquis de Puysegur. *Suite des mémoires pour servir à l'histoire et à l'établissement du magnétisme animal.* Paris and London: n.p., 1785.

Fischer, Friedrich. "Einige Beobachtungen über thierischen Magnetismus und Somnambulismus von F. Fischer." *Archiv für die Physiologie* 6 (1805): 264–81.

Gauld, Alan. *A History of Hypnotism.* Cambridge, UK: Cambridge University Press, 1995.

Gmelin, Eberhard. *Materialien für die Anthropologie: Band 1.* Tübingen: J. G. Cottische Buchhandlung, 1791.

Gruber, Bettina. *Die Seherin von Prevorst: Romantischer Okkultismus als Religion, Wissenschaft und Literatur*. Paderborn: Ferdinand Schöningh, 2000.
Hufeland, Friedrich. *Über Sympathie*. Weimar: Verlage des Landes- Industrie-Comptoirs, 1811.
Leys, Ruth. "The Turn to Affect: A Critique." *Critical Inquiry* 37 (2011): 434–72.
Luly, Sara. "Magnetism and Masculinity in E. T. A. Hoffmann's Der Magnetiseur." *The Germanic Review: Literature, Culture and Theory* 88, no. 3 (2013): 418–34.
Massumi, Brian. *Parables for the Virtual: Movement, Affect, Sensation*. Durham, NC: Duke University Press, 2002.
Mesmer, Franz Anton. "Dissertation by F. A. Mesmer, Doctor of Medicine, on His Discoveries." In *Mesmerism: A Translation of the Original Scientific and Medical Writings of F. A. Mesmer*, edited and translated by George Bloch, 43–80. Los Altos, CA: William Kaufmann, 1980.
——— *Mesmerismus: oder, System der Wechselwirkungen, Theorie und Anwendung des Thierischen Magnetismus als die Allgemeine Heilkunde zur Erhaltung des Menschen*. Edited by Karl Christian Wolfart. 1814, Reprint. Amsterdam: E. J. Bonset, 1966.
Schott, Heinz. "Über den 'thierischen Magnetismus' und sein Legitimationsproblem." *Medizinhistorisches Journal* 21 (1986): 104–21.
Steigerwald, Jörn. "Die Normalisierung des Menschen: Eine Anthropologische Problemskizze am Beispiel der Mesmerismusdiskussion des Jahres 1784." In *Reiz, Imagination, Aufmerksamkeit: Erregung und Steuerung von Einbildungskraft im klassischen Zeitalter, 1680–1830*, edited by Jörn Steigerwald and Daniela Watzke, 13–40. Würzburg: Königshausen und Neuman, 2003.
Tatar, Maria M. *Spellbound: Studies on Mesmerism and Literature*. Princeton: Princeton University Press, 1978.
von Eschenmayer, C. A. *Versuch die scheinbare Magie des thierischen Magnetismus aus physiologischen und psychischen Gesezen zu erklären*. Stuttgart: J. G. Cotta'schen Verlag, 1816.
von Schubert, Gotthilf Heinrich. "Dreizehnte Vorlesung: Von dem thierischen Magnetismus und einigen ihm verwandten Erscheinungen." In *Ansichten von der Nachtseite der Naturwissenschaft*, 193–224. Dresden and Leipzig: Arnoldischen Buchhandlung, 1840.
Weder, Katharine. *Kleists Magnetische Poesie: Experimente des Mesmerismus*. Göttingen: Wallstein, 2008.
Wolters, Gereon, and Walter Bongartz, eds. *Franz Anton Mesmer und der Mesmerismus: Wissenschaft, Scharlatanerie, Poesie*. Konstanz: Universitätsverlag Konstanz, 1988.

CHAPTER 2

Emotional Contagions
Franz Liszt and the Materiality of Celebrity Culture in the 1830s and 1840s

HANNU SALMI

The concert which took place in the Music Hall, on last Thursday, was beyond all doubt one of the most remarkable and interesting that we ever attended in this town. We have rarely witnessed a similar enthusiasm amongst our music-loving public. But who could possibly remain cold on hearing such a performer as Franz Liszt? Who would not be carried away by the fire and intenseness which pervades his play, or listen with delight to the harp-like tones which he draws from his instrument, as they softer and softer fall upon the ear, and gently die away. Cold critics, who affect a sober judgment, may find such a performance too wild and extravagant, but to us it is no such thing. For we not alone recognise in Liszt the great performer, who overcomes incredible technical difficulties, but we see in him the deeply reflecting artist, who well knows what stress to lay upon every individual note, and who stamps upon every composition which he plays, however various it may be, a distinct character. He intended to have concluded with the overture to "Wilhelm Tell," but, as the public by loud encores insisted on his re-appearing, he finished with "God save the Queen," in a style not to be excelled in grandeur.
—*The Leeds Mercury*, 12 December 1840

This is how *The Leeds Mercury* described the concert of Franz Liszt (1811–86) in Leeds on 10 December 1840. The critic emphasized the great enthusiasm of the "music-loving public" and "the fire and intenseness" of Liszt's art. There was irresistible emotionality in his playing, and he was able, at will, to transform the strings of the piano into a harp that gently swept the ear. At the same time, Liszt's music, but also his figure and his presence, was too "wild and extravagant" for the "cold," obviously unemotional, critics.

His biographer, Derek Watson, has characterized Liszt as "a dazzling wizard, a showman and superman of the keyboard."[1] In a world that was divided by political borders, Liszt travelled smoothly from place to place with his own wagon, later by train, and was recognized without any travel documents. According to the contemporary Viennese music critic Eduard Hanslick, Liszt's face was probably the most well-known in Europe at the time.[2] In his fame, Liszt equalled to the Italian violinist Niccolò Paganini, but he was able to target a wider geographical area in Europe than his colleague, thrilling audiences from Scotland to Spain, from France to Russia.[3] Franz Liszt was born in the village of Doborján in the Kingdom of Hungary. He was a child prodigy who aroused enthusiasm in London as early as 1824, as echoed by, amongst others, the Dutch daily *Arnhemsche courant* and the Finnish *Finlands Allmänna Tidning*.[4] Liszt became known for his extraordinary skills, tricks, and technique, and his amazing bravura.[5]

In his book *The Invention of Celebrity 1750–1850*, the French historian Antoine Lilti has traced the origins of celebrity culture and stressed the era of enlightenment as a decisive turning point. Already, Voltaire became a celebrity through the printing press and was known throughout Europe. Still, as I argue, as cultural phenomena, celebrities like Paganini and Liszt embarked on something new. They travelled at a hectic pace and allowed massive audiences to experience their performances. They usually performed in opera houses and other large venues. Literary figures, like Voltaire, were known through their writings, but Paganini and Liszt really toured around the continent and met tens of thousands of people, or even more. In this respect, Liszt was particularly active, and his fame was fostered and intensified by the rise of transport technology, newspaper publishing, and bourgeois music culture. Liszt seemed to have a strange appeal to the audiences: they were not only tempted to follow him on stage but were eager to know about his deeds also in private life. The mysterious attraction of these star-like figures was sometimes explained in terms of magnetism and other natural forces, sometimes, as in the case of Paganini, by supernatural and invisible *diablerie*, a pact with the devil.[6] Heinrich Heine coined the term "Lisztomania" to describe the active, even fanatic audiences who participated in the performances and were ready to express openly their emotions.[7] A devotion to Liszt was a mania, an obsession.

I have previously written on the rise of musical celebrities in nineteenth-century Europe and its resonance with and intervention in the concept of culture.[8] My aim is now to concentrate on Franz Liszt and especially on his emotional gravitation; with "gravitation," I refer to the ways in which his emotional appeal was amplified in mid-nineteenth-century culture, besides his music and musical performances, especially through technological changes in musical instruments as well as in both transport and media. I argue that this gravitation had striking, and complex, material ramifications, not only from the perspective of the emotional responses of the audience but already in regard to Liszt's body as a performer. Liszt became an emotional power field, fuelled by the on-going process of modernization. This chapter analyzes the materiality of emotions both from the perspective of the emotionality of the audience but also by focusing on how Liszt was interpreted, and how he functioned in the end, as a generator of emotionality, as an assemblage of human and nonhuman forces. As already argued in the introduction of this book, the mind does not form the limits of emotions. Therefore, Liszt's emotionality has to be studied not only by analyzing his body and its immediate extensions, like the piano, but also the larger environment that enabled and participated in the amplification of his emotional appeal. In this task, the chapter draws on contemporary public discourse, on books and articles, on digital newspaper repositories, and also on images and caricatures of his physical appearance.

The Body of the Performer

Alan Walker, the author of the seminal Franz Liszt biography, has emphasized the influence of Paganini on the young Liszt. In April 1832, cholera was raging in Paris, which generated widespread anxieties, but it did not prevent Paganini from presenting his concerts for large audiences. In one of these concerts, Franz Liszt was in the auditorium and was thrilled by the performance, especially by the inseparability of the virtuoso and his instrument. As a result, he began to exercise frantically to become "the Paganini of the piano."[9]

Liszt's teacher Carl Czerny has documented the great rapidity with which his pupil finally learned to master his instrument. Liszt became "an expert sight-reader that was capable of *publicly* sight-reading even compositions of considerable difficulty and so perfectly as though he had been studying them for a long time."[10] Liszt's technical virtuosity also aroused criticism, and it was sometimes seen as exaggerated, as an aim *per se*. Similar arguments were often presented against Paganini, who developed dashing tricks to astonish his audiences and seemed to have a completely new relationship to his instrument. Paganini, and later his follower Liszt, wanted to draw the attention of his audience exclusively. This created something new compared to other contemporary entertainments like grand opera, where the audience itself had to be visible and had to have the possibility for socializing. Erika Quinn has pointed out how Paganini, and Liszt, aimed to become spectacles themselves. Paganini forced the audience to watch him rather than each other.[11]

According to the contemporary sources, the audience genuinely paid attention to the physical appearance of both Paganini and Liszt. In Paganini's case, this is no wonder since his body was distorted by diseases. In 1822–23, he did not perform while recovering from syphilis. He had intestinal problems too and lost all the teeth of his lower jaw. When Paganini was touring in Bohemia in 1828, the local critic Joseph Sedlazek wrote, "His body is so strangely contorted that one fears any moment the feet will part company with the rest of him, and the whole frame fall suddenly to the ground, a heap of bones."[12]

At the same time, Paganini's physiognomy was described as an automaton, as a machine that could play forever.[13] This metaphor probably referred also to his inexhaustible pace in touring. His corporeality extended beyond his physical body; a man-machine could reach out his travels into the most distant areas in Europe. In fact, Liszt was finally able to tour even more extensively than Paganini, thanks to the rapid changes in transport technology in the 1830s and 1840s. There was much more to be harvested than had been possible for Paganini. In this respect, Liszt's career was an epitome of modernity—also in an emotional sense, since through his extensive itineraries he was able to address a wider audience than anyone before him.

Franz Liszt, like Paganini, was an eye-catcher among the public. When he visited Vienna after a long break in 1838, his presence was immediately noticed. Newspapers wrote on the "internal unrest" of the genius and on his majestic outer appearance.[14] His bodily fluids were in restless motion, but still he had particular calmness in his public behavior. On the other hand, his physicality was harshly critiqued during the concerts. In Paris, François-Joseph Fétis, one of the most powerful music critics of the nineteenth century, argued that Liszt had "converted music into a shell-game and conjuring show."[15] There are many caricatures that portray Liszt in action. The collections of the University Library of Strasbourg include an image entitled *Liszt jouant "Grand galop chromatique"* (1843, Figure 2.1), where Liszt seems to be unable to sit behind his piano and is jumping up during the course of the energetic gallop. His fingers are almost unnaturally long, and his gestures look edgy. Liszt himself seems to be taken away by his own compositions, and other musicians try to follow as well as they can.[16] Liszt is paralleled with a galloping rider, as in some other contemporary images. He is in a seemingly uncontrolled motion, and only he seems to be able to follow the logic of this restless ride. In this image, Liszt is not a star as an object of desire, but more like an irresistible artist, a natural phenomenon that cannot be controlled or held back.

Figure 2.1 is from 1843. There is evidence, however, that Franz Liszt became increasingly conscious of his body already in the 1830s, after his first successes in Paris. In fact, many later portraits show him in rather calm positions, playing an aristocratic type.[17] Dana Gooley argues that already the critiques Liszt confronted in Paris made him control his virtuosity, or merely the way he presented his skills for the audience during the shows. Because he was in search of affirmation as an artist, he gradually replaced his inspiration of Paganini with the commitment to Beethoven who was obviously a more noble figure to follow. It was important to emphasize that he, Franz Liszt, was not *only* a virtuoso. He wanted to be recognized both as a man of letters and as a composer.[18] All this shows that Liszt not only fashioned his body to arouse the

Figure 2.1. Liszt playing the *Grand galop chromatique* (1843). Image: Bibliothèque nationale et universitaire de Strasbourg, NIM35493, http://catalogue.bnf.fr/ark:/12148/cb41932328g. Public domain.

interest of his audiences but he also aimed at influencing on how his body and his emotionality were perceived by the public.

Despite these efforts, as the image from 1843 suggests, Franz Liszt's virtuosity remained essential for his reception. Liszt's amazing bravura occurred in conjunction with the development of piano as an instrument. This, in turn, offers the possibility to analyze the materiality of Liszt's emotionality not only in relation to his body but also from the perspective of his tangible instrument. In recent literature on the history of emotions, materiality has gained much attention,[19] although there are fewer studies on early nineteenth-century music and materiality.[20] In the 1820s, the so-called repetition lever was introduced to enable clear articulation and rapid playing of notes, which was particularly important for Liszt. It was also a precondition for his own compositions, which included very rapid passages and many notes within short timeframes.[21] While the piano was ready to respond to its player's virtuosity more precisely, it seems that the player and the piano looked like an inseparable whole for the audience. Liszt himself stresses the inseparability of his body and his instrument: "I have the same feeling for my piano that a sailor has for his frigate, that an Arab has for his horse—more than that . . . for me, it is my language, my life."[22] This material entanglement reminds of Gilles Deleuze and Félix Guattari's discussion on human/nonhuman assemblages: a rider on a horse is a "man-horse" who gets new faculties and is thus more than a sum of its parts.[23] Liszt on stage was a "man-piano," an assemblage of human and nonhuman forces that was capable of producing unexpected outcomes. Thus, if we interpret emotionality as communication, there was an essential material element to the emotionality in a piano recital by Franz Liszt. The new instrument with a repetition lever was more sensitive and nuanced in responding to the emotions of the artist, and, at the same time, the pianist had to be quicker, sharper, and, in the end, more physical to be able to fully exploit the potential of the instrument. For the audience, the "man-piano" was an inseparable entity that could produce something that previously had been unheard and unseen. The emotionality of both the instrument and the body, their close entanglement, constituted what I call the emotional gravitation of Liszt's presence in the concert hall.

The Audience Overwhelmed

In the case of Franz Liszt, the body of the performer and its material extensions is only one platform for the materiality of emotions. It is equally important to pay attention to the audience and its reactions. Liszt became one of the most celebrated public figures in nineteenth-century Europe. As already noted, he travelled extensively throughout the continent, especially in his so-called *Glanzperiode* after 1839.

Figure 2.2 shows Liszt's concert sites between 1839 and 1847. As the map indicates, he occupied an amazingly vast area through his personal activity. These tours were probably the most extensive and wide-reaching among the musicians of the time. They also reveal the interest of Liszt to build a relationship with audiences. He produced celebrity culture through his efforts to reach his listeners in different countries and language regions and to create an audience that was particularly devoted to his music. Liszt's fandom was based on his physical presence, which, in end, had an impact on a much wider geographical region because of the mobility of the audience. He did not only go to his audience, but people came to listen to him from even further away.

Emotional Contagions ~ 47

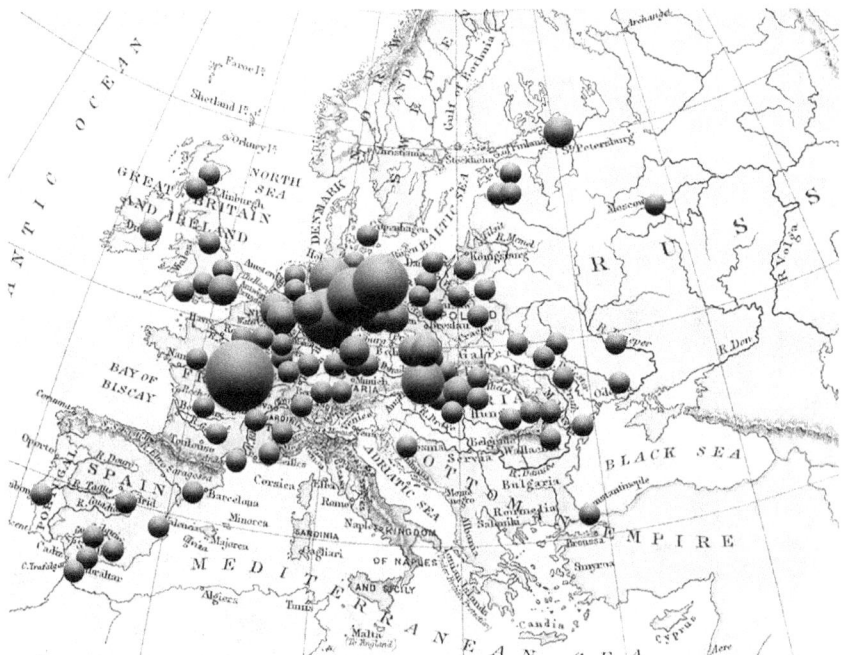

Figure 2.2. The sites of Franz Liszt's concerts, 1839–1847. The size of the ballot refers to the frequency of concerts during the time span. Image: Hannu Salmi.

This continued well into his later life. He never visited Norway, for example, but he met Edvard Grieg in Rome in 1870. Liszt showed his ability to play fluently directly from the notes and performed Grieg's piano concerto *ad hoc*.[24] Liszt did not visit Finland either, but the German-born musician Richard Faltin visited the first Bayreuth festival in 1876 and heard Liszt's playing in Villa Wahnfried. He wrote an article on this experience for a Finnish music journal and told, "Even today the maestro is able to put all his apprentices into his pocket."[25]

The contemporary audiences celebrated Liszt, as they had celebrated Paganini before. Still, the irresistible appeal that drew people to him was bound together with astonishment upon those forces that actually gave birth to this particularly powerful, unexpected interest among the public. The spectators were drawn to him, to experience his performances, which the press and other spectators already proclaimed as astonishing. The Paris-based, German-born author Heinrich Heine used the term "Lisztomania" to describe the hysterical relationship of the audience toward the famous pianist. Liszt's *Glanzperiode*, especially the visit to Berlin after Christmas 1841, became the climax of his popularity. The recital in Singakademie on 27 December evoked particularly

Figure 2.3. Franz Liszt at the Singakademie in Berlin (1847). Image: Lebrecht Music & Arts/Alamy Stock Photo.

strong emotions among the listeners, and Liszt decided to stay as long as ten weeks in the city. He performed at a hectic pace, and soon Lisztomania was like a virus among the public. Fervent admirers tried to cut curls from his hair, and even collected his cigar butts from the street.[26]

Liszt's concert at Singakademie has become an image of a turning point. The most famous depiction of this moment is a colored lithography, which was probably made a few years later in 1847 (Figure 2.3). The main focus of the image is not actually on Liszt, who is playing in a rather calm and relaxed manner, but instead on the audience that openly expresses its devotion.

It is obvious that the drawing wants to emphasize the great number of women in the audience. There are a few men, but only to take care of the fainting women or to observe the strange performance that is going on. Many of the women are using binoculars to have a closer look at their idol. Even in the first row, there seems to be a fan who has reserved a good place for viewing but still uses her binoculars. Some of the women are sending blowing kisses, some are throwing flowers. The concert situation is full of bodily activities, gestures, and facial expressions. Some members of the audience are so eager that they have stood up out of excitement. Some have raised their hands. There is even one woman listener who seems to want to leave the auditorium and rush onto the stage. According to this image, Liszt's concert was an emotionally loaded event where the "man-piano" evoked strong emotions from the audience, and the audience in turn responds by expressing its devotion to the star.

Heinrich Heine's notion "Lisztomania," or in French *Lisztomanie*, was a commentary on Liszt's huge success in Berlin. It originally appeared in one of Heine's Parisian musical feuilletons, dated 25 April 1844. It seems that, as a concept, *Lisztomanie* spread immediately around Europe. Already on 22 June 1844, *Wiener Zeitung* in Vienna published a short novella by an author who has given only his initials: J. D. The story is entitled "Die Hand des Herrn Liszt" ("The Hand of Mr. Liszt"). A two-page anecdote tells a story of Lelia, a girl who is completely devoted to Liszt. The author writes that the piano as an instrument does not exist for Lelia without Liszt: they form an inseparable whole. Without Liszt, a piano will remain completely silent and nonexistent. To express her love for Liszt, she has a model of Liszt's hand, which she treasures like a holy relic.[27] The setting seems to anticipate the novel *Madame Bovary* (1857) by Gustave Flaubert: like Bovary, Lelia is married and feels tempted to live in her own escapist fantasy world.[28] Her husband argues that Lelia is a fool, but she only answers that, then, the princess N. is a fool too, because she has a similar "hand" in her boudoir. Lelia's husband concludes that his wife's *Lisztomanie* has developed into a *monomanie*.[29] Finally, it appears that the hand is actually not Liszt's at all but a fake.

As the previous example shows, *Lisztomanie* was conceived as a women's disease in the same manner as *bovarisme*. Heine's original analysis of Lisztomania also had political ramifications. He saw the Berlin frenzy as "an indication of the politically unfree situation on that side of the Rhine."[30] Instead of Georg Herwegh, it was easy to turn to Liszt who was not a threat. Heine's feuilleton includes also a medical and physical view on Liszt's emotional contagiousness, with an ironic twist. After concluding that "the solution of this question belongs to the domain of pathology rather than that of aesthetics," he consulted a physician whose specialty was female diseases. The doctor "smiled in the strangest manner, and at the same time said all sorts of things about magnetism, galvanism, electricity, of the contagion of a close hall filled with countless wax lights and several hundred perfumed and perspiring human beings, of historical epilepsy, of the phenomenon of tickling, of musical cantharides, and other scabrous things."[31] The culture of fame is here explained as a contagion, as an infectious disease that seems to spread in an uncontrolled manner in the crush of the concert halls. If music lovers in the 1830s had to be afraid of cholera on their way to the concert hall, in the 1840s, they had to be aware of another kind of disease.

In trying to understand the infectiousness of *Lisztomanie*, Heine's physician friend paralleled the transmission of this contagion with physical forces like magnetism. In contemporary reviews, too, the notion of magnetism was associated with those mysterious powers that drew people toward Franz Liszt. This was articulated already before Heine's famous diagnosis. After Liszt had performed in Milan, the German *Allgemeine Musikalische Zeitung* wrote on 9 May 1838 that he was "a physiological-psychological-artistic triad," "an aggregate of all forces acting in his body with their peculiar circumstances, especially electricity and animal magnetism."[32] If this description is interpreted from the perspective of present-day cultural theory, the notion of an "aggregate" can be paralleled with Deleuze and Guattari's idea of an assemblage of human and nonhuman forces.[33] Liszt was a machinery that gained new faculties through its complicity with the instrument. *Allgemeine Musikalische Zeitung* mentioned also the notion of "animal magnetism." It refers to the late eighteenth-century idea of the German physician Franz Mesmer that there was an invisible force exerting from all animals and that this force could have concrete effects, for example, for healing. Mesmerism and animal magnetism had a profound impact on nineteenth-century art and literature, and also the interpretation of early celebrities and their appeal.[34] In the early nineteenth century, there was an idea that this invisible force between human beings had social implications. According to Alison Winter, there was a common claim that communication was in fact a kind of transfer of vital fluids between bodies and that people's minds touched each other in mysterious ways.[35] Furthermore, in the discussion on mesmerism, it was stressed that there were people who could develop the use of these forces in creating emotional connections between people.[36] Clearly, these different conceptual thoughts, mesmerism as well as the idea of infection and contagion, were efforts to try to get hold of the strange gravitation that drew people to the concert hall. There was new materiality in this emotional realm, corroborated by the changes in media landscape.

Affects beyond the Body

Franz Liszt's success took place at the time of turmoil. The 1830s and 1840s were characterized by revolutionary activities and political struggles—by the frightening cholera pandemic that eclipsed Europe from East to West, by monetary capitalism and the rise of stock exchanges, and by many technological leaps, the consequences of which were difficult to foresee. Both Paganini and Liszt took advantage of the new opportunities for travelling and exploited the new musical markets that had been emerging. Heinrich Heine had interpreted *Lisztomanie* as a Berlin phenomenon, but clearly Liszt's fandom had wider geographical resonance.

Steamboat and railway connections contributed in transforming the itineraries of early celebrities. It would be too straightforward to interpret these cultural ramifications as direct results of modernization. Instead, it seems that the culture of celebrity and the new mobile culture were constructed simultaneously. Transport technology had agency in shaping sense of spatiality, not only by enabling the mobility of bodies but also by fostering flows of information and goods.[37] An ever-growing number of people could see Liszt in person, but through the printing press they could also read about how he had given concerts somewhere beyond their everyday environment and attracted people in different corners of Europe. When we consider the role of emotional contagiousness, these conditions must be taken under consideration. In his classic book *Understanding Media* (1964), Marshall McLuhan interpreted media as "extensions of man." He also discussed railway as a medium—not as something that necessarily produced new, but as something that accelerated or amplified previous processes.[38] It seems that, in the 1830s and 1840s, transport technology was a material platform for emotional contagiousness of celebrity culture and participated in amplifying it into unexpected proportions. The technological change becomes obvious if Liszt's tours are compared to Paganini's tours a bit earlier. Paganini's itineraries were not yet based on railways. He used mainly horse-drawn transport, and of course maritime connections when crossing the English Channel and the North Channel. Liszt used horse-drawn carriages as well, but he was able to employ the emerging railway network efficiently and to extend his travels wider than Paganini. Therefore, Liszt's gravitation developed into a stronger field of power compared to Paganini's supposed *diablerie*.

Franz Liszt was also able to reach remote areas of Europe, performing in Lisbon and Moscow, Dublin and Constantinople within only a few years (Figure 2.2). The Mediterranean region and countries like Sweden, Finland, and Norway were out of his scope already because of travel conditions. Christopher Rueger has pointed out that although Liszt fever exploded in the era of the emergent railway networks, his *Glanzperiode* was not yet able to completely rely on train connections.[39] On the other hand, in 1837, the first long-distance railway was launched between Leipzig and Dresden, which were focal points of musical life in Germany. By 1849, there were already 5,000 kilometers of track in Germany, which was more than double compared to the network in France.[40] It is evident too that in choosing his places of residence, Liszt had to carefully consider transport connections since he led a mobile lifestyle. Weimar became his asylum from 1848 onward, and it is hardly a coincidence that the city opened its first railway line two years earlier. Liszt could easily make a trip to Leipzig or Berlin and return back home within the same day. He could visit Düsseldorf and Cologne with an overnight stop.[41] There was demand for Liszt's presence, and Weimar was an ideal node in the transportation network. It was probably favorable also because it was outside the already "infected" Berlin.

Liszt's tours were also molded in conjunction with the rising capitalism and culture of money. London and Paris were cradles of musical life, but they were also centers for stock exchange and business markets. These were the places to go if someone in the early nineteenth century wanted to make a profit. In cities such as London and Paris, there were wealthy members of the bourgeoisie who could afford the high prices of tickets. It is important to note, however, that it was not only the public sphere that tempted virtuosos, but also the semipublic salon scene was very much still alive, and Liszt in particular mingled easily in this society and gave concerts for smaller circles too. In this sense, Berlin was an important venue as well, and it seems that Liszt's success in Berlin had many indirect economic benefits, and the emotional turbulence he aroused was a vehicle in this process.

In the formation of music culture, it is obvious that new modes of business became visible in salons and private homes. *Salonmusik* was at its heights in the 1830s and 1840s, at the time when the salons of the high society in particular became stages for piano virtuosos. Short pieces, of which Frédéric Chopin's nocturnes, waltzes, and mazurkas are excellent examples, were composed for salon use. Many of Franz Liszt's compositions served similar purpose, let us only think of his six solo piano pieces entitled *Consolations*. At the same time, the production of pianos rapidly increased together with the commercialization of easy arrangements and piano transcriptions.[42] Franz Liszt participated in this material flow, as a musician and a composer, as a man of letters and an idol of his audience. Liszt was doubtless conscious of this on-going change of conditions. Furthermore, it has to be noted that in his musical production, Liszt emphasized programmatic ideas. He provided explicit programs for many of his piano pieces, like the series *Années de pèlerinage*, and he was also the initiator of symphonic poems that strongly opposed the idea of absolute music. His music entangled with poems, prose, and also visual arts, like in the case of *Hunnenschlacht*. Therefore, his works were perhaps emotionally more accessible to the audience than the nonprogrammatic music of the time.[43]

In critical theory, there has been recent discussion on affective capitalism, on how capitalism appeals to emotions through a plethora of things.[44] Brian Massumi has emphasized that the ability of affect produces "an economic effect more swiftly and surely than economics itself," which means "affect is itself a real condition, an intrinsic variable of the late-capitalist system, as infrastructural as a factory."[45] This might be the case in "late-capitalist system," but it seems that already in the early nineteenth century, this condition was taking shape and the ability to affect had obvious economic effects. It may be argued, too, that the nineteenth-century culture of emotions formed a material, bodily "infrastructure" for the rising economy. Such artists as Paganini and Liszt were well aware of their emotional magnetism and its economic ramifications.

They both also produced musical pieces that appealed to emotions and further radiated their fame.

Already, Heine noted Franz Liszt's magical skills and his striking appeal to the audience. Heine was convinced that Liszt had organized not only his tours but their almost unavoidable successes: "It seems to me at times that all this sorcery may be explained by the fact that no one on earth knows so well how to organize his successes, or rather their *mise en scene*, as our Franz Liszt. In this art he is a genius, a Philadelphia, a Bosco, a Houdin, yes, a Meyerbeer!"[46] For Heine, Liszt was a master of spectacle and *trompe l'œil*. Heine refers to the famous magician, alchemist, and juggler Jacob Philadelphia (1735–95), the illusionist Bartolomeo Bosco (1793–1863), the legendary magician Jean Eugène Robert-Houdin (1805–71), and the master of *grand opéra*, Giacomo Meyerbeer (1791–1864), whose works were often spectacular entertainment for bourgeois audience. They all also made economic success. The magic for the eye was not everything, as Heine argued; it required actions behind the scene: "The most distinguished persons serve him gratis as his colleagues, and his hired enthusiasts are models of training. Popping champagne corks, and a reputation for prodigal generosity, trumpeted forth by the most reliable newspapers, lure recruits to him in every city."[47] It is dubious if there ever were "hired enthusiasts," as Heine suspects, but already Heine's idea about a machinery, tailored to produce enthusiasm and *Lisztomanie*, reveals the possibility of evoking and even manipulating emotions through material conditions. Heine's reference to the press is of interest as well. The "most reliable press" seemed to be not particularly reliable in the way it amplified such phenomena as celebrity culture. It circulated information without critical editing. This was very much the case in the newspaper business of the nineteenth century since there was no effective copyright law: papers were used to copy texts from other papers, which lead to the fact that some texts were reprinted hundreds of times or even more.[48] It seems that newspapers were keen to report on Liszt's success in other cities and also on his plans for the future, so that editors either consciously or without further consideration promoted Liszt's tours. An illuminating example is a letter by Liszt, written in French, which was reprinted in the *Hamburger Nachrichten* on 3 April 1840: here, Liszt revealed that he will come to Hamburg next November and thus the reprinted letter cultivated a seed for his success by making locals wait for his appearance.[49]

Newspaper business was under rapid growth during the first decades of the nineteenth century. From the 1830s onward, high-speed presses allowed the printing of tens of thousands of newspaper copies in a day. Papers were shipped to faraway regions and distant continents. This information flow occurred in parallel, and was entangled with, the increase in transportation, the exploitation of new sources of power, and the growth of capitalism.

It is today possible to trace transcontinental information flows through digitized newspaper collections worldwide. They include many references to Liszt's globalizing fame. During his visit to Spain, for example, Liszt was honored with an exceptional prize. This was announced as far as in Singapore on 13 March 1845: "Liszt, the celebrated pianist, has had the supernumerary cross of Charles III. conferred upon him by the Queen of Spain, who presented him at the same time with a rich diamond pin, worth 1,000 piastres."[50] Liszt was already at the height of musical life. The previous year, in 1844, Gustav Schilling had published his biography, entitled *Franz Liszt: Sein Leben und Wirken, aus nächster Beschauung dargestellt*, although Liszt was only thirty-three years of age at the time of publication.[51] The book was noted as part of Liszt's success on the other side of the globe, when *Adelaide Observer* in Australia told its readers on 14 December 1844 about the publication of Schilling's biography. It also published Schilling's listing of all honorary titles Liszt had received so far.[52] Liszt's fame, his fandom, and the admiration of his deeds spread in an intermedial manner and were promoted by music, books, and newspapers.

The audience around the globe was also interested in Liszt's personal life. In New Zealand, *The Wellington Independent* gossiped in October 1847 that Liszt had just been married in Prague to "the daughter of a wealthy jeweller."[53] Many stories about Liszt stressed his success in society, but they also highlighted his hectic concert tours and astounding skills as a pianist. In Brazil, the paper *Diario Novo* drew its reader's attention in February 1848 to his recent *soirée* in Constantinople.[54] It is obvious that Franz Liszt became known through his newspaper coverage in areas where he never performed or visited, from Finland to Australia, from Mexico to Singapore. Liszt remained a public figure for decades. It did not restrict itself only to his *Glanzperiode*, and his deeds were followed by the press until his death in 1886. In fact, he was discussed after that as well almost as intensively as when he was still living.

Conclusion

This chapter has focused on the history of emotions from the perspective of the rise of musical celebrities in the early nineteenth-century Europe. It has concentrated on Franz Liszt and his affective gravitation, especially on his relationship with the active, often fanatic audience who participated in the performances and was ready to express its emotions and, of course, love for its idol. Heinrich Heine coined the term *Lisztomanie* to describe the hysterical relationship of the audience toward the famous virtuoso. This gravitation was not something inherent, however: as already discussed, it emerged from the complex assemblage of human and nonhuman elements.

As we have seen, in many contemporary reviews, Liszt's emotional contagiousness and those mysterious powers that drew people to him were intensively discussed. In 1838, the *Allgemeine Musikalische Zeitung* described him as "an aggregate of all in his body acting forces." This aggregate was like an inexhaustible engine that functioned without a break during the subsequent years. He toured particularly actively from 1839 to 1847. He stopped in places where the audience was emotionally committed and also economic benefits could be gained. In Berlin, he played ten weeks in a row. He became famous all over Europe, and soon in other continents, too, through the press.

This chapter has emphasized three aspects in the materiality of emotions. Firstly, Liszt's body was under continuous scrutiny, just like Paganini's distorted body before him. Liszt was a generator of emotionality whose gravitational field lured members of the audience, drew them closer, but also relieved them again after a while. Another material dimension, or the second pillar of the materiality of emotions, was the audience that was thrilled on Liszt's bravura and his skillful tricks on stage, the audience that expressed its emotions through shouts and gestures, and developed distinctive practices of fandom, like Lelia in the Austrian short story about the hand of Liszt. My argument has been that this emotional gravitation cannot be understood only in terms of emotional standards of the time, nor as an interconnecting glue of an emotional community formed by a star and his fans. Early nineteenth century was an era of rapid political, social, and economic changes. The third aspect of the Liszt case, or the ways in which materiality played a role in *Lisztomanie*, was the effectiveness of the mobile age itself—its increasing flows of money, information, and goods. Liszt's affective materiality is an expression of early nineteenth-century culture as a whole. That world lived in the process of continuous becoming, structuring, and restructuring due to the cultural explosion with its new forms of communication and transport. In this setting, an emotional aggregate called Franz Liszt reached its affective contagiousness far beyond his physical body, his musical impulses, and the societies where he resided and traveled.

Hannu Salmi is a Professor of Cultural History at the University of Turku and Academy Professor 2017–21. His current research interests focus on digital history, the cultural history of the nineteenth century, especially music history, media history, and the history of emotions and the senses. His current research projects include Viral Culture in Early Nineteenth-Century Europe (2017–21); Computational History and the Transformation of Public Discourse in Finland, 1640–1910 (2016–19); and Oceanic Exchanges: Tracing Global Information Networks in Historical Newspaper Repositories, 1840–1914 (2017–19). Professor Salmi has published fifteen books in Finnish, German, English, and Polish on nineteenth- and twentieth-century history.

Notes

1. Derek Watson, *Liszt* (London: J. M. Dent & Sons, 1989), 49.
2. Antoine Lilti, *The Invention of Celebrity 1750–1850* (Cambridge, UK: Polity, 2017), 236. Here, Lilti refers to Dana Gooley, "From the Top: Liszt's Aristocratic Airs," in *Constructing Charisma: Celebrity, Fame and Power in Nineteenth-Century Europe* (New York: Berghahn Books, 2010), 69–85.
3. For a visualization of Franz Liszt's tours in 1839–1847, see https://www.youtube.com/watch?v=GnnnaYaBXPc, accessed 9 August 2019.
4. *Arnhemsche courant* (6 March 1824); *Finlands Allmänna Tidning* (10 July 1824).
5. In Liszt's case, this was accompanied by technological changes in piano construction. In the 1820s, the so-called repetition lever was introduced to enable clear articulation and rapid playing of notes which was particularly important for Liszt. For further details, see Michael Chanan, *Musica Practica: The Social Practice of Western from Gregorian Chant to Postmodernism* (London: Verso, 1994), 204.
6. On Franz Liszt's magnetism, see "Liszt in Mailand," *Allgemeine Musikalische Zeitung* (9 May 1838). On Paganini's *diablerie*, see "Paganini," *The Gentleman's Magazine* 1 (1837): 68.
7. "Heinrich Heine's Musical Feuilletons," *The Musical Quarterly* 8 (July 1922): 458–59; Dana Gooley, *The Virtuoso Liszt* (Cambridge, UK: Cambridge University Press, 2009), 203.
8. Hannu Salmi, "Viral Virtuosity and the Itineraries of Celebrity Culture," in *Travelling Notions of Culture in Early Nineteenth-Century Europe*, ed. A. Nivala, H. Salmi, and J. Sarjala (New York: Routledge, 2016), 135–53.
9. Alan Walker, *Franz Liszt, Vol. 1: The Virtuoso Years 1811–1847*, revised edition (Ithaca: Cornell University Press, 1987), 173.
10. Quoted by Paul Metzner, *Crescendo of the Virtuoso: Spectacle, Skill, and Self-Promotion in Paris during the Age of Revolution* (Berkeley: University of California Press, 1998), 137–38.
11. Erika Quinn, *Franz Liszt: A Story of Central European Subjectivity* (Leiden: Brill, 2014), 31.
12. English translation in J. G. Prod'homme, *Nicolo Paganini* (New York: Fischer, 1911), 15. These words have been addressed to Paganini's biographer Julius Max Schottky who quoted them in his 1830 book *Paganini* (Prague: Taussig & Taussig, 1830). The quotation was however copied from *Neues Archiv für Geschichte, Staatenkunde, Literatur und Kunst* (5 January 1829), from the report of Sedlatzek, dated 4 December 1828. I have previously discussed Paganini's physiognomy in Salmi, "Viral Virtuosity," 135–53.
13. In 1837, the French inventor Marreppe presented his automaton violin-player that performed "airs à la Paganini." For further detail, see John Timbs, *Stories of Inventors and Discoveres in Science and the Useful Arts* (London: Kent and Co., 1860), 49.
14. "Franz Liszt in Wien," *Österreichisches Bürgerblatt für Verstand, Herz und gute Laune* (22 June 1838).
15. Quoted by Metzner, *Crescendo of the Virtuoso*, 139.
16. National Library of France, Gallica, http://gallica.bnf.fr/ark:/12148/btv1b10219978h.
17. See, for example, Quinn, *Franz Liszt*, 47.

18. Gooley, *The Virtuoso Liszt*, 22–24.
19. See, for example, Stephanie Downes, Sally Holloway, and Sarah Randles, eds., *Feeling Things: Objects and Emotions through History* (Oxford: Oxford University Press, 2018); and Caroline van Eck, *Art, Agency and Living Presence: From the Animated Image to the Excessive Object* (Boston: De Gruyter, 2015).
20. An important contribution is Susan Bernstein, *Virtuosity of the Nineteenth Century: Performing Music and Language in Heine, Liszt, and Baudelaire* (Stanford: Stanford University Press, 1998), 75–76, which also pays attention to Liszt's materiality. Liszt's anatomy is discussed in J. Q. Davies, *Romantic Anatomies of Performance* (Berkeley: University of California Press, 2014).
21. For further details, see Michael Chanan, *Musica Practica: The Social Practice of Western from Gregorian Chant to Postmodernism* (London: Verso, 1994), 204.
22. "Mein Klavier ist für mich, was dem Seemann seine Fregatte, dem Araber sein Pferd—mehr noch . . . meine Sprache, mein Leben," Rueger, *Franz Liszt*, 74.
23. Gilles Deleuze and Félix Guattari, *A Thousand Plateaus: Capitalism and Schizophrenia*, trans. and Foreword by Brian Massumi (Minneapolis: University of Minnesota Press, 1987), 89–90.
24. Adrian Williams, *Portrait of Liszt: By Himself and Contemporaries* (Oxford: Clarendon Press, 1990), 452–53.
25. For further detail, see Hannu Salmi, *Wagner and Wagnerism in Nineteenth-Century Sweden, Finland, and the Baltic Provinces: Reception, Enthusiasm, Cult* (Rochester, NY: University of Rochester Press, 2005), 206.
26. Walker, *Franz Liszt*, 371–72.
27. J. D., "Der Hand des Herrn Liszt," *Wiener Zeitung* (22 June 1844).
28. Hannu Salmi, *Nineteenth-Century Europe: A Cultural History* (Cambridge, UK: Polity Press, 2008), 82–83.
29. J. D., "Der Hand des Herrn Liszt," *Wiener Zeitung* (22 June 1844).
30. "Heinrich Heine's Musical Feuilletons," *The Musical Quarterly* 8 (July 1922), 158–59.
31. "Heinrich Heine's Musical Feuilletons," *The Musical Quarterly* 3 (1922): 458.
32. "Liszt in Mailand," *Allgemeine Musikalische Zeitung* (9 May 1838).
33. Manuel De Landa, *Deleuze: History and Science* (New York: Atropos Press, 2010), 10–13.
34. On animal magnetism, see Fred Kaplan, "'The Mesmeric Mania': The Early Victorians and Animal Magnetism," *Journal of the History of Ideas* 4 (1974): 691–702.
35. Alison Winter, *Mesmerized: Powers of Mind in Victorian Britain* (Chicago: University of Chicago Press, 1998), 119.
36. Winter, *Mesmerized*, 118–20.
37. On the changes in the notion of time and space, see Wolfgang Schivelbusch, *The Railway Journey: The Industrialization of Time and Space in the Nineteenth Century* (Berkeley: The University of California Press, 2014), xxiii.
38. Marshall McLuhan, *Understanding Media: The Extensions of Man* (Cambridge, MA: MIT Press, 1994), 8.
39. Christopher Rueger, *Franz Liszt: Des Lebens Widerspruch* (Munich: Langen Müller, 1997), 100.
40. Sung Jik Cha, *Railroads in 19th Century Europe: Great Britain, France, Germany, and Russia*, accessed 13 February 2015, http://www.zum.de/whkmla/sp/0910/csj/csj1.html.

41. Alan Walker, *Franz Liszt, Vol. 2: The Weimar Years 1848–1861*, revised edition (Ithaca: Cornell University Press, 1993), 6.
42. Andreas Ballstaedt and Tobias Widmaier, *Salonmusik: Zur Geschichte und Funktion einer bürgerlichen Musikpraxis* (Stuttgart: Steiner, 1989), 34–38, 60–78. See Salmi, *Wagner and Wagnerism*, 34–35.
43. Jonathan Kregor, *Program Music* (Cambridge, UK: Cambridge University Press, 2015), 99–128, 137.
44. Tero Karppi, Lotta Kähkönen, Mona Mannevuo, Mari Pajala, and Tanja Sihvonen, "Affective Capitalism: Investments and Investigations," *Ephemera: Theory and Politics in Organization* 16, no. 4 (November 2016): 1–13. On music, emotions, and capitalism, see Ori Schwarz, "Emotional Ear Drops: The music industry and technologies of emotional management," in *Emotions as Commodities: Capitalism, Consumption and Authenticity*, ed. Eva Illouz, 56–78 (New York: Routledge, 2017).
45. Brian Massumi, *Parables of the Virtual: Movement, Affect, Sensation* (Durham, NC: Duke University Press, 2002), 45.
46. "Heinrich Heine's Musical Feuilletons," *The Musical Quarterly* 3 (1922): 458.
47. "Heinrich Heine's Musical Feuilletons," *The Musical Quarterly* 3 (1922): 458.
48. For further details, see for example David A. Smith, Ryan Cordell, and Elizabeth Maddock Dillon, "Infectious Texts: Modeling Text Reuse in Nineteenth-Century Newspapers," *Proceedings: 2013 IEEE International Conference on Big Data, 6–9 Oct 2013, Santa Clara, CA, USA*, ed. Xiaohua Hu et al., 86–94 (Piscataway, NJ: Institute of Electrical and Electronics Engineers, 2013), DOI: 10.1109/BigData.2013.6691675; Ryan Cordell, "Reprinting, Circulation, and the Network Author in Antebellum Newspapers," *American Literary History* 27 (2015): 417–45; Aleksi Vesanto, Asko Nivala, Heli Rantala, Tapio Salakoski, Hannu Salmi, and Filip Ginter, "Applying BLAST to Text Reuse Detection in Finnish Newspapers and Journals, 1771–1910," *Proceedings of the 21st Nordic Conference of Computational Linguistics*. Gothenburg, Sweden, 23–24 May 2017 (Linköping 2017), 54–58, http://www.ep.liu.se/ecp/133/010/ecp17133010.pdf.
49. *Hamburger Nachrichten* (3 April 1840).
50. *The Singapore Free Press and Mercantile Advertiser* (13 March 1845).
51. Gustav Schilling, *Franz Liszt: Sein Leben und Wirken, aus nächster Beschauung dargestellt* (Stuttgart: A. Stoppani, 1844).
52. *Adelaide Observer* (14 December 1844).
53. *Wellington Independent* (30 October 1847).
54. *Diario Novo* (1 February 1848).

Bibliography

Newspapers and Magazines

Adelaide Observer, 14 December 1844.
Arnhemsche courant, March 1824.
Diario Novo, 1 February 1848.
Finlands Allmänna Tidning, 10 July 1824.

"Franz Liszt in Wien." *Österreichisches Bürgerblatt für Verstand, Herz und gute Laune*, 22 June 1838.
Hamburger Nachrichten, 3 April 1840.
"Heinrich Heine's Musical Feuilletons." *The Musical Quarterly* 8 (July 1922): 458–59.
J. D. "Der Hand des Herrn Liszt." *Wiener Zeitung*, 22 June 1844.
The Leeds Mercury, 12 December 1840.
"Liszt in Mailand." *Allgemeine Musikalische Zeitung*, 9 May 1838.
Neues Archiv für Geschichte, Staatenkunde, Literatur und Kunst, 5 January 1829.
"Paganini." *The Gentleman's Magazine* 1 (1837): 68.
The Singapore Free Press and Mercantile Advertiser, 13 March 1845.
Wellington Independent, 30 October 1847.

Literature

Ballstaedt, Andreas, and Tobias Widmaier. *Salonmusik: Zur Geschichte und Funktion einer bürgerlichen Musikpraxis*. Stuttgart: Steiner, 1989.

Bernstein, Susan. *Virtuosity of the Nineteenth Century: Performing Music and Language in Heine, Liszt, and Baudelaire*. Stanford: Stanford University Press, 1998.

Chanan, Michael. *Musica Practica: The Social Practice of Western from Gregorian Chant to Postmodernism*. London: Verso, 1994.

Cordell, Ryan. "Reprinting, Circulation, and the Network Author in Antebellum Newspapers." *American Literary History* 27 (2015): 417–45.

Davies, J. Q. *Romantic Anatomies of Performance*. Berkeley: University of California Press, 2014.

De Landa, Manuel. *Deleuze: History and Science*. New York: Atropos Press, 2010.

Deleuze, Gilles, and Félix Guattari. *A Thousand Plateaus: Capitalism and Schizophrenia*. Translation and Foreword by Brian Massumi. Minneapolis: University of Minnesota Press, 1987.

Downes, Stephanie, Sally Holloway, and Sarah Randles, eds. *Feeling Things: Objects and Emotions through History*. Oxford: Oxford University Press, 2018.

Gooley, Dana. "From the Top: Liszt's Aristocratic Airs." In *Constructing Charisma: Celebrity, Fame and Power in Nineteenth-Century Europe*, 69–85. New York: Berghahn Books, 2010.

——— . *The Virtuoso Liszt*. Cambridge, UK: Cambridge University Press, 2009.

Jik Cha, Sung. *Railroads in 19th Century Europe: Great Britain, France, Germany, and Russia*. Accessed 13 February 2015. http://www.zum.de/whkmla/sp/0910/csj/csj1.html.

Kaplan, Fred. "'The Mesmeric Mania': The Early Victorians and Animal Magnetism." *Journal of the History of Ideas* 4 (1974): 691–702.

Karppi, Tero, Lotta Kähkönen, Mona Mannevuo, Mari Pajala, and Tanja Sihvonen. "Affective Capitalism: Investments and Investigations." *Ephemera: Theory and Politics in Organization* 16, no. 4 (November 2016): 1–13.

Kregor, Jonathan. *Program Music*. Cambridge, UK: Cambridge University Press, 2015.
Lilti, Antoine. *The Invention of Celebrity 1750–1850*. Cambridge, UK: Polity, 2017.
Massumi, Brian. *Parables of the Virtual: Movement, affect, sensation*. Durham, NC: Duke University Press, 2002.
McLuhan, Marshall. *Understanding Media: The Extensions of Man*. Cambridge, MA: MIT Press, 1994.
Metzner, Paul. *Crescendo of the Virtuoso: Spectacle, Skill, and Self-Promotion in Paris during the Age of Revolution*. Berkeley: University of California Press, 1998.
Prod'homme, J. G. *Nicolo Paganini*. New York: Fischer, 1911.
Quinn, Erika. *Franz Liszt: A Story of Central European Subjectivity*. Leiden: Brill, 2014.
Rueger, Christoph. *Franz Liszt: Des Lebens Widerspruch*. Munich: Langen Müller, 1997.
Salmi, Hannu. *Nineteenth-Century Europe: A Cultural History*. Cambridge, UK: Polity Press, 2008.
——— *Wagner and Wagnerism in Nineteenth-Century Sweden, Finland, and the Baltic Provinces: Reception, Enthusiasm, Cult*. Rochester, NY: University of Rochester Press, 2005.
——— "Viral Virtuosity and the Itineraries of Celebrity Culture." In *Travelling Notions of Culture in Early Nineteenth-Century Europe*, edited by A. Nivala, H. Salmi, and J. Sarjala, 135–53. New York: Routledge, 2016.
Schilling, Gustav. *Franz Liszt: Sein Leben und Wirken, aus nächster Beschauung dargestellt*. Stuttgart: A. Stoppani, 1844.
Schivelbusch, Wolfgang. *The Railway Journey: The Industrialization of Time and Space in the Nineteenth Century*. Berkeley: The University of California Press, 2014.
Schottky, Julius Max. *Paganini*. Prague: Taussig & Taussig, 1830.
Schwarz, Ori. "Emotional Ear Drops: The music industry and technologies of emotional management." In *Emotions as Commodities: Capitalism, Consumption and Authenticity*, edited by Eva Illouz, 56–78. New York: Routledge, 2017.
Smith, David A., Ryan Cordell, and Elizabeth Maddock Dillon. "Infectious Texts: Modeling Text Reuse in Nineteenth-Century Newspapers." *Proceedings: 2013 IEEE International Conference on Big Data*, 6–9 Oct 2013, Santa Clara, CA, USA, edited by Xiaohua Hu et al., 86–94. Piscataway, NJ: Institute of Electrical and Electronics Engineers, 2013. DOI: 10.1109/BigData.2013.6691675.
Timbs, John. *Stories of Inventors and Discoverers in Science and the Useful Arts*. London: Kent and Co., 1860.
van Eck, Caroline. *Art, Agency and Living Presence: From the Animated Image to the Excessive Object*. Boston: De Gruyter, 2015.
Vesanto, Aleksi, Asko Nivala, Heli Rantala, Tapio Salakoski, Hannu Salmi, and Filip Ginter. "Applying BLAST to Text Reuse Detection in Finnish Newspapers and Journals, 1771–1910." *Proceedings of the 21st Nordic Conference of Computational Linguistics*. Gothenburg, Sweden, 23–24 May 2017. Linköping 2017, 54–58. http://www.ep.liu.se/ecp/133/010/ecp17133010.pdf.

Walker, Alan. *Franz Liszt, Vol. 1: The Virtuoso Years 1811–1847*, revised edition. Ithaca: Cornell University Press, 1987.

——— *Franz Liszt, Vol. 2: The Weimar Years 1848–1861*, revised edition. Ithaca: Cornell University Press, 1993.

Watson, Derek. *Liszt*. London: J. M. Dent & Sons, 1989.

Williams, Adrian. *Portrait of Liszt by Himself and Contemporaries*. Oxford: Clarendon Press, 1990.

Winter, Alison. *Mesmerized: Powers of Mind in Victorian Britain*. Chicago: University of Chicago Press, 1998.

CHAPTER 3

Reading Embodied Emotions in Rilke's *Die Aufzeichnungen des Malte Laurids Brigge*

DEREK HILLARD

"The days when they told stories, properly told stories, must have been before my time. I never heard anyone tell a story."[1] This comment by Malte, the protagonist of Rainer Maria Rilke's groundbreaking novel of 1910, *Die Aufzeichnungen des Malte Laurids Brigge* (*The Notebooks of Malte Laurids Brigge*), highlights his sense that his generation comes after the decline of proper storytelling. Implied in this comment is that the waning of traditional stories and experience calls out for a narrative capable of depicting social values in a time of dynamic technology, scientific investigation, body culture, and mass communication.[2] In attempting to answer this demand, Rilke turned to a new source, one that must have seemed due for a revision at a time when much seemed under assault by dynamic change—bodies.

Let me remain with the novel for a moment to continue this thought. In younger days, Malte's grandfather could still tell stories. Curiously, the grandfather's storytelling technique points to an embodied approach to narration. Unable to sit still, he narrates too quickly for Malte's aunt, Abelone, who, as a young girl, is tasked with writing down the stories: "Sometimes he would leap up and speak into the candles, . . . he would pace vigorously to and fro."[3] In telling the tale of an unconventional family member from his childhood, the grandfather lets the story content spill into the performance: "Trembling, the Count stood up and made a gesture as if putting something into the room, which remained."[4] Maniacally insistent that this eccentric character become visible, he thrusts the burning candlestick before Abelone's face and barks, "Can you see him?"[5] Presence is achieved through body-narrative. Gestures, including the physical dimensions of the voice, become an essential part of this narration. In other words, his story can only be conveyed through his kinetic body.[6]

Interestingly, for an idea of writing as a gesture—to which I will return—on the day on which the dictation abruptly ends, the Graf excitedly tells

Abelone of Julie Reventlow, another member of their peculiar family: "He took Abelone's hands and opened them out like a book. 'She had the stigmata,' he said, here, and here.' And he tapped her two palms quickly but firmly with his cold finger."[7] The tale, Abelone tells Malte, was forgettable, "'But I can still sometimes feel those spots in my palms,' she smiled."[8] The way in which kinetic bodies extend and create emotions by punctuating our lives becomes, I want to suggest, a source for narratives after the time of proper storytelling. In other words, Rilke's novel aims to be something akin to this impactful narrative touch. Gesture is a kind of writing into the body and writing is a gesture, one that Malte carries forward as he writes his own *Aufzeichnungen*. A contributing factor in the rise of this innovative novelistic form is an awareness of how the fabric of meaning and perception of events are indebted to bodies, on both the side of production and reception. The sense that bodies shape thinking, emotion, memory, writing, the arts, urban design, and a host of other segments of life becomes a powerful idea around 1900.

In Rilke's *Aufzeichnungen*, the range of emotions is broad, including joy, satisfaction, fear, disgust, anger, confusion, and mourning. My study does not dwell on such familiar and well-formed, what I am calling "classic," emotions, but instead looks at the embodied way in which emotions are manifested. While space considerations preclude an extensive discussion of "embodiment" in affective terms, some mention of this is warranted. In scientific emotion research, embodiment challenges views of the mind and body as distinct components, arguing instead "that the body helps to constitute the mind in shaping an emotional response."[9] In this view, emotions take shape through the body, instead of representing phenomena from a separate entity called mind. Emotions, such as fear or joy, rely on sensorimotor simulations and features from a variety of contexts and symbolic settings where fear or joy are encountered and "labeled" as such. In this way, bodies enable emotions and knowledge about them to arise. Presently, I will discuss one concept that formed a key moment of the prehistory of embodiment around 1900, the *Ausdrucksbewegung* (expressive movement).

From a traditional literary-interpretive perspective, the dominant emotion of Rilke's novel would seem to be *Angst* or *Furcht*, that is, fear, anxiety, or dread. Per this view, which one might call the "*Angst*-thesis," the narrative's primary affective concern is with anxieties. To be sure, there is much to fear in the city, the place where modernization is most clearly felt. Illness, loneliness, disability, social isolation, poverty, conflict, the transformation of the self, the hectic pace—these all contribute to the presence of *Angst* in the novel. It is not that the *Angst*-thesis has no merit, but that the presence of other emotions complicates any reading that would keep fear at the center. For instance, disgust is frequently commingled with fear and is as prevalent as *Angst*. As contemporary readers of the novel were only too eager to point out, Malte (or

Rilke) finds inordinate pleasure in writing abundantly and respectfully about disgusting things.[10] Readers read *Angst* but felt disgust. More to the point, as I will show, there is a different emotion, one that exists just below the surface, one that feels, so to speak, more anxious than anxiety, the feeling of fragmentation or decomposition.

I wish to suggest that the use of bodies to narrate emotions is Rilke's response to the question of writing in a poststorytelling age. As his reflections on Rodin show, Rilke was clearly aware that a traditional, idealistic approach to the emotional–physical relationship had to be modified to make room for the body-emergent provocations in our lives: "Layer upon layer of clothing had been laid upon it [the body] like constantly renewed varnish, but beneath these protecting incrustations the living soul, breathlessly at work upon the human face, had transformed the body too. It had become a different body."[11] Kinetic bodies, as imagined in the novel, are ways to make sense of our environments. And in the context of our historical endeavors (the living soul), bodies change.

Rilke was not alone in his fascination with the way in which kinetic bodies and emotions ineluctably interconnect. Psychologists, philosophers, and practitioners and thinkers of dance, photography, and early film were also drawn to kinetic bodies to describe a host of phenomena. The psychologist Wilhelm Wundt (1832–1920) emphasized a principle that became an irresistible concept for psychologists, graphologists, philosophers, and critics: the *Ausdrucksbewegung*.[12] As they grappled with various dimensions of the mind/body relationship and the place of emotions, in particular, the *Ausdrucksbewegung* became a central motif. Well into the early decades of the twentieth century, *Ausdrucksbewegung*, a term rarely used before Wundt, became a touchstone for the discussion of physical manifestations of inner processes in which terms emotions were nearly universally described.

In Wundt's understanding, all *Ausdrucksbewegungen*—including language—had their origins in emotions, or *Affekte*, per his, albeit, inconsistent terminology.[13] For Wundt, the origins of language and social groups are to be found in emotional expressions, such as facial or manual movements, which have become communicative vehicles. Wundt's basic observation regarding emotions and expression was laid out already in 1863.[14] Their undeniable communicative import notwithstanding, *Ausdrucksbewegungen*, for Wundt, were all about feelings: "the primary cause of natural gestures does not lie in the motivation to communicate a concept, but rather in the expression of an emotion. Gestures are first and foremost affective expressions."[15] Wundt assumes as a foundation for the *Ausdrucksbewegung* a psychophysical parallelism, according to which psychical events and systems have correlates in the physical events and systems.[16] Any inner feeling, which he frequently distinguished with reference to the figure of *Gemütsbewegung* (movement of temper), has a correlate in potentially perceivable, sensory or nervous, physical *Ausdrucksbewegungen*.[17] At the same time, however—and the literature on Wundt has not sufficiently stressed this—he viewed the value of *Ausdrucksbewegungen* as *symptomatic*. So, although *Ausdrucksbewegungen* corresponded to the inner *Gemütsbewegungen*, neither side, seen in isolation, permits comprehension of the other, or enjoys a priority of origin. Instead, for Wundt, it was most likely one process in which "the emotion and its physical correlative manifestation begin simultaneously."[18]

The second thinker whose work can be briefly discussed, the historian and philosopher of art Konrad Fiedler (1841–95), was drawn to Wundt's threads of psychophysical interplay as well as to the *Ausdrucksbewegung*. Despite offering neither an explicit account of emotion nor a model of artistic reception, his unique theory of knowledge and artistic production centered on something essential to the discourse of emotion around 1900: the relationship of bodies to what we would today refer to as the cognitive.

For Fiedler, the work of art results from a physical gesture. Fiedler radically extended the *Ausdrucksbewegung*, arguing that physical movements (*Gebärde*) and the artworks that depend on them are not reproductions or supplements to cognitive intentionality. Instead, they are productive. In other words, gestures have an autonomy that, while linking them to emotional intentionality, possess their own being and presence—one that does not depend on cognitive directives: "We concede that every intellectual work announces itself to our perception at the same time, as a bodily achievement, that everything the mind does is at the same time an activity of the lived bodily organism. . . . The constituent parts of the so-called mental life itself . . . are present in a sensuous form."[19] In other words, Fiedler did not see the mental and physical realms operating according to a representational model: "The logic of the *Ausdrucksbewegung* can therefore not be that a content with mental origins creates, in a movement of corporeal organs, a sign of its existence, an expression of its meaning."[20] Instead, both psychical (*seelisch*) and physical phenomena, which begin "with the excitation of the sensory nerves," find their manifestation, their unique "development," in the *Ausdrucksbewegung*.[21] So, the gesture presents something that would not otherwise have existed and whose existence does not lie in a cognitive realm separate from an expression that merely awaits a body to transmit it. This is possible because Fiedler theorizes the gesture as cognitive–intellectual, yet its purported origin as one that "takes place from the very beginning in bodily processes."[22]

For Fiedler, because of the key role of *Ausdrucksbewegung*, art begins where a hand moves. One can see emotion operating in ways consonant with this notion of the *Ausdrucksbewegung*. With Fiedler and against him, one can see how an expression contains an appraisal as much as it does an emotion's manifestation. In the context of Fiedler, one can see how emotion relies on the movement of a body, and that at no conceivable stage of an emotional process is there a moment of pure cognition that merely waits to be represented in physical space. Clearly, this anticipates contemporary theories of embodiment.[23] Fiedler's writings indicate a nascent cultural understanding of phenomena in terms of materiality and corporeality, one that German philosophy and psychology understood largely in mental–spiritual terms until around 1850.

Scholars in various fields have analyzed gesture. My approach to the concept of "gesture" differs not only through its emphasis on emotion, but also through its focus on body kinetics as a series of interrogations, repetitions, differences, and provocations. The typical approach to gesture in cultural and historical analysis, by contrast, focuses on formal codes of comportment resting on various sorts of controlled and standardized expectations aimed at reducing complexity.[24] While my notion of the gesture does not exclude such codes of conduct, it aims more broadly to encompass any observed kinetic act, voluntary or involuntary, wherein the observation itself enacts an emotion.

Having reviewed select theories of expression around 1900, we can better appreciate Rilke's turn to embodied literature, both the ways in which it confirmed and deviated from psychology and critique of his day. Regarding influence, it has yet to be determined whether Rilke read Wundt or Fiedler. Yet, as Ute Frevert observes, the "somatization" of emotions taking place under the gaze of experimental science in the late nineteenth century is one example of wide-ranging redefinitions of emotion around this time.[25]

I want to explore two specific dimensions: that of probing (searching) and decomposition. In depicting emotions in the novel, Rilke makes use of actions related to how bodies probe their surroundings and attempt to survive. Thus, I want to make a case for emotions that may be less familiar than fear, anger, joy, and the like. To underscore how these help to enact the value and the make-up of what they encounter in environments, instead of merely representing phenomena, I would like to call these "enactive" emotions.[26] The novel is brimming with figures who cannot rest and, through their bodies, cast about their environment to construct the value of what is there and what is thereby produced, such as Malte's grandfather, the fifteenth-century Duke of Burgundy, Charles "the Bold," the fourteenth-century king Charles VI, various animals, and Malte himself. While this might describe countless protagonists in world literature, in Rilke's novel it has become a principle not only of narration but also, by extension, one of perception and a way of living.

One of the first fleeting and anonymous figures that Malte encounters on the street shows us the hand in motion: "I saw a pregnant woman. With some difficulty she was shuffling along beside a warm, high wall that she sometimes reached out to touch as if to convince herself that it was still there. Yes, it was still there," adds the narrator, a remark that makes clear what this gesture seeks out.[27] In the "still there," the woman enacts continuity and embraces it. Echoing Fielder's analysis of art, her gesture does not merely express some existing anxiety for the benefit of voyeuristic observers (both Malte and the reader). Her affective probing of borders (walls), matter, and continuity emerges from the gesture, one that simultaneously projects fragility and strength. Look, the narrator seems to indicate, this manual searching, as if in the dark, is how she appraises the city. The searching hand forms the sensitivity to what matters and constitutes meaning and space. Whichever classical emotions are here at work—a commingling of anxiety, desire, and curiosity—they orient and assess material spaces in and through her body.

This search extends to a few scenes later as the woman falls in front of the narrator: "But the woman—the woman: she had completely collapsed into herself, forwards into her hands."[28] With this falling into her hands, the woman, as Malte and thus the reader too sees it, not only collapses but also looks for something. The abrupt shift from an externally focused gesture to one seemingly focused on the self is not by chance, for in doing so, her putative interior state occupies a surface. As Malte's footsteps on the quiet street stir her, "the woman was startled and lifted herself out of herself, too quickly, too fiercely, so that her face remained stuck in her hands."[29] To hold one's face in one's hands is to decompose, not to mention to reveal a transference from the role of the face to the hand. As Malte's eyes remain on the hands, he sees her face appear there. What does it mean to see her face in her hands, its "hollow" form? Of course, we can see in this something like the plaster cast for a sculpture.[30] Is this an exterior, to some extent controlled and protocoled, now seen as an open cipher? If Malte feels that if there is something to be seen in the hands, it must be legible.

By attending to kinetic bodies, a different, more nuanced construction of emotions emerges where they can be elusive and go (almost) unrecognized. At the same time, we can notice how their narrative function or motivations are not so easy to define. As we have seen, the general consensus among psychologists, aesthetic thinkers, and cultural theorists around 1900 was that a particular inner *Gemütsbewegung* determines the specific *Ausdrucksbewegung*. Rilke's novel departs from this consensus in a striking fashion. It asks us to pay attention to gestures, to *Ausdrucksbewegungen* in several new ways.[31] Deviating from the then typical interpretation of *Ausdrucksbewegungen*, Rilke's novel does not confirm a correlation between particular emotions and particular movements. Kinetic bodies revealed emotions but left the observer with the task to make sense of them.

The novel suggests that we are to regard them in their own right as affective phenomena, as emotions; see them as ways of living; instead of reactive, they are creative or "enactive"; instead of merely responding to appraisals, they appraise. In partial agreement with Fiedler, these gestures do not express emotional ideas but are emotions that create differences essential for the life out of which they come. While the modernist novel turned its gaze early on this phenomenon, it would only gain wider transmission with the appearance of phenomenological work after World War II, such as in the writings of Maurice Merleau-Ponty.

Readers relying primarily on conceptual references to classic emotions such as fear, anger, or joy may pass by this emotion without noting its force. Malte does not want to see "what had been ripped from them. I was terrified of seeing a face from the inside, but I was even more afraid of the naked, raw head with no face."[32] To the question of what this sore, raw, faceless head is, the answer can be loss, uncertainty, a horrifying evacuation of the self. This horror is as much a part of the woman's world as it is of Malte's.

Seeing the face from the inside turns this inside into an outside so that it receives a surface. One might see this as Rilke's own attempt at collapsing the distinction of inside and outside. Rilke commented in a similar vein in his writings on Rodin, wondering "whether everything before us, everything we observe, explain, and interpret, does not consist simply of surfaces? And what we call mind and spirit and love; are these things not only a slight change seen on the small surface of our neighbor's face?"[33] The interior is an exterior, and the exterior bears its interior; but instead of bearing this only spatially, it does so also kinetically and temporally. The expressivity of the face is transferred to the hands, which results in the woman's effacement.

The emotional sounding out of environments, which I have discussed, enjoys several echoes among other characters in the novel, which I can only briefly mention here. Consider, for instance, the "very tall, slim man" who comes around the corner from the Champs-Elysées: "he was carrying a crutch, . . . he held it out before him . . . banging the ground with it like a herald's staff,"[34] using the crutch to measure the city's space. Like the woman along the wall, yet with a joyful tone, this man seeks out the space of the city with his gestures, including a crutch as an extension of the body. At the same time, several further scenes in Rilke's novel could be discussed in an effort to highlight the emotion of self-dissolution and at the same time to demonstrate its intimate relationship to both bodies and classic emotions, such as fear or disgust. Recall, for instance, the episode with Malte at the doctor's office, the dying man in the crémerie, and Malte's childhood memory of struggling with his own hands.

That emotions are not merely reactive but enactive is suggested in a different scene from the *Aufzeichnungen*. It is the segment of the man with the hopping gait, or per the tradition of Rilke scholarship, the St. Vitus dancer. Before Malte can become aware of the man with the hopping gait, *Angst* begins to make sense of the ridicule and disgust over this man by the people in a café. With his attention stirred by the waiters who suddenly begin to gesture and laugh at something in the street, which Malte cannot yet see, anxiety is already making sense of this: "I felt a modicum of fear rising in me."³⁵ Instead of cognitively assessing an idea, Malte's fear identifies the man and object of the emotion. Perhaps the significance of many emotions lies in their tendency seemingly to intuit rather than merely react.

This man deserves special notice. Malte notes in detail how the two movements of his hands manipulate his collar, "a quick, secret one," with which he raises his collar, and the other "lengthier, more sustained, as if spelling something out exaggeratedly," while his stumbling feet move with a "terrible two-syllable hopping" that "wanders" across his body.³⁶ This not only hints at what we have seen is a turn-of-the century linkage of language with affective expressive movements. It may also suggest that Rilke considers gesture to be a kind of kinetic artifact not so different from impactful language, including the novel in question. The man seeks to stabilize his body and control "the terrible twitching"³⁷ by pushing the handle of his walking stick into his spine as he walks, so that "the way those hands looked was so grim and tight" (*der Ausdruck dieser Hände*), becoming "fierce and angry."³⁸ Per the law of the *Ausdrucksbewegung* operative in the novel, these hands do not convey feelings as if they were a position taken about something: they produce not only fury and wrath but they attempt to engage with the world in ways that are both trivial and striking. The episode is also fascinating because it explicitly depicts a struggle between the man's will, or cognition, and his body—one that a stunning image of dance attempts to resolve, where decomposition manifests itself, but does so in an aesthetic, and thus emotionally familiar form:

> He turned his head a little and his gaze ranged over sky, houses, and water without settling on anything, and then he gave way. The stick went, he stretched his arms out as if about to take wing, and it broke out from within him like a force of nature and bent him forwards and ripped him backwards and made him nod and tilt and hurled a dancer's energy out of him and into the crowd.³⁹

I cite this scene extensively to illustrate several components of my thesis. It shows the production of emotions from kinetic bodies. It gives one more example of gestures that are emotional explorations of environments—essentially ways in which to navigate social and material terrains. At the same time, it highlights Rilke's use of gestural expression, where emotions are not messages of someone's inner state, but they are both the uses of and the working through of these states. Not only that, but as the comparison with dance shows, gestures have an aesthetic quality to them, one that is felt by beholders. At the same time, this passage demonstrates Rilke's concern with messy, chaotic emotions that seem to exceed the neat boundaries of joy, fear, or anger. The man's complex whirlwind dissolves not only those boundaries but also customary boundaries between self and other, where the crowd is sprayed, as it were, with the energy of his dance. Finally, this scene exemplifies a kind of kinetic auto-destruction. Malte and the reader witness his struggle, isolation, and dissipation. Not just the man, but, as is so often the case, Malte, the literary observer, in a habit of dangerous empathy with destroyed figures, is also threatened: "I was empty. Like a blank sheet of paper I floated past the houses and back up the Boulevard."[40]

With Rilke, the concern is no longer with expressive movement as a correlation to emotions that are interior and classic. Instead, expression seeks to impact observers (readers, beholders) and bring meaning into material, spatial, and physical environments. By contrast, the notion of the *Ausdrucksbewegungen* in much of the scientific literature was reactive. They represented emotions instead of producing them or through them generating a meaningful environment.

With its attention to expressive movements, the novel establishes points of contact with early dance and film. Gabriele Brandstetter, for instance, has analyzed the overlapping concerns between modernist German literature and gestural movement in dance. She emphasizes notions of dance as "body writing," with particular reference to Aby Warburg's notion of the pathos formula (*Pathosformel*), which, for her "contains a poignant theory of the affective dynamics of movement expression."[41] Brandstetter too indicates how avant-garde dance was concerned with the properties of self-fulfillment and self-dissolution in space as well as how it developed an attachment to an "aesthetic of ugliness"[42]—both of which were shared and presaged by Rilke's novel, where it would be more suitable to speak of an "aesthetics of disgust." Similarly, Petra Löffler pursues the interest in early film and film theory with affective body movements.[43] Initially an object of fascination and a source for positivist knowledge gain, film had to wait until later to develop a sense that gesture makes sense of the world while at the same time exploring the boundaries of selves, which, as we have seen, literature was investigating around 1900.

As I have suggested in my discussion, one might regard Rilke's *Aufzeichnung* as an attempt at unifying emotion with the concept of *Ausdruck* so that there is no distinction between them. In this dynamic, the relational structure is shifted. Instead of bodies expressing an existent or nascent feeling of fear or anger, kinetic bodies are implicated in the production of fear and anger. At the same time, emotions require an other position—be it a city street, a wall, or other people, to establish a network or to be observed so that we can become attentive to what their ends or effects might be.

As such, emotion in Rilke comments on modernist notions of artworks and bodies, for these all form a material nexus, one that poses questions about life to which metaphysics, idealism, science, or religion offered unsatisfactory answers. Kinetic bodies and embodied emotions in the novel are not easily put at the service of various existing agendas—be they social, medical, psychological, political, or aesthetic. This is not to claim any kind of grand resistance for them, but to contend that neither bodies nor emotions were what society thought they were. They are not singular but doubled, tripled, multiplied. They do not allow familiar borders, for Malte's emotions show how his body is enmeshed with those of others. The emotions are not proprietary, for they course through the city's dwellers to spill over its boundaries where they stretch across time and space. All this calls for a different approach to writing.

Many episodes in the novel, such as the hopping man, are about kinetic bodies. A marginal concern in literature for so long, a kinetic body can be a mobile technology of effects and affects. Body writing creates new narratives and narrative effects as readers try to make sense of bodies and gestures. Atypical emotional clusters such as fear-disgust are employed to make sense of these puzzling situations, which in turn generate additional emotions. Furthermore, this attempt to use one's body to make sense of environments and materiality, such as with the woman who falls into her hands on the street or the hopping man on Boulevard St. Michel, is also on view in Malte's attempts at identification. In each of these instances, Malte involves himself in the drama of the gestures that he observes. He even modifies his body or contemplates doing so, though in each case nothing comes of this intervention but his *Aufzeichnungen*, that is, his embodied storytelling.

This essay began with narrative doubts. Yet this is not merely the familiar linguistic crisis, the turn-of-the-century *Sprachkrise* that has received much attention.[44] Let me offer a different perspective. Were the changing assumptions around 1900 regarding bodies and their relations to emotions *not* a central factor in the emergence of modernism and its concomitant rejection of existing linguistic and representational norms, then would we find such widespread fascination with bodies and emotions in the arts, the sciences, or philosophy? We would not find numerous investigations of the body or empirical approaches to philosophy, psychiatry, aesthetics, art, and other discourses and practices. Instead, we would expect to find a great many treatises about the inadequacy of linguistic models alongside abundant scientific, artistic, and cultural laments about the insufficiency of language. These laments would be unconcerned with the possibility that the bodies and things that language had been tasked with depicting had themselves been misunderstood or undergone change. If the focus were language, rather abstractly understood, would kinetic bodies be so frequently conceived as either at the origin of language or as utterances themselves?

Die Aufzeichnungen des Malte Laurids Brigge is deeply committed to an interrogation of our affective relations to bodies and things. There is a narrative anxiety that one may not be able to distinguish the exterior from interior, the self from its environment, one emotion from another. It is less the realization that language cannot represent reality than it is the sense that reality is not what we thought it was. This larger cultural moment is less a loss of faith in language than a growing sense, both as promise and a danger, of our ineluctable intertwining with bodies and things.

Derek Hillard is Professor of German at Kansas State University. His research concerns German modernism. In particular, he has investigated the languages of emotion and pain, the representation of violence and sacrifice, and discourses of the mind. He is the author of *Poetry as Individuality: The Discourse of Observation in Paul Celan* (2010), as well as recent essays on Alfred Döblin and Ernst Jünger.

Notes

1. Rainer Maria Rilke, *The Notebooks of Malte Laurids Brigge*, trans. Robert Vilain (Oxford: Oxford University Press, 2016), 85.
2. On changes to body culture, see Knut Dietrich, *Körpersprache: über Identität und Konflikt / Eichberg, Henning* (Frankfurt am Main/Griedel: Afra-Verlag, 1993), 257–58. For period reviews stressing this point, see H., "Rainer Maria Rilke: *Die Aufzeichnungen des Malte Laurids Brigge*," *Deutsche Arbeit*, November 1910, 10: 1 edition, stressed how "content determines form" (67), how the conventional naturalistic representation of life now yields in the novel to new forms adequate to "what reality is for us today" (66). All translations from German are my own unless indicated otherwise. On the end of storytelling, see Derek Hillard, "Rilke and Historical Discourse or the 'Histories' of Malte Laurids Brigge," *German Studies Review* 29, no. 2 (2006): 308.
3. Rilke, *Notebooks of Malte Laurids Brigge*, 85.
4. Rilke, *Notebooks of Malte Laurids Brigge*, 88.
5. Rilke, *Notebooks of Malte Laurids Brigge*, 89.
6. Thus, the Graf both represents vanished narrative practices and offers attributes that Rilke rediscovers and repurposes for new ends.
7. Rilke, *Notebooks of Malte Laurids Brigge*, 89.
8. Rilke, *Notebooks of Malte Laurids Brigge*, 89.
9. Lisa Feldman Barrett and Kristen A. Lundquist, "The Embodiment of Emotion," in *Embodied Grounding: Social, Cognitive, Affective, and Neuroscientific Approaches*. Edited Gün R. Semin and Eliot R. Smith, 237–62 (Cambridge, UK: Cambridge University Press, 2008), 237.
10. See for instance, Armin Friedmann, "Ein neues Buch von Rilke," *Wiener Abendpost*, 14 July 1910.
11. Rainer Maria Rilke, *Rodin and Other Prose Pieces* (London: Quartet Books, 1986), 6–7. For the idea that Rilke's Rodin texts were an attempt to overcome the conventional notion of expression, see G. (Georg) Braungart, *Leibhafter Sinn: der andere Diskurs der Moderne* (Tübingen: Niemeyer, 1995), 254.
12. While space considerations permit me to discuss only two figures, the list is long. See, for instance, Oskar Kohnstamm, *Kunst als Ausdruckstätigkeit: biologische Voraussetzungen der Ästhetik* (Munich: E. Reinhardt, 1907); Hermann Cohen, *Ästhetik des reinen*

Gefühls (Berlin: B. Cassirer, 1912); Susanne Rubinstein, *Zur Natur der Bewegungen* (Leipzig: A. Edelmann, 1890); Heinrich Rudolph, *Der Ausdruck der Gemütsbewegungen des Menschen; dargestellt und erklärt auf Grund der Urformen und der Gesetze des Ausdrucks und der Erregungen* (Dresden: Kühtmann, 1903); August Schmarsow, *Kompositionsgesetze in der Kunst des Mittelalters: Studien* (Leipzig: B. G. Teubner, 1915); Ludwig Klages, *Die Probleme der Graphologie; Entwurf einer Psychodiagnostik* (Leipzig: Barth, 1910); Hugo Münsterberg, *Hugo Munsterberg on Film: The Photoplay; A Psychological Study and Other Writings* (Abingdon-on-Thames: Routledge, 2013).

13. Wilhelm Max Wundt, *Grundzüge der physiologischen Psychologie* (Leipzig: W. Engelman, 1874), 429.
14. Wilhelm Max Wundt, *Vorlesungen über die Menschen- und Thierseele* (Leipzig: Voss, 1863), 387.
15. Wilhelm Max Wundt, *The Language of Gestures*, ed. George Herbert Mead (Berlin: De Gruyter Mouton, 1973), 146.
16. For a discussion of this parallelism, see Claudia Wassmann, "Physiological Optics, Cognition and Emotion: A Novel Look at the Early Work of Wilhelm Wundt," *Journal of the History of Medicine and Allied Sciences* 64, no. 2 (March 1, 2009): 234.
17. "The most general principle of psychophysical content, according to which *every change of psychical conditions is associated with changes in physical correlate-processes*," Wilhelm Max Wundt, *Völkerpsychologie*, vol. 1 (Leipzig: W. Engelmann, 1900), 84–85.
18. Wundt, *Völkerpsychologie*, 84.
19. Conrad Fiedler, *Schriften zur Kunst*, ed. Gottfried Boehm. Vol. 1 (Munich: Wilhelm Fink, 1971), 225.
20. Fiedler, *Schriften zur Kunst*, 193.
21. Fiedler, *Schriften zur Kunst*, 194.
22. Fiedler, *Schriften zur Kunst*, 193.
23. See for instance Andy Clark, *Supersizing the Mind: Embodiment, Action, and Cognitive Extension* (Oxford: Oxford University Press, 2008); Shaun Gallagher, *How the Body Shapes the Mind* (Oxford: Oxford University Press, 2005).
24. See, for instance, Jan Bremmer and Herman Roodenburg, eds., *A Cultural History of Gesture* (Ithaca: Cornell University Press, 1992). For a study of gesture in terms of embodiment, see Guillemette Bolens, *The Style of Gestures: Embodiment and Cognition in Literary Narrative* (Baltimore: Johns Hopkins University Press, 2012). For an exceptionally nuanced discussion of gestures in a historical context, one that crucially recognizes their ambiguity, see Michael J. Braddick, "Introduction: The Politics of Gesture," in *The Politics of Gesture: Historical Perspectives. Past and Present*, Supplement 4, ed. Michael J. Braddick, 9–35 (Oxford: Oxford University Press, 2009), esp. 11–12.
25. Ute Frevert, "Defining Emotions: Concepts and Debates Over Three Centuries," in *Emotional Lexicons: Continuity and Change in the Vocabulary of Feeling 1700–2000*, ed. Ute Frevert et al. (Oxford: Oxford University Press, 2014), 22.
26. Obviously, the term "enactive" is informed by enactive theories of cognition. See, Francisco J. Varela, Eleanor Rosch, and Evan Thompson, *The Embodied Mind: Cognitive Science and Human Experience* (Cambridge, MA: MIT Press, 1992); Giovanna Colombetti, *The Feeling Body: Affective Science Meets the Enactive Mind* (Cambridge, MA: MIT Press, 2014).
27. Rilke, *Notebooks of Malte Laurids Brigge*, 3.
28. Rilke, *Notebooks of Malte Laurids Brigge*, 5.

29. Rilke, *Notebooks of Malte Laurids Brigge*, 5.
30. Braungart sees Rilke's comments about "Gesichtsausdruck" as a reference to physiognomic theories about characters' inner qualities: Braungart, *Leibhafter Sinn*, 255. Yet this misses Rilke's concern with feelings and surfaces.
31. Braungart argues that Rilke's Rodin texts were an attempt to overcome the conventional contemporary notion of *Ausdruck*, understood as an internal event that seeks an exterior expression: Braungart, *Leibhafter Sinn*, 254. My discussion shows how this is a central concern of Rilke's novel.
32. Rilke, *Notebooks of Malte Laurids Brigge*, 5.
33. Rilke, *Rodin and Other Prose Pieces*, 49.
34. Rilke, *Notebooks of Malte Laurids Brigge*, 11.
35. Rilke, *Notebooks of Malte Laurids Brigge*, 39.
36. Rilke, *Notebooks of Malte Laurids Brigge*, 40.
37. Rilke, *Notebooks of Malte Laurids Brigge*, 41.
38. Rilke, *Notebooks of Malte Laurids Brigge*, 41.
39. Rilke, *Notebooks of Malte Laurids Brigge*, 41–42.
40. Rilke, *Notebooks of Malte Laurids Brigge*, 42.
41. Gabriele Brandstetter, *Poetics of Dance: Body, Image, and Space in the Historical Avant-Gardes* (Oxford: Oxford University Press, 2015), 17.
42. Brandstetter, *Poetics of Dance*, 18.
43. Petra Löffler, *Affektbilder: eine Mediengeschichte der Mimik* (Bielefeld: Transcript, 2004), 200.
44. Brandstetter, *Poetics of Dance*, 6. On the *Sprachkrise*, see George Steiner, *Von realer Gegenwart: Hat unser Sprechen Inhalt?* (Munich: Hanser, 2010); Philip Ajouri, *Literatur um 1900: Naturalismus—Fin de Siècle—Expressionismus* (Berlin: Akademie Verlag, 2009), 149–57.

Bibliography

Ajouri, Philip. *Literatur um 1900: Naturalismus—Fin de Siècle—Expressionismus*. Berlin: Akademie Verlag, 2009.
Bolens, Guillemette. *The Style of Gestures: Embodiment and Cognition in Literary Narrative*. Baltimore: Johns Hopkins University Press, 2012.
Braddick, Michael J. "Introduction: The Politics of Gesture." In *The Politics of Gesture: Historical Perspectives. Past and Present*, Supplement 4, edited by Michael J. Braddick, 9–35. Oxford: Oxford University Press, 2009.
Brandstetter, Gabriele. *Poetics of Dance: Body, Image, and Space in the Historical Avant-Gardes*. First edition. Oxford: Oxford University Press, 2015.
Braungart, G. (Georg). *Leibhafter Sinn: der andere Diskurs der Moderne*. Tübingen: Niemeyer, 1995.
Bremmer, Jan, and Herman Roodenburg, eds. *A Cultural History of Gesture*. Ithaca: Cornell University Press, 1992.
Clark, Andy. *Supersizing the Mind: Embodiment, Action, and Cognitive Extension*. Oxford: Oxford University Press, 2008.

Cohen, Hermann. *Ästhetik des reinen Gefühls*. Berlin: B. Cassirer, 1912.
Colombetti, Giovanna. *The Feeling Body: Affective Science Meets the Enactive Mind*. Cambridge, MA: MIT Press, 2014.
Dietrich, Knut. *Körpersprache: über Identität und Konflikt / Eichberg, Henning*. Frankfurt am Main/Griedel: Afra-Verlag, 1993.
Feldman Barrett, Lisa, and Kristen A. Lundquist. "The Embodiment of Emotion." In *Embodied Grounding: Social, Cognitive, Affective, and Neuroscientific Approaches*, edited by Gün R. Semin and Eliot R. Smith, 237–62. Cambridge, UK: Cambridge University Press, 2008.
Fiedler, Conrad. *Schriften zur Kunst*, edited by Gottfried Boehm. Vol. 1. Munich: Wilhelm Fink, 1971.
Frevert, Ute. "Defining Emotions: Concepts and Debates Over Three Centuries." In *Emotional Lexicons: Continuity and Change in the Vocabulary of Feeling 1700–2000*, edited by Ute Frevert et al., 1–35. Oxford: Oxford University Press, 2014.
Friedmann, Armin. "Ein Neues Buch von Rilke." *Wiener Abendpost*, 14 July 1910.
Gallagher, Shaun. *How the Body Shapes the Mind*. Oxford: Oxford University Press, 2005.
H. "Rainer Maria Rilke: Die Aufzeichnungen Des Malte Laurids Brigge." *Deutsche Arbeit*, November 1910, 10: 1 edition.
Hillard, Derek. "Rilke and Historical Discourse or the 'Histories' of Malte Laurids Brigge." *German Studies Review* 29, no. 2 (2006): 299–313.
Klages, Ludwig. *Die Probleme der Graphologie: Entwurf einer Psychodiagnostik*. Leipzig: Barth, 1910.
Kohnstamm, Oskar. *Kunst als Ausdruckstätigkeit: biologische Voraussetzungen der Ästhetik*. Munich: E. Reinhardt, 1907.
Löffler, Petra. *Affektbilder: eine Mediengeschichte der Mimik*. Bielefeld: Transcript, 2004.
Münsterberg, Hugo. *Hugo Munsterberg on Film: The Photoplay; A Psychological Study and Other Writings*. Abingdon-on-Thames: Routledge, 2013.
Rilke, Rainer Maria. *The Notebooks of Malte Laurids Brigge*. Translated by Robert Vilain. Oxford: Oxford University Press, 2016.
——— *Rodin and Other Prose Pieces*. London: Quartet Books, 1986.
Rubinstein, Susanne. *Zur Natur der Bewegungen*. Leipzig: A. Edelmann, 1890.
Rudolph, Heinrich. *Der Ausdruck der Gemütsbewegungen des Menschen; dargestellt und erklärt auf Grund der Urformen und der Gesetze des Ausdrucks und der Erregungen*. Dresden: Kühtmann, 1903.
Schmarsow, August. *Kompositionsgesetze in der Kunst des Mittelalters: Studien*. Leipzig: B. G. Teubner, 1915.
Steiner, George. *Von realer Gegenwart: Hat unser Sprechen Inhalt?* Translated by Jörg Trobitius. Munich: Hanser, 2010.
Varela, Francisco J., Eleanor Rosch, and Evan Thompson. *The Embodied Mind: Cognitive Science and Human Experience*. Cambridge, MA: MIT Press, 1992.

Wassmann, Claudia. "Physiological Optics, Cognition and Emotion: A Novel Look at the Early Work of Wilhelm Wundt." *Journal of the History of Medicine and Allied Sciences* 64, no. 2 (March 1, 2009): 213–49.

Wundt, Wilhelm Max. *Grundzüge der physiologischen Psychologie*. Leipzig: W. Engelman, 1874.

—— *The Language of Gestures*, edited by George Herbert Mead. Berlin: De Gruyter Mouton, 1973.

—— *Völkerpsychologie*. Vol. 1. Leipzig: Wilhelm Engelmann, 1900.

—— *Vorlesungen über die Menschen- und Thierseele*. Leipzig: Voss, 1863.

CHAPTER 4

Embodied Emotions
On the Communist Habitus of Agitprop

SABINE HAKE

Communist agitprop during the Weimar years relied heavily on the performance of embodied emotions. In very literal ways, the act of standing established a distinct communist habitus, a *Klassenstandpunkt* (class standpoint), through embodied practices in theater, dance, music, and agitprop created to distinguish the militant culture of the KPD from the communitarian culture of the SPD. This essay reconstructs this highly gendered communist habitus through the representation of the agitator in paintings by Conrad Felixmüller, Curt Querner, and Magnus Zeller; the performance of class consciousness by the "red dancers" Jean Weidt and Jo Mihaly; and the instructions on the right way of standing by the agitprop troupe Das Rote Sprachrohr. Closer attention to such embodied practices in performances of ideology, it will be argued, is not only essential for understanding the politics of emotion during the Weimar Republic but also key to opening up the study of emotions in history to notions such as embodiment, performance, and habitus.

Social movements are based on, and sustained by, emotions—emotions that, simply by being evoked in the name of politics, become political emotions.[1] Integral to new conceptions of community, society, and nation, these emotions function as sources of group unity and strength, as expressions of shared goals and beliefs, and sometimes even as political arguments themselves. Much of the power of emotions in social movements derives from their formative, if not transformative function—namely, to invite identifications and provide identities, including in gendered and classed terms. The symbolic politics of the German workers' movement and, more specifically, the intense competition over the working-class body between the Weimar-era SPD (Social Democratic Party of Germany) and KPD (Communist Party of Germany) offers almost ideal conditions for studying the historical configurations of politics and emotion. Gaining access to these symbolic politics, however, means paying close attention to the interplay of linguistic, visual, musical, and dramatic forms and tracing collective imaginaries across artistic media, aesthetic sensibilities, and emotional registers. In light of the KPD's confrontational course, nothing would be better suited for such an undertaking than the party's approach to political agitation, or agitprop, as a public performance, a form of embodiment, and an exercise in habitus.

During the Weimar years, KPD agitational campaigns depended to a large degree on techniques of the body that channeled anger and indignation into highly formalized—which also means, highly politicized—terms. For communist artists and writers, the declared goal was to transform physical bodies into classed bodies: by identifying political antagonists and obstacles, by modeling the process of moving and thinking as one, and by equating the various stages in this process with specific emotions. Given the importance attributed to the right (and wrong) ways of standing in what can be described as paradigmatic scenes of class mobilization, taking a very literal approach to what in Marxist theory is called *Klassenstandpunkt* might prove surprisingly productive—not least because it draws attention to larger questions of embodiment in the study of political emotions. In proposing such an approach, this essay draws on the visual archives of Weimar-era communism and examines in what ways the act of standing was treated as a public performance of the communist habitus. Based on a thematic reading of these agitational practices, the conclusion will argue for greater attention to questions of embodiment, performance, and habitus in the growing body of research on the history of emotions and on emotions in history.

In the polarized atmosphere of the late Weimar Republic, the very act of standing in political or politicized settings can be read as the most obvious manifestation of what dance historian Hannah Kosstrin calls embodied ideology.[2] KPD agitators appeared on the streets to articulate and, quite literally, perform their ideological positions in the confrontational terms of leftwing radicalism and dogmatism. In the groups dominated by the KPD, a thus defined *Klassenstandpunkt* functioned very much in the sense of what Pierre Bourdieu describes as embodied habitus: a "political mythology realized, *em-bodied*, turned into a permanent disposition, a durable manner of standing, speaking, and thereby of *feeling* and *thinking*."[3] Habitus, of course, is closely related to the German *Haltung*, a term denoting posture, bearing, attitude, or demeanor. Significantly, the gestural codes that produce *Haltung* on the theatrical stage have played a key role in the development of antipsychological approaches in line with Soviet behaviorist psychology and modern performance practices, including in epic theater. Delineating its potentialities in Bertolt Brecht's instructions for the *Lehrstücke* (teaching plays), Darko Suvin in fact designates *Haltung* as the "terminus technicus of a Marxist theory of behavior."[4] According to Suvin, *Haltung* and its cognate *Verhalten* (behavior) are closely related to discourses of power and control. Whether identified with an individual or a group, the term establishes a relationship between bodies and ideas in performative terms. It is inseparable from norms of public behavior and, while typically equated with an ethos of resistance, just as often associated with an attitude of inflexibility. In all cases, Haltung implies a strong sense of conviction that, by choosing steadiness over adaptability, has a tendency toward dogmatism. And precisely through this unwillingness to yield, Haltung, according to Suvin, is well suited for articulating a political position or, in this case, defining an agitational style.

At first glance, Haltung has much in common with the Brechtian practice of Gestus, which treats physical gestures as manifestations of political attitudes. Both modalities, in turn, are inseparable from the body cultures developed in the context of workers' sport, industrial labor, and military training and, in their insistence on influencing attitudes and behaviors through physical regimes, far removed from older bourgeois notions of psychological interiority. However, Brechtian Gestus typically involves a much more dialogic, process-based practice. As Marc Silberman points out, its function is to foreground the historical nature of social structures and institutions and to emphasize their availability to critical analysis and political critique.[5] By contrast, the performances of Haltung examined in this essay preclude the possibilities for open dialogue as they adhere to highly normative definitions of political emotions and make clear distinctions between constructive and destructive ones. Mobilized against the harmonious Gemeinschaftskultur (communitarian culture) promoted by the SPD's cultural socialists, the figure of the agitator gave a body and a voice to a recognizable communist Kampfkultur (militant culture) distinguished by its cult of militancy, discipline, and self-control. In defining the terms and conditions of standing like a communist, KPD agitprop advanced official party positions, including the denunciation of the "weak" Social Democrats as social fascists, but it also drew on specific emotional regimes, all of them related to hardness and coldness, to promote their "strong" ideological positions.[6] The presentation of radicalization as a process of masculinization played a key role in this process, a connection that unfortunately cannot be explored further because of considerations of space.

The performances of the communist habitus are based on two methods of interpellation: propaganda as a technique of persuasion (and available to interpretation through discourse analysis) and agitation in the double sense of physical and emotional stimulation. Agitprop emerged as the KPD's preferred method of mass mobilization through the enthusiastic reception of new cultural practices from the Soviet Union and the ever-closer alignment of the party with the Bolsheviks (and, later, Stalinists). A portmanteau word, agitprop is usually defined as a musical or theatrical performance distinguished by its improvised sets and settings, short pieces and mixed forms, and heavy reliance on parody, satire, and the grotesque; but it also entails a particular habitus: physical, loud, precise, disciplined, and confrontational. Combining posters, songs, speeches, dances, skits, and film clips in short programs and longer revues, KPD agitprop troupes appeared at election rallies, mass demonstrations, neighborhood events, and factory cell meetings to address working-class problems such as labor struggles, low wages, family strife, unemployment, homelessness, and poverty. Yet channeled through the artistic imagination of the historical avant-garde, agitprop also became a particular mode of enunciation, or form of presentation, adopted across a wide range of body practices in modern theater, music, and dance. Speaking to these connections, Richard Bodek rightly insists on the importance of proletarian performances to Weimar modernism as a whole; Robert Heynen makes a similar point about the class politics of embodiment and its little understood role in (the critique of) capitalist modernity in the most advanced forms of politically committed art.[7]

Whether in the theater or on the street, agitprop reorganized class-based experiences through confrontational performances that relied heavily on physical and psychological techniques developed in conscious opposition to bourgeois notions of interiority. In addition to rhetorical devices such as repetition, simplification, and direct address, aggressive body postures and gestures and forceful modes of speaking were considered essential to the making of proletarian identifications and, by extension, revolutionary energies. The dismissive description by Otto Rühle of the wrong kind of "proletarian whose facial expressions convey submission and resignation" and his praise for "the rebellious proletarian . . . as more likable and more beautiful but also more valuable to the class struggle"[8] confirms widespread awareness of the power of embodied ideology and can be used to introduce the examples presented in the next section through a few simple questions: What did the ideal proletarian look like—aside from the fact that he was young and male? How did his incarnation in the figure of the agitator establish a repertoire of typical gestures and postures? How did the agitator come to occupy a place, control a space, and move as part of a group or inside a crowd? And how did the appearance and performance of the agitator become recognizable in ideological terms? To begin with, the ideal proletarian was not supposed to look like council-communist-turned-anarchist Rühle (see Figure 4.1), portrayed with bulging, bloodshot eyes by Conrad Felixmüller in *Der Agitator/Otto Rühle spricht* (1920, The Agitator/O. R. Speaks). On the contrary, the examples presented here suggest that communist agitprop was intended to move political discourse beyond the pathos and ecstasy of the early postwar years and align the Bolshevik concept of vanguardism more closely with what Ernst Bloch once called the cold stream within Marxism—that is, an unemotional approach that implied both self-control and control of others.

Embodied Emotions ~ 81

Figure 4.1. Conrad Felixmüller, *Der Agitator: Otto Rühle spricht/The Agitator: Otto Rühle Speaks* (1920), oil on canvas, Nationalgalerie Berlin, 1946 reproduction. Copyright 2017 Artists Rights Society (ARS), New York/VG Bild-Kunst Bonn.

An almost ideal-typical performance of communist cool can be found in a large-scale oil painting, titled *Agitator* (1931), by the Dresden-based Curt Querner, a metalworker-turned-artist who worked in the New Objectivity style of his teacher Otto Dix (see Figure 4.2).[9] The composition focuses on a

Figure 4.2. Curt Querner, *Agitator* (1930), oil on canvas, Nationalgalerie Berlin. Copyright 2017 Artists Rights Society (ARS), New York/VG Bild-Kunst Bonn.

slender man in his thirties standing alone on a street corner in what looks like a working-class neighborhood. The cobblestone street and the gray walls, drainpipe, and tenement houses in the back suggest an overall mood of deprivation and desolation. Notwithstanding such a drab setting, the man's posture, with his legs slightly apart and knees tightly locked, conveys a sense of confidence and strength. His arms are extended forward, with both digit fingers pointing at an imagined audience beyond the frame. His wide corduroy pants and short light-brown jacket are not typical sartorial choices for a factory worker and suggest a party functionary. For Querner, an active member of KPD and ASSO (Association of Revolutionary Visual Artists), the proletariat was inseparable from its uniforms—the pea coats, simple tunics, and soft caps worn by the marching workers in his best-known work, *Demonstration* (1930), and the overalls and smocks donned by the artist himself in several probing self-portraits. Read in this context, the agitator's mountaineering-type jacket may even be an allusion to communism's heroic climb to the summit of world history, and his chiseled face and tight lips an expression of the self-control required of all party members. Clearly, Querner was interested less in the representation of a particular social milieu or political type than in the performance of an ideological position. The fact that his agitator does not even require the visible presence of an audience strengthens the implied connection between communist orthodoxy and aggressive militancy and adds some credence to the claim by Hellmuth Heinz that an earlier, larger version of the painting included a worker's hand wielding a gun.[10]

The revolutionary sounds and images produced in the Soviet Union and circulated widely throughout the communist lifeworld provided the main source of inspiration for the kind of agitprop considered best suited to Weimar-era sensibilities. Yet the communist discourse on position, stance, and posture was also greatly influenced by the different conceptions of collective bodies developed in the context of mass psychology, scientific management, and sport education. Thus, the bodily regimes shared by the modern penal system and factory system and transformed by the workers' movement in the context of workers' sport provided important points of reference through their shared assumptions about the body as both a site of discipline and an instrument of resistance. As Sander Gilman has shown, extensive medical research was conducted during the age of industrialization to prove the importance of good posture.[11] Related claims about physical exercises and psychological dispositions were made to persuade children, soldiers, as well as workers to willingly submit to state authorities and class hierarchies. During the same time, bodily practices from nudism to vegetarianism to calisthenics played a key role in various experiments with alternative ways of life started under the heading of life reform—primarily in the form of individual solutions to the problem of alienation and social anomie, but also in the context of social and socialist utopias.

Figure 4.3. Magnus Zeller, *Agitator/Volksredner* (1920), oil on canvas, Los Angeles County Museum of Art (LACMA). Copyright 2017 Artists Rights Society (ARS), New York/VG Bild-Kunst Bonn.

The performative nature of the communist habitus becomes clearer through a comparison of *Agitator* to earlier treatments of scenes of agitation that explicitly reference Christian iconographies of suffering. These are on full view in Magnus Zeller's expressionist *Agitator/Volksredner* (1920, Agitator/Orator, oil on canvas), which relies on religious tropes and symbols to depict agitation as a state of ecstatic communitarianism (see Figure 4.3). In choosing the subject matter, Zeller, who studied with Berlin Secession member Lovis Corith, drew on his personal experiences during the revolutionary uprisings in the capital and his close familiarity with the conventions of the expressionist stage. His reenactment of the transformative effect of agitation centers on a preacher-like figure, a young, slender man in a garish green suit, who is surrounded by an enraptured audience in what could be a religious revival—were it not for a large silhouetted man in the foreground ominously shaking his fist. The danger emanating from the scene is captured in the raw emotions on the faces of the worshippers and the formal dynamism of stark contrasts, diagonal lines, and elongated shapes. The constitutive tension between reverie and revolt, to cite the title of a related portfolio of Zeller lithographs, foregrounds what, for many expressionist artists, distinguished the intensely emotional nature of modern mass mobilizations.

The difficulties of contributing to the performance of classed bodies while overcoming their disciplinary regimes are on full view in the work of two communist dancers, Jean Weidt and Jo Mihaly. Descriptions, photos, and reviews of their choreographies suggest that Weidt and Mihaly drew upon a limited register of motion and emotion to present the worker as a distinct physical type. The fact that Mihaly bound her breasts to pass as a man, thereby signaling the primacy of class over gender, confirms the degree to which masculinist body practices sustained revolutionary fantasies despite the Weimar-era myth of the New Woman or the fashionable infatuation with androgyny. In fact, Mihaly's ability to make this choice without causing a scandal underscores the attractiveness of a masculine habitus even to women.

Jean (originally Hans) Weidt, known as "the red dancer," grew up in the Hamburg working class, worked as a gardener and a coal trimmer in the harbor, and became one of the few communists in the world of German *Ausdruckstanz* (expressionist dance). In 1925, he created a solo dance called *Der Arbeiter* (The Worker) that drew on his own experiences as a physical laborer. In his memoirs, Weidt describes the problems during the rehearsal phase with creating a dance piece that could at once be descriptive and prefigurative:

> After all, I myself worked as a professional gardener for eight to ten hours a day and felt it in my bones. But I did not want to present the worker who toils and labors but the worker who builds a more beautiful life. . . . I worked until I was ready to acknowledge that the worker should not be danced with a bowed head but that he has to be shown as proud, oriented toward the future.[12]

With his body not only marked by daily experiences of exploitation but also animated by his belief in radical change, Weidt tried to capture the movement, in the words of Marion Reinisch, "from feeling socially . . . to thinking politically."[13] Photographs from the performance at Hamburg's Komödienhaus show a slender man dressed in simple gray pants and an open shirt, with his bare feet evidence of his modern dance credentials (see Figure 4.4). His right arm is extended upward, and his left arm bent sideways across his chest—choices that recall the scene of agitation in Querner. While his downward glance conveys a feeling of hesitation or concentration, the clenched fists and strong legs suggest an unfurling of revolutionary energy. Despite negative reviews—one critic dismissively referred to him as the Ernst Toller of dance—Weidt was able to build on these early experiments in his later choreographic work with the Berlin-based Die roten Tänzer and in his collaboration with Erwin Piscator on the ambitious program of political theater at the Theater am Nollendorfplatz. The goal of the proletarian dancer, Weidt would later

Figure 4.4. Jean Weidt, *Der Arbeiter/The Worker* (1925), Sammlung Weidt. With permission of Universitätsbibliothek Leipzig, Tanzarchiv, Slg. Weidt.

explain, was "to visualize the surrounding world with the means of his body so that his embodied experience gives his fellow human beings spiritual nourishment!" His approach can be read as a succinct definition of the communist habitus: "Dance is struggle, and struggle is our language."[14]

In 1926, the Berlin-based dancer and poet Jo Mihaly created a similar piece also called *Der Arbeiter* (see Figure 4.5). One newspaper review

Figure 4.5. Jo Mihaly, *Arbeiter/Worker* from Feierliche Tänze, c. 1926. Photo: Atelier Stone. With permission of Deutsches Tanzarchiv Köln.

described a performance "in which the arduous life of the working proletarian and his breaking under the weight of oppression were brilliantly depicted."[15] Photographs show a slender woman reenacting proletarian masculinity through the tension between oppression and resistance. Knowledge of the dancer's gender only heightens the underlying sense of provocation. With her dark hair closely cropped and her breasts tightly bound, Mihaly exudes both strength and vulnerability; in so doing, she foregrounds the conventions that define the working class in highly gendered terms. Even as the fists raised to protect the chest suggest a defensive gesture, the feet firmly planted on the ground convey a sense of stability. She is clearly prepared for assaults by imagined enemies, including by those provoked by such a bold assumption of male privilege.

In their performances of class struggle, Weidt and Mihaly contributed to what dance historian Gabriele Brandstetter, building on Aby Warburg's notion of pathos formulas, has described as a selective appropriation of the discourse of pathos by the historical avant-gardes.[16] Pathos formulas, as defined by Warburg, are the primeval vocabulary of passionate gesticulation; in the arts, they establish highly codified (and universally valid) connections between emotions and bodies, especially in the form of body gesture and facial expression. In Brandstetter's reading, avant-garde writers and artists claim these pathos formulas for a modernist aesthetic arising out of the tension between body language and textual corpus. Very similar processes can be observed in the context of communist agitprop and its proletarian modernist credentials. Here, however, pathos formulas aim to escape the confines of bodies and texts and use expanded notions of performativity to affect real political change. Their function is always defined in relational and referential terms. Developed within the divided political landscape of the late Weimar Republic, particular gestures thus mean something very different, depending on whether they are performed in middle-class or working-class settings, whether they address KPD, SPD, or NSDAP audiences, and whether they treat embodied emotions as part of the political instrumentalization or the radical transformation of the work of art.

One way of assessing the communist appropriation of pathos formulas involves the instructions by practitioners of agitprop about the right (and wrong) ways of standing and speaking. *Das Rote Sprachrohr* (Red Megaphone), for one, came up with very clear recommendations for fellow performers in the art of embodied ideology. Founded in 1929 by the actor and director Maxim Vallentin, the troupe played a key role in turning agitprop into a multimedia practice that included extensive commentary on the proper class habitus. According to Vallentin, agitprop meant direct intervention into current political crises and critical engagement with the structural problems of capitalist societies. It also meant training performers in modeling the process of hardening and strengthening considered so necessary to proletarian mobilizations. Their journal, *Das Rote Sprachrohr* (1929–33), published songs and skits about labor struggles, political confrontations, and family problems and offered detailed advice on the types of programs best suited for factory settings, neighborhood events, and large rallies. When a makeshift stage was not available, the troupe performed on top of flatbed trucks, like construction workers on assignment. Easily recognized by their dark blue unisex overalls, known as *Kesselanzüge* (boilersuits), male and female performers cultivated the confrontational tones and gestures that, according to Vallentin, best conveyed the attitude of class struggle—and did so accompanied by folk instruments such as accordion, mandolin, and snare drum. Approvingly, a contemporary observer noted "a distinct toughness, a sharp awareness in their performance; their momentum resembled the blows of a hammer; their restraints had something of the reflective polish of metals and glass."[17] Speaking in general terms, Hanns Eisler identified as the distinctive characteristic of agitprop its "very tight, rhythmical, precise singing" and a "cold, sharp, and cutting delivery" more typical of political lectures.[18] Very few recordings by the Rote Sprachrohr have survived, but their unique style is on full display in Bertolt Brecht and Slatan Dudow's *Kuhle Wampe, oder Wem gehört die Welt?* (1932, *Kuhle Wampe, or Who Owns the World?*) where they perform a skit about the eviction of a working-class family during a workers' sport festival.

The performances by the Rote Sprachrohr were part of a systematic training of embodied habitus meant to distinguish the Communists from the Social Democrats, including through vocal intonation and enunciation. Already in the early 1920s, Gustav von Wangenheim, in instructions for *Chor der Arbeit* (1923, Chorus of Labor), proposed different modes of speaking for characters representing the rivaling leftist parties. "The KPD always speaks tersely and energetically, the SPD broadly and comfortably," he informed his actors and explained how to ridicule Social Democrats by giving them soft, effeminate voices. Not surprisingly, the superior strength of the KPD in that production was communicated through different vocal pitches, with "the masses [on the stage] once again divided into placidly thrashing SPD and quickly striking KPD."[19] Urgent calls for more emotional restraint became a recurring feature in critical comments on proletarian performance, with too much expressivity seen as a sign of bourgeois decadence and social reformism and with terseness, coolness, and remoteness extolled as essential communist virtues.

For instance, the actors in a play by Hans Marchwitza were instructed not to succumb to sentimental or melodramatic impulses and to "deliver all sentences in a clear, hard, untheatrical tone."[20] Elsewhere Johannes R. Becher warned performers not to present political slogans as if frozen in time and place. Instead, he recommended: "Add movement. But only movements modeled on reality. Don't stage symbolic dances."[21] It was as part of a coordinated campaign against too much emotion on which *Der Agitator* (1931–32, The Agitator), a short-lived journal published by the Rot Front organization, offered practical advice for effective public speaking and street agitation. No detail was deemed irrelevant, with one program for the KPD's 1932 election campaign even offering tips on how not to extend one's hand: "A class-conscious worker will never extend his hand, never! Because he cannot be found begging; instead, he must demand. I tell you again, you must understand that you demean yourselves endlessly in the eyes of the bourgeoisie, the ruling class, when you stand in front of their doors and ask for scraps from their tables."[22]

How can embodiment in agitprop shed new light on the role of emotions in history and the complicated relationship between politics and emotions? In the past decades, the burgeoning interdisciplinary field known as the history of emotions has drawn attention to the importance of symbolic politics in establishing what scholars have called emotional communities, emotional regimes, and emotional practices—terms that are central to many of the essays in this anthology.[23] Historians have shown how legal, medical, educational, literary, and philosophical discourses are inseparable from theories of emotion; how definitions of public and private spheres and experiences of class identity are dependent on (gendered) hierarchies of emotions; and how both the minor rituals of belonging and the grand narratives of nation are contingent upon performances of public emotion. Focusing on ideas about emotions, intellectual historians have shed light on how theories of the passions, sentiments, affects, and drives have profoundly influenced modern definitions of subjectivity, individuality, and identity. More recently, literary scholars have insisted that aesthetic emotions be treated as an integral part of the historical constellation of Enlightenment thought, idealist aesthetics, and bourgeois emancipation. All of these connections are important not only to the study of dominant culture (whether feudal or capitalist, aristocratic or bourgeois) but also of social movements that rely on the literary, visual, and performing arts in their struggles for representation in the literal and figurative sense.

Here, political emotions—how they are defined, interpreted, evaluated, and represented—open up new perspectives on the culture of socialisms and its competing sensibilities and mentalities. Functioning as a heuristic device, emotions allow us, first of all, to move beyond the underlying assumptions informing much scholarship produced during the 1970s and 1980s. These include the equation of working-class culture with the workers' movement, the privileging of political and economic categories in the study of class identifications, and the treatment of symbolic practices as mere extensions of working-class reality or Marxist theory. Secondly, focusing on the aesthetic manifestations of political emotions draws our attention to the highly politicized divides between then-dominant discourses of collectivity and community and the equally contested practices related to gender and sexuality. Reading the communist habitus along these lines means highlighting the tension in proletarian performances between the presumed expressivity and authenticity of embodiment and the highly formalized rules of agitprop and to use that very tension to gain a better understanding of the emotional appeal of the KPD's militant culture during the Weimar years and beyond. Based on this two-pronged approach, this essay has used KPD agitprop practices to shed new light on the formative and transformative role of emotions in modern social movements, to assess their liberating and disciplining functions in performances of class and masculinity, and to uncover the close connection both between embodiment and ideology and between performance and habitus in what still remains the largely unexplored field called embodied ideology in twentieth-century mass mobilizations.

Sabine Hake is Professor and Texas Chair of German Literature and Culture in the Department of Germanic Studies at The University of Texas at Austin. A cultural historian working on nineteenth and twentieth century Germany, she is the author of six monographs, including *Topographies of Class: Modern Architecture and Mass Society in Weimar Berlin* (2008) and *Screen Nazis: Cinema, History, and Democracy* (2012). This essay is based on a chapter in *The Proletarian Dream: Socialism, Culture, and Emotion in Germany 1863–1933* (2017), which won the 2016–17 MLA Aldo and Jeanne Scaglione Prize for Studies in Germanic Languages and Literatures.

Notes

This essay is a shorter, revised version of Chapter 13 in *The Proletarian Dream: Socialism, Culture, and Emotion in Germany, 1863–1933* (Berlin: De Gruyter, 2017), and appears here with permission of the publisher.

1. In this chapter, I will use the term "emotion" rather than "affect," given the difficulty of the latter to account for the dialectics of emotion and cognition so central to Marxist thought; for an *incisive* critique of affect theory in general. For instance, see Ruth Leys, "The Turn to Affect: A Critique," *Critical Inquiry* 37 (Spring 2011): 434–72.
2. Hannah Kosstrin, "Inevitable Designs: Embodied Ideology in Anna Solokow's Proletarian Dances," *Dance Research Journal* 45, no. 2 (2013): 5–23.
3. Pierre Bourdieu, *Outline of a Theory of Practice*, trans. Richard Nice (Cambridge, UK: Cambridge University Press, 1977), 93–94. Bourdieu uses the Greek word *hexis* to describe the embodied habitus; emphasis in the original.
4. Darko Suvin, "Haltung," in *Historisch-kritisches Wörterbuch des Marxismus*. Vol. 5. Ed. Wolfgang Fritz Haug (Berlin: Argument, 2001), 1134. Also see his "*Haltung* (Bearing) and Emotions: Brecht's Refunctioning of Conservative Metaphors for

Agency," in *Zweifel—Fragen—Vorschläge* (Frankfurt am Main: Peter Lang, 1999), 43–58. All translations from the German are mine unless noted otherwise.
5. Marc Silberman, "Gestus," in *Historisch-kritisches Wörterbuch des Marxismus* 5 (2001): 659.
6. The term "emotional regimes" is taken from William M. Reddy, *The Navigation of Feeling: A Framework for the History of Emotions* (Cambridge, UK: Cambridge University Press, 2001).
7. See Richard Bodek, *Proletarian Performance in Weimar Berlin: Agitprop, Chorus, and Brecht* (Columbia, SC: Camden House, 1997); and Robert Heynen, "Revolution and the Degeneration of the Weimar Republic: Worker Culture and the Rise of Fascism," in *Degeneration and Revolution: Radical Cultural Politics and the Body in Weimar Germany*, 496–583 (Leiden: Brill, 2015). For a comprehensive account of proletarian theater, including agitprop during the early Weimar Republic, also see Richard Weber, *Proletarisches Theater und revolutionäre Arbeiterbewegung 1918–1925* (Cologne: Prometh, 1976).
8. Otto Rühle, *Illustrierte Kultur- und Sittengeschichte des Proletariats* (Berlin: Neuer Deutscher Verlag, 1930), 29.
9. On coolness in Weimar culture, see Helmut Lethen, *Cool Conduct: The Culture of Distance in Weimar Germany* (Berkeley: University of California Press, 2002).
10. Hellmuth Heinz, *Curt Querner* (Dresden: Verlag der Kunst, 1968), 24. On the figure of the agitator (also from a GDR perspective), see Dieter Schmidt, "Die Figur des Agitators in der proletatisch-revolutionären Kunst," *Bildende Kunst* 11 (1964): 576–83.
11. See Sander Gilman, "'Stand Up Straight': Notes Toward a History of Posture," *Journal of Medical Humanities* 35 (2014): 57–83.
12. Jean Weidt, *Der Rote Tänzer: Ein Lebensbericht* (Berlin: Henschel, 1968), 10.
13. Marion Reinisch, *Auf der großen Straße: Jean Weidts Erinnerungen; nach Tonbandprotokollen aufgezeichnet und herausgegeben von Marion Reinisch* (Berlin: Henschel, 1984), 5.
14. Reinisch, *Auf der großen Straße*, 184 and 186.
15. Quoted in Yvonne Hardt, *Politische Körper: Ausdruckstanz, Choreographien des Protests und die Arbeiterkulturbewegung in der Weimarer Republik* (Münster: Lit, 2004), 87. For the only English-language article on Weidt, see, by the same author, "Ausdruckstanz, Workers Culture, and Masculinity in Germany," in *Why Men Dance: Choreographing Masculinities Across Borders*, ed. Jennifer Fisher and Anthony Shay, 258–275 (Oxford: Oxford University Press, 2009).
16. See Gabriele Brandstetter, *Poetics of Dance: Body, Image, and Space in the Historical Avant-gardes*, trans. Elena Polzer (Oxford: Oxford University Press, 2015), especially the introduction.
17. Quoted in Dieter Steinke, *Die Entwicklung der Agitprop-Truppe "Das Rote Sprachrohr"* (Leipzig: Zentralhaus für Volkskunst, 1958), 17.
18. Hanns Eisler, "Einige Ratschläge zur Einstudierung der Maßnahme," in *Musik und Politik: Schriften 1924–1948*, ed. Günter Mayer (Leipzig: Deutscher Verlag für Musik, 1973), 168.
19. Gustav von Wangenheim, *Chor der Arbeit* (Berlin: Vereinigung Internationaler Verlagsanstalten, 1924), 110.
20. Hans Marchwitza, "Die rote Schmiede," *Das rote Sprachrohr* 1, no. 4 (1929): 10.

21. Johannes R. Becher, "Die Partei," *Das rote Sprachrohr* 1, no. 4 (1929): 4.
22. *Das rote Sprachrohr: Material für Agitproptruppen und Arbeiter-Theatervereine* (Berlin: Zentralagitprop der KPD und des KJVD, 1932), 16. For a brief introduction to Weimar-era agitprop, see Erika Funk-Hennigs, "Die Agitpropbewegung als Teil der Arbeiterkultur der Weimarer Republik," *Beiträge zur Popularmusikforschung* 15–16 (1995): 82–117. Two lesser-known agitprop troupes, Truppe im Westen and Nordwest ran, are the focus in Susanne Seelbach, *Proletarisch-revolutionäres Theater in Düsseldorf 1930–1933: Die Bühne als politisches Medium* (Frankfurt am Main: Peter Lang, 1994). For more personal recollections, see Daniel Hoffmann-Ostwald, ed., *Auf der roten Rampe: Erlebnisberichte und Texte aus der Arbeit der Agitproptruppen vor 1933* (Berlin: Henschel, 1963).
23. The term "emotional communities" is taken from Barbara H. Rosenwein, *Emotional Communities in the Early Middle Ages* (Ithaca: Cornell University Press, 2007), and Barbara H. Rosenwein, *Generations of Feeling: A History of Emotions, 600–1700* (Cambridge, UK: Cambridge University Press, 2015).

Bibliography

Becher, Johannes R. "Die Partei." *Das Rote Sprachrohr* 1, no. 4 (1929): 4–7.
Bodek, Richard. *Proletarian Performance in Weimar Berlin: Agitprop, Chorus, and Brecht*. Columbia, SC: Camden House, 1997.
Bourdieu, Pierre. *Outline of a Theory of Practice*. Translated by Richard Nice. Cambridge, UK: Cambridge University Press, 1977.
Brandstetter, Gabriele. *Poetics of Dance: Body, Image, and Space in the Historical Avant-gardes*. Translated by Elena Polzer. Oxford: Oxford University Press, 2015.
Das Rote Sprachrohr: Material für Agitproptruppen und Arbeiter-Theatervereine. Berlin: Zentralagitprop der KPD und des KJVD, 1932.
Eisler, Hanns. "Einige Ratschläge zur Einstudierung der Maßnahme." In *Musik und Politik: Schriften 1924–1948*, edited by Günter Mayer. Leipzig: Deutscher Verlag für Musik, 1973.
Funk-Hennigs, Erika. "Die Agitpropbewegung als Teil der Arbeiterkultur der Weimarer Republik." *Beiträge zur Popularmusikforschung* 15–16 (1995): 82–117.
Gilman, Sander. "'Stand Up Straight': Notes Toward a History of Posture." *Journal of Medical Humanities* 35 (2014): 57–83.
Hardt, Yvonne. "Ausdruckstanz, Workers Culture, and Masculinity in Germany." In *Why Men Dance: Choreographing Masculinities Across Borders*, edited by Jennifer Fisher and Anthony Shay, 258–275. Oxford: Oxford University Press, 2009.
———. *Politische Körper: Ausdruckstanz, Choreographien des Protests und die Arbeiterkulturbewegung in der Weimarer Republik*. Münster: Lit, 2004.
Heinz, Hellmuth. *Curt Querner*. Dresden: Verlag der Kunst, 1968.
Heynen, Robert. "Revolution and the Degeneration of the Weimar Republic: Worker Culture and the Rise of Fascism." In *Degeneration and Revolution: Radical Cultural Politics and the Body in Weimar Germany*, 496–583. Leiden: Brill, 2015.

Hoffmann-Ostwald, Daniel, ed. *Auf der roten Rampe: Erlebnisberichte und Texte aus der Arbeit der Agitproptruppen vor 1933*. Berlin: Henschel, 1963.
Kosstrin, Hannah. "Inevitable Designs: Embodied Ideology in Anna Sokolow's Proletarian Dances." *Dance Research Journal* 45, no. 2 (2013): 5–23.
Lethen, Helmut. *Cool Conduct: The Culture of Distance in Weimar Germany*. Berkeley: University of California Press, 2002.
Leys, Ruth. "The Turn to Affect: A Critique." *Critical Inquiry* 37 (Spring 2011): 434–72.
Marchwitza, Hans. "Die rote Schmiede." *Das Rote Sprachrohr* 1, no. 4 (1929): 10–12.
Reddy, William M. *The Navigation of Feeling: A Framework for the History of Emotions*. Cambridge, UK: Cambridge University Press, 2001.
Reinisch, Marion, ed. *Auf der großen Straße: Jean Weidts Erinnerungen; Nach Tonbandprotokollen aufgezeichnet und herausgegeben von Marion Reinisch*. Berlin: Henschel, 1984.
Rosenwein, Barbara H. *Emotional Communities in the Early Middle Ages*. Ithaca: Cornell University Press, 2007.
——— *Generations of Feeling: A History of Emotions, 600–1700*. Cambridge, UK: Cambridge University Press, 2015.
Rühle, Otto. *Illustrierte Kultur- und Sittengeschichte des Proletariats*. Berlin: Neuer Deutscher Verlag, 1930.
Schmidt, Dieter. "Die Figur des Agitators in der proletatisch-revolutionären Kunst." *Bildende Kunst* 11 (1964): 576–83.
Seelbach, Susanne. *Proletarisch-revolutionäres Theater in Düsseldorf 1930–1933: Die Bühne als politisches Medium*. Frankfurt am Main: Peter Lang, 1994.
Silberman, Marc. "Gestus." In *Historisch-kritisches Wörterbuch des Marxismus* 5 (2001): 659.
Steinke, Dieter. *Die Entwicklung der Agitprop-Truppe "Das Rote Sprachrohr."* Leipzig: Zentralhaus für Volkskunst, 1958.
Suvin, Darko. "Haltung." In *Historisch-kritisches Wörterbuch des Marxismus*. Vol. 5, edited by Wolfgang Fritz Haug, 1134–42. Berlin: Argument, 2001.
——— "Haltung (Bearing) and Emotions: Brecht's Refunctioning of Conservative Metaphors for Agency." In *Zweifel—Fragen—Vorschläge*. Frankfurt am Main: Peter Lang, 1999.
Vallentin, Maxim. "Agitpropspiel und Kampfwert." *Linkskurve* 2, no. 4 (1930): 15–16.
von Wangenheim, Gustav. *Chor der Arbeit*. Berlin: Vereinigung Internationaler Verlagsanstalten, 1924.
Weber, Richard. *Proletarisches Theater und revolutionäre Arbeiterbewegung 1918–1925*. Cologne: Prometh, 1976.
Weidt, Jean. *Der Rote Tänzer: Ein Lebensbericht*. Berlin: Henschel, 1968.

CHAPTER 5

A Skin of Hatred
How Bodies Are Involved in the Memory of Emotions and Anti-Semitic Practice of the Weimar Republic

RUSSELL SPINNEY

"Goose pimples." Those are the words that Anny Kessler used in her visual history interview for the USC Shoah Foundation to recall her feeling the moment one of her high school teachers asked her to pronounce her father's name, "Isaak." Speaking almost fifty years later to an interviewer, the image of Anna is reduced to her face and shoulders through the lens of the camera. With her eyes focused on the interviewer off to the side, she continues to relate a collection of memories that she locates in that feeling of her skin. At the start of the new school year in 1925, as she explained, she "got the shivers because she knew the other boys and girls would make fun of her." The teacher, as she recalled further, knew her father's name very well, but made a point of repeating the name nonetheless so that the students could make fun of her a little more. She then felt a sense of relief, however brief, every time the teacher called out her mother's more German-sounding name, "Hilde." It was not always this way, as she noted later in her interview. Born in 1915 in the central German town of Gotha, Anny also remembered early Jewish and gentile friendships. But with these memories of the mid-1920s, she "already felt the difference between Jewish and not-Jewish" at the local private coed Humanist high school she attended; and it continued to worsen as she lost her gentile friends, and classmates increasingly played little tricks on her like taking away her pencils. By age eleven, as she specifically dated the memory and the emotions in that memory, she felt lonely and different. She also recalls that this compelled her to study even harder in order to show her classmates that she could succeed academically. Then things abruptly changed around 1930, when her father decided to move the family to another town in the hope that the change would do them good.[1]

Placing the larger history of the Weimar Republic and its familiar tropes of deterioration and doom aside for the moment, the recollection of a bodily feeling presents an often overlooked and useful, yet challenging, approach to what has constituted and continues to shape emotions long after an event has occurred. Despite the unavoidable problems of language, time, and space that a video history interview presents, the recollections of those goose pimples and bodily shivers offer a way to explore the key themes of this volume at one of the most immediate sites of interaction where corporeality and materiality meet. In this instance, it is the memory of the skin that links an individual to another time and place, which in turn may offer a way to recover what the historian Barbara Duden noted as the "vanished reality of the 'corporal self'" enmeshed in the origins of our own perceptions.[2] By bringing the body back into view, this case thus raises a question about how emotions are initially formed where bodies and materiality meet, and how the body can continue to help shape and reify emotions long after the original event. In peeling back these layers of a specific memory, this case raises additional questions about the importance of bodies in the affective practices of anti-Semitism in the Weimar Republic, and, in the process, points out areas for future research, especially about the role of emotions in the appeal of emerging fascism among youth and their families, and the emotional "ecologies" of self and community in a cluster of small towns and cities in the heart of central Germany.

Approaching Emotions through Visual History Testimonies

Emotions are elusive, complex, and messy, to say the least from a historian's perspective, as the example of the visual history testimony offered at the start of this chapter suggests. Yet despite the challenges that visual history testimonies present, in terms of temporal, spatial, and linguistic distances from the event itself, let alone the iterative, subjective, and even aggrandizing nature of memory, that subjectivity, as the historian Konrad Jarausch has recently argued, also provides access to representations of "earlier events and emotions through the lens of later reflection and evaluation" and the idiosyncratic ways in which people narrate history.[3] Given my research interest in locating firsthand accounts of everyday life and experience in the Weimar Republic, the USC Shoah Foundation's Visual History Archive offers not only the world's largest collection of video history testimonies on the Holocaust, but also a way to cross-search their collections for people who were born in the Central German communities, which are at the center of my dissertation and post-dissertation research.[4] It was through that research that I first noticed the occasional reference to bodily memories of sensation and other evidence of emotional practices that deserve further consideration and study.

In accessing the emotions present in historical records, scholars have already developed a range of approaches from which to draw, approaches grounded in a whole host of human-generated social relations, cultures, and politics, which in turn present perhaps the most readily observable forms of historical evidence in terms of language, discourse, and, more recently, practices. Approaching emotions through the concept of practices, especially by thinking of emotions as ways of doing and being, appears especially useful because they open the way to study what scholars of the "New Materialism" would call the "ecological self," reminiscent of Wilhelm Dilthey's living body interacting with the external world discussed in this book's introduction—that is, the intersections of the internal and external dimensions of emotions involving what people are sensing around them (including other people, material objects, and the surrounding environment) and what they are feeling and thinking internally, able to draw from different words, sounds, gestures, and other cultural sources of emotions.[5]

As I hope to demonstrate below, visual history testimonies, and more specifically the information that this memory of goose pimples contains, lend themselves well to a more ecological conception of a person's emotions, such as the constructed view to emotions proposed by the contemporary psychologist Lisa Feldman Barrett. From this approach, people create their emotions and their sense of reality itself through the sensations of their bodies in relationship to their cognitive practices of memory, personal goal setting, and perception of the world around them. As Feldman Barrett warns, however, emotions are also highly idiosyncratic and subjective, and in no way fully capture what was really going on in a situation.[6] But those idiosyncrasies and subjectivities matter both in terms of historical experience and how emotions can affect social relationships, communities, politics, and power.[7]

Within that memory of Anny's physical response to her class, there is evidence of the construction of that memory in a different time and place, with the specific purpose of posterity—that is, bearing witness to the Holocaust for future use. There is also evidence of how that original sensation informed her emotions at the time, and evidence that can help illuminate the ways in which anti-Semitic practices operated via what people sensed through their bodies. Moreover, the historical forms of evidence encapsulated in these memories can be corroborated with other forms of archival evidence from pamphlets, newspaper accounts, police records, and other forms of semiprivate and public evidence. As will be demonstrated further below, such triangulated approaches show why tracking archival evidence of the physical sensations of the body can not only help show how feelings are initially perceived and formed over time and place, but also how those feelings and other details embedded in them are really important to a fuller understanding of larger questions about what happened in the past; and in this case, what was happening in the communities of central Germany in the 1920s.

The Body, Emotions, and Self-Fashioning in Imperial Germany and the Weimar Republic

The role of the body in human subjectivity, long distrusted in European intellectual history, only became an object of more scientific interest in the late nineteenth century with the proliferation of the natural sciences, leading to what the historian Ute Frevert has called the "somatization of emotions."[8] The professional development of physiology, for example, significantly influenced how people might perceive, name, and translate the experience of goose pimples into a range of meaning and action. Naming a sensation, in this case goose pimples, suggests nearly universal folk etymologies and practices of sensing what the body feels that can be found across many cultures around the world that all draw metaphorical comparisons between human sensation and avian species and their skin.[9] In fact, the sensation of the hairs on one's skin rising up can be found across much, if not all, of humanity, and even among other mammalian species.[10]

In Late Latin, for example, it was known as *horripilātiō*, or *horripilātiōn-*, from the Latin *horripilātus*, and its past participle, *horripilāre*, which interestingly, in terms of the body, combines *horrēre (to tremble)* with *pilāre (to grow hair*—from *pilus, hair*) in order to mean *to bristle with hairs*.[11] The medical terms *cutis anserine*, *arasing*, *piloerection*, the *pilomotor reflex*, and *horripilation*, in part not only reflect that Late Latin etymological history, but also demonstrate an increasingly nineteenth- and twentieth-century scientific and transnational understanding of the bumps that form on a person's skin at the base of body hairs as an involuntary function of what a person senses—in particular, the feeling of being cold. Charles Darwin, for example, considered the formation of these goose bumps in human bodies as a vestigial reflex of human evolution designed to raise the body's hair, thereby making the ancestral human body appear larger and more able to scare off predators.[12] Similarly, late eighteenth-century and nineteenth-century German language reflects cultural metaphors of goose skin, or *Gänsehaut*, as well as early modern and scientific discoveries and understandings that acknowledged the physical phenomenon of the hair follicles and skin rising in association with a wide variety of sensations including feeling cold, being frightened, or the psychological condition of hysteria, which could be found by the mid-nineteenth century in German medical, physiology, anthropology, and even homeopathy publications.[13]

Interest in the historical construction of the human body has only grown with the proliferation of studies across a wide array of contemporary disciplines. Drawing from their respective work in US and early modern European history, some historians, such as Peter and Carol Stearns and Barbara Rosenwein, notice that societies or other definable groups cultivate attitudes, standards, and codes about what people should feel and how they should or should not express what they are feeling.[14] For example, in his study on the documented cases of neurasthenia and how notions of nerves influenced Imperial German society and politics, the historian Joachim Radtkau, has illuminated a complex landscape for scholars to think about in their examination of emotions, showing how medical professionals generated knowledge about nervousness and how that knowledge permeated popular culture, even private diaries, in both everyday experience and national politics. Many contemporary observers believed that nervous conditions did in fact stem from modern, industrial, urban society or the crisis of imperial politics. They influenced how people conceived of their own thoughts and feelings in terms of nerves and nervous conditions and invoked larger thoughts of hopeless cultural decline, decadence, or downfall. Yet Radtkau also points out the ambivalence about nerves in German society and politics. There were also those who sought to reclaim older romantic German values of sensitivity or *Gemütlichkeit*, or valorized nerves as an advantageous prerequisite for great ideas and general progress. And there were still others who countered with alternative discursive traditions about security and health, denigrated nervousness as a sign of feminine weakness, and even proclaimed a new type of German person: one who conveyed a cooler, less nervous, and more hardened image of men.[15]

Given such inherent ambivalence and the array of cultural sources available in Imperial German society and politics, the number of emotional styles and codes that Germans could draw from, as the historian Moritz Föllmer has shown, greatly expanded in the wake of World War I with the complex interplay of wide-ranging desires for individual experience and different kinds of collectivism in a modern mass society.[16] For minority groups and individuals, as the historian Sharon Gillerman has argued, the inherent ambiguity in such emotional concepts could offer not only the opposing possibilities for inclusion or exclusion, but also chances for cultural creativity and innovative self-fashioning.[17] As the philosopher Judith Butler theorized, such "intelligible bodies" never quite comply with the constraints to which they are subject and open up possibilities at the same time that other bodies become unthinkable and unlivable.[18]

A great deal of work has therefore been done to understand how the human body has been constructed in terms of gender, religion, class, sport, consumerism, entertainment, and war.[19] However, based on this preliminary study of the history of goose bumps, there is arguably more work to be done on how the human body itself has actively influenced and continues to influence historical constructions of the body and related emotional styles and codes. Beyond the skin, such a project could further map out how different parts of the body, like the face, eyes, ears, nose, stomach, and heart, just to name a few, inform human subjectivity and emotions. Moreover, how the human body informs the subjectivity of experience, history itself, and historiography deserves further consideration—in this case, in the resurgence of anti-Semitism in the Weimar Republic. There is already an existing range of studies that can help, like some of the work on the history of the body, the social dynamics in neighborhoods, and political forms of violence.[20] But there is also more work to be done in terms of how the human body itself was involved in anti-Semitic practice in everyday life, and how ordinary Germans, both Jewish and gentile, responded to the resurgence of anti-Semitism after World War I in varied efforts.

Peeling Back the Layers of History in the Memory of a Bodily Feeling

In that memory of her skin, there are arguably details from the recollection's original context that come up immediately without much additional interpretation from the interview subject. There are also details that the interview subject has had time to think about and translate, which in turn reveal a more active set of cognitive practices over time and space, as anthropologist Monica Scheer might suggest, to identify, name, and express feelings.[21] In this instance, the act of recalling a physical sensation also includes making note of additional details, like Anny Kessler's age at an exact time and place in her life that formed the event. Within these recollections also lie important notes about the physical sensations of the interview subject's body—in this case, goose bumps and shivering—which Feldman Barrett arguably might view as revealing examples of the *interoceptive* processes (i.e., feeling what the body senses that informs the cognitive construction of emotions).[22]

The memory indicates additional "emotion-work," as historian Joanna Bourke terms such practices—for example, the search for words to name those physical sensations of the body, to translate them into more specific emotions in English, in this case, namely, to reify those sensations into memories of personal goals and feelings of loneliness and being different, and thereby mask or even shed other potential meanings of sensations in the process.[23] Beyond these direct details of her body and how those parts of her body inform her memory of the occasion, there are also glimpses of what her other senses were taking in around her from repeated efforts to humiliate her in the classroom, from the images and sounds of her teacher and coed classmates, particularly their laughter, to what mattered most to her in looking back, particularly the meaning of school in her life, how she reacted by choosing to set a goal to study harder, and how her family eventually responded to what was happening to their daughter and most likely themselves in the larger society of that little town of Gotha by moving away. Finally, the interview yields valuable information on several external factors in this memory of feeling that need more consideration and future research, including the evidence about the space itself, the people who were present (i.e., her teachers and coed classmates), and their own individual and collective emotional efforts (i.e., the audibly, visibly, and physically directed practices aimed to affect not only how the interview subject might feel lonely and different [whether intentionally or not], but also how they themselves might begin to feel the same or at least included in the increasingly ethnic, if not racialized, group).[24]

In the case of Anny Kessler, her family came to Gotha around 1901 from Poland, when anti-Semitism was rising again in Central and Eastern Europe. It was therefore still a time when local Jewish communities like nearby Erfurt could still pronounce a sense of hope in safety, prosperity, integration, and even belonging in Germany, as to be found in the dedications of their new synagogue before the turn of the century.[25] Her father thus followed a familiar immigrant trajectory of volunteering for his new country's military in World War I, as dozens of local Jewish male citizens in the region did. He developed a small clothing store in Gotha that allowed his daughter to attend a private, coed, humanist high school, and helped create a life for his family in Gotha that Anny recalled as lovely and beautiful, including both Jewish and non-Jewish German friendships.

The memory of goose pimples thus marked an important moment in a young teenage woman's life at the school on which she and her family pinned their hopes for her future in Germany. On their own, those bodily reactions are ambivalent. In looking back to a different time and place, Anny not only articulated very clearly the feelings of loneliness and being different, but also her own personal goals—that is, the determination to persevere and succeed despite such daily harassment. At the time, she may not have expressed those feelings and goals in exactly such terms (and in German no less), but that at least is what she believes she wanted to show her peers and teachers at the time and let viewers of her video history testimony know for posterity. Interestingly, she does note that the shivers reminded her of anticipating her peers' mocking encouraged by their teacher. However, any more explicit expression of fear or any other emotion is omitted, if not entirely absent, throughout the account, and there are few other signs of her corporal responses and expressions, or those of anyone else.

Triangulating Emotions through Local Archives and Visual History Testimonies

Beyond Anny's own construction of emotions, more than anything else, I would suggest these goose pimples reveal profound changes taking place in some German communities and elsewhere in central Europe in the mid 1920s.

These changes affected how people felt about themselves and each other in a wide variety of ways—not necessarily always intended or expected. What first marked the return of anti-Semitism at the everyday level were often changes in the anonymous affective practices shaping the materiality of local spaces in order to express the apparently masked feelings of anti-Semitic actors, and affect local Jewish citizens and their non-Jewish acquaintances that they targeted. In Erfurt and surrounding areas, it began in the fall of 1923, around the time of the lead up to and failure of the Nazi Beerhall Putsch, as local magistrate's confidential reports and Jewish newspapers reveal and visual histories confirm. On the night of 19 September 1923, for example, an unknown number of people assaulted some of the Jewish residents in Erfurt, breaking some of their windows and damaging their doors and gardens.[26]

These anonymous practices continued to escalate in the mid-1920s. The local police noted the dissemination of leaflets on train car seats and graffiti drawn on alley walls intended to threaten Jewish citizens, which prompted train authorities to publicly state their disapproval of such activities.[27] The most shocking event in this period, at least for local newspapers, might have been the desecration of the old Jewish cemetery in Erfurt in 1926, which the police traced back to a group of local German Nationalist youth and most likely the actions of their group leaders and some of their parents behind the scenes.[28] However, local sources also show that affective practices became increasingly interpersonal among ordinary people in everyday spaces during this time. In the fall of 1923, for example, the Erfurt police noted repeated insults directed at Jewish citizens in the streets; and in the fall of 1924, the police observed swastikas inscribed on the sides of children's lanterns at the annual festival of *Martinstag*.[29] Even some of the local unemployed had been seen roaming the streets wearing the black-white-red insignia of the *völkisch* nationalists and harassing innocent Jewish pedestrians.[30] More importantly, such interpersonal forms of anti-Semitic harassment began to manifest in local institutions like the school that Anny's family had chosen for her in Gotha that ostensibly emphasized the humanities. Most immediately, they reveal the efforts of a single teacher to create a nearly daily practice of identifying the Jewish children in the classroom. These affective practices directed by the teacher involved her peers in ways that began to change Jewish and gentile German interpersonal dynamics in the school, permitted some of her peers to perform an ethnic nationalist sense of belonging marked by the sounds of some students' laughter, and left Anny feeling isolated and foreign—glimpses of affective practices and performances among those doing what one might otherwise just call bullying.

Challenging more simplistic assumptions of passivity, fear, and doom rooted in hindsight, Jewish youth articulated a wide range of responses that drew from a range of emotional concepts in response to these increasing forms of interpersonal harassment, as the video history accounts of the USC Shoah Foundation's Visual History Archives reveal, ranging from shock, anxiety, and desperation over their sense of difference and inferiority to feelings of exclusion, isolation, invisibility, the urge to flee, or even commit suicide. Still many others recall feeling offended, angry, and, like Anny, determined to persevere and even fight back.

The interviews also reveal evidence of the wide range of emotional practices in the responses of their parents. Some Jewish parents began to create more sheltered worlds for their families and friends, transferring their children to different schools, sending them away to family members in the relative anonymity of urban centers, the isolation of rural life, or abroad. Some told their children not to worry about the hatred and malice they perceived or to simply accept increasing everyday forms of anti-Jewish persecution as their historically Jewish fate. Some told their children to persevere, guarded them with dogs on their way to school, or trained them in boxing or martial arts to fight back. Yet others armed themselves to protect their families and communities and even became known as "Nazi bashers."[31]

Conclusions

At the center of this study is the memory of a person's skin recorded within a person's video testimony designed to bear witness to the much larger history of the Holocaust. To someone watching that video-recorded testimony, the mention of those goose pimples may not catch the viewer's attention at all. If the viewer heard Anny mention that detail about her skin, they may have disregarded it as a minor detail of little significance, or if they attached any meaning to it at all, the memory of her goose pimples may have simply confirmed a feeling that fits with one's understanding in hindsight of the horrific nature of Nazi persecution and genocide. Yet upon closer examination, that memory of one's skin is an interesting starting point for exploring how the body is involved in both sensing the environment that was originally involved in creating those goose pimples in the first place, *and* how that sensation continued to shape how that person actively assembled her memories of that past and reified more specific emotions over time and space in the process, including specific words, personal goals, images, sounds, and so on.

Concepts of emotions and their internalization are crucial cultural sources that inform how we perceive and express what we feel.[32] As put forward above, the concept of emotions as practice, as experiencing, doing, and being, can potentially be very useful. But where possible, the practices of the body, both naturally evolved and cultivated, must be brought back more into consideration in order to provide further insights into the range of factors that constitute emotions and make emotions such an important, albeit often neglected or shorthand, factor in history alongside ideas, social structure, culture, politics, and power.[33] How feelings become more specifically named emotions is also rooted in the materiality of our bodies and their sensations, which often work with other memories, personal goals, and cultural concepts in relationship with the complex material world and the people and things present and active in those specific historical contexts. Paying more attention to the historical evidence of the body and its sensations could further illuminate those initial historical contexts, showing how people articulate more specific emotions from those original experiences over the distances of time and space. And in this particular memory of a person's skin is evidence for competing, emotionally charged efforts and practices at the everyday level that are indicative of a contested, changing world.

As a few scholars like Barbara Rosenwein, Monica Scheer, Jan Plamper, and others have suggested, turning greater attention to bodies and emotions in times and places of conflict where different affective practices collide may yield further insights about both the failures and successes of "doing" certain emotions versus other emotions, as well as about unspoken rules of societies and competing efforts to regulate, if not control, what people felt and thought.[34] In hindsight, the resurgence of everyday forms of anti-Semitism in the early Weimar Republic that targeted bodies meets the criteria for the prerequisite stages of genocide—that is, the classification, symbolization, and discrimination against a minority group, as suggested by the political scientist Gregory Stanton.[35] In effect the resurgence points to the creation of an ecology of hatred; but upon closer examination, those stages also mark a time where communal emotional practices, codes, and concepts were in flux *and* creatively contested.

Jewish adults and youth responded to this resurgent anti-Semitism in a wide range of ways, revealing an array of emotional concepts and practices that should challenge more reductive assumptions of passivity and doom in the face of a growing threat. Moreover, the threat of anti-Semitism itself worked through affective practices that specifically targeted people, their bodies and emotions. There was still room, albeit diminishing, that allowed for different trajectories, like displays of civic courage among some Jewish and gentile German friends and acquaintances who chose not to disassociate themselves from each other in the face of growing harassment and persecution. But such decisions in everyday life also reinforced the fact that enough ordinary Germans from all strata of society, particularly parents, adult mentors, and a new generation of many youth, were increasingly codifying people in their everyday interactions in more polarizing ways that cut across everyday forms of respectability and conviviality to cultivate more radical ultranationalist emotional communities. Future research could therefore challenge simplistic linear transformations of the old imagined fears and anxieties of a racialized enemy (i.e., "the Jew," into an attractive *völkisch* racialized sense of belonging) by peering beneath the appearances of such emotional displays and looking more closely for what ordinary people were actually thinking, feeling, and doing about the rise of more radical forms of nationalism.[36]

The affective practices of anti-Semitism were by no means the only ways in which emotions were involved in many of these places, as the historian Sabine Hake's work on communist affective practices in this anthology shows so well. There were multiple, iterative sources of emotions and emotional practices that varied across different public and private spaces, neighborhoods, and institutions.[37] But the practices of anti-Semitism increasingly involved a range of different types of spaces, such as schools, businesses, streets, and homes. More importantly, they involved many adult leaders, parents, and peers in practices that affected their bodies and minds, as well as the bodies and minds of others through a range of emotional concepts and affective practices that could inspire closer examination of the individual and collective dynamics of ultranationalist affective practices elsewhere. Examined individually, each case remains idiosyncratic and seemingly limited in effect; but in sum, these cases further segregated and isolated people in the small towns and cities in which they lived across Central Germany. Indeed, the prevalence of anti-Semitism contributed to making those spouting racism verses those affected feel as if they could belong, or as if they were to be excluded, and thereby raises the question about how this may have contributed to more radical regimes with the potential to seize the power of the state from the ground up.

Russell Spinney is an independent historian and instructor at the Thacher School in Ojai, California, and he is a coorganizer of the Emotions Studies network for the German Studies Association. His research interests include emotions, particularly fear and courage, in the political practices of the Weimar Republic and the US. He has coauthored and edited a special journal issue on the history of emotions in twentieth-century European social movements, political protests, and revolutions for the Cambridge journal, *Contemporary European History* (Fall 2014). Additional publications include "Through the Sons of the Old Chiefs: Surveying Space, Identity and European-American Relationships in the 'New Purchase' Territory (Centre County, Pennsylvania 1769-1778)," in *Pennsylvania's Revolution*, ed. William Pencak (University Park, PA: Penn State Press, 2010); and "Fear, Courage and Civic Behavior in the Weimar Republic," *Revue Suisse d'Histoire* (Swiss Historical Review) 61 (2011): 74–89.

Notes

For the development of this article, the author would especially like to thank his wife Nicole Stern for helping carve out time from the intense collaborative efforts of raising two young children to pursue a career; the generous professional support of Santa Fe Prep for travel, research, and writing; and the helpful comments of the anonymous reviewers.

1. Anny Toni Kessler, interview by Randy Lichtman, Sunrise, FL, 21 July 1997, interview 31140, segments 4–8, *Visual History Archive* (VHA), USC Shoah Foundation, Los Angeles, CA.
2. Barbara Duden, *The Woman Beneath the Skin: A Doctor's Patients in Eighteenth-Century Germany*, trans. Thomas Dunlap (Cambridge, MA: Harvard University Press, 1991), 1–3.
3. Konrad Jarausch, *Broken Lives: How Ordinary Germans Experienced the 20th Century* (Princeton: Princeton University Press, 2018), 7–9.
4. The study of the USC Shoah Foundation Institute's Visual History Archives (VHA) examined the testimonies from more than one hundred interview subjects who were born in the towns of Erfurt, Gotha, Weimar, Magdeburg, and Nuremberg between 1902 and 1930. The study's Nuremberg group is the largest subgroup with sixty-seven interview subjects, followed by Magdeburg with twenty, Erfurt with ten, and Gotha and Weimar with two each; thirty-eight are men and sixty-three are women; sixteen were born before World War I, fourteen during the war, and the majority, seventy-one, between the years of 1920 and 1930; thirty-three people can recall their communities to some degree before the Nazi seizure of power, if those interview subjects born in 1919 are included.
5. See for example, Katie Barclay, "New Materialism and the New History of Emotions," *Emotions: History, Culture, Society* 1, no. 1 (2017): 161–83.
6. For some of the most recent research on the constructionist stance on emotions, see Lisa Feldman Barrett, *How Emotions Are Made: The Secret Life of the Brain* (Boston: Houghton Mifflin Harcourt, 2017), 56–83. For Barrett's discussion about the subjectivity of emotions, see also Hannah Rosin and Alix Spiegel, hosts, "Emotions," *Invisibilia*, NPR, 1 June 2017, accessed 28 December 2018, *NPR*, www.npr.org/programs/invisibilia/530718193/emotions.
7. Compare Ute Frevert's discussion of "The economy of emotions: How it works and why it matters," in *Emotions in History—Lost and Found* (Budapest: Central European University Press, 2011), 3–18.
8. Ute Frevert, "Defining Emotions: Concepts and Debates over Three Centuries," in *Emotional Lexicons: Continuity and Change in the Vocabulary of Feeling 1700–2000*, ed. Ute Frevert et al. (Oxford: Oxford University Press, 2014), 16–24.
9. There is still no vetted, comprehensive study of the use of "goose pimples" or "goose bumps" to identify the physical sensation. The best work on this subject so far may be found on Wikipedia, which notes how many languages other than English also use "goose", and includes additional references for further research. For example, "Goose skin" is used in German (*Gänsehaut*), Swedish (*gåshud*), Danish and Norwegian (*gåsehud*), Icelandic (*gæsahúð*), Greek (*χήνειο δέρμα*), Italian (*pelle d'oca*), Russian (гусиная кожа), Ukrainian (гусяча шкіра), Polish (*gęsia skórka*), Czech (*husí kůže*), Slovak (*husia koža*), Slovene (*kurja polt*), Latvian (*zosāda*), and Hungarian (*libabőr*).

This Wikipedia entry also tracks how "goose" skin may also be replaced by other kinds of poultry. For instance, "hen" is used in Spanish (*piel de gallina*), Portuguese (*pele de galinha*), Romanian (*piele de găină*), French (*chair de poule*), and Catalan (*pell de gallina*). "Chicken" is used in Dutch (*kippenvel*), Chinese (雞皮疙瘩, lit. *lumps on chicken skin*), Finnish (*kananliha*), Estonian (*kananahk*), Afrikaans (*hoendervleis*), and Korean (닭살, *daksal*). In Hindi/Urdu, it is called *rongtey khade ho jaana*. The equivalent Japanese term, 鳥肌 (*torihada*), translates literally as "bird skin." In Arabic, it is called *kash'arirah*, while in Hebrew, it is called "duck skin" (זווּרב רוע). See "Goose Bumps," *Wikipedia*, last modified 16 June 2017, https://en.wikipedia.org/wiki/Goose_bumps.

10. Studies of many mammals, including chimpanzees, porcupines, otters, mice, rats, and cats, show similar reactions of raising hairs or quills when they encounter perceived sources of stress from predators or other threats. See, for example, Y. Masuda, et al., "Developmental and Pharmacological Features of Mouse Emotional Piloerection," *Experimental Animals* 48 (July 1999): 209–11.
11. See "Goosebumps," *Online Etymology Dictionary*, accessed 26 June 2017, http://www.etymonline.com/index.php?term=goosebumps&allowed_in_frame=0.
12. Charles Darwin, *The Expression of the Emotions in Man and Animals* (London: John Murray, 1872), 101–3.
13. A search of Google NGrams Viewer for the term "Gänsehaut" in German between 1500 and the present yields a history of the term's use, particularly in scientific literature from the 1760s onward. The primary source texts that this search yields are quite extensive and deserve much more in-depth treatment than can be developed in this paper. See "Gänsehaut," *Google NGrams Viewer*, accessed 26 June 2017, https://books.google.com/ngrams/graph?content=Gänsehaut&year_start=1500&year_end=2000&corpus=20&smoothing=3&share=&direct_url=t1%3B%2CG%C3%A4nsehaut%3B%2Cc0. For a more specific example from this research, see the entry for "Gänsehaut," in *Real-encyclopadie der gesammten Heilkunde: medicinisch-chirurgisches Handwörterbuch für praktische Ärzte*, vol. 8, ed. Albert Eulenburg (Wien: Urban and Scwarzenberg, 1995), 192–94. Compare the entry for "Gänsehaut" in the online version of Jakob and Wilhelm Grimm, *Deutsches Wörterbuch*, accessed on 3 July 2017.
14. Peter N. Stearns and Carol Z. Stearns, "Clarifying the History of Emotions and Emotional Standards," *American Historical Review* 90, no. 4 (October 1985): 813–36. See also Barbara H. Rosenwein, "Worrying about Emotions in History," *American Historical Review* 107, no. 3 (June 2002): 821–45. Compare Judith Butler's notion of the "productive constraints" on "intelligible bodies"; see Judith Butler, *Bodies That Matter* (New York City: Routledge, 2011), vii–xxx.
15. Joachim Radtkau, *Das Zeitalter der Nervosität: Deutschland zwischen Bismarck und Hitler* (Munich: Hanser, 1998), 263–353.
16. Moritz Föllmer, *Individuality and Modernity in Berlin: Self and Society from Weimar to the Wall* (Cambridge, UK: Cambridge University Press, 2013). See also Kathleen Canning, "The Politics of Symbols, Semantics, and Sentiments in the Weimar Republic," *Central European History* 43, no. 4 (December 2010): 567–80.
17. Sharon Gillerman, "A Kinder Gentler Strongman? Siegmund Breitbart in Eastern Europe," in *Jewish Masculinities: German Jews, Gender, and History*, ed. Benjamin Maria Baader, Sharon Gillerman, and Paul Lerner (Bloomington: Indiana University

Press, 2012), 197–98. Compare Stefanie Schüler-Springorum, "A Soft Hero: Male Jewish Identity in Imperial Germany through the Autobiography of Aron Liebeck," in *Jewish Masculinities*, 101–2.
18. Butler, *Bodies That Matter*, xii.
19. Wolfgang Hardtwig, "Einleitung: Politische Kulturgeschichte der Zwischenkriegszeit," *Geschichte und Gesellschaft: Sonderheft* 21 (2005): 14. Compare Edward Ross Dickinson, *Dancing in the Blood: Modern Dance and European Culture on the Eve of the First World War* (Cambridge, UK: Cambridge University Press, 2017).
20. Compare Cornelia Hecht, *Deutsche Juden und Antisemitismus in der Weimarer Republik* (Bonn: Dietz, 2003); Anthony Kauders, *German Politics and the Jews. Düsseldorf and Nuremberg 1910–1933* (Oxford: Clarendon Press, 1996), 91–92; Richard S. Levy, "Continuities and Discontinuities of Anti-Jewish Violence in Modern Germany, 1819–1938," in *Exclusionary Violence: Antisemitic Riots in Modern German History*, ed. Christhard Hoffmann et al., 185–202 (Ann Arbor: The University of Michigan Press, 2002); and Dirk Walter, *Antisemitische Kriminalität und Gewalt: Judenfeindschaft in der Weimarer Republik* (Bonn: Dietz, 1999), 151–76. See also Michael Wildt, *Volksgemeinschaft als Selbstermächtigung: Gewalt gegen Juden in der deutschen Provinz 1919 bis 1939* (Hamburg: Hamburger Edition, 2007), 72–100; and Patricia Heberer, *Children during the Holocaust* (Lanham, MD: AltaMira Press, 2011).
21. See, for example, Monique Scheer, "Are Emotions a Kind of Practice (and Is That What Makes Them Have a History)? A Bourdieuan Approach to Understanding Emotion," *History and Theory* 51, no. 2 (2012): 193–220.
22. Barrett, *How Emotions Are Made*, 56–83.
23. Joanna Bourke, *Fear: A Cultural History* (London: Virago Press, 2005), 353–54. Compare the cultural anthropologist William Reddy's notion of "emotives" and its transformative capacities in naming and performing an emotion. See William M. Reddy, *The Navigation of Feeling: A Framework for the History of Emotions* (Cambridge, UK: Cambridge University Press, 2001). See also Deborah B. Gould, *Moving Politics: Emotion and ACT UP's Fight against AIDS* (Chicago: The University of Chicago Press, 2009), 31–39.
24. The emotions of those who were involved as perpetrators of anti-Semitism, especially in this period before the Nazi seizure of power, deserve much greater attention than can be offered here. For rich details of what this might look like, from the perspective of a young person, see, for example, Franz Fühmann's memories of school and classmates in 1929: Franz Fühmann, *The Jew Car*, trans. Isabel Cole (London: Seagull Books, 2013), 1–14. Compare Andrew Donson, *Youth in the Fatherless Land: War Pedagogy, Nationalism, and Authority in Germany, 1914–1918* (Cambridge, MA: Harvard University Press, 2010).
25. See Leo Baeck Institute, DS 135 G4 E74 K76, "Festschrift zur Einweihung der neuen Synagoge in Erfurt am 4. September 1884 auf Wunsch der Gemeinde-Collegien verfasst von Dr. Th. Kroner."
26. *Stadt- und Verwaltungsarchiv Erfurt* (StVAE), 1-2/154-2, Vol. 1, "Geheime Akten des Magistrats zu Erfurt," 37.
27. "Antisemitismus im Eisenbahnbetrieb," *Israelitisches Wochenblatt* (Erfurt), 21 November 1924, 55.
28. Most local gentile newspapers reported on this event. See, for example, "Antisemitische Grabschänder," *Thüringer Allgemeine Zeitung* (Erfurt), 14 March 1926. No report has

yet been discovered from the fragmented collections of the local Jewish newspaper, the *Israelitisches Wochenblatt*. Compare StVAE, 1-2/154-2, Vol. 1, 70–81.

29. Compare StVAE, 1-2/154-2, Vol. 1, 37; and "Völkische Geschmacklosigkeit," *Israelitisches Wochenblatt*, 14 November 1924, 47.
30. "Unfug," *Israelitisches Wochenblatt*, 19 December 1924, 87.
31. Anny Toni Kessler, interview by Randy Lichtman, Sunrise, FL, 21 July 1997, interview 31140, segments 4–8, *Visual History Archive* (VHA), USC Shoah Foundation, Los Angeles, CA. Compare Arnold Friedman, interview by Dave Kells, Hadley, MA, 1 August 1996, interview 18039, segment 7, VHA; see also Friedman, segment 2; Werner Hausmann, interview by Barbara White, Englewood, NJ, 7 October 1996, interview 20734, segment 1, VHA; Arno Kahn, interview by Judith Friedman, interview 3776, Florham Park, NJ, 6 July 1995, segment 18, VHA; Ruth Heiman, interview by Kathy Strochlic, Flushing, NY, 13 December 1995, interview 10051, segment 13, VHA; Jack Minc, interview by Arlene Adler, Wellington, FL, 30 April 1996, interview 14699, segments 26–29, VHA; Kurt Wallach, interview by Andrew Hartmann, Vero Beach, FL, 31 May 1996, interview 15863, segment 9, VHA; and Susan Schachori, interview by Marianne Bergida, Givataim, Israel, 16 June 1997, interview 32555, segment 51, VHA.
32. See Barrett, *How Emotions*, 84–111; compare Ute Frevert et al., eds., *Learning How to Feel: Children's Literature and Emotional Sozialization, 1870–1970* (Oxford: Oxford University Press, 2014), 5–9.
33. For an earlier published discussion from this author on the application of the concept of practices to emotions studies, see Joachim C. Häberlen and Russell A. Spinney, "Introduction," *Contemporary European History* 23, no. 4 (November 2014): 489–503.
34. Compare Jan Plamper, *History of Emotions: An Introduction* (Oxford: Oxford University Press, 2017), 269–70; and Barbara Rosenwein, *Emotional Communities in the Early Middle Ages* (Ithaca: Cornell University Press, 2007), 196–200.
35. See Gregory Stanton, "The Ten Stages of Genocide," *Genocide Watch*, accessed 28 December 2018, http://www.genocidewatch.org/genocide/tenstagesofgenocide.html.
36. Carl Schmitt, for example, in laying out concepts of the friend and enemy in his definition of the political, dismissed "private emotions and tendencies." Focusing on these more personal emotional practices, however, may have helped shape Nazi emotional practices—what Peter Fritzsche termed the "dramaturgy of Nazism," or what Alf Lüdtke called the "sensory qualities" of symbols and the practices of domination, with space for individuals to make their own sense of what Nazism meant for them. See Fritzsche, *Rehearsals for Fascism, Populism and Political Mobilization in Weimar Germany* (Oxford: Oxford University Press, 1990), 71–109; compare Alf Lüdtke, "The 'Honor of Labor': Industrial Workers and the Power of Symbols under National Socialism," in *Nazism and German Society 1933–1945* (London: Routledge, 1994), 71–74; and Carl Schmitt, *The Concept of the Political* (Chicago: The Chicago University Press, 2007), 27–28. See also Dickinson, *Dancing in the Blood*, 214–19.
37. Compare Pamela E. Swett, *Neighbors and Enemies: The Culture of Radicalism in Berlin, 1929–1933* (Cambridge, UK: Cambridge University Press, 2007); and Andrew Stuart Bergerson, *Ordinary Germans in Extraordinary Times: The Nazi Revolution in Hildesheim* (Bloomington: Indiana University Press, 2004).

Bibliography

Archival Sources

Deutsches Wörterbuch von Jacob Grimm und Wilhelm Grimm online.
Google Books Ngram Viewer online.
Israelitisches Wochenblatt, Erfurt, Germany.
The Leo Baeck Institute, New York City, NY, USA.
Stadt- und Verwaltungsarchiv *Erfurt* (StVAE), Erfurt, Germany.
Thüringer Allgemeine Zeitung, Erfurt, Germany.
Visual History Archive (VHA), USC Shoah Foundation, Los Angeles, CA, USA.

Literature

Baader, Benjamin Maria, Sharon Gillerman, and Paul Lerner, ed. *Jewish Masculinities: German Jews, Gender, and History*. Bloomington: Indiana University Press, 2012.
Barclay, Katie. "New Materialism and the New History of Emotions." *Emotions: History, Culture, Society* 1, no. 1 (2017): 161–83.
Barrett, Lisa Feldman. *How Emotions Are Made: The Secret Life of the Brain*. Boston: Houghton Mifflin Harcourt, 2017.
Bergerson, Andrew Stuart. *Ordinary Germans in Extraordinary Times: The Nazi Revolution in Hildesheim*. Bloomington: Indiana University Press, 2004.
Bourke, Joanna. *Fear: A Cultural History*. London: Virago Press, 2005.
Butler, Judith. *Bodies That Matter*. New York City: Routledge, 2011.
Canning, Kathleen. "The Politics of Symbols, Semantics, and Sentiments in the Weimar Republic." *Central European History* 43, no. 4 (December 2010): 567–80.
Darwin, Charles. *The Expression of the Emotions in Man and Animals*. London: John Murray, 1872.
Dickinson, Edward Ross. *Dancing in the Blood: Modern Dance and European Culture on the Eve of the First World War*. Cambridge, UK: Cambridge University Press, 2017.
Donson, Andrew. *Youth in the Fatherless Land: War Pedagogy, Nationalism, and Authority in Germany, 1914–1918*. Cambridge, MA: Harvard University Press, 2010.
Duden, Barbara. *The Woman Beneath the Skin: A Doctor's Patients in Eighteenth-Century Germany*. Translated by Thomas Dunlap. Cambridge, MA: Harvard University Press, 1991.
Eulenburg, Albert, ed. *Real-encyclopadie der gesammten Heilkunde: medicinisch-chirurgisches Handwörterbuch für praktische Ärzte*. Vol. 8. Wien: Urban and Schwarzenberg, 1995.
Föllmer, Moritz. *Individuality and Modernity in Berlin: Self and Society from Weimar to the Wall*. Cambridge, UK: Cambridge University Press, 2013.

Frevert, Ute. *Emotions in History—Lost and Found*. Budapest: Central European University Press, 2011.
Frevert, Ute, et al., eds. *Emotional Lexicons: Continuity and Change in the Vocabulary of Feeling 1700–2000*. Oxford: Oxford University Press, 2014.
——— *Learning How to Feel: Children's Literature and Emotional Sozialization, 1870–1970*. Oxford: Oxford University Press, 2014.
Fritzsche, Peter. *Rehearsals for Fascism, Populism and Political Mobilization in Weimar Germany*. Oxford: Oxford University Press, 1990.
Fühmann, Franz. *The Jew Car*. Translated by Isabel Cole. London: Seagull Books, 2013.
Gillerman, Sharon. "A Kinder Gentler Strongman? Siegmund Breitbart in Eastern Europe." In *Jewish Masculinities: German Jews, Gender, and History*, edited by Benjamin Maria Baader, Sharon Gillerman, and Paul Lerner, 197–209. Bloomington: Indiana University Press, 2012.
Gould, Deborah B. *Moving Politics: Emotion and ACT UP's Fight against AIDS*. Chicago: The University of Chicago Press, 2009.
Häberlen, Joachim C., and Russell A. Spinney. "Introduction." *Contemporary European History*, 23, no. 4 (November 2014): 489–503, doi: 10.1017/S0960777314000289.
Hardtwig, Wolfgang. "Einleitung: Politische Kulturgeschichte der Zwischenkriegszeit." *Geschichte und Gesellschaft: Sonderheft* 21 (2005): 14.
Heberer, Patricia. *Children during the Holocaust*. Lanham, MD: AltaMira Press, 2011.
Hecht, Cornelia. *Deutsche Juden und Antisemitismus in der Weimarer Republik*. Bonn: Dietz, 2003.
Jarausch, Konrad. *Broken Lives: How Ordinary Germans Experienced the 20th Century*. Princeton: Princeton University Press, 2018.
Kauders, Anthony. *German Politics and the Jews: Düsseldorf and Nuremberg 1910–1933*. Oxford: Clarendon Press, 1996.
Levy, Richard S. "Continuities and Discontinuities of Anti-Jewish Violence in Modern Germany, 1819–1938." In *Exclusionary Violence: Antisemitic Riots in Modern German History*, edited by Christhard Hoffmann et al., 185–202. Ann Arbor: The University of Michigan Press, 2002.
Lüdtke, Alf. "The 'Honor of Labor': Industrial Workers and the Power of Symbols under National Socialism." In *Nazism and German Society 1933–1945*. London: Routledge, 1994.
Masuda, Y., et al. "Developmental and Pharmacological Features of Mouse Emotional Piloerection." *Experimental Animals* 48 (July 1999): 209–11.
Plamper, Jan. *History of Emotions: An Introduction*. Oxford: Oxford University Press, 2017.
Radtkau, Joachim. *Das Zeitalter der Nervosität: Deutschland zwischen Bismarck und Hitler*. Munich: Hanser, 1998.
Reddy, William M. *The Navigation of Feeling: A Framework for the History of Emotions*. Cambridge, UK: Cambridge University Press, 2001.

Rosenwein, Barbara. "Worrying about Emotions in History." *American Historical Review* 107, no. 3 (June 2002): 821–45.

——— *Emotional Communities in the Early Middle Ages*. Ithaca: Cornell University Press, 2007.

Rosin, Hannah, and Alix Spiegel, hosts. "Emotions." *Invisibilia*, NPR, 1 June 2017. NPR, www.npr.org/programs/invisibilia/530718193/emotions.

Scheer, Monique. "Are Emotions a Kind of Practice (and Is That What Makes Them Have a History)? A Bourdieuan Approach to Understanding Emotion." *History and Theory* 51, no. 2 (2012): 193–220.

Schmitt, Carl. *The Concept of the Political*. Translated by George Schwab. Chicago: The Chicago University Press, 2007.

Schüler-Springorum, Stefanie. "A Soft Hero: Male Jewish Identity in Imperial Germany through the Autobiography of Aron Liebeck." In *Jewish Masculinities: German Jews, Gender, and History*, edited by Benjamin Maria Baader, Sharon Gillerman, and Paul Lerner, 90–113. Bloomington: Indiana University Press, 2012.

Stanton, Gregory. "The Ten Stages of Genocide." *Genocide Watch*. http://www.genocidewatch.org/genocide/tenstagesofgenocide.html.

Stearns, Peter N., and Carol Z. Stearns. "Clarifying the History of Emotions and Emotional Standards." *American Historical Review* 90, no. 4 (October 1985): 813–36.

Swett, Pamela E. *Neighbors and Enemies: The Culture of Radicalism in Berlin, 1929–1933*. Cambridge, UK: Cambridge University Press, 2007.

Walter, Dirk. *Antisemitische Kriminalität und Gewalt: Judenfeindschaft in der Weimarer Republik*. Bonn: Dietz, 1999.

Wildt, Michael. *Volksgemeinschaft als Selbstermächtigung: Gewalt gegen Juden in der deutschen Provinz 1919 bis 1939*. Hamburg: Hamburger Edition, 2007.

PART II

Emotions, Spaces, and Material Interests

CHAPTER 6

Early Modern Embodiments of Laughter
The Journal of Felix Platter

JOY WILTENBURG

Laughter is an ambiguous element in the history of emotions. Although a corporeal sign of emotional response, it cannot be tied to a single emotion or even to predictable relationships with specific emotional states. As Mary Beard has remarked in her study of laughter in ancient Rome, many have come to grief in the attempt to construct a unified theory of laughter.[1] Even within the body of one who laughs, it can reflect a wide variety of emotional reactions: happiness, surprise, embarrassment, pride, and malice, to name a few. At the same time, laughter is social and communicative, reflecting and affecting relationships. But its social meaning is contested. Is it a tool of hegemony used by the "masters of discourse" as a means of social control? Is it a subtly subversive weapon of the lowly who mock the flaws of the powerful? Is it an innocent easer of social relations? Or is it an aggressive means of exclusion and scapegoating? One can find laughter in all these modes; it is too slippery to pin down to one.[2] Yet because it is social and communicative as well as physical, it is embedded in cultural systems of meaning and subject to historical change. Its historical dimension quickly becomes obvious to those who attempt to grasp the jokes of yesteryear. What can it tell historians about the emotional life of the past?

The elusive quality of laughter is just one of the factors that have hampered historical study. Another obvious one is source material. Laughter is a common element in everyday interactions, but most of it goes unrecorded. We hear only the faintest echoes of everyday laughter, even as the production of comic texts exploded in the early modern era. With the spread of printing, there was money to be made in the growing market for jestbooks and other textual prompts to laughter. At the same time, as Quentin Skinner has argued, laughter "mattered" in the Renaissance, with new attention among humanists to its rhetorical power.[3] To approach the emotional meaning of laughter, however, we need to step back from the parsing of jokes to look at the social sites of laughter. Where did people laugh, with whom? What functions did laughter serve within the social spaces where we find it in the historical record? One might frame these questions in the context of Monique Scheer's concept of emotions as a form of practice—an embodied combination of action and experience, responding to and shaped by social and historical context.[4] All emotion, in this view, is corporeal, enacted—and laughter, which combines feeling with visible bodily movement, still more obviously so. Everyday laughter, grounded in materiality, contrasts sharply with the joke—a reproducible, discrete, and exchangeable provoker of laughter. Increasingly commodified in the popular jestbook genre, from erudite humanist facetiae to vernacular chapbooks, the joke was a disembodied extract from social laughter, detached from its context. Its marketability gave it an artificial prominence in public discourse, just as the permanence of textual comedy has distracted attention from laughter as it was socially performed.

A valuable window into everyday laughter appears in the autobiography of the early modern Swiss physician Felix Platter (1536–1614). A gifted memoirist, he was also linked to a remarkable nexus of laughter lore through his medical studies at Montpellier. Thus, although his memories are personal to him, they are embedded in broader cultural patterns. Platter's accounts of laughter fully embrace its materiality. The practices of laughter here are a far cry from the verbal, exchangeable joke: you literally had to be there. At the same time, Platter highlights the emotional resonance of laughter, showing its importance in forging and modifying relationships. In spaces of domestic intimacy as well as semipublic encounters, laughter was a powerful shifter of meanings, operating especially at sites of social anxiety. His account shows its uses across boundaries of gender, age, and status. The laughter of Platter's historical moment and social space could hardly be more different from the laughter of the collectible jestbook anecdote or the combative humor of Renaissance polemics.

Son of the self-made Swiss humanist Thomas Platter, Felix studied medicine at Montpellier in the 1550s and became a prominent professor of medicine at the University of Basel. Montpellier, one of the oldest medical schools in Europe, holds a noteworthy place in the history of laughter. François Rabelais, studying there in the 1530s, performed with a troupe of medical students in a comedy that later made its way into his masterwork, *Gargantua and Pantagruel*. Rabelais's work famously provided the inspiration for Mikhail Bakhtin's seminal exploration of the popular culture of laughter.[5] Platter's closer contemporary, Laurent Joubert, authored the most influential treatise on laughter of the early modern period.[6] A year or two ahead of Platter as a student, Joubert went on to become a professor and administrator of the school, as well as a prolific medical author. Another Montpellier graduate, the Englishman Andrew Boorde, was later credited with authorship of two hugely popular jestbooks: *Scoggin's Jests* and *The Merry Tales of the Mad Men of Gotham*—another hint of the school's comic reach.⁷ These Montpellier men linked the humanist interest in the power of laughter with the physician's awareness of the body. Rabelais's laughter was full of unruly bodies and belly laughs; Joubert was fascinated by its physiology. Platter shared with these fellow medical graduates a view of laughter as physical, memorable, and important—but his account goes beyond them to show how laughter was embedded in specific social and emotional relationships.

Writing his account late in life, Platter recalled many instances of laughter and jest, particularly from his youth. The detail of Platter's reconstruction owes much to the daily journal he began keeping in his teens. His original diaries have not survived, but were reworked into his autobiography. Recording one's life was a high priority for Felix; not only did he energetically document his own life, but he also pressed his father and brother to produce their own autobiographies. He clearly envisioned an audience, composed at the very least of family members and friends, and likely more. He felt he had important things to say. While writing his own account, he shared his father Thomas's shorter memoir with a family friend, to whom he wrote about how pleased he was "that it has so moved you to read my late father's *Life*," adding, "I am writing my own *Life* also, in which are many rare and wonderful things that I have seen."⁸ The memoir as a genre can be doubtful as reportage because events are filtered through memory and adapted for self-presentation. However, these very features add to its value as a reflection of the social meaning of laughter, particularly in regard to its impact on an individual's negotiation of social relationships, including his self-presentation in the autobiography itself. Platter's account, given its grounding in diary entries, is likely more accurate than most memoirs in terms of actual events as well. Writing before the eighteenth-century embrace of interiority (*Innerlichkeit*), Platter does not dwell on "inner" emotional states. Instead, he depicts emotions and relationships through their material performance.

Platter's memorable laughter—the laughter important enough to record—was firmly grounded in material life. It could not be separated from its physical spaces and specific social relations; that is, in Scheer's terms, it was laughter as emotional practice. Jest was very much embodied—whether in scenes of courtship, practical jokes, physical occurrences, social encounters, or clownish performances that depended on absurdities of dress and gesture.⁹ The laughter that mattered was social and relational: it could occur because of specific social relationships, but it also helped form them, in courtship as in the bonding among student friends.¹⁰ Laughter here was not about jokes of the kind that could become exchangeable funny stories, divorced from social context; it was embodied and enacted.

Courtship was a privileged site for laughter, and multiple occasions for hilarity appear in Platter's account of events surrounding his wedding in 1557. During the period of betrothal, he was allowed frequent access to the home of his fiancée, Magdalena Jeckelmann, daughter of a neighboring surgeon. He even expressed some surprise, looking back, at his freedom of entry, since it "was not yet a completed marriage and could easily have fallen through." But their meetings "took place in all honor and decency," filled with conversation and joking. Felix even felt free to joke about debts he had contracted in France, claiming to have wasted a lot of money. He enjoyed teasing his fiancée's brother about his own future wife. He especially relished the story of a gift-giving game in which he sneaked into the house to hide and surprise his lover. He crept in through the back and hid shivering for three hours; but she hid even better, under the stairs, and surprised him to win the prize. Such games were the prerogative of youth, fondly remembered in age: "so we had our play for a while, as young folks do."[11] The element of jest helped defuse the anxieties of the serious business of courtship, which as he says might still have gone wrong, while also easing the progression of the young couple's acquaintance. Although Felix tells more about his own joking—it is his story, after all—Magdalena was an active player in this early negotiation of relationship.[12] Both the physical spaces and the participants mattered.

On the wedding day itself, it was customary for young friends to play merry tricks on the newlyweds, and Felix hid to avoid "much noise and foolery." His mother helpfully led the bride and groom up the back stairs to his bedroom where the young revelers could not find them, and they went to bed. After a while, though, they heard his mother come up to the nearby privy, where she "loudly sang out, like a young girl, though she was already very old, at which my bride laughed heartily."[13] Felix associated mirth with the young, but his "very old" mother (sixty at the time) played the trick that roused the greatest, most heartfelt laughter. In this account, women were at least as active in nuptial jesting as men—and while one might hide from the pack of young rowdies, one could not hide from the women. In the morning, the bride's maid came to bring her a change of clothes, "and since she was a pleasant person, made many rare jokes."[14]

The jesting here is tied to specific social spaces of the courtship and wedding, and also to enclosed spaces with connotations of intimacy—the inner space of the betrothed's house where only the privileged suitor could enter, the hiding places (closets under the stairs in the gift-giving episode), and the even more secret privy to which his mother could creep quietly before surprising them with song.[15] The wedding laughter is a celebration of fertility and means of cementing the new relationships; mother, maidservant, and even frustrated rowdies participated in semiritual comedy that asserted communal ownership of the shift in social and sexual relations. Magdalena's heartfelt laughter in the bedroom—recounted only a few sentences after her tears at parting from her father—underscores the embrace of her new marital ties.

Of course, laughter and celebration at a wedding are no surprise; such customs span many centuries and cultures. Noteworthy elements here include the gender mutuality in the use of laughter to forge emotional bonds and reframe anxieties, as well as the grounding of laughter in scenes of material specificity. For Platter, it was not so much the vexatious roisterers who mattered, but the jesting that took place in intimate spaces behind the scenes, with particular relational meanings for the participants. In the account of his life, specific occasions of laughter had special meaning, although there was plenty of other laughter—from his mother, for instance, who "was always merry."[16] The important laughter emerged in telling scenes that both revealed and informed relationships.

There were bad jokes that failed to foster relationship; these too were material and enacted, but in ways that caused disharmony. Again in the realm of courtship, but unsuccessful, was a woman's practical joke of placing a hackle (a comb with long metal teeth used in textile preparation) in a man's bed. Felix strongly disapproved—the trick could easily have caused injury and was a sign of the woman's ill nature.[17] It was also an intimate jest, secreting a foreign object in the bed, a space of bodily vulnerability and sexual suggestiveness. According to Platter, this woman, a widow, had been hoping to marry the man in question, but he was put off by her shrewishness. Because she had money, she still was able to attract the physician Philipp Bechius, who married her but complained about her often.

His view of another courtship jest was more ambiguous. Here too the humor was enacted in private, domestic space: the table, a site of mixed-gender sociability that was ripe for jest.[18] Shortly after his marriage, Felix visited another doctor in Strasbourg and was entertained with a feast. The doctor's wife had a pretty sister whom they had teasingly told that Felix was coming to Strasbourg as a suitor for her. She was very friendly to him. "But when at midnight I said to the company, 'if my wife at Basel knew that I was banqueting so late, she would worry,' I completely spoiled the game and was no longer so valued."[19] Her family had conspired to fool her and apparently thought it a good joke, but the girl was clearly not amused.

Disapproval of the bad joke may also play a role in Platter's treatment of a "nasty [*wiest*]" Basel custom that prevailed in his youth, particularly in domestic space: the groping of women's breasts: "it was so general, even in distinguished houses, that seldom a maid left the house without the master having done her this honor."[20] His phrasing implies that one would expect such behavior from lower social groups; but no, it was a prerogative of social superiority, master to maid, which he sarcastically calls an honor. Felix evidently considered it an assault; did the older Basel householders think it was just good fun? The first mention of this custom is merely general, describing the time of his childhood. But it recurs later in his account of a trip he took with his father some years after his marriage, to visit Thomas's birthplace in the Valais. At one point, a female relative who kept an inn hosted them: "There was also a pretty woman there in the inn, whom a Platter grabbed very rudely, which made her angry."[21] One of them groped her—probably the father, an adherent of the old custom, embarrassing his disapproving son. Or might it have been the son, raised to see such groping as normal and surprised by the woman's anger? The text's indirection leaves some doubt about the event, but not about Felix's ultimate judgment that this was not funny.

Although there is no mention of laughter or jest in this account, it suggests a cultural shift that meshes with hints that appear elsewhere in the text. Clearly, the grabbing of breasts was no longer considered acceptable at the time he wrote, at least among those who aspired to social distinction. This shift was part of a general trend toward more restrictive sexual mores, which had already begun in the late fifteenth century but intensified in the Reformation era. In relation to laughter, gender relations were in one sense a privileged area, as shown in the license for play in courtship and wedding. On the other hand, questionable jests cluster around courtship and sexual relations also: the shrewish joker with the hackle, the Strasbourg doctor's deluded sister-in-law, and perhaps those young maids with their tempting breasts. The text suggests that sexual relations were an area of higher risk in jest, where things could easily go wrong.

Platter's depiction of homosocial relations among male youth was also marked by jest, both among the boarders in his father's household and among the medical students in Montpellier in more public spaces. Again, the comedy was inseparable from its social setting, and Felix did not shrink from recounting occasions of being laughed at himself. He remembered the laughter here as benign camaraderie—just as much when he himself was its target as when the laughter mocked the folly of another. On first arriving as a student in Montpellier, for instance, Felix made rather a fool of himself. Proud of his poetry, he read his Latin verses to fellow student Peter Lotichius, then offered to teach his skills to the other. Little did he know that Lotichius already was an accomplished, published poet: "When other Germans [fellow students] learned of this, they laughed at me."[22] Felix's response was to go to Lotichius and tell him how royally he had been had.[23] The incident became a lasting source of jesting nicknames between the two, a founding moment of their relationship.

As in the courtship game of hide-and-seek, Felix could relish being fooled. He recounts his favorite practical joke among the German students at Montpellier, valued for how hard it made him laugh. One Three Kings' Day, two of his friends, Ludovicus Hechstetter and Melchior Rotmundt, got drunk and quarreled, Hechstetter calling Rotmundt a *"milchmaul"* (milkmouth)." "I'll make you a *milchmaul*," Rotmundt replied, and hauled him to a barber to have his bushy beard shaved off. The next day, seeing Hechstetter was unrecognizable, they dressed him up in disguise, and Rotmundt introduced him to the others as a new German who had just arrived bringing them letters. Following custom, they treated him with great respect and invited him to the tavern.

"As we were about to sit at the table, Hechstetter threw off his cloak and said, 'you fools, don't you know me, it's Hechstetter!' at which we all fell into such laughter, that for my part I thought I would burst."[24]

The boarders in his father's house were young men with a penchant for jocularity. They loved mummery and play-acting, often dressing up as devils or fools. On one occasion at a wedding, they staged an outdoor play that Felix remembered as the funniest ever: "my father's boarders, and among them Jacob Truckses in fool's clothing played so many funny tricks that Myconius later confessed he had nearly pissed his pants with laughter."[25] Felix cites the involuntary physical response as testimony to the comedy's success. As with the laughter at Hechstetter's disguise that made Felix nearly burst, the physical effect was a sign of especially strong enjoyment that placed an event among the best and most memorable laughter occasions.[26]

These incidents highlight several notable elements of Platter's treatment of laughter: the embrace of physicality, the association with youth, and a self-presentation that appears to shrug off any fear of ridicule. The laughter incidents cluster most thickly in Platter's youth, and he explicitly emphasizes the appropriateness of jest for the young in his comments on his courtship and wedding. He also recounted occasions from his childhood when his naivety amused adults. The focus on youth reflected cultural norms, while also highlighting the role of laughter in forging social bonds. On the other hand, the emphasis on youth also hints at self-distancing by the now-elderly author. It was good to laugh, even to bursting, and good to be laughable; we hear no strictures on the loss of bodily control or dignity. But the focus on youth suggests a following period of greater sobriety, possibly less comfort with laughter over time.

In addition to laughter associated with courtship, laughter in the family, and laughter among his youthful male peers, Platter recalled his use of laughter in negotiating relationship across boundaries of status. He proudly recounted his jesting exchanges with the fun-loving abbess of Olsberg, Katharina von Hersberg. The abbey where she presided was a distinctive space, a home but also a semipublic religious property, into which Felix entered as professional consultant and as guest. Probably he found laughter there especially memorable because it showed his ease of sociability with his noble client, testifying to his professional and social success. He felt free to joke even about a matter that touched on their religious difference. A kinsman of the abbess had commissioned a painting for the abbey church and, as pious patrons often did, had his own portrait added among the kneeling figures. Platter laughingly said to the abbess that she must look at that saint more than the others when praying. A *"frölich"* (merry), cheerful woman (like Felix's mother), she took the jest in good part. Felix and his wife were often invited to the abbey for merrymaking, as at carnival time, for music, mummery, and other fun. On one occasion, the abbess sent Felix's wife into her chamber to fetch a baby from its cradle, a foundling she said had been left with her. But it was really a realistically carved doll: "my wife thought it was alive, then finally noticed the trick, at which we all laughed." The abbess must have gone to some trouble and expense to create such an artistic replica of a living child, all for the sake of laughter. The three of them shared in delighted amusement at the trick. But for the Protestant Platter, the incident also evoked reformers' critiques of monastic morality: "I thought, in some cloisters it was a custom to hide real children this way."[27] Surely the abbess was aware of these overtones, and they may even have heightened her amusement in playing this trick on a Protestant couple. She was far from the model of somber claustration that was to gain prominence with the Council of Trent.

* * *

What was the significance of Platter's laughter, remembered as so strikingly embodied and relational? Some of the vividness of these scenes of laughter must be ascribed to Felix Platter's literary gifts: no one had to advise him that he should "show, not tell" in recounting the significant experiences of his life. The challenge for the historian is to avoid becoming laborious in analyzing his economical yet evocative anecdotes. Partly also, of course, as in any personal narrative, the lens of the author's individual personality shapes our view. At the same time, however, the picture is very much of Platter's own time and place. In contrast to the exchangeable currency of the joke, this laughter depended completely on enactment. We do not get direct evidence about the gestural qualities of laughter, its loudness or facial expressions; but the materiality of laughter goes beyond its effects on the body. The possibilities of laughter were shaped by interaction within social spaces. These included domestic spaces of implied intimacy, especially in courtship jest, as well as more public sites of male homosocial interaction in the tavern, and even the semipublic, semireligious space where an abbess entertained diverse guests. The license of laughter offered both men and women means of negotiating relationships while reframing potential sources of social anxiety. Though specially associated with youth, it could operate widely and even across seemingly sharp divides of status and religion.

Though a single case, Platter's evidence casts intriguing reflections on theories of broader change. In relation to laughter, the most influential approaches have derived from the work of Mikhail Bakhtin and Norbert Elias. Bakhtin, taking Rabelais as his core source of evidence, argued that the Renaissance offered a unique moment of convergence between popular and elite cultures. In Rabelais, he read signs of a joyous popular hilarity that celebrated the body, in a moment of freedom sandwiched between the repressive religiosity of the Middle Ages and the alienating individualism of bourgeois society. Bakhtin's imaginative analysis has stimulated much research, although parts of his thesis—particularly the class basis of the culture he analyzed and the political implications of carnival laughter—are open to question. In Platter's journal, the corporeality of laughter appears to point neither to the timeless fertility of bodily functions, nor to a subtly subversive culture of the masses, but to sociability and the forging of relationships. Possibly Bakhtin would have read him as already bourgeois.

Perhaps even more far-reaching, the civilizing process theorized by Elias traced increasing bodily control as elites adopted new modes of behavior in the early modern period.[28] The theory has been applied to analyze a retreat from rowdy practical joking in Elizabethan England, as well as a shift away from the placement of laughter among the passions.[29] Although medievalists have debunked the notion that earlier behaviors signified a primitive lack of self-control,[30] there is empirical evidence of behavioral change, in what Eckhart Schörle has called "the civilizing of laughter."[31] This same trend can be connected with the modern privileging of "inner" experience. However, as Barbara Rosenwein has argued, the picture of unidirectional development can be overdrawn.[32] Platter could in some ways fit Elias's scheme as a transitional figure. In his own life, he was a straddler of social boundaries—a man of elite humanist education, only one generation removed from his father's humble roots as an orphaned shepherd boy. He was also living in a time of change in manners, with the groping of women perhaps less funny than before. At the same historical moment when commodified laughter was creating new means of laughing alone, Platter's social laughter kept to a different path. Yet we need not posit a real decline in the enacted and relational mode. At least, the question of practice has yet to be investigated for social locales much beyond the court and salon. Elite views of laughter certainly came to privilege verbal wit. But the tendency of texts to preserve more abstract humor has likely obscured the everyday. How far did the raised eyebrow really supplant the belly laugh?

Joy Wiltenburg is Professor of History at Rowan University in New Jersey, with a research specialty in the social and cultural history of early modern Europe. Her publications include *Crime and Culture in Early Modern Germany* (2012), *Women in Early Modern Germany: An Anthology of Popular Texts* (2002), and *Disorderly Women and Female Power in the Street Literature of Early Modern England and Germany* (1992). Her current project explores cultural practices of laughter in the early modern period.

Notes

1. Mary Beard, *Laughter in Ancient Rome: On Joking, Tickling, and Cracking Up* (Berkeley: University of California Press, 2014). A historical survey of laughter theories appears

in Michael Billig, *Laughter and Ridicule: Towards a Social Critique of Humour* (London: Sage Publications, 2005).
2. For differing interpretations of the social and historical meanings of laughter, see Mikhail Bakhtin, *Rabelais and His World*, trans. Hélène Iswolsky (Cambridge, MA: MIT Press, 1968); Madahev L. Apte, *Humor and Laughter: An Anthropological Perspective* (Ithaca: Cornell University Press, 1985); Susan Purdie, *Comedy: The Mastery of Discourse* (Toronto: University of Toronto Press, 1993); Jan Bremmer and Herman Roodenburg, eds., *A Cultural History of Humour* (Cambridge, UK: Polity Press, 1997); Eckart Schörle, *Die Verhöflichung des Lachens: Lachgeschichte im 18. Jahrhundert* (Bielefeld: Aisthesis Verlag, 2007); Indira Ghose, *Shakespeare and Laughter: A Cultural History* (Manchester, UK: Manchester University Press, 2011).
3. Quentin Skinner, "Why Laughing Mattered in the Renaissance: The Second Henry Tudor Memorial Lecture," *History of Political Thought* 22 (2001): 418–47.
4. See Monique Scheer, "Are Emotions a Kind of Practice (and Is That What Makes Them Have a History)? A Bourdieuan Approach to Understanding Emotion," *History and Theory* 51, no. 2 (2012): 193–220.
5. Bakhtin, *Rabelais and His World*.
6. See Laurent Joubert, *Treatise on Laughter*, trans. Gregory David de Rocher (Tuscaloosa: University of Alabama Press, 1980).
7. See *Oxford Dictionary of National Biography*, s.v. "Andrew Boorde," www.oxforddnb.com/search?q=Andrew+Boorde&searchBtn=Search&isQuickSearch=true.
8. "das ich (=Euch) meins lieben vatters seligen vita zelesen also zu hertzen gangen"; "Ich schrib auch mein vitam, dorin vil seltzam sachen und herlicheit, so ich gesechen"; Valentin Lötscher, "Introduction," in *Tagebuch (Lebensbeschreibung) 1536–1567*, by Felix Platter, vol. 10 of *Basler Chroniken*, ed. Valentin Lötscher (Basel: Schwabe & Co., 1976), 33.
9. For example, Platter, *Tagebuch*, 82, 93, 465.
10. For example, Platter, *Tagebuch*, 182–84, 203, 239–40.
11. "noch kein beschloßene ee war und alß baldt hindersich hette gon kennen"; "Geschach doch in allen züchten und eeren"; "Hatten also unser spil ein zeit lang, wie die jungen leuth thun"; Platter, *Tagebuch*, 312–13.
12. Cf. Emmanuel Le Roy Ladurie, *The Beggar and the Professor: A Sixteenth-Century Family Saga*, trans. Arthur Goldhammer (Chicago: University of Chicago Press, 1997), 314; Ladurie says that she "listened in indulgent silence" at an earlier stage in the courtship, but Platter indicates her active participation as they "conversed and jested honorably about all sorts of things" ["von allerley sachen eerliche gesprech hielten, vexatz driben"] (Platter, *Tagebuch*, 312). Even earlier in their acquaintance, his description emphasizes mutuality: "I could speak with my future bride and she with me" ["ich mit meiner zukünftigen reden kente und sy mit mir"] (Platter, *Tagebuch*, 297).
13. "vil gschär und vexatz"; "haupthelig sang, wie ein junge dochter, do sy doch schon in höchstem alter war, dorab mein hochzyteren hertzlich lachen thet," (Platter, *Tagebuch*, 327).
14. "und wie es ein holdtselig mensch, drib es vil seltzame schnocken," (Platter, *Tagebuch*, 328).
15. On the emotional resonance of differing social and physical spaces, see Benno Gammerl, "Emotional Styles—Concepts and Challenges," *Rethinking History* 16, no. 2 (June 2012): 161–75.
16. "allzyt frölich was," (Platter, *Tagebuch*, 327).

17. Platter, *Tagebuch*, 363.
18. For an analysis of jest at the table and elsewhere, see Susan C. Karant-Nunn, "The Masculinity of Martin Luther: Theory, Practicality, and Humor," in *Masculinity in the Reformation Era*, ed. Scott H. Hendrix and Susan C. Karant-Nunn, 167–89 (Kirksville, MO: Truman State University Press, 2008).
19. "Alß ich aber um mitnacht sagt zu der gselschaft, wan mein frauw zu Basel wißte, das ich so lang panquetiert, wurde sy in ängsten sein, hatt ich das spyl gar verderbet und war nit mer so wert," (Platter, *Tagebuch*, 353–54).
20. "Das was also gemein, auch in firnemmen hüseren, das selten ein magt aus dem haus kam, deren nit der husherr dise eer angethon hette," (Platter, *Tagebuch*, 106).
21. "Es wahre sonsten auch ein hüpsche frauw da im wirdtshauß, die griffe ein Platter gar grob an, daß verdroße sie," (Platter, *Tagebuch*, 416–17).
22. "Wie solches andre Teutschen innen warden, lachten sy meinen," (Platter, *Tagebuch*, 203).
23. Platter, *Tagebuch*, 204.
24. "Alß wir zum disch sitzen wellen, wirft Hechstetter sein mantel von sich und sagt: 'ir narren, kennen ir mich nit, daß ich der Hechstetter bin?' Doruf wir alle also in ein glechter kamen, das ich fir mein theil meint, ich mießte zerspringen," (Platter, *Tagebuch*, 239–40).
25. "meins vatters dischgenger und under denen Jacob Truckses in narrenkleidern so vil boßen reis, das Myconius hernoch bekant, er hette vor lachen schier in die hosen gebruntzt," (Platter, *Tagebuch*, 93).
26. As, for example, when in ignorance of local custom he refused to be kissed by a girl in greeting, and was laughed at; Platter, *Tagebuch*, 143.
27. "do hatt sy ein gmacht geschnitzlet nacket kindlin, gar zierlich, alß lebte eß und schlief; hatt es in ein wiegen, zeigt es meiner frauw mit vermelden, eß were geschickt. Main frauw vermeint, eß were lebendig, marckt doch zlest den drug, deßen wir alle lachten," (Platter, *Tagebuch*, 373). "Ich gedocht, in klösteren ettlichen wer das ein bruch, die rechte kinder also mit zeverbergen."
28. Norbert Elias, *The Civilizing Process*, trans. Edmund Jephcott (Oxford: Blackwell, 1994).
29. See Chris Holcomb, *Mirth Making: The Rhetorical Discourse on Jesting in Early Modern England* (Columbia: University of South Carolina Press, 2001); Anca Parvulescu, *Laughter: Notes on a Passion* (Cambridge, MA: MIT Press, 2010); for a later period, see Schörle, *Die Verhöflichung des Lachens*.
30. See, for example, Gerd Althoff, "Vom Lächeln zum Verlachen," in *Lachgemeinschaften: Kulturelle Inszenierungen und soziale Wirkungen von Gelächter im Mittelalter und in der Frühen Neuzeit*, ed. Werner Röcke and Hans Rudolf Velten, 3–16 (Berlin: De Gruyter, 2005).
31. Schörle, *Die Verhöflichung des Lachens*.
32. See Barbara H. Rosenwein, *Generations of Feeling: A History of Emotions, 600–1700* (Cambridge, UK: Cambridge University Press, 2016).

Bibliography

Apte, Mahadev L. *Humor and Laughter: An Anthropological Perspective*. Ithaca: Cornell University Press, 1985.

Bakhtin, Mikhail. *Rabelais and His World*, trans. Hélène Iswolsky. Cambridge, MA: MIT Press, 1968.
Beard, Mary. *Laughter in Ancient Rome: On Joking, Tickling, and Cracking Up.* Berkeley: University of California Press, 2014.
Billig, Michael. *Laughter and Ridicule: Towards a Social Critique of Humour.* London: Sage Publications, 2005.
Bremmer, Jan, and Herman Roodenburg, eds. *A Cultural History of Humour.* Cambridge, UK: Polity Press, 1997.
Elias, Norbert. *The Civilizing Process*, trans. Edmund Jephcott. Oxford: Blackwell, 1994.
Gammerl, Benno. "Emotional Styles—Concepts and Challenges." *Rethinking History* 16, no. 2 (June 2012): 161–75.
Ghose, Indira. *Shakespeare and Laughter: A Cultural History.* Manchester, UK: Manchester University Press, 2011.
Holcomb, Chris. *Mirth Making: The Rhetorical Discourse on Jesting in Early Modern England.* Columbia: University of South Carolina Press, 2001.
Joubert, Laurent. *Treatise on Laughter*, trans. Gregory David de Rocher. Tuscaloosa: University of Alabama Press, 1980.
Karant-Nunn, Susan C. "The Masculinity of Martin Luther: Theory, Practicality, and Humor." In *Masculinity in the Reformation Era*, edited by Scott H. Hendrix and Susan C. Karant-Nunn, 167–89. Kirksville, MO: Truman State University, 2008.
Ladurie, Emmanuel Le Roy. *The Beggar and the Professor: A Sixteenth-Century Family Saga*, trans. Arthur Goldhammer. Chicago: University of Chicago Press, 1997.
Parvulescu, Anca. *Laughter: Notes on a Passion.* Cambridge, MA: MIT Press, 2010.
Plamper, Jan. *The History of Emotions: An Introduction.* Oxford: Oxford University Press, 2015.
Platter, Felix. *Tagebuch (Lebensbeschreibung) 1536–1567.* Vol. 10 of *Basler Chroniken*, edited by Valentin Lötscher. Basel: Schwabe & Co., 1976.
Purdie, Susan. *Comedy: The Mastery of Discourse.* Toronto: University of Toronto Press, 1993.
Röcke, Werner, and Hans Rudolf Velten, eds. *Lachgemeinschaften: Kulturelle Inszenierungen und soziale Wirkungen von Gelächter im Mittelalter und in der Frühen Neuzeit.* Berlin: De Gruyter, 2005.
Rosenwein, Barbara. *Generations of Feeling: A History of Emotions, 600–1700.* Cambridge, UK: Cambridge University Press, 2016.
Scheer, Monique. "Are Emotions a Kind of Practice (and Is That What Makes Them Have a History)? A Bourdieuan Approach to Understanding Emotion." *History and Theory* 51, no. 2 (2012): 193–220.
Schörle, Eckart. *Die Verhöflichung des Lachens: Lachgeschichte im 18. Jahrhundert.* Bielefeld: Aisthesis Verlag, 2007.
Skinner, Quentin. "Why Laughing Mattered in the Renaissance: The Second Henry Tudor Memorial Lecture." *History of Political Thought* 22 (2001): 418–47.

CHAPTER 7

Beyond Interiority
Shame and Empathy in Karl Philipp Moritz's Anton Reiser

CHRISTIAN SIEG

Karl Philipp Moritz's novel *Anton Reiser*, published between 1785 and 1790, takes stock of the eighteenth century's literary culture, which had been characterized by its turn toward emotions. Novels by Johann Wolfgang Goethe, Jean-Jacques Rousseau, Samuel Richardson, or Laurence Sterne; plays by Gotthold Ephraim Lessing or Richard Cumberland; and poetry by Edward Young or Friedrich Gottlieb Klopstock exemplify the literary preoccupation with emotions that has been described as a "cult of sensibility." The German term *Innerlichkeit* (interiority) emerges in this cultural context, drawing on discourses that prioritized an inner realm like the soul, the spirit, or the *res cogitas* over the corporeal or physical world.[1] The importance of emotions for the very idea of interiority in the late eighteenth century becomes apparent in Johann Gottfried Herder's reformulation of Descartes' dictum: *cogito ergo sum*. In 1769, Herder exclaims: "I feel my own self! I am!"[2] The celebrated poet of German Sentimentalism (*Empfindsamkeit*) Friedrich Gottlieb Klopstock (1724–1803) uses interiority to designate the "authentic inner core of a thing," partaking in the aforementioned tradition for which interiority is the locus of truth.[3] In their recent publication, Julia Weber and Rüdiger Campe have stressed that the notion of interiority altered the way we think about emotions: "Emotions, for their part, have been understood, ever since the eighteenth century, essentially by means of the distinction between inner experience and outward forms of expression."[4] This chapter shows how Karl Phillip Moritz, who was important in early empirical psychology, moves beyond interiority.

Like other novels of the time, Moritz's *Anton Reiser* depicts a protagonist who writes sentimental letters to his friends, and poems that express his emotions. Yet, rather than elaborating on the depths of the protagonist's interiority, the novel foregrounds the social encounters, educational regimes, and rituals that produce emotions. Rather than an authentic expression of an inner core sealed from the "outside" world, emotions appear to be a product of these practices, always in need of being reproduced in performative ways. Turning to shame and empathy,[5] Moritz's novel shows that we emotionally and cognitively relate to ourselves through practices that involve intersubjective experiences. The recognition by others serves as a medium of our self-recognition—transgressing the inner/outer differentiation. Moving beyond interiority, Moritz's empirical psychology anticipates anthropological discourses on shame from the early twentieth century. Similar to anthropologists like Max Scheler and Helmuth Plessner or sociologists like Georg Simmel, Moritz scrutinizes the emotional dimension of social integration and takes the corporeal dimension of the life world into account. According to Moritz, social interactions always take place under specific material conditions and produce emotions.

Interiority

The notion of "interiority" draws on many discourses that long predate the eighteenth century. The theological prehistory of the term goes back to Paul and Augustin and finds an important proponent in Martin Luther. In *On Christian Liberty*, Luther distinguishes between the "spiritual, inner, or new man" and the "carnal, outward, or old man."[6] Pietism builds on this differentiation by pointing to the inner realm as the very locus of Christian faith. In the eighteenth century, many authors explored their inner selves in autobiographical texts as a means of religious identification—a process on which the psychological novel could subsequently build. Not surprisingly, the juxtaposition of inside and outside informs the theory of the novel as well. Hegel, in his *Aesthetics* (1823), contrasts the prosaic conditions of modern life with the inner truth of the individual: the rebellious spirit of the novel's protagonist only complies with the "infinite rights of the heart."[7] In the twentieth century, Georg Lukács echoes this idea in his *Theory of the Novel* (1916) when he defines the novel as the aesthetic form that expresses the adventure of interiority in a foreign world.[8] More recently, Martin Swales has argued that the major novels of the *Bildungsroman* genre exemplify how "practical reality continues to impinge on the cherished inwardness of the hero."[9] Karl Philipp Moritz's *Anton Reiser* (1785–90) has been understood along these lines. In *The German Bildungsroman* (1997), Michael Minden emphasizes with terms reminiscent of Lukács that a "constitutional homelessness of the subject" emerges from the secularist critique of religion in *Anton Reiser*.[10]

While there can be no doubt that the dichotomy between interiority and exteriority has been highly influential in constructing and presenting individual emotional life, alternative accounts were known around 1800 as well.

Rather than dichotomizing individual interiority and the outside world, Moritz's *Anton Reiser* shows how emotions—believed to be the very core of interiority—are produced in social interactions as well. The novel does not demonstrate the transcendental homelessness of the modern world, but presents a protagonist who lacks the social recognition on which processes of identity formation rely. Moritz's account of his protagonist's upbringing, religious education, as well as passion for literature and theatre testifies to an understanding of emotions that anticipates current sociological approaches. Anton is not the autonomous individual for whom the Enlightenment wished. More adequately he is characterized by practice theory's take on subjectivity as a subject that is "not viewed as prior to practices"[11] and that is "—even in his or her inner processes of reflection, feeling, remembering, planning, etc.—the sequence of acts in which he or she participates."[12] Practice theory as understood by Scheer and Reckwitz does not only point to the social conditioning of individuality but views emotional life itself as a form of practice: "The materiality of the body provides not only the locus of the competence, dispositions, and behavioral routines of practice, it is also the 'stuff' with and on which practices work."[13] Moritz's *Anton Reiser* focuses on such emotional practices. Parts of the book appeared in the *Magazin zur Erfahrungsseelenkunde* (1783–93), which Moritz at times edited. It stands at the intersection of novelistic discourse and the advance of empirical psychology in Germany.

Moritz's magazine sheds new light on the eighteenth-century's take on emotions since it follows an empirical agenda. Rather than suggesting definitions of terms, it presents various case histories. The same holds true for Moritz's novel, which draws on the experiences of the author himself and therefore has been regarded as an autobiographical case study.[14] If we focus on conceptually driven writing of the eighteenth century, such as lexicons and philosophical treatments, the inner/outer dichotomy figures grow larger. The new term *Gefühl* refers to processes that take place entirely within interiority. In line with this, emotions are defined as mental conditions that express "the subjectivity of the human being."[15] According to Johann Nikolaus Tetens, who was among the first to emphasize the self-referentiality of emotions, *Gefühle* does not refer to an outside (like perceptions), but rather to the inner reality of the subject itself.[16] While contemporary philosophical discourses informed Moritz's writing, the many references to shame do not indicate such theoretical presuppositions. A widespread form of cultural criticism appears more influential: the critique of religious and secular enthusiasm (*Schwärmertum*) as well as of religious melancholy. While this criticism is clearly informed by the inner/outer dichotomy, it at the same time draws attention to the religious or secular rituals—relating to how emotions are produced. Likewise, Moritz's focus on shame in *Anton Reiser* relies primarily on narratives rather than on concepts.

Shame

Moritz's *Anton Reiser* has been credited with conveying the social conditioning of culturally cherished individuality. In shame, much more is at stake.[17] The many shame scenes of the novel do not operate with the inner/outer dichotomy. Rather than pointing to the social causes of individual emotional experiences, the scenes of shame show how subjectivity itself rests on intersubjective recognition. Part and parcel of shame is a change of perspective that transgresses the inner/outer dichotomy: the ashamed person believes to see him or herself through the eyes of the others and suddenly observes a truth that he or she cannot accept. Therefore, Moritz's narrator describes shame as an annihilating experience:

> Among all sensations, the highest degree of embarrassment [*Beschämung*—CS] to which one can be subjected must be one of the most agonizing. Reiser has felt this more than once in his life; he has had more than one moment when he felt, as it were, annihilated in his own eyes for example, when he thought of somebody's greeting, praise, or invitation was meant for him when it was not.—The embarrassment [*Beschämung*—CS] and confusion to which such a misunderstanding could subject him were indescribable.[18]

The passage refers to an incident that takes place in a rich merchant's home: The merchant invites someone in the room to dinner. Anton, who thinks that he has been invited, politely rejects—only to be told that he had not been addressed. Consequently, Anton feels ashamed: How could he have possibly imagined that the esteemed merchant would invite the irrelevant and socially minor Anton Reiser? The passage stresses the change of perspective, which is essential to shame. Anton sees himself through the imagined eyes of the others. He cannot cope with the impression that "he cuts the stupidest, most contemptible of figures as he stood there, and at the same time was much more keenly and powerfully aware of his stupid and contemptible conduct than anyone else."[19] Moritz depicts the incident as if it were a theatre scene. The visual dimension of shame—stressed by theoreticians from Jean-Paul Sartre to Jacques Lacan—explains why theatre can serve as a model to bring the structures of shaming to the fore. Moritz's protagonist does not only play a role, thereby concealing his inner self, rather his emotional life and true self itself also depend on observations by himself and others. Along these lines, self-realization is understood in its intersubjective dimension: the self needs the recognition of others.[20]

Shame possesses a cognitive function. It brings those norms and values to the fore by which we judge ourselves. Since shame is often contrasted with guilt, morality and religion appear to be the primary field from which norms are drawn. Yet material conditions function as a source of shaming as well. Moritz's Anton Reiser feels ashamed when he is forced to follow his employer through the streets heavily burdened with manufactured goods. His parents are likewise ashamed of the poor clothing they provided for their son. Many scenes of the novel emphasize that observational regimes produce emotions. The protagonist experiences disapproval by real and imagined audiences, but approval as well. This is not to say that Anton is only passive. His emotional states are not caused by the outside world. As part of what we today would call emotional self-management, Anton seeks to be recognized and to alter his mood. Following Anton's emotional ups and downs, the narrator moves beyond the dichotomy of interior/exterior. Anton's engagement with literature and theatre and also his religious practices are active attempts of self-constitution. While shame possesses a negative evaluative dimension, these practices aim at approval of the self by the self.

Religion and the Construction of Interiority

The very beginning of *Anton Reiser* further demonstrates how much weight Moritz gives to the importance of social practices for the analysis of the individual psychic life. While the Preface argues along the lines of Friedrich von Blanckenburg's *Versuch über den Roman* (1774) and promises "man's internal history,"[21] the novel does not begin with an insight into Anton's inner life or a portrait of his family, but rather with a sober description of an aristocrat who presides over a Quietist community. The reader learns about the affiliations and traditions of German Quietism, and only on page three does the narrator reveal that Anton's father is part of the depicted religious community. Focusing on the emotional practices of the Quietist community, the novel quotes programmatic passages from Quietist leaders.[22] Quietism, it states, aims at "*annihilating* all their passions, and eradicating all *selfhood*."[23] By foregrounding the emotional regime of the Quietist community to which Anton's father belongs, the narrator interrelates the inner history of Anton to the religious practices to which his father has introduced him. Through the religious techniques of self-observation and a religiously grounded education, Anton acquires not only a sense of his self but also a "feeling of the self" (*Selbstgefühl*) that is highly paradoxical.[24] In the Quietist context, the loss of individuality alongside the feeling of worthlessness and despair acquires a positive connotation and functions as a prerequisite for salvation. With regard to Germany, this mixed emotional regime is better known from Pietism. Pietistic conversion narratives exemplify similar emotional dynamics, as Andreas Bähr has succinctly argued—the fear that they generate is at the same time the prerequisite for the turn to God: "In the texts of early Pietism, fear and anxiety are not psychic events caused or vanquished by religion, but basic concepts for personal and social self-constitution which gain their shape only through religious categorization."[25] Along these lines, Anton follows his spiritual mentor's way of praying and aims to produce "repentance, contrition, yearning for God, and the like."[26] Throughout the novel, the narrator emphasizes that these psychological states entail a reflexive stance. Repentance, contrition and the extermination of individual traits are considered positive since they are believed to be steps toward salvation. It would be one-sided to criticize this conscious effort to generate religious emotions as theatrical behavior. To be sure, the recognition for which Anton strives presupposes an approving audience, yet Anton is not simply acting. He follows the emotional regime in which he has been socialized. As the narrator states, Anton is incapable of distinguishing whether he is deceived by his imagination or truly feels what he feels.[27] The emotional practice itself generates recognition—in his eyes as well as in the eyes of the religious community—since it displays the desired Quietist interiority.

Religion, like other social spheres as well, introduces agents to emotional practices that are not limited to specific religious settings. For example, Anton, being left alone by his parents who feel ashamed of his poor clothing and consequently do not take him with them, happens to open a religious songbook by Jeanne Guyon, a leading Quietist authority, and suddenly feels at ease. The Quietist teaching addresses his situation since it allows him to soothe the pain resulting from his parents' neglect. Reading the songs, Anton considers his pain a necessary step toward God: "According to this hymn, a sense of annihilation such as he was feeling at that moment was necessary before one could lose oneself in the abyss of eternal love, like a drop in the ocean."[28] The scene comments on the relation between shame and Quietism. Anton learns that the extinction of all character traits not only characterizes the experience of shame but at the same time is stipulated and, thus, recognized by the Quietist community. The scene also points to reading as a practice that combines emotional and cognitive aspects. On the one hand, Anton empathizes with the emotions expressed in the song. Moritz's protagonist practices what Adam Smith called "sympathy," which we refer to today with the term "empathy." On the other hand, he recognizes that his own emotions resemble the emotional outline of the song. The scene captures in a nutshell the emotional and cognitive function ascribed to reading throughout the novel: it gives consolation.

Reading as Therapy

Moritz's novel partakes in the critique of Sentimentalism, which had become widespread at the end of the eighteenth century. According to their critics, the

Sentimentalists followed theatrical routines. They only acted their emotions, mimicked literary figures, and lacked an authentic emotional life. In *Über Empfindsamkeit und Empfindelei* (1779), Joachim Heinrich Campe, for example, identifies theatrical gestures on the part of the Sentimentalists: "proclamations, maxims, sighs, tears, hand-wringing and fainting."[29] This critic of Sentimentalism reiterates the dichotomy between interiority and merely outward-directed bodily behavior. While Moritz's novel is in no way uncritical of his protagonist's enthusiastic Sentimentalism, Anton's engagement with theatre and his sentimental rituals are not depicted as theatrical elements that conceal a truer inner self remaining hidden inside the body. Anton's strolls at midnight, his nightly reading of Shakespeare, and his readings in front of idyllic waterfalls are subjected to the narrator's satirical mockery; nevertheless, these rituals do produce the desired emotions. Instead of choosing sides in the quarrel over Sentimentalism in his discussion of Anton's love for Shakespeare and Goethe, Moritz asks why Anton engages in sentimentalist activities.[30]

One of the major intertexts by which the novel takes part in the discourse on Sentimentalism is Johann Wolfgang Goethe's *Die Leiden des jungen Werthers* (*The Sorrows of Young Werther*). Moritz's protagonist reads Goethe's novel with enthusiastic joy and mimics the writing style of Werther's letters. What claims to be a "natural" writing style thereby proves to be cultural artifice. To write as "naturally" as Werther, Anton reproduces the writing scene of Goethe's novel: he buys a tea pot, a cup, and fuel for a stove; prepares the tea; and only then starts writing.[31] He also writes to his father in the sentimental style—using so many dashes that the addressee fails to understand him. The letter, as the narrator comments, "was a theatrical role played by Reiser."[32] Using the term "role," the narrator emphasizes what many scenes convey as well: Anton's longing to present "the scenes of life in himself" pertains not only to the theatre but to everyday life in which sociologists from Mead to Dahrendorf have discerned behavioral roles.[33] Since his life lacks the desired roles for him, Anton turns to reading and theatre as emotional practices. As a child, he already aims to flee domestic struggles by reading novels: "Reading suddenly opened up to him a new world, the enjoyment of which afforded some compensation for the unpleasant things in his real world."[34] Goethe's novel has an ongoing impact on Anton, for he mimics Werther at several occasions—when he reads Homer, for example: "Whether this reading of Homer was an idea left over from *The Sorrows of Werther* or not, in Reiser's case it was certainly not affectation, but gave him pure and genuine pleasure."[35] Anton identifies with Werther and follows Goethe's counsel as expressed in the preface to his novel: "let this book be your friend if, due to fate or personal responsibility, you can find no closer one."[36] Through this line, Goethe's novel offers a dialogic relationship to the reader, and Anton accepts.[37] Goethe, Katja Mellmann argues, uses emotive patterns of discourse to facilitate the empathy of the reader. "The reader must respond to the question as who Werther is with the answer: 'He is my equal.'"[38] Moritz's novel does not only illustrate this form of empathetic reception; it also stresses that such empathy leads to the justification of the reader's sorrows. Feeling with Werther, Anton finds his own emotions justified.

Anton's reading experience with Shakespeare exemplifies this therapeutic dimension as well. In Shakespeare's tragedies, Anton recognizes his own suffering and, consequently, no longer considers it as insignificant and a cause for shame. With analytic interest, the narrator points to the reason for this change in perception: "he had shared in the feelings felt by thousands of others when reading Shakespeare."[39] Thus, it is this "imagined community" with other (absent) readers that ends Anton's negative self-assessment. He no longer feels marginalized. The narrator, who at times is also critical of Anton's reading practices, justifies Anton's reaction to Goethe and Shakespeare by pointing to the emotional recognition realized by reading. Reading produces empathetic communities that help Anton not to see himself any longer as "an insignificant, forsaken being," but to be "proud of his humanity."[40] It allows for an imaginary recognition that compensates for the contempt that Anton has experienced through his parents, mentors, teachers, and classmates. In all these groups, Anton frequently feels ashamed. Empathizing with the sorrows of Werther or Hamlet, though, legitimizes his own sorrows. Identifying with their problematic individuality allows participation in the recognition that Goethe's and Shakespeare's protagonists could expect. Anton's reading of Friedrich Maximilian Klinger's *Die Zwillinge* (1776) likewise shows how reading functions as an antidote to shame. Suffering from the discrepancy between his ego ideal and his social identity, and moreover burdened with the guilt of murdering his brother, Klinger's protagonist Guelfo—in a crucial scene of the drama—destroys the mirror in which he catches sight of himself. The narrator emphasizes the identificatory potential of this scene for Anton Reiser: "The self-loathing that Guelfo feels when he breaks the mirror . . . all this seemed to Reiser so true, such an echo of his own soul, which was always laden with such black fantasies, that he identified with the role of Guelfo and inhabited it for a while with all his thoughts and emotions."[41] Anton's identification with Guelfo highlights the low self-esteem of Moritz's protagonist, which can be traced back to the failed intersubjective recognition expressed in the many shame scenes of the novel, since the sight a person glimpses of herself in the experience of shame causes self-loathing. Shame threatens one's self-perception and questions one's ego. It triggers the urgent desire to sink into the ground and to retreat from all social relations.

Moritz's focus on reading as a social practice offers an alternative answer to what had been a pressing concern of the Enlightenment: Why do tragic plots elicit pleasure? While Schiller points in a Kantian manner to the faculties of the mind, Moritz draws attention to reading as a social practice.[42] The empathic relationship with literary figures rests on—imagined or real—similarities and thereby entails justification for the emotions that we identify in the reading process. Reading acquires a therapeutic dimension and comforts the suffering.

Beyond Interiority: Recognition, Empathy, and Shame

Increased literacy and the proliferation of print characterize the culture of the eighteenth century. In *Körperströme und Schriftverkehr*, Albrecht Koschorke has linked the evolution of media to fundamental transformations in our understanding of the human body.[43] Through print, direct bodily interaction increasingly gave way to mediated communication. Before this backdrop of a less integrated social body, Koschorke conceptualizes German Sentimentalism as an attempt to establish a new, more abstract form of collectivity. While the actual bodies are isolated from each other—as exemplified by the silent reader—reading aims at integration on an emotional level. Koschorke points to the notion of "sympathy" as an intellectual means of imagining this emotional integration. According to Adam Smith, "sympathy" allows us to feel what the other might feel: "By the imagination we place ourselves in his situation, we conceive ourselves enduring all the same torments, we enter as it were into his body, and become in some measure the same person with him, and thence form some idea of his sensations, and even feel something which, though weaker in degree, is not altogether unlike them."[44] Since sympathy is based on the imagination, it refers to direct social interactions as well as reading processes. Smith's conceptualization of "sympathy"—imbued by the literary culture of this time—even considers narrativity a prerequisite. While the direct display of pain might hamper our sympathy and cause disgust, the narrative account provides us with the causes for pain and, thereby, motivates sympathetic responses.

The importance of the arts becomes apparent in Smith's wording and examples as well. Speaking of the "spectator," Smith borrows the term for the sympathizing agent from the sphere of theater, and he, moreover, frequently refers to tragedies for examples of sympathetic responses. The "spectatorial structure"[45] of Smith's notion of "sympathy" concerns, as Helmut J. Schneider has rightfully emphasized, "the specific quality that the (real or fictional) object must possess in order to arouse the spectator's sympathy."[46] Since our sympathetic response rests on our capacity to identify with the expressed emotion, we encounter difficulties if we are confronted with emotions that are unknown to us. Likewise, the "theatrical relation to others" urges us to adapt our body language so as to arouse sympathy on the part of the "audience."[47] Before the backdrop of sympathy's reciprocal nature, Schneider summarizes that individual feelings become an object of sympathy only if they are transformed into "socially compatible qualities."[48] What we accept as socially compatible differs historically. The sentimental reader was probably more open to strong emotions than readers in other epochs. Yet literature does not only express what is compatible, but must also be considered a testing ground for social compatibility. The success of a novel or play depends to a certain degree on the acceptance the emotional makeup of a protagonist could gain from the audience. Goethe's Werther is a case in point. The book became a scandal based on the critique that too many readers empathetically identified with the protagonist—sometimes with deadly consequences. From the perspective of the reader, mimicry of Werther's suicide was fortunately the exception. To experience certain similarities with the protagonist in the reading process might also alter the reader's self-judgment in positive ways—as Moritz's *Anton Reiser* demonstrates. Through figures like Werther, Hamlet, and Guelfo, Anton feels vindicated. Smith's notion of sympathy explains this process, since it "consists in the *concurrence* of our emotions with another's emotions" and thus combines emotional and cognitive aspects.[49] We only empathize with behavior we find appropriate, and we find behavior appropriate if it resembles our own conduct. Thus, the empathetic identification with a protagonist who has also found approbation from other readers vindicates us to a certain degree. The imagined community of readers serves as a medium for such a form of recognition.

Moritz's take on emotions in *Anton Reiser* clearly breaks with notions of affective contagion according to which emotions are directly triggered by the bodily behavior of others. For Moritz, we do not simply mimic the emotions we encounter. Moritz as well as Smith point to our imagination as the place where empathy—or sympathy to use Smith's term—is based. We only connect to the other's emotions if we can imagine that we would feel the same way; "fiction itself has to bring about the similarity-effect," as Fritz Breithaupt has argued.[50] The compulsive element of reading triggered by this experience of similarity was stressed by contemporaries of Moritz who warned that the compulsion to read (*Lesewut*) results in utter passivity. Smith, on the contrary, emphasized the emotional gains of empathy. In his account, similarity is rewarded by a "sentiment of approbation," which is "always agreeable and delightful."[51] Moritz's novel shows that empathy allows us to partake in the social recognition fictional characters could gain. The "self" operative in this psychological process is of intersubjective origin—generated in social practices on the basis of comparisons, interpretations, and identifications, which transgress the borders between the inside and outside.

Moritz's approach to shame is fueled by the desire to overcome shame. It points to the politics of emotions, which characterizes the preoccupation with emotions in the eighteenth century.[52] The utopian promise of a society free of shame fascinated not only Moritz. Surprisingly, it is an aphorism by Friedrich Nietzsche that captures the political dimension of this endeavor: "What do you consider most humane? To spare someone shame."[53]

Christian Sieg studied at the Freie Universität Berlin and received his PhD from Stanford University in 2008. He holds a research position at Westfälische Wilhelms-Universität Münster, where he is part of the Cluster of Excellence "Religion and Politics." He is the author of *The Ordinary in the Novel of German Modernism* (2011) and has published on twentieth- and twenty-first-century literature, culture, and philosophy. In 2015, he completed his habilitation, published in 2017 as *Die "engagierte Literatur" und die Religion*, an analysis of political authorship in postwar Germany. Other publications include *Zukunftsvisionen zwischen Apokalypse und Utopie* (2016); "'Klar wie der Tag!' Evidenz und Recht in Friedrich Schillers Maria Stuart," in *Zeitschrift für deutsche Philologie* (2016); "Beyond Foundational Myths: Images from the Margins of the European Memory Map," in *The Changing Place of Europe in Global Memory Cultures: Usable Pasts and Futures* (2016).

Notes

1. Monique Scheer shows how these terms support the inner/outer dichotomy in the lexicons of the eighteenth century: Monique Scheer, "Topographies of Emotion," in *Emotional Lexicons: Continuity and Change in the Vocabulary of Feeling 1700–2000*, ed. Ute Frevert et al., 32–61 (Oxford: Oxford University Press, 2014).
2. "Ich fühle mich! Ich bin!" Johann Gottfried Herder, "Zum Sinn des Gefühls," in *Werke*, vol. 2 (Munich: Hanser, 1985), 244. My translation.
3. Klopstock writes: "eigentliche innerste Beschaffenheit einer Sache." My translation. See the entry "Innerlichkeit" by Renate von Heydebrand, "Innerlichkeit," in *Historisches Wörterbuch der Philosophie*, vol. 4, ed. Joachim Ritter and Karlfried Grunder (Basel: Schwabe, 1976), 386.
4. Rüdiger Campe and Julia Weber, eds., *Rethinking Emotion: Interiority and Exteriority in Premodern, Modern, and Contemporary Thought* (Berlin: De Gruyter, 2014), 2.
5. I use the terms "empathy" and "sympathy" as synonyms. Our contemporary usage of empathy refers to a practice in which "we feel what we believe to be the emotions of others," (Suzanne Keen, *Empathy and the Novel* [Oxford: Oxford University Press, 2007], 5). In the eighteenth century, the term was unknown and Adam Smith, to whom I will turn later, used the historically older term "sympathy," synonymous to this definition of empathy. Suzanne Keen emphasizes that both David Hume's and Adam Smith's "accounts of sympathy include clearly recognizable aspects of empathy," (42).

6. Martin Luther, *On Christian Liberty* (Minneapolis: Fortress Press, 2003), 3.
7. G. W. F. Hegel, *Aesthetics: Lectures on Fine Art*, vol. 1 (Oxford: Clarendon Press, 1975), 593.
8. Georg Lukács, *Die Theorie des Romans* (Darmstad: Luchterhand, 1971 [1916]), 56–57.
9. Martin Swales, *The German Bildungsroman from Wieland to Hesse*, (Princeton, N.J.: Princeton University Press, 1978), 29.
10. Michael Minden. *The German Bildungsroman: Incest and Inheritance* (Cambridge: Cambridge University Press, 1997), 85.
11. Monique Scheer, "Are Emotions a Kind of Practice (and Is That What Makes Them Have a History)? A Bourdieuan Approach to Understanding Emotion," *History and Theory* 51, no. 2 (2012): 200.
12. Andreas Reckwitz, "Grundelemente einer Theorie sozialer Praktiken: Eine sozialtheoretische Perspektive," *Zeitschrift für Soziologie* 32 (2003): 296. I quote Scheer's translation of Reckwitz. See Monique Scheer, "Are Emotions a Kind of Practice (and Is That What Makes Them Have a History)? A Bourdieuan Approach to Understanding Emotion," History and Theory 51, no. 2 (2012): 200.
13. Scheer, "Are Emotions a Kind of Practice," 200.
14. For the relationship between the autobiographical dimension and the scientific approach of empirical psychology, see Hans Esselborn, "Der gespaltene Autor: 'Anton Reiser' zwischen autobiographischem Roman und psychologischer Fallgeschichte," *Recherches germaniques* 25 (1995): 69–90.
15. Ute Frevert, "Defining Emotions: Concepts and Debates over Three Centuries," in *Emotional Lexicons: Continuity and Change in the Vocabulary of Feeling 1700–2000*, ed. Ute Frevert et al. (Oxford: Oxford University Press, 2014), 19.
16. Johann Nikolaus Tetens, *Philosophische Versuche über die menschliche Natur und ihre Entwicklung*, vol. 1 (Hildesheim: Olms, 1979 [1777]).
17. Lothar Müller, *Die kranke Seele und das Licht der Erkenntnis* (Frankfurt am Main: Athenäum Verlag, 1987), 272–80.
18. Karl Phillip Moritz, *Anton Reiser: A Psychological Novel*, trans. Ritchie Robertson (London: Penguin, 1997), 119.
19. Moritz, *Anton Reiser*, 120.
20. Schäfer and Wild miss this aspect and thus predominantly see vanity and simulation in Anton's enthusiasm for theater. See Martin Jörg Schäfer, *Das Theater der Erziehung: Goethe's "pädagogische Provinz" und die Vorgeschichte von Bildung* (Bielefeld: transcript, 2016), 187–92. See also the similar argument in Christopher J. Wild, "Theorizing Theater Antitheatrically: Karl Philipp Moritz's Theatromania," *MLN* 120 (2005): 512.
21. Moritz, *Anton Reiser*, 3.
22. Moritz also comments on the function of reading in the Quietist community. Cf. Lothar Müller, "Die Erziehung der Gefühle im 18. Jahrhundert: Kanzel, Buch und Bühne in Karl Phillip Moritz' 'Anton Reiser,' (1785–1790)," *Der Deutschunterricht* 48 (1996): 5–20.
23. Moritz, *Anton Reiser*, 5. Emphasis in the original.
24. See Johannes F. Lehmann, *Im Abgrund der Wut: Zur Kultur- und Literaturgeschichte des Zorns* (Freiburg i. Br.: Rombach, 2012), 181–84.
25. Andreas Bähr, "Fear, Anxiety and Terror in Conversion Narratives of Early German Pietism," *German History* 32, no. 3 (2014): 369.

26. Moritz, *Anton Reiser*, 47.
27. Moritz, *Anton Reiser*, 47f.
28. Moritz, *Anton Reiser*, 15f.
29. Joachim Heinrich Campe, *Über Empfindsamkeit und Empfindelei* (Potsdam: Becker, 2012 [1779]), 20. My translation.
30. Ironically, Moritz's sensitive protagonist himself writes a pamphlet against Sentimentalism, giving weight to the suspicion that the critics loathed Sentimentalism because they themselves fell prey to its temptations.
31. Moritz, *Anton Reiser*, 344.
32. Moritz, *Anton Reiser*, 147.
33. Moritz, *Anton Reiser*, 291.
34. Moritz, *Anton Reiser*, 11f.
35. Moritz, *Anton Reiser*, 272.
36. Johann Wolfgang Goethe, *The Sorrows of Young Werther*, in *The Collected Works*, vol. 11 (Princeton: Princeton University Press, 1995), 3.
37. Katja Mellmann, "Das Buch als Freund—der Freund als Zeugnis," in *Bürgerlichkeit im 18. Jahrhundert*, ed. Hans-Edwin Friedrich, Fotis Jannidis, and Marianne Willems (Tübingen: Niemeyer, 2006), 207.
38. Mellmann, "Das Buch als Freund," 211.
39. Moritz, *Anton Reiser*, 186.
40. Moritz, *Anton Reiser*, 207.
41. Moritz, *Anton Reiser*, 242.
42. Friedrich Schiller, "Über den Grund des Vergnügens an tragischen Gegenständen," in *Schillers Werke*, vol. 20 (Weimar: Böhlau, 1962), 133–47.
43. Albrecht Koschorke, *Körperströme und Schriftverkehr: Mediologie des 18. Jahrhunderts*, 2nd ed. (Munich: Fink, 2003).
44. Adam Smith, "The Theory of Moral Sentiments [1759]," in *Glasgow Edition of the Works and Correspondence*, vol. 1 (Indianapolis: Liberty Fund, 1982), I.I.2.
45. Helmut J. Schneider, "Humanity's Imaginary Body: The Concept of Empathy and Sympathy and the New Theater Experience in the 18th century," *Deutsche Vierteljahrsschrift für Literaturwissenschaft und Geistesgeschichte* 82, no. 3 (2008): 388.
46. Schneider, "Humanity's Imaginary Body," 388.
47. David Marshall, *The Figure of Theater: Shaftesbury, Defoe, Adam Smith, and George Eliot* (New York: Columbia University Press, 1986), 174.
48. Schneider, "Humanity's Imaginary Body," 389.
49. Imola Ilyes, "Empathy in Hume and Smith," in *The Routledge Handbook of Philosophy of Empathy*, ed. Heidi L. Maibom (New York: Routledge, 2017), 101. Emphasis in the original.
50. Fritz Breithaupt, "How I Feel Your Pain: Lessing's 'Mitleid,' Goethe's 'Anagnosisis,' and Fontane's 'Quiet Sadism,'" in *Deutsche Vierteljahrsschrift für Literaturwissenschaft und Geistesgeschichte* 82 (2008): 408.
51. Smith, "Theory of Moral Sentiments," III.I.9 (footnote).
52. See Nikolaus Wegmann, *Diskurse der Empfindsamkeit: Zur Geschichte eines Gefühls in der Literatur des 18. Jahrhunderts* (Stuttgart: Metzler, 1988), 56–70.
53. Friedrich Nietzsche, *The Gay Science* (New York: Vintage Books, 1974), § 274, 220.

Bibliography

Bähr, Andreas. "Fear, Anxiety and Terror in Conversion Narratives of Early German Pietism." *German History* 32, no. 3 (2014): 353–70.
Breithaupt, Fritz. "How I Feel Your Pain: Lessing's 'Mitleid,' Goethe's 'Anagnosisis,' and Fontane's 'Quiet Sadism.'" *Deutsche Vierteljahrsschrift für Literaturwissenschaft und Geistesgeschichte* 82 (2008): 400–23.
Campe, Joachim Heinrich. *Über Empfindsamkeit und Empfindelei*. Potsdam: Becker, 2012 (1779).
Campe, Rüdiger, and Julia Weber, eds. *Rethinking Emotion: Interiority and Exteriority in Premodern, Modern, and Contemporary Thought*. Berlin: De Gruyter, 2014.
Esselborn, Hans. "Der gespaltene Autor: 'Anton Reiser' zwischen autobiographischem Roman und psychologischer Fallgeschichte." *Recherches germaniques* 25 (1995): 69–90.
Frevert, Ute. "Defining Emotions: Concepts and Debates over Three Centuries." In *Emotional Lexicons: Continuity and Change in the Vocabulary of Feeling 1700–2000*, edited by Ute Frevert et al., 1–31 Oxford: Oxford University Press, 2014.
Goethe, Johann Wolfgang. *The Sorrows of Young Werther*. In *The Collected Works*. Vol. 11, 1–88. Princeton: Princeton University Press, 1995.
Hegel, G. W. F. *Aesthetics: Lectures on Fine Art*. Vol. 1. Oxford: Clarendon Press, 1975.
Herder, Johann Gottfried. "Zum Sinn des Gefühls." In *Werke*. Vol. 2, 243–51. Munich: Hanser, 1985.
Ilyes, Imola. "Empathy in Hume and Smith." In *The Routledge Handbook of Philosophy of Empathy*, edited by Heidi L. Maibom, 98–109. New York: Routledge, 2017.
Keen, Suzanne. *Empathy and the Novel*. Oxford: Oxford University Press, 2007.
Koschorke, Albrecht. *Körperströme und Schriftverkehr: Mediologie des 18. Jahrhunderts*. 2nd edition. Munich: Fink, 2003.
Lehmann, Johannes F. *Im Abgrund der Wut: Zur Kultur- und Literaturgeschichte des Zorns*. Freiburg i. Br.: Rombach, 2012.
Lukács, Georg. *Die Theorie des Romans*. Darmstadt: Luchterhand, 1971 (1916).
Luther, Martin. *On Christian Liberty*. Minneapolis: Fortress Press, 2003.
Marshall, David. *The Figure of Theater: Shaftesbury, Defoe, Adam Smith, and George Eliot*. New York: Columbia University Press, 1986.
Mellmann, Katja. "Das Buch als Freund—der Freund als Zeugnis." In *Bürgerlichkeit im 18. Jahrhundert*, edited by Hans-Edwin Friedrich, Fotis Jannidis, and Marianne Willems, 201–40. Tübingen: Niemeyer, 2006.
Minden, Michael. *The German Bildungsroman: Incest and Inheritance*. Cambridge, UK: Cambridge University Press, 1997.
Moritz, Karl Phillip. *Anton Reiser: A Psychological Novel*. Translated by Ritchie Robertson. London: Penguin, 1997.

Müller, Lothar. "Die Erziehung der Gefühle im 18. Jahrhundert: Kanzel, Buch und Bühne in Karl Phillip Moritz' 'Anton Reiser,' 1785–1790." *Der Deutschunterricht* 48 (1996): 5–20.

———. *Die kranke Seele und das Licht der Erkenntnis*. Frankfurt am Main: Athenäum Verlag, 1987.

Nietzsche, Friedrich. *The Gay Science*. New York: Vintage Books, 1974.

Reckwitz, Andreas. "Grundelemente einer Theorie sozialer Praktiken: Eine sozialtheoretische Perspektive." *Zeitschrift für Soziologie* 32 (2003): 282–301.

Schäfer, Martin Jörg. *Das Theater der Erziehung: Goethes "pädagogische Provinz" und die Vorgeschichte von Bildung*. Bielefeld: transcript, 2016, specifically 187–92.

Scheer, Monique. "Are Emotions a Kind of Practice (and Is That What Makes Them Have a History)? A Bourdieuan Approach to Understanding Emotion." *History and Theory* 51, no. 2 (2012): 193–220.

———. "Topographies of Emotion." In *Emotional Lexicons: Continuity and Change in the Vocabulary of Feeling 1700–2000*, edited by Ute Frevert et al., 32–61. Oxford: Oxford University Press, 2014.

Schiller, Friedrich. "Über den Grund des Vergnügens an tragischen Gegenständen." In *Schillers Werke*. Vol. 20, 133–47. Weimar: Böhlau, 1962.

Schneider, Helmut J. "Humanity's Imaginary Body: The Concept of Empathy and Sympathy and the New Theater Experience in the 18th Century." *Deutsche Vierteljahrsschrift für Literaturwissenschaft und Geistesgeschichte* 82, no. 3 (2008): 382–99.

Smith, Adam. "The Theory of Moral Sentiments [1759]." In *Glasgow Edition of the Works and Correspondence*. Vol. 1. Indianapolis: Liberty Fund, 1982.

Swales, Martin. *The German Bildungsroman from Wieland to Hesse*. Princeton: Princeton University Press, 1978.

Tetens, Johann Nikolaus. *Philosophische Versuche über die menschliche Natur und ihre Entwicklung*. Vol. 1. Hildesheim: Olms, 1979 (1777).

von Heydebrand, Renate. "Innerlichkeit." In *Historisches Wörterbuch der Philosophie*. Vol. 4, edited by Joachim Ritter and Karlfried Grunder, 386–88. Basel: Schwabe, 1976.

Wegmann, Nikolaus. *Diskurse der Empfindsamkeit: Zur Geschichte eines Gefühls in der Literatur des 18. Jahrhunderts*. Stuttgart: Metzler 1988.

Wild, Christopher J. "Theorizing Theater Antitheatrically: Karl Philipp Moritz's Theatromania." *MLN* 120 (2005): 507–38.

CHAPTER 8

Gambling and Emotion

JARED POLEY

Writing in the introduction to his 1986 collection *The Social Life of Things*, Arjun Appadurai isolates the logic of commodification to explain the genesis of value. "Economic exchange creates values," he explains. "Value is embodied in commodities that are exchanged. Focusing on the things that are exchanged ... makes it possible to argue that what creates the link between exchange and value is *politics*."[1] Noting the generous contributions of German intellectuals to our understanding of the cognitive and social process through which humans assign value, Appadurai focuses first on Georg Simmel and then on Karl Marx. Writing fifteen years later, amidst the fallout of the linguistic turn, Bill Brown writes in his essay "Thing Theory" that "the story of objects asserting themselves as things, then, is the story of a changed relation to the human subject and thus the story of the thing really names less an object than a particular subject-object relation."[2] He concludes the essay with a telling gesture toward another German thinker: "if thinking the thing, to borrow Heidegger's phrase, feels like an exercise in belatedness, the feeling is provoked by our very capacity to imagine that thinking and thingness are utterly distinct."[3]

What I find useful about Brown's Thing Theory—and why I find it an increasingly helpful way to think about subject–object relations, things that are "ready-to-hand," and embedded in contextual and temporal frameworks—is the way that this approach allows us to perform a kind of intellectual jujitsu. Rather than thinking about how we invest value in objects, we can begin to imagine instead the ways that these objects force their value on us. When the subject–object distinction collapses, we are forced to imagine the material world in a different way. No longer merely mute objects that we invest with value, things transform their humans too. This insight, contentious as it may be, reveals new ways to investigate the historical, seeking to understand not how humans transformed the material world, but how the material world transformed us. And in terms of the history of emotions, we may begin to ask: Do things make us feel, or do we feel because we have things?

Gambling is an emotionally dramatic activity that arises in close proximity to the material context of the gaming room. Gambling was made illegal in France following the 1830 Revolution in France, and this provided the nascent casinos of the Rhineland an opportunity to attract thrill seekers to their tables. When the Blanc brothers—Louis and François—arrived in the region in the 1840s, they quickly instituted modern gaming systems oriented around leisure, heterosociability, and games of chance—most significantly roulette. The modern casino was born in the Rhineland in the 1840s. Until the creation of Blanc's casino at Monte Carlo (and the illegalization of gambling in the unified Germany in 1873), the Rhineland possessed the world's most significant concentration of casinos. This chapter examines the ways gambling in the nineteenth century acted as a foundation upon which larger claims about the emotions, the body, and psychology were developed. If we consider casino gambling, which arguably was invented in its modern form in the German-speaking states in the Rhineland (Wiesbaden, Bad Homburg, etc.) in the mid-nineteenth century, we can begin to investigate the ways that emotions, material objects, and the body interacted in this sphere of human behavior. The oscillation between material cue and emotional response, like the one between the gambler's passionate exhibition and exhaustion, or the individual and society, tells us much about the ways the emotions and the material world interacted in the nineteenth century.

In his 1910 essay on "Sociability," Georg Simmel argues that play was a critical element in the building of sociability. "It is an obvious corollary," Simmel argues at one point in the essay, "that everything may be subsumed under sociability which one can call sociological play-form; above all, play itself, which assumes a large place in the sociability of all epochs." Continuing, Simmel notes:

> For even when play turns about a money prize, it is not the prize, which indeed could be won in many other ways, which is the specific point of the play; but the attraction for the true sportsman lies in the dynamics and in the chances of that sociologically significant form of activity itself. The social game has a deeper double meaning—that it is played not only *in* society as its outward bearer but that with its help people actually "play" society.[4]

Playing games, arguably the *raison-d'être* of a casino, allowed the players to create society. What that society looked like, and how it functioned, was the process of nineteenth-century trajectories that brought together a new transnational social class, a new transportation system based on steam, a new culture of leisure and play, and a set of new political circumstances that permitted legal gambling in only a few circumscribed places. Simmel's argument about the significance of play in the creation of sociability demands that we investigate more closely the ways in which the casino operated. For some a source of fun, for others, the casino may have been best described by inventor Hiram Maxim, who wrote in 1904 about Monte Carlo: "This institution must live; it feeds off the players, and as in the case of the lamb, is disastrous to them. It lives on disasters; without them it could not exist."[5]

Critics of gambling, writing in the early nineteenth century, were attuned to the ways that gambling and emotion were connected. Happiness—generated by winning—is in fact an organizing principle of play when players attempt to calculate probability in the course of a game. Money might make one happy, but it also exposed one to avarice. Money won at the gambling table represented more than just additional means. It was not just instrumental, it was also a vector for the emotion and imagination of the player—and it could be very dangerous. The passions unleashed by play also weaken the resolve of the player, exposing him or her to greater degrees of moral danger. The mental and emotional drama of gambling hints at a type of behavioralism in which the repetition of certain practices was a key to understanding why a person kept returning to the table. Gambling set the stage for a remarkable emotional drama, one that drew its power from the way in which emotional abstraction could be made real, the anguish of loss put on exhibition.

Gambling was a highly emotional activity, and it shaped the player in profound ways. In E. T. A. Hoffmann's 1819 story "Spielerglück" ("Gambler's Luck"), the reader is told that various gamblers are not only "excited and heated by play," but that the act of gambling transformed the range of possible human emotions that one could experience.[6] One gambler is said to be a "a stranger to every human feeling," while gamblers generally are said to be "alien to all human emotion." One way of interpreting these descriptions is to say that the environment of the gambling hall—like the act of gambling itself—commits the gambler to two conflicting emotional trajectories: gambling intensifies the emotions and then deadens them.

"Gambler's Luck" tells the story of Baron Siegfried, a man who is completely virtuous and always lucky. People hate him because of his good fortune, so he hits on a plan to lose money at the faro table and thereby to improve his reputation among people. But he fails at this task, and despite his best efforts, he wins. Siegfried notices an old man staring at him over the course of successive nights. Siegfried invites the uncanny visitor to dine with him, and the man tells him the story of a Chevalier, very similar to the baron, who also unfailingly wins and who bankrupts an old man named Vertua (who in turn had been extremely lucky at the gambling tables, but whose luck was no match for the Chevalier). The Chevalier forgives his debt when he sees Vertua's beautiful daughter, Angela (whom he later marries after giving up gambling altogether). But the Chevalier cannot stay away from the tables, and he eventually loses his entire fortune to a French colonel, who in one last wager puts up 20,000 francs against the right to take the Chevalier's wife (Vertua's daughter). The colonel wins, and when he goes to the Chevalier's house, the two find Angela dead. The Chevalier is of course the old man talking to Baron Siegfried, whom he is trying to warn away from the gambling tables.

In this story, there are several points of importance to this discussion of emotion and gambling. One passage describes Siegfried's first foray to the gambling rooms, and it indicates how the game attracted him, not so much for the lure of money but for the pleasures of playing. Most important, the game absorbs his attention, keeping him playing through a series of rewards. Hoffmann writes,

> Without his being conscious of it, there began to be awakened in his mind a strong liking for faro, which with all its simplicity is the most ominous of games; and this liking continued to increase more and more. He was no longer dissatisfied with his good-luck; gambling fettered his attention and held him fast to the table for nights and nights, so that he was perforce compelled to give credence to the peculiar attraction of the game, of which his friends had formerly spoken and which he would by no means allow to be correct, for he was attracted to faro not by the thirst for gain, but simply and solely by the game itself.[7]

The pleasures of play only intensify, and as the rewards compound, new emotions—perhaps most important, avarice—take over his emotional life and fundamentally change Siegfried.

Siegfried's emotional trajectory in the story is shaped by his experiences at the gaming tables. Hoffmann writes that a second character, the chevalier, "being thus comforted at heart, could not fail to develop again all the charms of manner which had once been so peculiarly his own before he was led astray by his insane, pernicious passion for gambling."[8] Other passages confirm this idea that one's confrontation with the pleasures of gambling reconfigure the player's emotional economy. Siegfried is warned: "In a single word, you are on the point of becoming a confirmed and passionate gambler and ruining yourself."[9] And perhaps most alarming to Hoffmann, gambling and the passions that it unleashed might do lasting damage to the ability to feel emotions at all. The intensity of the player's emotional life could reach a breaking point. The dramatic intensity of the gambling tables, and the addictive qualities of play, could damage a person's emotional life in unforeseen ways.

These descriptions of how gambling interacted with the emotions were written before the advent of Louis Blanc-style resort gambling as he developed the system first at Bad Homburg and then at Monte Carlo. But even early observers of that system, like George Sala who wrote about the Rhenish casinos in 1860, were alert to the emotional dynamics of gambling in that context.[10] Sala, for instance, wrote about Bad Homburg as a place where the casino functioned as machine that could systematically wear down players through emotional distress. Sala writes:

> in the bank being, from chime to chime, always at it, always gambling, whereas you can only devote a certain number of hours per diem to making your game; in the bank, in its personnel of dealers and croupiers, being always calm, collected, sober, and indifferent as to gain or loss, whereas you, the player, are generally nervous and excited, never indifferent, and frequently, after the vesper bell has done chiming, considerably flushed with champagne.[11]

The player's emotions were often turned against them, weaponized by the casino, which was typically described as passionless. This way of understanding the emotional contexts of casino gambling remained a way to understand the dynamics of the casino by focusing on the emotional disequilibrium generated at the table.

Sala recognized an important fact about the casino was that passionlessness could be a key tool in the player's workshop, and earlier observers of gambling, like Hey and Hoffmann, also saw that the heightening and deadening of a player's emotions were outcomes of the process. Fyodor Dostoyevsky's 1866 novella *The Gambler* offers a deeper analysis of the dynamic effects of emotion in the casino.[12] *The Gambler* tells the story of a group of Russians enjoying the casino at "Roulottenburg," a veiled description of Wiesbaden. The text has been described as "frankly autobiographical"[13] and "a historical document . . . of the highest value,"[14] but it is most useful here for its descriptions of the emotional responses of gamblers to the material objects of the casino. Some gamblers express stoic resignation in the face of loss. "A true gentleman," Dostoyevsky writes, "even if he loses his entire fortune, must not show emotion. Money is supposed to be so far beneath a gentleman that it's almost not worth thinking about."[15] Others cannot contain their emotions, and they display their emotional reactions to the game in the form of somatic response: "Feeling as though I had a fever, I moved this entire pile of money on to red—and suddenly I came to my senses! And only this once during the whole of the evening, during all the time that I was playing, did fear course through me like a chill and cause my arms and legs to tremble."[16] Similar descriptions appear in other sections of the novel: "*Rouge!* the croupier cried—and I took a deep breath, fiery pins and needles ran up and down my body. . . . that same evening I set off for the roulette table. Oh, how my heart pounded! No, it was not the money that was dear to me!"[17] As it is in this passage, the casino's environment is seen to trigger all sorts of emotional changes: "I swear that I felt sorry for Polina [a woman with whom the Gambler is in love], but strangely enough, from the moment I touched the gaming table yesterday and started raking in packets of money—my love seemed to have retreated into the background."[18]

Dostoyevsky, who experienced his own deeply emotional response to the gaming tables, has been described as "so excitable that when he entered the casino he became nervous and uncontrolled."[19] The Russian countess Sophie Kissilev (who provided the template upon which the character of the Grandmother in *The Gambler* was patterned) was also described as expressing a raw emotionality when confronted with the roulette table: "the moment she heard the rattle of the fateful ball, she suddenly became rejuvenated, followed the course of the little ivory ball with glowing and bated breath, and staked sums which often amounted to hundreds of thousands."[20] Even if Dostoyevsky was "stimulated to a state of morbid excitement by the vicissitudes of the game," his characters were not always so lucky.[21] At the conclusion of the novella, the Gambler is shown to be emotionally shattered by his gambling, no longer able to feel. He is told:

> You've become apathetic, . . . not only have you renounced life, your interests both personal and social, your duty as a man and a citizen, your friends (and all the same you did have friends); not only have you renounced any goal whatsoever, apart from winning, you have even renounced your own memories. I remember you at an ardent and intense moment of your life; but I'm certain that you've forgotten all your best impressions of that time; your dreams, your most urgent desires now don't go further than *pair* and *impair*, *rouge*, *noir*, the twelve middle numbers and so forth and so on, I'm certain of it![22]

Indeed, Dostoyevsky's Gambler describes himself as having an emotional hollowness caused by the repeated elevation of his passions: "I live in constant anxiety, I play for the smallest stakes and wait for something; I make calculations, I stand for days on end by the gaming table and *observe* the play, I even see them playing in my sleep, but all that notwithstanding I seem to have become numb, as it were, as if I'd become mired in some sort of mud."[23]

By the late nineteenth century, the emotional regimes produced by the modern casino were understood to be of a recent historical vintage. The constant fluctuation of emotional extremes—often associated with modernity in general—is evidence of how a person could be driven to the edge of sanity while at the casino. Emotional overstimulation, or the idea that the machinery of emotion could wear out through overuse, meant that an emotional deadness could set in. And ultimately, death was the most worrisome outcome of this emotional trajectory. Conclusions about the ways gaming and play provided the context within which emotions unfolded and were experienced indicate an important way to think about the meanings of gambling in the late nineteenth century. Gambling, it was recognized, encouraged a deeply emotional relationship to the material world and to other people. Sometimes that emotionality culminated in a deadening of the emotions; at other times it led to an overwhelming of the subject that only ended in insanity or suicide. Indeed, gambling generally and the casino specifically represented a historically novel way to experience emotion. Understanding the microdynamics of this emotionality surfaced in gambling-oriented texts produced in the nineteenth century in a variety of ways; but together, they attempt to map the emotional trajectory of a gambler. The psychological mechanisms used to handle emotions of loss meant that there was a recognition that loss at the gaming table held some deeper meaning. If the game was truly random and did not respond to human intervention, skill, or intellect, observers were left to ponder the larger implications of chance for human agency.

The vision of the gambling table as a machine for intensifying emotion beyond any capacity for a human to bear was only one way that nineteenth century commentators viewed the connection between gambling and emotion. Others focused on emotional disconnection instead, looking at the ways gambling generated boredom or culminated in what the sociologist Georg Simmel called the "blasé attitude." In *The Philosophy of Money*, written in 1900, Simmel describes the attitude toward money characteristic of the rich gambler who loses vast sums but affects the demeanor of carelessness. "The blasé person," Simmel writes, "has completely lost the feeling for value differences. He experiences all things as being of an equally dull and grey hue, as not worth getting excited about, particularly where the will is concerned. . . . As a rule, the blasé attitude is rightly attributed to satiated enjoyment because too strong a stimulus destroys the nervous ability to respond to it."[24] This type of gambler, in Simmel's estimation, no longer experienced the proper emotional connection to money because he or she had reached a saturation point and was no longer capable of enjoyment.

Of course, Georg Simmel was not just interested in gambling, and his overall project centered on an exploration of money and its significance in a range of areas. Yet he was also aware of the special significance that money held for gamblers. In fact, money lent any game a special quality and elevated its psychological importance to the players. In this way, money and gambling represented a paradox. Money made gambling fun, but it also meant that money held a transformed importance to the gambler. Simmel writes in *Philosophy of Money*, "We have here one of those interesting cases in which the disease determines its own form of the cure. A money culture signifies such an enslavement of life in its means, that release from its weariness is also evidently sought in a mere means which conceals its final significance—in the fact of 'stimulation' as such."[25] Money stimulates, but it also enslaves—a duality that appears in a number of descriptions of gambling in the nineteenth century.

Simmel also described gambling as a form of ersatz exchange. Gambling represents a monetization of chance and luck—money could be used as a ruthless and merciless tool to quantify the random elements of the universe. As Simmel argues,

> Money is the purest reification of means, a concrete instrument which is absolutely identical with its abstract concept; it is a pure instrument. The tremendous importance of money for understanding the basic motives of life lies in the fact that money embodies and sublimates the practical relation of man to the objects of his will, his power and his impotence; one might say, paradoxically, that man is an indirect being.[26]

The idea that money achieves some kind of amphibious status and can perform almost any type of cultural work is borne out in Simmel's analysis of the "calculating character of modern times," in which he asserts: "By and large, one may characterize the intellectual functions that are used at present in coping with the world and in regulating both individual and social relations as *calculative* functions. Their cognitive ideal is to conceive of the world as a huge arithmetical problem, to conceive events and the qualitative distinction of things as a system of numbers."[27] Money, Simmel explains, had not only achieved a historically novel claim to emotional life, but it also directly represents what Appuradai would later recognize as the power of the material over the emotional.

Simmel recognized that the conversion of the world into a set of monetized numerical functions was a novel departure from previous methods of ascertaining reality. He writes that this "psychological feature of our times which stands in such a decisive contrast to the more impulsive, emotionally determined character of earlier epochs seems to me to stand in a close causal relation to the money economy. The money economy enforces the necessity of continuous mathematical operations in our daily transactions."[28] However, it is only in the casino that the calculative function of the modern money economy is obscured and emotionalized on the one hand and deeply calculative on the other. In the first case, the gambler and his or her somatic responses to gambling and the intense emotional investment in gambling unfold in an environment in which the usual markers of money have been removed through the use of proxy signifiers of money like chips. In the second case, money is used to quantify and rationalize probability and chance, and that is why the casino specifically and gambling generally appeal as a theoretical experimental space for statisticians.[29] In an important coda to this argument, critic Sara Ahmed describes the circulation of the material as a way of storing emotional value. "Affect does not reside in an object or sign," she argues, "but is an affect of the circulation between objects and signs (= the accumulation of affective value over time). Some signs, that is, increase in affective value as an effect of the movement between signs: the more they circulate, the more affective they become, and the more they appear to 'contain' affect."[30]

Simmel dealt with the dual quality of money in another section of the *Philosophy of Money* in which he notes the "relations between external stimuli and emotional responses in the field of money."[31] In particular, Simmel sought to probe the "threshold of the awareness of money," and he suggests that the emotional content of money is related to our awareness of money and its meaning to us in very localized ways. Emotions about money are essentially latent until some exogenous force—like a wager at the gambling table—crystalizes them and generates a form in which they are expressed (and this can be either positive or negative).[32] He explored this idea further in an essay published in 1904, titled "Fashion," in which he takes up the question of envy as an emotion related specifically to the possession of objects. Simmel describes the emotional dynamism of envy in the following way: "The moment we envy an object or a person, we are no longer absolutely excluded from it; some relation or other has been established—between both the same psychic content now exists—although in entirely different categories and forms of sensations."[33] While Simmel was not talking about gambling in the essay, his insight into the emotional power that objects exert over us remains a useful way to understand the lure that gambling held in the nineteenth century. In the emotional connections between players, or between players and the mechanical objects of the gambling hall, we see a tightly forged emotional connection. This connection was not always positive, and indeed it was not always reciprocal, but the powerful nature of games and play—and the social spaces in which these games were played—contributed much to the way in which nineteenth century observers noted the intensely emotional nature of gambling.

Simmel viewed gambling as a relationship to money that was unlike any other. "All money outlays for the purposes of acquisition fall into two categories—with risk and without risk. Viewed abstractly, both forms exist in every single outlay if one excludes gambling."[34] Gambling represented more than just a calculation of odds, because money was involved it also was complicit in a highly emotional process in the midst of which a person could lose track of rationality. "A personal factor must also be considered. In every economic situation," Simmel writes, "a certain fraction of one's possession should not be risked at all, regardless of how large and how probable the chances of profit might be. The desperate risk of the final gamble, which is usually justified by the statement that one 'has nothing more to lose,' indicates by this very argument that any vestige of rationality has been deliberately abandoned here."[35] In the heat of the wager, chance overwhelmed the senses, and money's ability to dissolve and reconstitute social relations was diminished in favor of pure emotion.

The materiality of the casino forcefully channeled emotions. On one hand, "The roulette wheel is . . . the most potent of mesmeric instruments. Under its influence a man ceases to be a responsible being."[36] But on another, as the Austrian Viktor Silberer argued at the end of the century: "In gambling, temper is stronger than reason. That is why men will always be far behind the Bank, which has no soul, no temper, no sentiments. . . . The human player is no match for a machine. . . . to compete with the Bank on even terms they must be a machine like the Bank, they must have unlimited capital like the Bank, they must play every 'coup' like the Bank."[37] To beat the machine, become the machine—a passionless cyborg in which the distinction between subject and object dissolves and the emotions are overwhelmed by the power and presence of dead material. If players were often described as being overwhelmed by emotion, carried away on torrents of feeling that they could not control or at times even understand, the opposite affect was cultivated by the house. Time and again, nineteenth century observers described the passionlessness of the house, and noted its machine-like qualities, unlike those hapless players ruthlessly crushed by the casino's roulette wheels.

Gambling was thought to affect the sense of self, one's relations with others, and even the degree to which one apprehended the world in realistic ways that were free of psychoses. We have also considered the ways in which gambling—in that it represented a way to interact with the unknown—also facilitated a larger reckoning with the external world that was at once pleasurable and disturbing, thus reinforcing the attractiveness of the practice. But we also need to consider other ways that gambling facilitated a set of psychologically powerful connections in players. Money, perhaps unsurprisingly, was a key factor in the process of encouraging players to return to the gaming table. Georg Simmel notes in *The Philosophy of Money*: "Money builds a bridge between such people and objects. In crossing the bridge, the mind experiences the attraction of their possession even if it does in fact not attain it."[38] Simmel goes on to argue that the act of payment exerts a stamp of ownership and personality on an object, but that money retains a special power because it is psychologically fluid. Money can represent anything. As Simmel explains:

> The greedy soul who seeks complete satisfaction and wants to penetrate the ultimate, innermost and absolute nature of things, is painfully rejected by them. Objects are, and remain, something for themselves which resists their complete integration into the sphere of the self and allows the most passionate ownership to end in dissatisfaction. The possession of money is free of this hidden contradiction that exists in all other kinds of possession. . . . It is only money that we own completely and without reservations; it is only money that merges completely into the function we assign to it.[39]

Money, in other words, is the most psychologically satisfying medium because it can be converted into anything, and it therefore represents something special to the gambler.

In his O notebook (Prostitution, Gambling) for the *Arcades Project*, Walter Benjamin referenced Simmel's thoughts on the psychology of the gambler.[40] While it is impossible to know how Benjamin would have connected all the issues he raised in the notes on gambling, the fragments appearing at the end of that section give some indication of how the pieces might fit together. One passage in particular highlights the themes animating this essay. "The peculiar feeling of happiness in the one who wins," Benjamin wrote, "is marked by the fact that money and riches, otherwise the most massive and burdensome things in the world, come to him from the fates like a joyous embrace returned to the full."[41] Winning did not just cue a flood of pleasant feelings, but hinted at the existence of a transformed emotional relationship between the gambler and his or her world forged in the powerful environment of the nineteenth-century casino.

Jared Poley is Professor of History at Georgia State University. He is the author of the books *The Devil's Riches: A Modern History of Greed* (2016) and *Decolonization in Germany: Weimar Narratives of Colonial Loss and Foreign Occupation* (2005), and a coeditor of the collections *Money in the German-speaking Lands* (2017); *Migrations in the German Lands, 1500–2000* (2016); *Kinship, Community, and Self* (2015); and *Conversion and the Politics of Religion in Early Modern Germany* (Berghahn, 2012). He is currently working on a history of gambling in nineteenth-century Europe.

Notes

1. Arjun Appadurai, ed., *The Social Life of Things: Commodities in Cultural Perspective* (Cambridge, UK: Cambridge University Press, 1986), 3.
2. Bill Brown, "Thing Theory," *Critical Inquiry* 28, no. 1 (2001): 4.
3. Bill Brown, ed., *Things* (Chicago: University of Chicago Press, 2004), 16.
4. Georg Simmel, *Georg Simmel on Individuality and Social Forms* (Chicago: University of Chicago Press, 1972), 134.
5. Hiram Stevens Maxim, *Monte Carlo: Facts and Fallacies* (London: Grant Richards, 1904), 173.
6. Léon Vallée, *The International Library of Famous Literature: Selections from the World's Great Writers, Ancient, Mediaeval, and Modern, with Biographical and Explanatory Notes and Critical Essays by Many Eminent Writers*, vol. XVI (Issued by The Standard, 1899), 7378, 7381.
7. Vallée, XVI: 7370.
8. Vallée, XVI: 7386.
9. Vallée, XVI: 7372.
10. George Augustus Sala, *Make Your Game, Or, The Adventures of the Stout Gentleman, the Slim Gentleman, and the Man with the Iron Chest: A Narrative of the Rhine and Thereabouts* (London: Ward and Lock, 1860).
11. Sala, *Make Your Game*, 219–20.
12. Fyodor Dostoyevsky, *The Gambler and Other Stories* (New York: Penguin, 2010).
13. Egon Caesar Corti, *The Wizard of Monte Carlo* (Boston: E. P. Dutton, 1935), 211.

14. Corti, *The Wizard of Monte Carlo*, 212.
15. Dostoyevsky, *The Gambler and Other Stories*, 136.
16. Dostoyevsky, *The Gambler and Other Stories*, 239.
17. Dostoyevsky, *The Gambler and Other Stories*, 264.
18. Dostoyevsky, *The Gambler and Other Stories*, 250.
19. Corti, *The Wizard of Monte Carlo*, 210.
20. Corti, *The Wizard of Monte Carlo*, 55.
21. Corti, *The Wizard of Monte Carlo*, 211.
22. Dostoyevsky, *The Gambler and Other Stories*, 267.
23. Dostoyevsky, *The Gambler and Other Stories*, 265.
24. Georg Simmel, *The Philosophy of Money*, 3rd enl. ed. (London: Routledge, 2004), 256.
25. Simmel, *The Philosophy of Money*, 257.
26. Simmel, *The Philosophy of Money*, 211.
27. Simmel, *The Philosophy of Money*, 443–44. Emphasis in the original.
28. Simmel, *The Philosophy of Money*, 444.
29. Statisticians like Karl Pearson used the results of Monte Carlo's roulette tables—tabulated and published weekly—as a data set that could be used to probe the logic of chance. Karl Pearson, *The Chances of Death: And Other Studies in Evolution* (London: Edward Arnold Publishers, 1897).
30. Sara Ahmed, "Affective Economies," *Social Text* 22, no. 2 (May 14, 2004): 120.
31. Simmel, *The Philosophy of Money*, 269.
32. Simmel, *The Philosophy of Money*, 269–70.
33. Simmel, *Georg Simmel on Individuality and Social Forms*, 304.
34. Simmel, *The Philosophy of Money*, 260.
35. Simmel, *The Philosophy of Money*, 260.
36. Norwood Young, "Systems of Gambling," *National Review* 18 (Dec. 1891): 451.
37. Quoted in Maxim, *Monte Carlo*, 168.
38. Simmel, *The Philosophy of Money*, 327.
39. Simmel, *The Philosophy of Money*, 327–28.
40. Walter Benjamin, *The Arcades Project*, trans. Howard Eiland and Kevin McLaughlin (Cambridge, MA: Harvard University Press, 1999), 489–515, in particular 510–11.
41. Benjamin, *The Arcades Project*, 513.

Bibliography

Ahmed, Sara. "Affective Economies." *Social Text* 22, no. 2 (May 14, 2004): 117–39.
Appadurai, Arjun, ed. *The Social Life of Things: Commodities in Cultural Perspective*. Cambridge, UK: Cambridge University Press, 1986.
Benjamin, Walter. *The Arcades Project*. Translated by Howard Eiland and Kevin McLaughlin. Cambridge, MA: Harvard University Press, 1999.
Brown, Bill. "Thing Theory." *Critical Inquiry* 28, no. 1 (2001): 1–22.
———, ed. *Things*. Chicago: University of Chicago Press, 2004.
Corti, Egon Caesar. *The Wizard of Monte Carlo*. Boston: E. P. Dutton Publishers, 1935.
Dostoyevsky, Fyodor. *The Gambler and Other Stories*. New York: Penguin, 2010.

Maxim, Hiram Stevens. *Monte Carlo: Facts and Fallacies*. London: Grant Richards, 1904.
Pearson, Karl. *The Chances of Death: And Other Studies in Evolution*. London: Edward Arnold Publishers, 1897.
Sala, George Augustus. *Make Your Game, Or, The Adventures of the Stout Gentleman, the Slim Gentleman, and the Man with the Iron Chest: A Narrative of the Rhine and Thereabouts*. London: Ward and Lock, 1860.
Simmel, Georg. *Georg Simmel on Individuality and Social Forms*. Chicago: University of Chicago Press, 1972.
——— *The Philosophy of Money*. 3rd enl. edition. London: Routledge, 2004.
Vallée, Léon. *The International Library of Famous Literature: Selections from the World's Great Writers, Ancient, Mediaeval, and Modern, with Biographical and Explanatory Notes and Critical Essays by Many Eminent Writers*. Vol. XVI. Issued by The Standard, 1899.
Young, Norwood. "Systems of Gambling." *National Review* 18 (Dec. 1891): 449–60.

CHAPTER 9

Emotions and Material Interests in the Sales Talk of German Spa Guides, 1830–1900

HEIKKI LEMPA

In his analysis of Paris in the nineteenth century, Walter Benjamin made a thought experiment: "If the soul of the commodity, which Marx occasionally mentions in jest, existed, it would be the most empathetic ever encountered in the realm of souls, for it would have to see in everyone the buyer in whose hand and house it wants to nestle."[1] The idea of things having soul and agency is, however, not only an experiment or delusion. Works of art, as Caroline van Eck has recently reminded, often move us in a way that justifies a claim that things have agency. They are experienced as living presences, which is often incomprehensible and confusing. "It is this experience," she argues, "that causes the feelings of discomfort, shame and so forth."[2] The premise that things, objects, and physical environments can move us by generating emotions guides the following analysis. The case is German spas in the nineteenth century. Considering their steadily increasing popularity, German spas exercised a special charm over the clientele who hailed not only from German principalities but also from other European regions, Asia, Africa, and the United States. How was this possible? How did the German spas move so many?

To trace the emotions the spas generated in their clientele, it is not enough to look at their living presence, their immediate and unmediated impact on the spa guests, because the spas were not art works but commodities; they satisfied needs. The materiality of emotions, I argue, is not only in the physicality of the things that generate these emotions but also in their embeddedness in the process of satisfying human needs. Wolfgang Fritz Haug has delineated a critical juncture in this process: the interaction between the consumer and the seller. The seller, according to Haug, makes a use-value promise for the commodity he is selling to extract the highest exchange value from the consumer. The consumer is interested in how much the commodity serves as a use-value and satisfies his/her needs. An important function in this relationship is the seller's use of aesthetic imagination that appeals to and moves the consumer.

In his/her sales talk, the seller makes a promise of use-value to the consumer.[3] It is this promise, I argue, that increasingly modified and shaped the needs and emotions of the spa consumers in nineteenth-century Germany. To explore how the use-value promises changed between 1830 and 1900, I take a look at the use of emotions and especially at what Peter and Carol Stearns have called "emotional expectations."[4]

Since the Middle Ages, German spas had established themselves first as sites to do a healing pilgrimage and then, since the late eighteenth century, as places to restore one's health.[5] Between 1830 and 1900, German spas became increasingly commercial enterprises. The spa guides provide a clear testimony. What is intriguing in these guides is the use of emotional language to entice the spa guests' interests. The question is how this language changed between 1830 and 1900. How were emotions shaped in the intersection of three forces: the material, profit interests of the spa operators; the objects—the spa facilities and environments to which the emotions referred; and the curative interests of the patients? The materials I use are the spa guides from five leading spas of the German-speaking world: Carlsbad, Marienbad, Pyrmont, Baden-Baden, and Kissingen. I argue that the classic model of spa guides that projected *Ruhe* (calmness, tranquility) und *Heiterkeit* (cheerfulness but also serenity) was, in the course of the nineteenth century, replaced by the emotions of excitement and pleasure. This transformation was possible because the sales talk, the technique of attaching emotional expectations to material objects—in this case, the spas—changed. I will first take a short look at the early history of the specific genre that generated sales talk for spas: the *Brunnenschriften* (spa literature). Then I will shift the attention to the ways *Brunnenschriften* raised certain emotional expectations in the first half of the nineteenth century. The last section traces the complicated transformation of emotional expectations for spa guests in the late nineteenth century.

The sales talk of spas had a specific genre (*Brunnenschriften*) that had emerged as a well-structured body of knowledge in the sixteenth century. The first *Brunnenschrift* in German that I have located is Alexander Seitz's *Menschlichs lebens art vnd vrsprung vnd wie man daß befristen soll und die Wildbäder beuor zu Oberbaden: Ouch von deren crafft tugent und eygentschafft*, which Adam Petri published in Basel in 1516. The book framed the use of spas and baths in physiology, pharmacology, and therapeutics. This *locus communis* remained dominant until the late eighteenth century. The use of baths and spas was justified in scientific discourse; but at the same time, it was accessible to lay people combining medical knowledge with short historical descriptions, religious advice, proverbial instructions, and personal testimonials. In the late eighteenth-century, the *Brunnenschrift* went through a transformation. In the so-called Hippocratic renaissance, doctors moved away from pharmacological therapies to practical, life-style therapies, especially the ones that manipulated the six nonnatural things of the human body: air, food and drink, awake and sleep, rest and motion, evacuation, and emotions.[6] In dietetic thinking, the nonnaturals were seen as the necessary mediators between the body and its environment. Dietetics promised the cure by offering the restoration of the balance between the body and its environment by regulating the nonnaturals. Emotions, as the sixth nonnatural, were an important tool in this healing.

The chief physician of the Pyrmont spa, Heinrich Matthias Marcard, was a classic representative of dietetic thinking. He saw the nonnaturals as the most important tool of healing because they helped merge the curative treatment with social life. In his two-volume *Beschreibung von Pyrmont*, published in 1785, Marcard reflected the status of the spa doctor as a medical professional and also the primary spokesperson for the entire spa. In the beginning of his book, he described vividly and with great detail the mall of the spa:

> On both sides, there are small boutiques in which one can find all kinds of goods one can think of. The pharmacy, the bookstore, the coffee house, both large halls for entertainment, conversation circles, casino, theater, and the springs; all are here close by. Even the best apartments of the guests are almost all close to the mall, and so are certain conveniences necessary for those who drink waters close by but still unseen. Therefore one finds company on the mall at a good weather from early morning till night. The mall is the stock exchange for Pyrmont where one finds everyone else and where everything starts.[7]

Although all the amenities clearly invited the guests to enjoy their time, Marcard saw them as part of the medical therapy as well. They contributed to healing, which consisted of bathing, drinking of waters, and also following a scheduled regimen. Spa cure was ritualized control of time. In this time regimen, sociability varied with drinking and bathing cures so that, for instance, after the morning drink and breakfast, Marcard recommended, "one should once again undertake exercise (*Bewegung*) when the air is comfortable; when one doesn't take baths, one should go riding or find pleasant conversation in the society that still congregates on the mall, in the boutiques, and the ballrooms. Writing and demanding reading I would not recommend to anybody."[8] The mall was the main site of drinking waters that was combined with slow walking, which spa doctors universally recommended as moderate exercise.[9] But also, the amenities themselves contributed to healing by restoring one's emotional balance, and Marcard claimed, "A place like Pyrmont which situates in a beautiful environment, has pleasant social life, and provides amusements and pastime and where not only the crippled and paralyzed frequent but also cheerful people who are looking for amenities, such an advantage over" the other spas.[10] Joyful, vivid, and pleasant social life was instrumental to one's cure; it was a part of the regimen, not a diversion from it.

It is the dietetic *Brunnenschrift* that provided the platform for sales talk of spas in the first half of the nineteenth century. The rapid growth of spas, both in numbers and visits, induced a flurry of spa guides that tried to inform and entice the public in the Germanic world and beyond—many German spas had a strongly international clientele. It is this point that marks the beginning of my analysis. How did the dietetic *Brunnenschrift* present and appropriate the emotions? And why did it do so? In the center of this genre was the promise of healing embedded in the sixth nonnatural: the emotions. Calmness and tranquility were its main emotions. This was paired with the quest for cheerfulness and serenity. The physician of the Carlsbad spa, Eduard Hlawaczek, is representative in his 1838 recommendation "that above all the patient should distance himself from his customary business circles and avoid everything that could disturb the peace and cheer of his mind."[11] In 1840, Karl Theodor Menke recommended for his patients in Pyrmont spa a morning filled with solemn choral music that "tunes the minds of the drinking patients [*Trinkende*] to a devout and quiet meditation [*frommen und stillen Andacht*] which transfers them gradually through more joyful melodies to the cheerfulness of a lively day."[12] These two examples of the common sales talk reveal the leading emotions; but even more important is their proverbial location. The emotions were in the center of the cure; they were part of the therapy prescribed by the physician; they framed the entire healing process of the patient; they were the antidote to the everyday emotions of agitation and restlessness caused by professional and business worries.[13]

How then did a spa evoke emotions in spa guests? Harris and Sørensen have developed an archaeological model for tracing the emotional impact of an object or space on individuals. An architectural structure or space, they argue, creates an atmosphere in which people are attuned to an emotion created by an affective field.[14] In the case of the Pyrmont spa, the mall as the architectural design combined with the solemn spa music attuned the guests to the affective field that invited them to tranquility. The picture of emotional agency of a space would then be complete. Yet this picture comes with several caveats. It applied only to those who attended the spring and had their drinking cure after six o'clock in the morning; the peasants and poor came often already at 3 a.m. when the orchestra had not started playing.[15] The affective field was different at noon when the music was more cheerful. Finally, we don't know what exactly the spa guests felt, whether they perhaps were annoyed because the music was too solemn or whether they found the spring and the mall too crowded to get attuned to a tranquil mood. Yet they had arrived knowing the emotional expectations so clearly mentioned by the spa doctors.[16] And the atmosphere was there to allow them to get attuned. This was intentional—and the intention was not only healing but also a successful sales talk. All major and many minor German spas were important economic enterprises for their owners—often, local princes whose domains were short of other revenue sources. This was also the case with the Pyrmont spa. Regardless of the financial mismanagement, the spa was a tremendous source of revenue for the County of Waldeck and Pyrmont.[17] It was not the absence of economic motives but their intertwinement with the emotional economy that framed the sales talk at German spas in the early nineteenth century.

Just at the time when German spas started to see the payoff for their work in rapidly increasing numbers of visits, new factors entered the stage and the sales talk began to change. In 1828, Hippolyt Schreiber, an advocate of the Baden-Baden spa, put the Assembly Hall (*Conversationshaus*) in the center of his sales talk: "The large and splendid assembly room and casino makes the center of the society house."[18] Gambling was now an important draw. The modernization of Baden-Baden facilities had started in 1810 when Weinbränner, the main architect of the Duke, made a plan for new buildings and facilities; by the early 1820s, it was mostly finished.[19] The economically most important facility was the casino, which, in 1809, contributed as rent 10,000 guldens, and in 1822, already 27,000 guldens, 2,000 guldens more than the annual budget of the city.[20] All this paid off handsomely. In 1802, Baden-Baden could attract only 282 guests; in 1820, there were 5,138 visits; and then in 1857, the numbers climbed to a staggering 50,097 guests.[21] Baden-Baden had become the most successful spa in the Germanic world, especially popular among the Parisian elite.[22] The success came with a price. The statistics of 1868 showed that of 56,013 guests total, only 3,875 were taking the cure; the rest were finding other attractions: gambling, entertainment, and tourism.[23] This change was echoed in the emotional expectations of the sales talk. Schreiber promoted the town as an exciting place "to which one is transferred as if through a magic touch and the wealth and luxury fill the scene with their loud followers."[24] In 1836, the English version made an even clearer pitch: "You fancy yourself transported into the midst of a large capital, where all springs of enjoyment are copiously flowing for the benefit of the happy."[25] A later English edition from 1867 continued the same sales talk. After a very short description of the waters and their healing qualities, Schreiber described in detail the amusements of the spas: "The centre of the life and gaiety of Baden during the season is of course to be found in the Assembly rooms, which direct all the movements of society. The rooms are devoted to the amusement of the visitors, and no expense or trouble is spared that they may be entirely satisfied with what is here provided for them."[26] Enjoyment, excitement, and happiness had replaced serenity and tranquility.

Baden-Baden was not the norm. At the Austrian spas, Carlsbad and Marienbad among others, gambling remained illegal. But Baden-Baden showed the direction. In 1847, when Baden-Baden's success had become clear, Adalbert Danzer promoted Marienbad as a spa that would fulfill both the expectations of healing and entertainment. It provided the "enjoyment of free air and beautiful nature, the cheerfulness and joy of society, the intercourse with people full of joie de vivre, exercise, outings, music, games, in short entertainment."[27] This new sales talk appealed to the desires of the potential visitors without abandoning the promise of healing—serenity and cheerfulness (*Heiterkeit*) were connected with the expectation of the pleasures of life (*lebensfroh, Lebensfreude*). For Kissingen Hermann Welsch recommended in 1888: "Bad habits, business, grief and sorrow are to be left at home as much as possible; a quiet life, cheerful society and innocent amusements ought not to be undervalued, as being powerful auxiliaries to the beneficial effects of mineral waters."[28] Rodolphe Mannl enticed the potential visitors to Carlsbad by emphasizing that there were amusements—music especially—but that they were all moderate and rational.[29] The emotions of healing were complemented by the appeals to the desires for excitement and pleasure. Importantly, the atmosphere, the architectural structures, did not change. It was the attunement of the guests and the affective fields that had changed—to set new emotional expectations.

In 1872, the rapid growth and financial success of many German spas came to an abrupt end. By federal law, all casinos were closed at German spas. The time of reorientation started. Symptomatic is the Conference of Silesian Spas in December 1873. A large number of administrators and spa doctors attended. After a lively debate, Privy Council Dr. Langer asked the critical question. He wanted a resolution on the question whether "the Silesian baths should be only for healing [*Heilanstalten*] or, at the same time, also pleasant resorts for the healthy."[30] The resolution never came to a vote but later, when the delegate discussed the promotion of Silesian spas, the consensus was to promote the Silesian spas as sites of therapy, "whereas Korn's original idea to advocate them only to tourist was rejected."[31] In the subsequent conferences, the questions of tourism, amusements, amenities, and social arrangements were absent from the debates. The spa doctors set the tone, and topics centered exclusively on healing and healing in a new, medicalized sense that resorted to the new standards of balneology, the chemical composition of the waters, the climate, the diseases, and baths. The traditional dietetic discourse with its six nonnatural things had disappeared.

But the appeals to emotions, the sales talk did not disappear. The minutes of the Conference of Silesian Spas is a case in point. Whereas the doctors set the tone for the official debates and minutes, the administrators took over the section on advertisements appended to the end of the volumes under the title "Improvements." Here, the administrators continued to emphasize the importance of the amenities, the splendor of their assembly halls or reading rooms, or, as an administrator from the Flinsberg spa reported in 1884, that the spa "is visited by foreigners, that is recreational guests, but not by spa guests."[32]

Moreover, when a commission prepared a volume to exhibit German spas at the Paris World Fair in 1900, the official information on 206 German spas was strictly medical. But at the end of the volume, the spas received space for advertisements. In these advertisements, the tone was clear. For instance, the Sool- und Thermalbad Münster advertised its excellent train connections to Frankfurt, Paris, Holland, Cologne, Basel, and Milano. Then followed a long list of diseases that would be treated, a detailed description of environment, and, finally, that there was "a spa house and a park with large playing fields. Hunting. Fishing."[33] Besides healing, the expectations were raised to enjoy and find pleasure in playing and sports.

For the German spas, the genre of the *Brunnenschrift* had come to an end. Thereby also, the delicate connection between emotions of healing and emotions of excitement had come to an end. The vigorous adherence to the healing emotions of calmness, cheerfulness, and serenity, or the careful balancing between entertainment and tranquility, had switched to an open appeal to customer satisfaction. In 1892, the Kissingen spa was advertised as the place of international excitement and fun with sports combined with music and theater.[34] And some twenty years later, Rosenau appealed to the English-speaking customers with an image of a place where "entertainments and amusements are numerous (excellent music, new theatre for light operas and comedies, dancing reunions, good tennis and golf-links); besides, there is a fair opportunity for riding, fishing, hunting, and swimming sport."[35] This is also the time Carlsbad was promoted as the spa for sports and rigorous exercise.[36]

What had happened? The emotions had been externalized from the medical discourse. They had become part of the commodity aesthetics that promised the intensification of the preexisting everyday desires rather than the healing of the pathological emotions of the everyday through an antidote. The spa had been commodified as a new type of product by shifting the emotional expectations from tranquility and serenity to pleasure and excitement, from the emotional antidote to emotional intensification. But why did this happen? Clearly, the rise of capitalist mass markets and tourism explains part of the change. The increase in spa visits in Germany in the nineteenth century is staggering, from a few thousand visitors in 1800 to hundreds of thousands of guests by 1914. The easy access allowed by railroad connections made spas accessible for short term visits and for a clientele that hailed further away than before. The spa discourse had changed. The externalization of emotions from the cure allowed the marketing to associate emotions with different objects and practices than before. And these objects and their emotions were more enticing than the healing emotions of the early nineteenth century. Pleasure and excitement had replaced calmness and serenity. In fact, a certain doubling took place. An aggressive medicalization was complemented with an increasing commodification. The emotionalized sales talk targeted explicitly the tourist who was expected to find pleasure and excitement in the spas. At the same time, the discourse of healing was strictly medicalized, resorting to the de-emotionalized language of balneology.

Heikki Lempa is a Professor of Modern European and German History at Moravian College. His interests are in German cultural and social history, the history of emotions, the body, education, masculinity, and honor. He is the author of *Beyond the Gymnasium: Educating the Middle-Class Bodies in Classical Germany* (2007), and *Bildung der Triebe: Der deutsche Philanthropismus (1768– 1788)* (1993).

Notes

1. Walter Benjamin, "The Paris of the Second Empire in Baudelaire," in *Selected Writings* (Cambridge, MA: Belknap Press, 2006), 31.
2. Caroline van Eck, "Living Statues: Alfred Gell's Art and Agency, Living Presence Response and the Sublime," *Art History* 33 (2010): 646. Van Eck's theory is based on Alfred Gell's anthropology of art. On the emotion generating agency of objects and material spaces, see also an important conceptual intervention by Oliver J. T. Harris and Tim Flohr Sørensen, "Rethinking Emotion and Material Culture," *Archaeological Dialogues* 17 (2010): 145–63.
3. Wolfgang Fritz Haug, *Warenästhetik und kapitalistische Massenkultur (I) "Werbung" und "Konsum:" Systematische Einführung in die Warenästhetik* (Berlin: Argument-Verlag, 1980), esp. Chapters 8, 9, and 10. Haug introduced the concept of "commodity aesthetics" in the 1970s and became a seminal figure in the development of the theory of commodification. It is the link between material interests and aesthetic expression that is so appealing in Haug's theory and its application to the understanding of emotions.
4. Peter N. Stearns and Carol Z. Stearns, "Emotionology: Clarifying the History of Emotions and Emotional Standards," *The American Historical Review* 90 (1985): 815–20. It is critical to understand that both sales talk and emotional expectations did not determine how and whether the clients experienced these emotions.
5. There is an expanding body of scholarship on German spas. See, for instance, Reinhold Kuhnert, *Urbanität auf dem Lande: Badereisen nach Pyrmont im 18. Jahrhundert* (Göttingen: Vandenhoeck & Ruprecht, 1984); Miriam Zadoff, *Next Year in Marienbad: The Lost Worlds of Jewish Spa Culture* (Philadelphia: University of Pennsylvania Press, 2012); and contributions in Susan C. Anderson and Bruce H. Tabb, eds. *Water, Leisure and Culture: European Historical Perspectives* (New York: Berg, 2002).
6. James C. Riley, *The Eighteenth-Century Campaign to Avoid Disease* (London: MacMillan, 1987), 34–44. Cf. Mary Lindemann, *Health and Healing in Eighteenth-Century Germany* (Baltimore: Johns Hopkins University Press, 1996), 65–71. See

also Roy Porter, "Introduction," in *The Popularization of Medicine 1650–1850*, ed. Roy Porter (London: Routledge, 1992), especially 6–10; and in the same volume, Antoinette Emch-Dériaz, "The Non-Naturals Made Easy," 136–39.
7. "Zu beyden Seiten liegen die Boutiquen daran herunter, in denen allerley erdenkbare Dinge feil sind. Die Apotheke, der Buchladen, das Kaffehaus, die beyden großen Säle, die den Lustbarkeiten und den Conversationscirkeln bestimmt sind, und worin die Pharaobank ist, das Comödienhaus und der Brunnen selbst, alles ist hier dichte bey; auch die besten Wohnungen der Fremden sind fast alle ganz nahe um die Allee her, und sogar gewisse für Brunnentrinker sehr nothwendige Bequemlichkeiten sind, zwar ungesehn, aber gleich dabey. Daher, vom frühesten Morgen bis des Abends hinzu, findet man, bey heiterm Himmel, beständig Gesellschaft in der Allee; sie ist die Börse für Pyrmont, wo man jedermann findet und wo man alles abthut," Henrich Matthias Marcard, *Beschreibung von Pyrmont*. Vol. 1 (Leipzig: Weidmanns Erben und Reich, 1784), 15–16. Translation mine.
8. "macht man noch wieder einige Bewegung, wenn die Luft angenehm ist, geht zu Pferde, wenn man nicht badet, oder findet sonst eine angenehme Unterhaltung in der Gesellschaft, die sich gewöhnlich noch in der Allee in den Boutiquen, und in den beyden Ballhäusern verweilet. Schreiben, und mit einiger Anstrengung lesen, rathe ich Niemanden an," Henrich Matthias Marcard, *Beschreibung von Pyrmont*. Vol. 2 (Leipzig: Weidmanns Erben und Reich, 1785), 298. Translation mine.
9. Marcard, *Beschreibung von Pyrmont*. Vol. 2, 303–20, 296–8.
10. "hat auch ein Ort wie Pyrmont, der in einer schönen Gegend liegt, der angenehme Gesellschaft, Unterhaltung und Zerstreuung gewährt, wo nicht blos Krüppel und Lahme hinkommen, sondern auch fröhliche Menschen, die Vergnügungen suchen, . . . so viel Vorzügen vor den Bädern," Marcard, *Beschreibung von Pyrmont*. Vol. 2, 313. Translation mine.
11. "Vor allem andern hat sich der Kranke aus seinem früher gewohnten Geschäftskreise heraus zu reissen, und alles zu vermeiden, was die Ruhe und Heiterkeit seines Gemüths stören könnte," Eduard Hlawaczek, *Karlsbad in medicinischer, pitoresker und geselliger Beziehung: Für Kurgäste* (Prague: Kronbergers Wittwe und Weber, 1838), 42. Translation mine.
12. "stimmt die Gemüther der Trinkenden zu einer frommen und stillen Andacht, die sie allmälig, durch fröhlichere Melodien, zur Heiterkeit des regsameren Tages hinüberführet," Karl Theodor Menke, *Pyrmont und seine Umgebungen mit besonderer Hinsicht auf seine Mineralquellen; historisch, geographisch, physikalisch und medicinisch dargestellt* (Pyrmont: Georg Uslar, 1840), 144. Translation mine. Although Menke's description evokes the emotional language of German classicism with its emphasis on peace and tranquility, the taxonomy here is from earlier dietetic tradition that we can find, for instance, in Marcard, *Beschreibung von Pyrmont*. Vol. 1, 52–54.
13. Menke, *Pyrmont und seine Umgebungen*, 318.
14. Harris and Sørensen, "Rethinking Emotion," 153.
15. Menke, *Pyrmont und seine Umgebungen*, 445–48. Cf. Henrich Matthias Marcard, *Kleines Pyrmonter Brunnenbuch für Curgäste zu Hause und an der Quelle* (Pyrmont: Helwingsche Buchhandlung, 1805), 95–107; and Karl Friedrich Heinrich Straß, *Pyrmont und dessen Umgebungen: Ein Taschenbuch für Curgäste und Reisende. Aus Dankbarkeit gegen die kräftigenden Quellen des herrlichen Bades* (Pyrmont: Georg Uslar, 1850), 42–45. In Pyrmont, the peasants could use the spring from 4 to 6 a.m.

16. Heinrich Laube was in his early spa experiences in the 1830s and everyone was very much aware of the prescriptions and regimens when he, on his second day, missed the early drinking. Heinrich Laube, *Reisenovellen I*. Vol. 4. of *Gesammelte Werke* (Leipzig: Max Hesse, 1908), 99. See also Rudolf von Jhering who arrived on 7 August 1854 in Kissingen to heal his melancholy, *Briefe und Erinnerungen 1852–1868* (Berlin: H. W. Müller, 1907), 36.
17. Kuhnert, *Urbanität auf dem Lande*, 100–3. On the financial impact of the Ems spa, see Hermann Sommer, *Zur Kur nach Ems: Ein Beitrag zur Geschichte der Badereise von 1830 bis 1914* (Stuttgart: Franz Steiner Verlag, 1999), 42–46. On Wiesbaden and Carlsbad, see Burkhard Fuhs, *Mondäne Orte einer vornehmen Gesellschaft: Kultur und Geschichte der Kurstädte 1700–1900* (Hildesheim: Georg Olms Verlag, 1992), 368.
18. "Die Mitte des neuen Gesellschaftshauses bildet der große, prächtige Gesellschafts- und Spielsal," Hippolyt Schreiber, *Baden im Großherzogthum und seine Umgebungen: Ein Führer für Reisende* (Carlsruhe und Baden: Verlag der D. R. Marx'schen Buchhandlung, 1828), 25. Translation mine.
19. Rolf Gustav Haebler, *Geschichte der Stadt und des Kurortes Baden-Baden* (Baden-Baden, W. Schmidt, 1969), 41.
20. Haebler, *Geschichte der Stadt*, 42.
21. Haebler, *Geschichte der Stadt*, 42, 104.
22. Haebler, *Geschichte der Stadt*, 72.
23. Haebler, *Geschichte der Stadt*, 104.
24. "wie durch einen Zauberschlag, in den Mittelpunkt einer glänzenden Hauptstadt versetzt, und der Reichthum und Luxus hüllen mit ihrem lärmenden Gefolge die Scene," Schreiber, *Baden*, 26. Translation mine.
25. Hippolyt Schreiber, *A New Guide through Baden and Its Environs for Travelers and Visitors: Together with a History of the Town* (Carlsruhe and Baden: J. Velten, 1836), 38.
26. Hippiolytus Schreiber, *A Guidebook through the Town and Neighbourhood of Baden-Baden* (Baden: D. R. Marx, 1867), 14–16.
27. "Genuss der freien Luft und schönen Natur, Heiterkeit, Fröhlichkeit der Gesellschaft, Umgang mit lebensfrohen Menschen, Bewegung, Lustfahrten, Musik, Spiele, kurz einerseits Zerstreuungen," Adalbert Danzer, *Topographie von Marienbad als Führer im Curorte selbst und in den Umgebungen: Für Badegäste* (Prague: Ignaz Jackowitz, 1847), 109. Translation mine.
28. Hermann Welsch, *The Springs and Baths of Kissingen* (Kissingen: Author, 1888), 58.
29. Rodolphe Mannl, *Carlsbad in Bohemia and Its Mineral Springs: A Guide of Strangers at the Most Reputed Spa of Germany* (Carlsbad: Brothers Franieck, 1858), 134.
30. "Sollen die schlesischen Bäder nur Heilanstalten sein, oder auch gleichzeitig angenehme Aufenthaltsorte für Gesunde"? *Die Verhandlungen des Schlesischen Bädertages der II. Sitzung am 4. Dezember 1873 zu Breslau*, ed. Paul Dengler (Reinerz: Commissions-Verlag der Platz'schen Buchhandlung, 1874), 3. Translation mine.
31. "während die ursprüngliche Korn'sche Absicht, dieselben nur für Touristen zu beschreiben, fallen gelassen wurde," *Die Verhandlungen des Schlesischen Bädertages*, 12. Translation mine.
32. "von Fremden, d.h. von Erholungsgästen, nicht aber von Kurgästen besucht sein wird," *Der zwölfte schlesische Bädertag und seine Verhandlungen am 15. December 1883 nebst dem Medizinisch-statistischen General-Berichte, dem Bericht über die Witterungs-*

Verhältnisse im Sommer 1883, dem statistischen Vewaltungs-Berichte über die schlesischen Bäder für die Saison 1883 und einer colorirten Karte (Reinerz: Verlag des schlesischen Bädertages, 1884), 153. Translation mine.

33. "Curhaus und -Park mit grossen Spielplätzen. Jagd. Fischerei," in *Deutschlands Heilquellen und Bäder = Bains et sources minérales d'Allemagne = The baths and mineral springs of Germany*, ed. Kaiserliches Gesundheits-Amt of Berlin (Berlin: Seehagen, 1900), 290.

34. Anonymous, *Kissingen Spa: The International Health-Resort, in Its Medical and Social Aspects* (Munich: Kurverein Bad Kissingen, 1892), 54.

35. Albert Rosenau, *Bad Kissingen as a Health Resort, with Notes on the Diseases Most Benefited by Its Baths and Mineral Waters* (London: Baillière, 1913), 30.

36. Edward Stephanides, *Karlsbad: Seine Thermen und übrigen Heilfactoren deren Bedeutung, Wirkung und Anwendung bei verschiedenen chronischen Krankheiten* (Karlsbad: Hermann Jakob, 1888), 54.

Bibliography

Anderson, Susan C., and Bruce H. Tabb, eds. *Water, Leisure and Culture: European Historical Perspectives*. New York: Berg, 2002.

Anonymous. *Kissingen Spa: The International Health-Resort, in Its Medical and Social Aspects*. Munich: Kurverein Bad Kissingen, 1892.

Benjamin, Walter. "The Paris of the Second Empire in Baudelaire." In *Selected Writings*. Cambridge, MA: Belknap Press, 2006.

"Curhaus und -Park mit grossen Spielplätzen. Jagd. Fischerei." In *Deutschlands Heilquellen und Bäder = Bains et sources minérales d'Allemagne = The baths and mineral springs of Germany*, edited by Kaiserliches Gesundheits-Amt of Berlin, 290. Berlin: Seehagen, 1900.

Danzer, Adalbert. *Topographie von Marienbad als Führer im Curorte selbst und in den Umgebungen: Für Badegäste*. Prague: Ignaz Jackowitz, 1847.

Der zwölfte schlesische Bädertag und seine Verhandlungen am 15. December 1883 nebst dem Medizinisch-statistischen General-Berichte, dem Bericht über die Witterungs-Verhältnisse im Sommer 1883, dem statistischen Vewaltungs-Berichte über die schlesischen Bäder für die Saison 1883 und einer colorirten Karte. Reinerz: Verlag des schlesischen Bädertages, 1884.

Die Verhandlungen des Schlesischen Bädertages der II. Sitzung am 4. Dezember 1873 zu Breslau, edited by Paul Dengler. Reinerz: Commissions-Verlag der Platz'schen Buchhandlung, 1874.

Emch-Dériaz, Antoinette. "The Non-Naturals Made Easy." In *The Popularization of Medicine, 1650–1850*, edited by Roy Porter, 136–39. London: Routledge, 1992.

Fuhs, Burkhard. *Mondäne Orte einer vornehmen Gesellschaft: Kultur und Geschichte der Kurstädte 1700–1900*. Hildesheim: Georg Olms Verlag, 1992.

Haebler, Rolf Gustav. *Geschichte der Stadt und des Kurortes Baden-Baden*. Baden-Baden: W. Schmidt, 1969.

Harris, Oliver J. T., and Tim Flohr Sørensen. "Rethinking Emotion and Material Culture." *Archaeological Dialogues* 17 (2010): 145–63.

Haug, Wolfgang Fritz. *Warenästhetik und kapitalistische Massenkultur (I) "Werbung" und "Konsum:" Systematische Einführung in die Warenästhetik.* Berlin: Argument-Verlag, 1980.

Hlawaczek, Eduard. *Karlsbad in medicinischer, pitoresker und geselliger Beziehung: Für Kurgäste.* Prague: Kronbergers Wittwe und Weber, 1838.

Kuhnert, Reinhold. *Urbanität auf dem Lande: Badereisen nach Pyrmont im 18. Jahrhundert.* Göttingen: Vandenhoeck & Ruprecht, 1984.

Laube, Heinrich. *Reisenovellen I.* Vol. 4 of *Gesammelte Werke.* Leipzig: Max Hesse, 1908.

Lindemann, Mary. *Health and Healing in Eighteenth-Century Germany.* Baltimore: Johns Hopkins University Press, 1996.

Mannl, Rodolphe. *Carlsbad in Bohemia and Its Mineral Springs: A Guide of Strangers at the Most Reputed Spa of Germany.* Carlsbad: Brothers Franieck, 1858.

Marcard, Henrich Matthias. *Beschreibung von Pyrmont.* Vol. 1. Leipzig: Weidmanns Erben und Reich, 1784.

——— *Beschreibung von Pyrmont.* Vol. 2. Leipzig: Weidmanns Erben und Reich, 1785.

——— *Kleines Pyrmonter Brunnenbuch für Curgäste zu Hause und an der Quelle.* Pyrmont: Helwingsche Buchhandlung, 1805.

Menke, Karl Theodor. *Pyrmont und seine Umgebungen mit besonderer Hinsicht auf seine Mineralquellen; historisch, geographisch, physikalisch und medicinisch dargestellt.* Pyrmont: Georg Uslar, 1840.

Porter, Roy. "Introduction." In *The Popularization of Medicine 1650–1850*, edited by Roy Porter. London: Routledge, 1992.

Riley, James C. *The Eighteenth-Century Campaign to Avoid Disease.* London: MacMillan, 1987.

Rosenau, Albert. *Bad Kissingen as a Health Resort, with Notes on the Diseases Most Benefited by Its Baths and Mineral Waters.* London: Baillière, 1913.

Schreiber, Hippolyt. *Baden im Großherzogthum und seine Umgebungen: Ein Führer für Reisende.* Carlsruhe und Baden: Verlag der D. R. Marx'schen Buchhandlung, 1828.

——— *A Guidebook through the Town and Neighbourhood of Baden-Baden.* Baden: D. R. Marx, 1867.

——— *A New Guide through Baden and Its Environs for Travelers and Visitors: Together with a History of the Town.* Carlsruhe and Baden: J. Velten, 1836.

Sommer, Hermann. *Zur Kur nach Em: Ein Beitrag zur Geschichte der Badereise von 1830 bis 1914.* Stuttgart: Franz Steiner Verlag, 1999.

Stearns, Peter N., and Carol Z. Stearns. "Emotionology: Clarifying the History of Emotions and Emotional Standards." *The American Historical Review* 90 (1985): 813–36.

Stephanides, Edward. *Karlsbad: Seine Thermen und übrigen Heilfactoren deren Bedeutung, Wirkung und Anwendung bei verschiedenen chronischen Krankheiten*. Karlsbad: Hermann Jakob, 1888.

Straß, Karl Friedrich Heinrich. *Pyrmont und dessen Umgebungen: Ein Taschenbuch für Curgäste und Reisende. Aus Dankbarkeit gegen die kräftigenden Quellen des herrlichen Bades*. Pyrmont: Georg Uslar, 1850.

van Eck, Caroline. "Living Statues: Alfred Gell's Art and Agency, Living Presence Response and the Sublime." *Art History* 33 (2010): 642–59.

von Jhering, Rudolf. *Briefe und Erinnerungen 1852–1868*. Berlin: H. W. Müller, 1907.

Welsch, Hermann. *The Springs and Baths of Kissingen*. Kissingen: Author, 1888.

Zadoff, Miriam. *Next Year in Marienbad: The Lost Worlds of Jewish Spa Culture*. Philadelphia: University of Pennsylvania Press, 2012.

PART III

Emotions and Things

CHAPTER 10

The Paper Bird
Emotions and Things in the Pedagogy of Johann Heinrich Pestalozzi and Friedrich Fröbel

ANN TAYLOR ALLEN

During the Romantic Era of the early nineteenth century, emotions transported some to fantastic realms of the imagination but bound others more closely to home, soil, and everyday objects. The Swiss educator Johann Heinrich Pestalozzi was among the latter. In his book *How Gertrude Teaches Her Children* (first published in 1801), he referred his readers to a homely object taken from the material culture of Swiss peasants. We are not so advanced, he told them, as the "Appenzell woman, who hangs a large paper bird, painted with many colors, over her child's cradle" during the first three weeks of life and thus "begins the process by which art must begin to bring natural objects into the child's firm and clear consciousness."[1] For the mother and child, the paper bird is not merely a passive object of observation, but an active agent that orients the child's spatial perceptions and cognitive abilities. Pestalozzi therefore called it a "sacred object" that was endowed with the power to initiate that most important of all creative processes: the development of the self.[2]

Although we usually understand emotions chiefly as feelings that arise in the inner world of the individual psyche, emotions also shape interactions with the environment, including material things.[3] When the mother used a material thing—the paper bird—to teach her child about the world, she channeled her emotion—maternal love—into a pedagogical practice. Pestalozzi and his student Friedrich Fröbel, who became famous as the creator of the kindergarten, were among the most internationally influential of all nineteenth-century educators. Both rejected traditional teaching methods based on stern discipline and theoretical learning. Instead, they called on teachers to continue the work of mothers by introducing children to the world of objects in a secure and loving environment. Separated in age by a generation, the pedagogues developed their ideas during two successive eras: Pestalozzi (1746–1827) during the French Revolution of 1789 and the Napoleonic and restoration periods, and Fröbel (1782–1852) during the German *Vormärz* (the period leading up to the 1848 revolutions).

Pestalozzi was reluctant to acknowledge his intellectual debts—he once boasted that he had read no books in thirty years—but in fact he shared many ideas with his own and past generations of educators.[4] He was born in Zurich in 1746, began as an educator of local peasant children, and later became internationally famous as the author of treatises on pedagogy, ethics, and politics and as a trainer of teachers.[5] Pestalozzi was deeply influenced by his compatriot Jean-Jacques Rousseau, whose *Émile*—a novel about a boy whose education was driven by his own intellectual curiosity rather than a set curriculum—was the era's most widely read treatise on pedagogy and child-rearing.[6] Pestalozzi also owed much to the philosophers John Locke and Immanuel Kant as well as to the educational reformers known as the Philanthropists (*Philanthropen*) who developed and popularized Rousseau's pedagogy in the German-speaking world. He agreed with these authorities that all knowledge originated in the senses; that conventional teaching methods that required children to memorize material that was meaningless to them were worse than useless; that corporal punishment in schools was cruel; and that teaching was most effective when it mobilized children's energy and curiosity.[7]

Pestalozzi adapted these familiar ideas to a new context—the turbulent history of the French Revolution and the Napoleonic era. Though initially optimistic about the French Revolution's promise of liberty, equality, and fraternity, he concluded from the horrors of the Reign of Terror and the Napoleonic wars (including Napoleon's invasion of Switzerland) that the promise had been betrayed. Pestalozzi blamed this tragic outcome largely on a faulty educational system that, in France and the rest of Europe, had created the narrow intellectual elite of the Enlightenment "republic of letters" and left the masses in ignorance. In Pestalozzi's view, the Enlightenment intellectuals were mere "letter men," who derived their knowledge from books rather than life experience. As the ideologues of the revolution, they had promoted abstract principles (such as those contained in the *Declaration of the Rights of Man and Citizen*), without concern for the human consequences of their actions. Despite their claims to virtue, such leaders spoke only "lies and folly," and their words encouraged fanaticism and hatred more than liberty and progress.[8] Pestalozzi therefore insisted that a primary purpose of education must be to inculcate a different kind of ethical consciousness—one that was based on practical as well as theoretical knowledge and affirmed compassion and human ties.

What kind of education could create such a consciousness? Although he shared Rousseau's conviction that children were gifted with energy and curiosity, Pestalozzi did not agree that they were by nature so good that if removed from the corruption of society they could almost teach themselves. Education, he insisted, was the only bulwark against lawlessness and disorder. Pestalozzi also developed Rousseau's epistemology, which was largely based on Locke's idea that knowledge came entirely through the senses. Mere sense perception was, in Pestalozzi's view, an essential but not sufficient means of learning, for sensory data entered the mind in a disordered and chaotic state (what William James later called "blooming, buzzing confusion").[9] Like Kant, Pestalozzi argued that the human mind had faculties for ordering and assessing sense perceptions, and that the aim of education was to develop those faculties.[10]

Pestalozzi held that education must start with the first sensory perceptions, and therefore in the first days of life. The mother (Pestalozzi hardly mentioned any other parent or caretaker) was therefore the first teacher. This view owed something to eighteenth-century pedagogical theories. Philosophers such as John Locke extolled the family as the source of benevolent and socially constructive behavior.[11] Rousseau exhorted mothers to be the educators of their children and advised them to train infants' senses by encouraging them to handle and manipulate objects.[12] Some of the Philanthropists also instructed mothers on the raising of infants. The pedagogue Joachim Heinrich Campe, though chiefly concerned with the hygienic management of pregnancy and lactation, anticipated Pestalozzi by portraying the mother as the child's first teacher who guided the development of sensory perceptions, speech, and the social sense.[13]

All these pedagogues, however, took a highly cautious and sometimes even negative view of motherly love, which they regarded as yet another symptom of female moral weakness and irrationality. Rousseau and Campe believed that too much affection was a danger to the child's moral development, and admonished mothers to avoid spoiling by exercising "a wise severity."[14] Both also assumed that the mother's duties were exclusively domestic and saw no way to apply nurturing skills outside the home.[15]

Not until the revolutionary era of the late eighteenth century did moralists, including some feminists such as Mary Wollstonecraft and the female activists of the French Revolution, upgrade the mother's prestige by making her responsible for the vital task of educating children in the duties and responsibilities of citizenship. This was the version of the maternal role that Pestalozzi incorporated into his pedagogy.[16]

Although he, too, warned against spoiling, Pestalozzi did not regard maternal love as a source of moral corruption, but rather as the indispensable basis of all ethical as well as cognitive development. "Maternal love," he wrote to his British colleague Greaves, was "the most powerful agent" and "the primitive motive in early education."[17] Pestalozzi shared his theoretical understanding of emotions with Kant. Both held that human nature had both an animal and a spiritual side. Emotions (*Gefühle*), which arose in response to pleasure and pain, originated in the animal nature, which craved only the satisfaction of physical needs. The child's first positive emotion toward the mother was an intense animal pleasure when fed and comforted. Though originally selfish, however, emotions also empowered the spiritual side of human nature, including the all-important capacity for altruism.[18] The child's pleasure in the mother's presence gave rise to the first experience of love. "The child knows the footstep of the mother, it smiles at her shadow, it loves whoever looks like her . . . it smiles at the mother's form, it smiles at the human form." The child who learned to love the mother learned first to love the people whom she loved, and then the community of which they were a part. Similarly, the child's feeling of responsibility toward the mother laid the foundation for a broader civic consciousness. The mother also opened the way to the highest of all ethical commitments, religious faith, by providing an earthly premonition of divine love.[19]

What was the connection between maternal love and material objects? Pestalozzi saw that infants were endowed with an intense and unceasing drive to explore their material environment. Babies acquired their first knowledge of the world when they reached for, touched, and manipulated things. Mothers did not need to force children to learn, but only to direct and gently supervise their development. The mother provided a secure environment for the exploration of a new and sometimes frightening world—an environment in which learning was a joyous and spontaneous process. "Now there is an object that the child has never seen; it is astonished, it is afraid, it cries; the mother clasps the child to her breast . . . and the weeping stops; the object appears again—the mother holds the child in her sheltering arms and smiles—now the child does not weep but returns the mother's smile."[20]

By explaining the function, the origin, the attributes, and the uses of each object, the mother laid the foundation for later education in many areas: the "mother tongue," mathematics, science, craft skills. Wise mothers nurtured "the first traces . . . of that mental activity which will hereafter employ itself in the numberless observations or combinations of events, or in the search for their hidden causes."[21] Pestalozzi's pedagogy was based on an idealized conception of the peasant household, which during his era was a center of agricultural and artisanal as well as domestic work. In this rich environment, children could develop all their powers—in a famous and much-quoted phrase, "head, heart, and hand."[22]

Pestalozzi acknowledged that schooling outside the home was necessary for older children, but indignantly rejected the traditional schools of his era. Schools killed children's spontaneous love of learning by confining them in "stinking rooms," engaging them in the "contemplation of unattractive and monotonous letters," and forcing them to learn material that they did not understand (such as Latin grammar or the catechism) by shaming or beating them. "In all civilized countries, cruelty of every description is forbidden. . . . How, then, comes cruelty to children to be so generally overlooked, or rather thought a matter of course?" he asked.[23] Continuing a campaign for educational reform that had begun in the eighteenth century, he called such schools instruments of tyranny that stunted individual initiative by using violence to enforce meaningless learning.[24]

In order to develop new methods and train teachers to use them, Pestalozzi set up teacher-training institutes in Burgdorf (1800–4) and in Yverdon (1804–25), which offered instruction to teachers and provided experimental schools in which they could put theories into practice. The role-model that Pestalozzi prescribed for these student teachers was not that of the stern, punitive schoolmaster, but that of the mother. In Pestalozzi's popular novel entitled *Leonard and Gertrude*, Gertrude was a fictional peasant mother who taught the village children reading, writing, household tasks, and cotton-spinning. The male teacher of the village school visited Gertrude and modeled his classroom as nearly as possible on her methods.[25] By prescribing behavior which the culture defined as female for teachers of both sexes, Pestalozzi helped to transform the traditionally male image of pedagogical authority.

How did Pestalozzi's method work out in practice? Because he himself never developed his techniques systematically and failed to formulate lesson plans, most of what we know about his actual pedagogical comes from accounts written by the diverse group of educators who flocked to his training institute at Yverdon from many different nations—the German lands, France, Britain, the United States, Russia, and others.[26]

Pestalozzi insisted that all schooling, at whatever level, must derive its energy from love. He himself occasionally administered corporal punishment, but forbade it to his assistants, and also discouraged shaming.[27] Methods that encouraged competition and emulation among children, though popular among some contemporary educators, were in Pestalozzi's view designed to promote only selfish ambition rather than a true desire to learn. Students must be motivated by interest in the subject and by love for the teacher.[28] Emotional engagement was crucial. If their students failed, teachers must blame themselves for the lack of "that real interest in the task of instruction" and of the appropriate emotional expression: "kind words and kinder feelings—the very expression of the features and the glance of the eye," which are "never lost upon children."[29]

Like mothers, teachers guided their pupils' development and stimulated energy and curiosity in learners of all ages. Tangible, visible, or familiar examples provided a basis for teaching theoretical concepts. When objects were lacking, the teachers were allowed to use pictures, but an object that children could touch and manipulate was always preferable. While other progressive educators of the time had also encouraged observation, Pestalozzi integrated it more systematically into a pedagogical method.[30] Describing and manipulating objects taught concepts such as form (description), language (vocabulary), and number, and also developed manual coordination.

Pestalozzi's French student Roger Guimps praised "the very practical inventions by which he [Pestalozzi] sought to make teaching easier." Children learned reading by using movable alphabet blocks; arithmetic by counting familiar objects; fractions by looking at "squares, some whole, others divided into two, three, or even ten parts."[31] Teachers used these concrete objects to demonstrate theoretical concepts. In other areas, too, teachers began on the level of the near and familiar and progressed to a higher level of complexity and abstraction. Children learned speaking before reading, and the mother tongue before other languages such as Latin.[32] Familiar songs introduced children to notation and harmony. "Indeed, singing was one of our chief sources of pleasure in the Institute," recollected Guimps. "We sang everywhere . . . and this singing together contributed in no small measure to the harmony and good feeling that prevailed among us."[33]

The same methods were also used to teach more advanced students who based theoretical learning on concrete observation. For example, teachers at Yverdon led students on hikes through the striking Alpine valley where the school was located, and then required them to draw maps of the area they had seen. Exploration of the natural environment introduced the general principles of geology, geography, and natural history, and also educated the emotions by expanding the attachment to home and family to include a wider love for the homeland or nation.[34]

Although Pestalozzi rejected much of the Enlightenment heritage because he held it responsible for the horrors of the French Revolution, he was in his own way a revolutionary. Rousseau had detested all schools, and the Philanthropists had educated chiefly the sons of gentlemen. Pestalozzi, by contrast, became his era's most famous and charismatic advocate of universal education for children regardless of gender, religion, and class. Earlier generations had found this idea inconceivable, but in the early nineteenth century, it gained wider acceptance among progressive educators. Educational opportunity, Pestalozzi insisted, must not depend on class: both manual and academic training must be part of a curriculum designed for all. "We must bear in mind, that whatever class of society a pupil may belong to, whatever calling he may be intended for, there are certain faculties common to all. . . . We have no right to withhold from anyone the opportunities of developing all their faculties," he wrote to his friend Greaves.[35]

Pestalozzi included girls among the children who had a right to develop all their faculties. Yverdon, Pestalozzi's most famous training institute, began as an all-male community, but expanded in 1806 to include a school for girls headed by the Zurich teacher Rosette Kasthofer (after her marriage to one of Pestalozzi's colleagues, Niederer-Kasthofer).[36] Although Pestalozzi specified that the curriculum should prepare girls for their most important profession, motherhood, he also called for the training of young women as teachers.[37] In 1806, another teacher, Betty Gleim, introduced Pestalozzian methods into her girls' school in Bremen.[38] These educators claimed that the emotional capacities that the culture identified as female and maternal made women more qualified than men to teach girls and young children. Crucially, they attributed these gifts not only to biological mothers, but also to the large group of unmarried and childless women who aspired to careers in teaching.[39] Pestalozzi's female colleagues were among the earliest educators to challenge the male domination of the teaching profession. The organized women's movements that emerged later in the century continued this challenge by working to open educational and professional opportunities to women teachers.[40]

In 1806, Friedrich Fröbel, born the son of a pastor in the town of Oberweissbach in Thuringia, set out for Switzerland to study with the now famous Pestalozzi, and he returned several times in subsequent years along with two of his pupils. Fröbel accepted many of his Swiss colleague's ideas. Because the loss of his own mother had overshadowed his childhood, Fröbel felt great sympathy for Pestalozzi's exalted view of the mother–child bond. The student teacher also shared his master's preference for objects over words in the classroom.[41]

Separated from Pestalozzi by an entire generation, however, Fröbel based his pedagogy on some new developments in science and philosophy to which his rather eclectic academic studies had exposed him. He owed his understanding of the relationship of the human individual to the material world largely to the idealist philosopher Friedrich Wilhelm Joseph Schelling. Whereas Kant and Pestalozzi had assumed that the individual mind was separate from the material world and observed it objectively, Schelling's "natural philosophy" (*Naturphilosophie*) held that the human individual was part of an immense organism that encompassed all nature, animate and inanimate. All elements of this organism were shaped by the same evolutionary processes and shared a common consciousness, of which human self-consciousness was the highest stage. Human beings could know the material world intuitively because they belonged to it.[42]

Fröbel became most famous as the inventor of the kindergarten, which he began to develop in Blankenburg, Thuringia, in 1837 and named in 1840. In addition to this institution, however, he also created songs, games, and toys to be used by mothers in the home. These were contained in a book of verses, songs, and pictures entitled *Mother- and Nursery Songs*, which became one of his most popular works and was often used in kindergartens.[43] The book began with a paean to the mother-love that initiated and guided the learning process. It then provided mothers with a series of games, accompanied by songs, pictures, and diagrams, that stimulated children's cognitive, emotional, and physical development in the first years of life.

The text introduced material things not merely as instruments, but as active participants in the learning process. One song instructed children, under their mother's guidance, to imitate a weather vane by moving their hands. The weather vane taught not only physical coordination but also the emotion of joy. "Baby can bend his hand and learn, to get joy at every turn." Similarly, a clock taught children not only to move their arms in imitation of the pendulum, but also to appreciate moral values such as punctuality. The child addressed the clock, imploring it never to "tell me wrong, But [tell] the right time by your song." Love pervaded the natural and material worlds. Things felt empathy with people: for example a compassionate moon comforted a child, promising that although it could not come for a visit it would send its "clear and silvery light, to make you glad, my little Child." A moon that felt sympathy did not seem strange to children, whose keen intuition enabled them to feel connections that the duller senses of adults could no longer recognize. "Do not disturb the child in his sweet dreams," Fröbel admonished mothers. "At one with all the universe he seems."[44]

The kindergarten offered a half-day program that admitted children between about three and six years of age (German children started elementary school at seven). Children learned chiefly from exercises using objects. Continuing the work of Pestalozzi, who had provided material teaching aids, Fröbel designed a complex and ingenious set of educational playthings. Unlike such typical playthings of the era as dolls and hobby-horses, these toys were abstract. Fröbel drew on his studies of mathematics and crystallography to design a set of blocks of many shapes, which children could put together to create various forms. Other playthings such as beads, sticks, puzzles, and colored paper developed spatial perceptions and manual dexterity.[45]

Fröbel's toys taught manual, quantitative, and cognitive skills, but also communicated philosophical concepts that he believed children could understand intuitively. He prescribed a specific sequence of activities, or "occupations." Children began by playing with the ball, symbol of oneness, and then went on to such toys as blocks and puzzles—concrete objects designed to demonstrate theoretical concepts such as geometrical shapes, spatial relationships, and the relationship of parts to the whole. The curriculum was not limited to such sedentary and intellectual activities. Group games that required children to take turns taught social skills; songs and stories appealed to the imagination; gardening and animal care encouraged respect for nature. There was, however, no formal academic instruction and (very unusually for the time) no prescribed religious teaching. Many of the first kindergartens admitted children of all religions—Catholics, Protestants, and Jews.[46]

Like Pestalozzi, Fröbel insisted that teaching must be motherly, but his conception of maternal pedagogy reflected the changes in women's status and self-consciousness that had occurred over the forty years since Pestalozzi had founded his first schools. The Swiss educator had connected nurturing gifts with biological motherhood, and had therefore insisted that the first education must take place in the family. Since then, however, a substantial group of educated women had followed the example first set by Pestalozzi's female disciples and claimed that all women possessed maternal gifts that they could use in two socially valuable ways: in the home as mothers or outside it as teachers. In the 1830s, disciples of the French utopian socialists Saint Simon and Fourier admonished women to emerge from their domestic confinement and to uplift society through their nurturing and compassionate influence.[47] The dissenting German religious movements known as the Free Congregations (*Freie Gemeinde*), which sponsored many early kindergartens, incorporated this and other utopian aspirations into their theology and social-reform activism.[48]

Fröbel had originally supposed that the teachers in the kindergartens, as in the great majority of German elementary schools, would be men. When his male colleagues showed little interest in his methods, however, he called on "all German women and maidens" to "aid in the founding of a "general institution for the nurture of child life until school age."[49] He praised the mostly unmarried women who became kindergarten teachers for a gift that he and his disciples called "spiritual motherhood." This gift, though innate, was not purely instinctual, but required development and training. Fröbel set up the first courses that trained kindergartners (as the teachers, not the pupils were called) for their calling.[50]

This proved to be a major step in the process that Pestalozzi's female disciples had begun—the regendering of teaching. The educated women of the German-speaking world were particularly in need of professional opportunities because German male elementary school teachers resisted the feminization of their profession (a process that had already begun in other countries) and public schools hired few women.[51] German kindergartners created one of the first distinctively female professions that offered women, particularly single women and widows, the opportunity both to engage in useful work and (sometimes) to achieve economic independence and personal autonomy.[52]

The influence of Pestalozzi and Fröbel was by no means confined to the German-speaking world, but was and remains international. According to the American John Dewey, probably the best-known educator of the twentieth century, these pedagogues "influenced school practice more than any other modern educators."[53] Their theories and methods gained global popularity because they both reflected and shaped two major historical developments of the nineteenth and twentieth centuries.

The first was the rise of public schools and mass education. Educational reformers usually cited Pestalozzi to support the founding of public school systems in the nineteenth century, first in Prussia and Denmark and then throughout Europe and North America. The kindergarten launched a new method of early childhood education, which a movement led chiefly by women brought to most European countries and North American by the 1870s and to many non-Western countries by 1900.[54]

The second was the development of curricula and methods for these school systems, and here the relationship of emotions and objects was of central importance. The nineteenth-century educators who founded public school systems shared the German educators' dissatisfaction with traditional methods that taught abstruse material that most students found irrelevant to their lives after school. These educational reformers worked to create a new kind of school that cultivated more practical competence, including work skills, and trained children in the responsibilities of citizenship. The use of objects and hands-on experience in teaching could fit into vocational as well as academic programs. Humane pedagogy, the reformers insisted, produced good citizens by encouraging social responsibility, individual initiative, and cooperation.[55]

"Only life educates," said Pestalozzi in his last major work, *Swan Song* (*Schwanengesang*), and this was surely the thought that guided his own and Fröbel's work.[56] Traditional methods, they charged, produced one-sidedly intellectual people who were alienated from life and its practical and emotional demands. A learning process that integrated theoretical and practical learning and included the heart and the hand along with the head could encompass the full range of life experience—family and community, child-rearing, social responsibility, nature, science, music, industry, manual and intellectual work. Such pedagogy took learning out of the classroom and into the wider world. It also provided a basis for extending education backward into infancy and forward into adulthood, for life never stops educating. In the years since these two great teachers lived, educators have discussed, modified, and often discarded their theories. The questions that they raised—What should be the relationship of teacher and student? How do children learn? What is the role of the emotions in learning? At what age should education begin? How can schooling be made relevant to the student's life experience? How does the home environment influence the child's school performance?—still engage us today.

Ann Taylor Allen, who received her bachelor's degree from Bryn Mawr College and her doctorate from Columbia University, is a Professor Emerita of History at the University of Louisville, Kentucky. She is the author of *Satire and Society in Wilhelmine Germany* (1984); *Feminism and Motherhood in Germany, 1800–1914* (1991); *Feminism and Motherhood in Western Europe, 1890–1970: The Maternal Dilemma* (2005); and *Women in Twentieth-Century Europe* (2008). She has published many articles on international feminist movements and on the history of the kindergarten in Germany and the United States. Her latest book is *The Transatlantic Kindergarten: Women's*

Movements and Education in Germany and the United States, published by Oxford University Press in January 2017.

Notes

1. Johann Heinrich Pestalozzi, *Wie Gertrud ihre Kinder lehrt, ein Versuch, den Müttern Anleitung zu geben, ihre Kinder selbst zu unterrichten, in Briefen von Heinrich Pestalozzi* (Bern and Zurich: Heinrich Gess, 1802), 286.
2. On the agency of material things, see Oliver J. T. Harris and Tim Flohr Sørensen, "Rethinking Emotion and Material Culture," *Archaeological Dialogues* 17, no. 2 (2010): 145–63.
3. Monique Scheer, "Are Emotions a Kind of Practice (and Is That What Makes Them Have a History)? A Bourdieuian Apporach to Understanding Emotion," *History and Theory* 51, no. 2 (2012): 193–220; Richard Grassby, "Material Culture and Cultural History," *The Journal of Interdisciplinary History* 35, no. 4 (2005): 591–603.
4. Johann Heinrich Pestalozzi, *How Gertrude Teaches her Children*, trans. Lucy E. Holland (Washington, D.C.: University Publications of America, 1977), 56.
5. On Pestalozzi's life and times, see Jürgen Oelkers, "Das Jahrhundert Pestalozzis? Zum Verhältnis von Erziehung und Bildung in der europäischen Aufklärung," in *Pestalozzi: Umfeld und Rezeption: Studien zur Historisierung einer Legende*, ed. Jürgen Oelkers and Fritz Osterwalder (Weinheim: Beltz Verlag, 1995), 25–90; Käte Silber. *Pestalozzi, the Man and His Work* (London: Routledge and Kegan Paul, 1960); Gerald Lee Gutek, *Pestalozzi and Education* (New York: Random House, 1968), 387; Daniel Tröhler, *Pestalozzi and the Educationalization of the World* (New York: Palgrave Macmillan, 2013).
6. Jean-Jacques Rousseau, *The Émile of Jean-Jacques Rousseau*, trans. and ed. William Boyd (New York: Teachers' College Press, 1958).
7. Heikki Lempa, *Bildung der Triebe: der deutsche Philanthropismus (1768–1788)* (Turku: Turun yliopisto, 1993).
8. Pestalozzi, *Wie Gertrud ihre Kinder lehrt*, 280–81 (quotation 280); Jürgen Oelkers, "Ja und Nein: Pestalozzis Stellung zur franzosischen Revolution," in *Pestalozzi*, ed. Oelkers and Osterwalder, 148–63.
9. James quoted in "James, William," in Ted Honderich, ed., *Oxford Companion to Philosophy* (Oxford: Oxford University Press, 1995), 424–26.
10. G. Felicitas Munzel, "Kant on Moral Education, or 'Enlightenment' and the Liberal Arts," *The Review of Metaphysics* 57, no. 1 (2003): 43–73; Tröhler, *Pestalozzi and the Educationalization of the World*, 70–71; Gutek, *Pestalozzi and Education*, 80–100.
11. Cf. Ann Taylor Allen, *The Transatlantic Kindergarten: Education and Women's Movements in Germany and the United States* (New York: Oxford University Press, 2017), 10–12.
12. Rousseau, *The Émile of Jean-Jacques Rousseau*, 21–25.
13. Christa Kersting, *Die Genese der Pädagogik im 18. Jahrhundert: Campes "Allgemeine Revision" im Kontext der neuzeitlichen Wissenschaft* (Weinheim: Deutscher Studien Verlag, 1992), 24–56.
14. Rousseau, *The Émile of Jean-Jacques Rousseau*, 17.
15. Kersting, *Die Genese der Pädagogik*, 325.

16. Allen, *The Transatlantic Kindergarten*, 14; Heidi Koenig. "Die Mutter: Anthropologische Konzept oder Konvention," in *Pestalozzi: Umfeld und Rezeption: Studien zur Historisierung einer Legende*, ed. Jürgen Oelkers and Fritz Osterwalder (Weinheim: Beltz Verlag, 1995), 133–46.
17. Johann Heinrich Pestalozzi, *Letters on Early Education, Addressed to J. P. Greaves, Esq. by Pestalozzi* (London: Longman, Brown, Green, and Longmans, 1851), 57.
18. Munzel, "Kant on Moral Education;" "Kant, Immanuel," in Honderich, *Oxford Companion to Philosophy*, 434–35.
19. Pestalozzi, *Wie Gertrud ihre Kinder lehrt*, 352–57.
20. Pestalozzi, *Wie Gertrud ihre Kinder lehrt*, 353.
21. Pestalozzi, *Letters on Early Education*, 8.
22. Johann Heinrich Pestalozzi, "Journal für die Erziehung 1807 mit nachgelassenem Text zu den darin enthaltenen Briefen der damals geplanten 'Neuen Auflage der Schrift: Wie Gertrud ihre Kinder lehrt,'" in *Sämtliche Werke: Kritische Ausgabe*, ed. Stefan Graber, vol. 17 B (Zurich: Verlag der Neuen Zürcher Zeitung, 1996), 129.
23. Pestalozzi, *Letters on Early Education*, 151.
24. Pestalozzi, *Wie Gertrud ihre Kinder lehrt*, 38–41; Keiichi Takaya, "The Method of Anschauung: From Johann H. Pestalozzi to Herbert Spencer," *The Journal of Educational Thought* 37, no. 1 (2003): 77–99.
25. Johann Heinrich Pestalozzi and Eva Channing, *Pestalozzi's Leonard and Gertrude* (Boston: D.C. Heath, 1985), 152–59.
26. Johann Heinrich Pestalozzi, *Letters on Early Education*, xxix.
27. George Edward Biber, *Henry Pestalozzi, and His Plan of Education, Being an Account of His Life and Writings. With Copious Extracts from His Works and Extensive Details Illustrative of the Practical Parts of His Method* (London: Sherwood, Gilbert and Piper, 1833), 32.
28. Pestalozzi, *Letters on Early Education*, 166–67.
29. Pestalozzi, *Letters on Early Education*, 15 and 73.
30. Takaya, "The Method of Anschauung."
31. Roger Guimps and John Russell, *Pestalozzi: His Life and Work* (New York: D. Appleton, 1890), 179, 231.
32. Biber, *Henry Pestalozzi*, 218; Guimps and Russell, *Pestalozzi*, 179–81.
33. Biber, *Henry Pestalozzi*, 218.
34. Biber, *Henry Pestalozzi*, 67; Guimps and Russell, *Pestalozzi*, 414.
35. Pestalozzi, *Letters on Early Education*, 86.
36. Yvonne Leimgruber, *In pädagogischer Mission: Die Pädagogin Rosette Niederer-Kasthofer (1779–1857) und ihr Wirken für ein "frauengerechtes" Leben in Familie und Gesellschaft* (Bad Heilbrunn: J. Klinkhardt, 2006), 64–132.
37. Johann Heinrich Pestalozzi, "Bericht an die Eltern und an das Publikum über den gegenwärtigen Zustand und die Einrichtung des Pestalozzischen Anstalt in Iferten: Zusatz, das Töchterinstitut betreffend," In *Sämtliche Werke*, vol. 21 (Zürich, 1964), 82–83.
38. Juliane Jacobi, *Mädchen- und Frauenbildung in Europa von 1500 bis zur Gegenwart* (Frankfurt: Campus Verlag, 2013), 185–98.
39. Leimgruber, *In pädagogischer Mission*, 252–53; Rosette Niederer-Kasthofer, *Blicke in das Wesen der weiblichen Erziehung: Für gebildete Mädchen und Töchter* (Berlin: Rucker, 1828), 10; Betty Gleim and Ruth Bleckwenn, *Erziehung und Ubterricht des*

weiblichen Geschlechts: Ein Buch für Eltern und Erzieher (Paderborn: M. Hüttemann, 1989), 90.
40. Allen, *The Transatlantic Kindergarten*, 19–20.
41. On Fröbel's early life and relationship to Pestalozzi, see Allen, *The Transatlantic Kindergarten*, 23–26.
42. "Schelling, Friedrich Wilhelm Joseph von," in Honderich, ed., *The Oxford Companion to Philosophy*, 188–201.
43. On the founding of the first kindergartens, see Helmut Heiland, *Friedrich Wilhelm August Fröbel (1782–1852)* (Baltmannsweiler: Schneider-Verlag Hohengehren, 2002), 64–71; Allen, *The Transatlantic Kindergarten*, 26–31.
44. Friedrich Fröbel, *Mothers' Songs, Games, and Stories (Fröbel's Mutter- und Kose-Lieder)*, trans. Frances and Emily Lord (London: William Rice, 1888), 8, 16, 22, 56, 56, 58; on the agency of material things, see Harris and Sørensen, "Rethinking Emotion and Material Culture."
45. On Fröbel's pedagogy see Heiland, *Friedrich Wilhelm August Fröbel*, 54–70, 220–66; Barbara Beatty, *Preschool Education in America : The Culture of Young Children from the Colonial Era to the Present* (New Haven: Yale University Press, 1995), 38–51.
46. On Fröbel's methods in historical context, see Allen, *The Transatlantic Kindergarten*, 28–31.
47. Claire Goldberg Moses, *French Feminism in the Nineteenth Century* (Albany: State University of New York Press, 1984), 41–88.
48. Catherine M. Prelinger. *Charity, Challenge, and Change: Religious Dimensions of the Mid-Nineteenth-Century Women's Movement in Germany* (New York: Greenwood Press, 1987), 79–104; Sylvia Paletschek, *Frauen und Dissens: Frauen im Deutschkatholizismus und in den freien Gemeinden 1841–1852* (Göttingen: Vandenhoeck & Ruprecht, 1990), 153–222.
49. Friedrich Fröbel, *Entwurf eines Planes zur Begründung und Ausführung eines Kinder-Gartens* (Leipzig: Obraldruck Brandstetter, n.d.), 5.
50. For much, much more on this history, see Allen, *The Transatlantic Kindergarten*.
51. James C. Albisetti, "The Feminization of Teaching in the Nineteenth Century: A Comparative Perspective," *History of Education* 22, no. 3 (1993): 253–63.
52. Prelinger, *Charity, Challenge, and Change*, 79–104; Allen, *The Transatlantic Kindergarten*, 37–45.
53. John Dewey and Evelyn Dewey, *Schools of Tomorrow* (New York: Dutton, 1915), 61.
54. Tröhler, *Pestalozzi and the Educationalization of the World*, 73–94; Karl A. Schleunes, "Enlightenment, Reform, Reaction: The Schooling Revolution in Prussia," *Central European History* 12, no. 4 (1979).
55. Among many other works on changing pedagogies: Heinz Stübig, "Diesterweg und das Problem der deutschen Nationalerziehung," *Paedagogica Historica* 17, no. 2 (2001): 341–45; David Hogan, "Modes of Discipline: Affective Individualism and Pedagogical Reform in New England, 1820–1850," *American Journal of Education* 99, no. 1 (1990): 1–56.
56. Johann Heinrich Pestalozzi, *Schwanengesang* (Berlin: Contumax Hofenberg 2014), 30.

Bibliography

Albisetti, James C. "The Feminization of Teaching in the Nineteenth Century: A Comparative Perspective." *History of Education* 22, no. 3 (1993): 253–63.

Allen, Ann Taylor. *The Transatlantic Kindergarten: Education and Women's Movements in Germany and the United States.* New York: Oxford University Press, 2017.

Beatty, Barbara. *Preschool Education in America: The Culture of Young Children from the Colonial Era to the Present.* New Haven: Yale University Press, 1995.

Biber, George Edward. *Henry Pestalozzi, and His Plan of Education: Being an Account of His Life and Writings. With Copious Extracts from His Works and Extensive Details Illustrative of the Practical Parts of His Method.* London: Sherwood, Gilbert and Piper, 1833.

Dewey, John, and Evelyn Dewey. *Schools of Tomorrow.* New York: Dutton, 1915.

Fröbel, Friedrich. *Entwurf eines Planes zur Begründung und Ausführung eines Kinder-Gartens.* Leipzig: Obraldruck Brandstetter, n.d.

——— *Mothers' Songs, Games, and Stories (Fröbel's Mutter- und Koselieder).* Translated by Frances and Emily Lord. London: William Rice, 1888.

Gleim, Betty, and Ruth Bleckwenn. *Erziehung und Unterricht des weiblichen Geschlechts: Ein Buch für Eltern und Erzieher.* Paderborn: M. Hüttemann, 1989.

Grassby, Richard. "Material Culture and Cultural History." *The Journal of Interdisciplinary History* 35, no. 4 (2005): 591–603.

Guimps, Roger, and John Russell. *Pestalozzi: His Life and Work.* New York: D. Appleton, 1890.

Gutek, Gerald Lee. *Pestalozzi and Education.* New York: Random House, 1968.

Harris, Oliver J. T., and Tim Flohr Sørensen. "Rethinking Emotion and Material Culture." *Archaeological Dialogues* 17, no. 2 (2010): 145–63.

Heiland, Helmut. *Friedrich Wilhelm August Fröbel (1782–1852).* Baltmannsweiler: Schneider-Verlag Hohengehren, 2002.

Hogan, David. "Modes of Discipline: Affective Individualism and Pedagogical Reform in New England, 1820–1850." *American Journal of Education* 99, no. 1 (1990): 1–56.

Honderich, Ted, ed. *Oxford Companion to Philosophy.* Oxford: Oxford University Press, 1995.

Jacobi, Juliane. *Mädchen- und Frauenbildung in Europa von 1500 bis zur Gegenwart.* Frankfurt: Campus Verlag, 2013.

Kersting, Christa. *Die Genese der Pädagogik im 18. Jahrhundert: Campes "Allgemeine Revision" im Kontext der neuzeitlichen Wissenschaft.* Weinheim: Deutscher Studien Verlag, 1992.

Koenig, Heidi. "Die Mutter: Anthropologische Konzept oder Konvention." In *Pestalozzi: Umfeld und Rezeption: Studien zur Historisierung einer Legende,* edited by Jürgen Oelkers, and Fritz Osterwalder, 133–46. Weinheim: Beltz Verlag, 1995.

Leimgruber, Yvonne. *In pädagogischer Mission: Die Pädagogin Rosette Niederer-Kasthofer (1779–1857) und ihr Wirken für ein "frauengerechtes" Leben in Familie und Gesellschaft.* Bad Heilbrunn: J. Klinkhardt, 2006.

Lempa, Heikki. *Bildung der Triebe: der deutsche Philanthropismus (1768–1788).* Turku: Turun yliopisto, 1993.

Moses, Claire Goldberg. *French Feminism in the Nineteenth Century.* Albany: State University of New York Press, 1984.

Munzel, G. Felicitas. "Kant on Moral Education, or 'Enlightenment' and the Liberal Arts." *The Review of Metaphysics* 57, no. 1 (2003): 43–73.

Niederer-Kasthofer, Rosette. *Blicke in das Wesen der weiblichen Erziehung: Für gebildete Mütter und Töchter.* Berlin: Rücker, 1828.

Oelkers, Jürgen, and Fritz Osterwalder, eds. *Pestalozzi: Umfeld und Rezeption: Studien zur Historisierung einer Legende.* Weinheim: Beltz Verlag, 1995.

Paletschek, Sylvia. *Frauen und Dissens: Frauen im Deutschkatholizismus und in den freien Gemeinden 1841–1852.* Göttingen: Vandenhoeck & Ruprecht, 1990.

Pestalozzi, Johann Heinrich. "Bericht an die Eltern und an das Publikum über den gegenwärtigen Zustand und die Einrichtung des Pestalozzischen Anstalt in Iferten: Zusatz, das Töchterinstitut betreffend." In *Sämtliche Werke*, vol. 21, 82–83. Zurich: Hansebooks, 1964.

——— *How Gertrude Teaches Her Children.* Translated by Lucy E. Holland. Washington, D.C.: University Publications of America, 1977.

——— "Journal für die Erziehung 1807 mit nachgelassenem Text zu den darin enthaltenen Briefen der damals geplanten 'Neuen Auflage der Schrift: Wie Gertrud ihre Kinder lehrt.'" In *Sämtliche Werke: Kritische Ausgabe*, edited by Stefan Graber, vol. 17 B, 129. Zurich: Verlag der Neuen Zürcher Zeitung. 1996.

——— *Letters on Early Education, addressed to J. P. Greaves Esq., with a Memoir of Pestalozzi.* London: Longman, Brown, Green, and Longmans, 1851.

——— *Schwanengesang.* Berlin: Contumax Hofenberg, 2014.

——— *Wie Gertrud ihre Kinder lehrt, ein Versuch, den Müttern Anleitung zu geben, ihre Kinder selbst zu unterrichten, in Briefen von Heinrich Pestalozzi.* Bern and Zurich: Heinrich Gess, 1802.

Pestalozzi, Johann Heinrich, and Eva Channing. *Pestalozzi's Leonard and Gertrude.* Boston: D.C. Heath, 1985.

Prelinger, Catherine M. *Charity, Challenge, and Change: Religious Dimensions of the Mid-Nineteenth-Century Women's Movement in Germany.* New York: Greenwood Press, 1987.

Rousseau, Jean-Jacques. *The Émile of Jean-Jacques Rousseau.* Translated and edited by William Boyd. New York: Teachers' College Press, 1958.

——— *Emile, or On Education.* New York: Basic Books, 1979.

Scheer, Monique. "Are Emotions a Kind of Practice (and Is That What Makes Them Have a History)? A Bourdieuian Approach to Understanding Emotion." *History and Theory* 51 no. 2 (2012): 193–220.

Schleunes, Karl A. "Enlightenment, Reform, Reaction: The Schooling Revolution in Prussia." *Central European History* 12, no. 4 (1979).
Silber, Käte. *Pestalozzi, the Man and His Work*. London: Routledge and Kegan Paul, 1960.
Stübig, Heinz. "Diesterweg und das Problem der deutschen Nationalerziehung." *Paedagogica Historica* 17, no, 2 (2001): 341–45.
Takaya, Keiichi. "The Method of Anschauung: From Johann H. Pestalozzi to Herbert Spencer." *The Journal of Educational Thought* 37, no. 1 (2003): 77–99.
Tröhler, Daniel. *Pestalozzi and the Educationalization of the World*. New York: Palgrave Macmillan, 2013.

CHAPTER 11

Reading Early German Photographs for Histories of Emotion

SARAH L. LEONARD

The static, restrained, almost uniform portraits produced by German daguerreotypists and photographers in the middle of the nineteenth century would seem to be unlikely sources for writing a history of emotions. Squeezed into dark suits and dresses, heads and hands situated in stylized postures, sitters traveled distances and tolerated difficult conditions to walk out of the studio with a likeness of themselves. The result, as historian of photography Timm Starl has pointed out, were portraits that were unspectacular by design. They provided images of people quietly settled in domestic interiors; the fantasy of stability seemed to disavow the political and economic eruptions that marked this period.[1] Rather than differentiate and individuate, the success of these portraits hinged upon sitters' ability to occupy conventional gestures and spaces and to perform a particular emotional style, characterized by bodily discipline and reserve, leavened by discreet gestures of affection or connection.

This reserved portraiture was not determined by technological restraints. Some of the earliest photographers of the 1840s, working with the challenges of long exposures and natural light, produced creative, emotionally spirited daguerreotypes. In Saxony, an important center of photographic innovations in the nineteenth century, early professional photographers like Hermann Krone and Bertha Wehnert-Beckmann made playful portraits capturing a wide range of bodily gestures and emotional expressions.[2] The new medium lent itself as much to experimentation with multiple emotional styles as it did to standardization. Krone produced beautiful, expressive daguerreotypes of his wife and brothers, and a remarkable range of self-portraits. Wehnert-Beckmann, one of several professional women photographers in the German States, experimented with daguerreotype self-portraits, nudes, and still-life studies of ordinary objects. Over the course of four decades, she developed a style of portraiture that attracted a steady stream of clients that included aristocrats, comfortable members of the urban *Bürgertum*, as well

Figure 11.1. Portrait of government administrator Otto Weise by Bertha Beckmann, Daguerreotype, 1843. From the collection of the Stadtgeschichtliches Museum Leipzig.

as nonelites—among them men and women, as she put it in her client book, "in service" (maids, housekeepers, and the like).[3] By the 1860s, sitters paid to pose in the carefully arranged photographic settings (we might call them sets) provided in her studio. In these sets, designed to emulate orderly domestic spaces, clients engaged with the props provided by the studio. These included a limited range of wooden chairs, tables, plants, and books. Dressed in formal attire, sitters formed their bodies into expressions, postures, and gestures that would be captured and memorialized.

It would be easy to conclude that the formal postures struck in early German photographic portraits yield very little historical insight into the affective lives of their sitters, or more generally into the emotional styles of the period. They have none of the spontaneity we associate today with "authentic" expressions of emotion. Early daguerreotype portraits involved effort, skill, patience, and even discomfort—subjects needed to sit perfectly still and refrain from blinking, their bodies arranged in postures designed to display clothes well. If they were lucky, their faces would express a contemplative depth of character.

This essay examines German photographic portraits from the middle of the 1840s through the 1860s to understand what these sources reveal about emotional practices and styles in this period.[4] I have chosen to focus here on the portraits of Wehnert-Beckmann because her activity as a photographer is richly documented. Wehnert-Beckmann's work is technically and aesthetically accomplished, and it seems likely that she attracted a steady clientele because she took beautiful portraits. However, I focus on her work not to highlight what is unique about it, but instead because of the size and scope of existing archives. A large body of images produced by Wehnert-Beckmann after she began her career as a professional photographer in 1842—daguerreotypes, negatives, and photographs—are held at the Stadtgeschichtliches Museum Leipzig. Other sources in this collection lend context to the photographs: books she kept on the supplies she used, a fascinating (if incomplete) list of the clients who visited her studio, and documents related to land purchases and building. While these written documents are not shortcuts for understanding the emotional import of Wehnert-Beckmann's images, they do provide hints from both sides of the lens about how these portraits were made. I have also examined the photographic portraits of Wehnert-Beckmann's contemporaries, and therefore have a sense of her professional context.

Early German photographic portraits required the performance of particular emotional styles, which could be difficult to achieve in the space of the studio. An advertisement from 1851 promised clients comfort: they would enjoy heated waiting rooms and ample reading materials, should it take several tries to produce a good portrait.[5] Handbooks and manuals provided tips on how to comfort sitters and elicit desired facial expression and postures of bodily ease.[6] Small pieces of textual evidence provide hints about the attitudes of those who sat for photographs. A handwritten note to Wehnert-Beckmann by the prominent Leipzig publisher Rudolf Brockhaus in 1867, for example, explained that he was in a rush to have his portrait taken: "I would like to have photographs taken in *carte-de-visite* format, but I have very little time. Nonetheless I would like to know on what day and at what hour I can come to your studio.... The best time for me would be the hour from one to two o'clock."[7] Achieving the static, purposeful posture of the *carte-de-visite* portraits would have required Brockhaus to stand still, relax, and forget his haste.

Large archives of often-anonymous sitters arranged in seemingly identical postures present a challenge to the historian who wants to understand the emotional histories they illustrate. A recent body of scholarship on vernacular photography argues that such photographs should not be ignored because they seem formulaic. Historian Tina Campt, for example, writes that photographs in a series are important for what they reveal about communities and their desire to be represented in particular ways. "Unpacking what motivated a community's attachment to the serial reproduction of certain kinds of images and specific image-making practices . . . gives us a different appreciation of the reappearance of familiar or similar (albeit never exact) reproductions of the same types of images over time."[8] Furthermore, photographs in a series are only apparently the same; a closer look reveals important variations in the choices of both sitters and photographers.[9] She urges us to "listen" to the emotional register of these images—they may be quiet, but quiet should not be mistaken for silence.

The images at the heart of this study are two varieties of the formal studio photograph: the individual portrait, and the family portrait. The individual photographic portrait became part of a transnational visual vocabulary of the mid-nineteenth century. Sitters in many geographical contexts had such photographs taken of themselves in dark suits and dresses, often seated in wooden chairs and at tables, holding flowers or books. Although one is tempted to read sitters as members of the bourgeoisie because of their dress and settings, clothes and bearing did not always correlate with social or financial status. Historians have shown that slaves, domestic servants, and colonized peoples also sat for such portraits.[10] Indeed, one of the appeals of these images was the way they held out the promise of casting most sitters as members of the respectable bourgeoisie. As historian Laura Wexler has written: "Photography was part of the master narrative that created and cemented cultural and political inequalities of race and class."[11] The classic portrait cast sitters in relatively homogenous styles that seemed to both erase difference (because everyone was cast in the image of the bourgeoisie), and to highlight it (those who could not quite perform this role were conspicuous in their difference).

As a second variation, early photographs of families shared many features of the individual portrait. Clothes were typically the same, as were the sets created in the studio to mimic the semiprivate spaces of bourgeois homes. However, family photographs also represented relations between people. Patterns and choices of touch, positioning, and order spoke to hierarchies, attachments, and relationships between people. Like individual portraits, they tell us about how families *wanted* to appear, the emotional registers they hoped to set down in order to share, keep, and revisit them. Campt writes, "Family photography thus functions as an affective and material practice that constructs and reproduces the family not necessarily as it is or was, but rather as it would like to be seen."[12] Relationships between people were practiced in the studio through touch, bodily proximity, and playfulness (and conversely through bodily reserve, physical distance, and formality).

Scholars also urge us to attend to the emotional value of these photographs as objects that were meant to be held, displayed, worn, and exchanged. As unique images that captured the light emanating from the photographed person, and as objects often held close to or worn on the body, their emotional import was tied to touch, to the haptic.[13] Furthermore, the burgeoning field of "thing theory" draws our attention to the agency of objects and to the coconstruction of things and people: just as people make things, things also make people. As the editors of a recent collection on objects and emotions explain: "One of the main points emphasized in the recent 'material turn' in historical scholarship is the importance of reciprocity in the object subject relationship."[14] Photographs, for example, are objects made by people, but they also "make people": because they were being photographed, people dressed and posed in particular ways, and adapted their limbs and faces to perform potent norms of comportment. As objects of gift and exchange, they worked to mediate relationships between people and between generations; they also provided important visual markers of belonging and difference.

Historian Monique Scheer argues that emotions are brought into being through material practices in the world—feelings are done and not simply had.[15] People engage in practices (and often these are physical practices) designed to evoke and shape particular emotions. Bodily gestures and movements, built environments, and forms of sociability can bring emotions into being. Furthermore, emotions are embodied. This has implications for the way we think about the physical practices associated with the seemingly standard photographic portraits of the mid-nineteenth century.[16] On the topic of emotions as practices, Scheer disputes the idea that "real emotions" are those experienced privately and inside the self.[17] Scholars have argued that, in the West, emotions have often been imagined as internal and private, associated with the mind rather than the body. Authentic affective states are thought to be distinct from those that are performed, compulsory, or ritualized. Thus, the historian trying to access histories of emotion through conventional images seems to be missing real, spontaneous, internal states. Drawing on practice theory, Scheer asserts that the habits, gestures, and phrases we use, and the spaces we produce and inhabit, are what bring us into being. Emotions therefore proceed in part from the things we do in the world: "Emotional practices," Scheer writes, "are habits, rituals, and everyday pastimes that aid us in achieving a certain emotional state—this includes the striving for a desired feeling as well as the modifying of one that is not desirable."[18]

The bodily practices of those who sat for portraits were not the stuff of everyday habit; for most, these were occasional performances. Yet the fact that they were captured on silver plates, displayed, and viewed again and again gave these practices power and longevity. Though the act of sitting for a portrait was extraordinary in this era, photographers sought to create the illusion of ordinary spaces, gestures, and emotions. Presumably, these were the kinds of images people wanted to see of themselves.

Turning to a detailed analysis of some of Wehnert-Beckmann's portraits, we can consider how the content of these photographs, their status as objects, and the bodily performances involved in producing them provide us with tools for understanding their material import.

The Emotional Language of Objects

Sorting through the hundreds of portraits taken by Wehnert-Beckmann from the late 1840s through the 1860s, one is immediately struck by the presence of objects meant to be worn or held close to the body. Necklaces, rings, walking sticks, watches, books, hats, and clothing occupied places of prominence in these portraits. The bodies of men and women alike were arranged to show off rings of various kinds—from signet to wedding rings, worn in no discernable pattern on the first three digits of the hand. While women wore jewelry—often broaches, hair ornaments, necklaces, and rings—men actively displayed rings and pocket watches. Clothing and jewelry claimed space in the small daguerreotype portraits that were necessarily focused closely on sitters. Portraits were composed to emphasize clothing and fabric—the ruching and tiny buttons of many sitters' best dresses, the striped pants and plaid waistcoats that were fashionable among men in the late 1840s and 1850s. Laying close on the body like jewelry, but generally more standardized, clothing captured the outer layer that determined the boundary between the body and the spaces around it.[19]

While sitters themselves were still and carefully composed and their faces generally impassive, the objects on their bodies pointed to potent human attachments and memories. Rings and hair ornaments did more than signal status; they embedded these sitters in a network of social relations. Objects in the photographs signaled the importance of people who were absent, bearing witness to human connections.

Indeed, it seems as though one of the functions of portrait photography may have been to teach people how to read for the meaning of objects. While jewelry and clothing were distinct to each sitter and presumably individual property, other stock props were used repeatedly. Chairs and tables, a curtain, sometimes flowers and plants occupied the space of the sitter. Occasionally, clients would wear a broach with a photograph in it. More often, they wore lockets that may have held tiny photographs close to the skin. These props were touched by sitters and acted as temporary extensions of their bodies.

Figure 11.2. Portrait of singer and actress Auguste Götze by Bertha Wehnert-Beckmann, Daguerreotype, c. 1856–65. From the collection of the Stadtgeschichtliches Museum Leipzig.

Such props bore several functions. On the one hand, they seemed to establish that those being photographed occupied spaces of respectability associated with bodily comfort (this comfort did not necessarily extend beyond the studio). Upholstered chairs, wooden desks, books, curtains, and plants imitated the space of the bourgeois home. Wehnert-Beckmann's studio staged bodies in areas protected from cold, clutter, difficult work, and the rowdy interruptions of others. The photographs suggested that because these bodies were supported, their subjects' minds were free to range—to the narratives or memories contained in the books or pictures they held, or simply to the thoughts that sat lightly on calm, composed faces. Historian Annelie Ramsbrock argues that beauty in this period was associated with interiority and "the cultivation of the soul."[20] In these portraits, the illusion of interior depth required, somewhat paradoxically, the strategic use of objects. The materiality of emotions—that is, the way affective performance depended upon the presence of objects attached to or surrounding the body—complicates historians' arguments that the German self in this period was imagined primarily in terms of interiority. Material things and social gestures were clearly legible (and portraits played a role in making them so) as markers of social belonging and exclusion. Objects worn on the body spoke pointedly to the attachments and personal histories of individual sitters, even as their expressions remained largely impassive.

Some people appeared more at ease in standard postures. Certain sitters commanded the space, looking thoroughly at home in the photographer's studio. Others (who show signs of being from a different class—including chapped hands, less expensive clothing and jewelry, and variations in posture) looked uncomfortable. We are less likely as historians to know the identities of lower-status sitters, making it difficult to establish links between emotional performances and the social position of those who had their portraits taken. Particular details do allow us to make some educated guesses about the status of some sitters. Signs of hard work and bodily tension, for example, alert us to the potential emotional or physical discomfort of people in photographs.[21] Hands that have been worked hard, postures that are less straight, gazes directed away from the camera—these hint at a lack of ease embodying the emotional and physical conventions of the bourgeois portrait.

Emotions and Body Gestures

The people in these portraits also used their bodies in distinct ways. For example, their hands rested on other sitters in a limited series of gestures that are worth considering for what they suggest, as well as for what they obscure, about bodies and emotions. In portraits featuring more than one person, touch was notable for its presence in small, often predictable gestures, but also for its total absence in some photographs. Like objects, gestures carried the weight of emotional expression. Examining these portraits by the hundreds, one begins to see that rituals of posture and touch formed recognizable patterns that made sitters' relationships to one another legible.

Though affectionate portraits of married couples exist from this period—suggesting that such representations of marriage were imagined by some—the vast majority of marriage portraits cast wives and husbands in reserved postures.[22] In early daguerreotype portraits, which are more tightly framed, these couples regularly sit side-by-side, looking in different directions, their bodies sometimes touching at the hip or waist, but otherwise not physically engaged. By the 1860s, Wehnert-Beckmann's married couples were positioned in a style inherited from eighteenth-century painted portraits: the man sitting at a table looking at or resting his hands on a book, facing away from the woman standing in profile behind his chair. In what became part of the iconography of the married couple in many of Wehnert-Beckmann's portraits, men and women did not touch, nor did they engage with each other. What they did do, however, was cast an immediately recognizable shape—one that displayed the woman's dress, and suggested the purposefulness of the partnership (his engagement with books, her quiet support of these activities).

Portraits of adults and children were more varied in gestures and direct engagement. Nonetheless, gestures of affection were still quiet and efficient— the arms of siblings linked in comradery, the hands of children resting on their mother's lap. Often, the older women in these portraits (presumably the mothers, though this is difficult to tell) gazed at books of photographic albums while flanked by older children who sometimes placed a hand on their mothers' shoulders. Portraits of men with younger children were more physically demonstrative, with a father holding a child's hand or resting their own hands on their child's shoulder. In general, adult men were accorded a wider range of openly affectionate gestures than adult women, and their bodies were often set in postures of greater ease. Portraits of men even involved an element of play.

Gestures and postures also reveal something about hierarchies—about who could touch whom, and in what ways. While siblings were regularly depicted holding hands or linking arms, fathers often rested hands or elbows on younger members of the family, presumably their children. Patriarchs also engaged in a kind of self-touch by resting their hands on their abdomen or chest, inside their clothing. While this was certainly borrowed from earlier norms of male portraiture, it is nonetheless a reminder that subtle hierarchies were expressed through the quiet gestures of photographs. It also seems likely that hierarchy was bound up with the affective resonance of these images, for affection can carry with it relationships of dependence and authority.

We cannot conclude from such images that mothers in this period were distracted by books and unaffectionate to their children, or that married life was marked by physical disengagement. Still, these practices of the body cannot be dismissed as sheer artifice, for following Wexler, they tell us a great deal about how people wanted to present their family in the few photographic portraits they would own. Furthermore, these were images that would be displayed in homes and become part of the visual narrative of the family. Through repeated viewing, emotions and histories likely attached themselves to photographs.

A striking exception to this reserve was found in the demonstrative, playful portraits that depicted groups of adult men (presumably friends, perhaps

Figure 11.3. Portrait of an unknown family by Bertha Wehnert-Beckmann, Daguerreotype, c. 1845–50. From the collection of the Stadtgeschichtliches Museum Leipzig.

also brothers); such pictures presented an entirely different range of emotions in the gestures of the face and the body. In group portraits of men, bodies are closely grouped; men touch each other's shoulders and arms affectionately. Humor and theatricality play an important role in this genre, with men holding cigars or cards, moving their bodies in ways that break out of the disciplined postures of the formal portrait or the family portrait. In a style of presentation that extended beyond Wehnert-Beckmann's studio, male friendships were often cast against painted backdrops that mimicked nature rather than the bourgeois salon. Sometimes they were actually taken outside. There appears to have been no equivalent style for adult women. While portraits of sisters contained elements of play—sometimes a costume or a gesture, and more direct engagement with each other—they did not share the overlapping bodies and free gestures contained in the portraits of male friends. Here again, we cannot conclude from these portraits that relationships between male friends were close while those between women were reserved. Still, the clear

Figure 11.4. Portrait of six men, a boy, and a small child by Bertha Wehnert-Beckmann, albumen print, c. 1855. From the collection of the Stadtgeschichtliches Museum Leipzig.

existence of this genre of male friendship—and its longevity—show us that the portraits of the period were not reserved because the range of emotional expression was inherently limited. Rather, we are able to see how these bodily performances were distinct and situation specific. These images of male friends were a marked exception to the otherwise restrained portraits of the period.

This brings us back to the question: What emotional work were these portraits designed to do? On the one hand, they were memory objects, produced to capture a particular image of a person; their potency rested on the inclusion of recognizable objects and gestures. Their emotional import was bound up with the performances in which sitters engaged in order to produce these photographs—that is, with the process of taking the photograph rather than the end product. They were by no means "mere" performances, but ways of knowing the body in its social contexts. Following Scheer, we might argue that the bodily practices of these photographs were ways of thinking about the self. As people shaped their bodies in particular gestures and spaces, they also learned an art of being (some likely learned about their exclusion from that art of being). Adopting standardized postures in these photographs meant that the scenes they depicted were immediately recognizable as expressing particular modes of kinship. One did not need to scrutinize the photograph to ponder the relationship expressed—the basic shape, the simple outline, repeatedly conveyed that information. Having one's portrait taken was a way to learn that social language.

We know from Wehnert-Beckmann's books that her clientele was socially wide-ranging; yet the studio cast them all in the uniform space of the bourgeois interior, failing to mark social difference through props or setting. Despite the studio's best efforts, subtle gestures of the body, and the unmistakable evidence of clothing quality, the evidence of hands (some looking like they performed hard work) and faces revealed more than intended about the social status of sitters. In subtle ways, the subjects of these photos could fail to inhabit the prescribed postures convincingly, marking their separation from those who could. In this way, these photographs provided evidence of the emotional experience of class, with its subtle realities of inclusion and exclusion.

The photographic products of the portrait studio became retrospective documents of something real that had taken place: sitters and photographers had worked together in a studio to produce relatively scarce images. They had made a series of choices about the objects to bring, those at the studio to use, and the postures to adopt. The studio brought into being a reality that took on the form of the photographic image. In this process, as "thing" theorists help us see, objects were involved in the cocreation of realities. Even within the narrow conventions of the genre, people made subtle decisions about dress, comportment, touch, and expression. Existing photographs continued to attract emotions through touching, viewing, and display, becoming part of the fabric and narrative of relationships of kinship, belonging, and selfhood.

If we imagine emotions as interior, as something that people are privately subject to, then photographs seem like superficial documents of false performances. Yet a focus on the materiality of emotions—both on the way emotions are embodied practices, and on the relationships between objects and emotions—suggests ways we might use photographs as a way to understand histories of feeling. For even formal, seemingly uniform photographs tell us about the affective stances sitters went to great lengths to perform. Thus we learn about how people wanted to appear, and about a formal range of bodily expression embodied in touch.

Sarah L. Leonard is Associate Professor of History at Simmons University. She specializes in German cultural history. Her book *Fragile Minds and*

Vulnerable Souls: The Matter of Obscenity in Nineteenth-Century Germany was published in 2015 by University of Pennsylvania Press. She is working on two related projects on early German photography. The first explores the relationship between the new medium and the history of emotions; the second considers the position of women and Jews as photographers and sitters in the 1840s and 1850s.

Notes

1. Timm Starl, "Fortschrit und Phantasma: Zur Entstehung der photographischen Bildwelt," in *Silber und Salz: Zur Frühzeit der Photographie im deutschen Sprachraum*, ed. Bodo von Dewitz and Reinhard Matz (Heidelberg: Edition Bras and Cologne: Agfa Foto-Historama, 1989), 80–81.
2. Jochen Voigt and Christoph Kaufmann, *Der gefrorene Augenblick: Daguerreotypie in Sachsen, 1839–1860: Inkunabeln der Photographie in sächsischen Sammlungen: gemeinsamer Bestandskatalog "Daguerreotypie"* (Chemnitz: Edition Mobilis, 2004), 81–82.
3. On the career of Wehnert-Beckmann, see Jochen Voigt, *A German Lady: Bertha Wehnert-Beckmann, Leben und Werk einer Fotographiepionieren* (Chemnitz: Edition Mobilis, 2014). A sample of the clients she served at her photographic studio in Leipzig is found in the list of clients who visited her studio, contained in a book she began in 1848: *Kundenbuch*, Nachlaß Wehnert-Beckmann, Stadtgeschichtliches Museum Leipzig.
4. For insightful discussions about how to work with photographs as historical evidence, see in particular Elizabeth Harvey and Maiken Umbach, eds., Special Issue: "Photography and Twentieth-Century German history," *Central European History* 48 (2015); and Jennifer Tucker, ed., Special Issue: "Photography and Historical Interpretation." *History and Theory* 48 (2009).
5. See the advertisement for Frederike Pommer's photographic studio reproduced in Voigt, *A German Lady*, 91.
6. Handbooks for producing daguerreotypes (and later photographs) began to circulate in the German States beginning in the 1840s. They offered information on the technical aspects of producing photographs as well as advice on how to work with clients and set up a photographic studio. See, for example, Anton Martin, *Handbuch der gesammten Photographie*, 4th ed. (Wien: Carl Gerold und Sohn, 1854); and Christian Friedrich Schmidt, *Handbuch der Photographie*, 2nd ed. (Weimar: B. F. Voigt, 1858).
7. *Kundenbuch*, Nachlaß Wehnert-Beckmann. The note from Brockhaus is unnumbered, slipped loose inside the book. We know from inventories of Wehnert-Beckmann's photographs that members of the Brockhaus family had their portraits taken several times in her studio.
8. Tina Campt, *Image Matters: Archive, Photography, and the African Diaspora in Europe* (Durham, NC: Duke University Press, 2012), 17.
9. Tina Campt, *Listening to Images* (Durham, NC: Duke University Press, 2017). Campt writes that looking at serial photographs is a practice in "engaging in the counterintuitive." Photographs that are quiet are not silent—one must listen for slight variations in rhythm and tone.

10. On these different subjects and contexts, see for example Laura Wexler, "Seeing Sentiment: Photography, Race, and the Innocent Eye," in *The Familial Gaze*, ed. Marianne Hirsch (Hanover: University Press of New England, 1999), 52–93.
11. Wexler, "Seeing Sentiment," 252.
12. Campt, *Image Matters*, 50.
13. On haptics and photography, see Campt, *Image Matters*; and Geoffrey Batchen, *Forget Me Not: Photography and Remembrance* (New York: Princeton Architectural Press, 2004).
14. Stephanie Downes, Sally Holloway, and Sarah Randles, eds., *Feeling Things: Objects and Emotions Through History* (Oxford: Oxford University Press, 2018), 3.
15. Monique Scheer, "Are Emotions a Kind of Practice (and Is This What Makes Them Have a History)? A Bourdieuian Approach to Understanding Emotion," *History and Theory* 51, no. 2 (2012): 194.
16. Scheer, "Are Emotions a Kind of Practice?," 193–220.
17. Scheer, "Are Emotions a Kind of Practice?," 196. On the western notion that "authentic" emotions are rooted in interiority, see also Lila Abu-Lughod and Catherine A. Lutz, "Introduction: Emotion, Discourse, and the Politics of Everyday Life," and Arun Appadurai, "Topographies of the Self: Praise and Emotion in Hindu India," both in Abu-Lughod and Lutz, eds., *Language and the Politics of Emotion* (Cambridge, UK: Cambridge University Press, 1990).
18. Scheer, "Are Emotions a Kind of Practice?," 209.
19. On dermic boundaries, see Madeline H. Caviness and Charles G. Nelson, *Women and Jews in Medieval German Law: The Sachsenspiegel Books* (Turnhout, Belgium: Brepolis Press, forthcoming).
20. Annelie Ramsbrock, *The Science of Beauty: Culture and Cosmetics in Modern Germany, 1750–1930*, trans. David Burnett (New York: Palgrave Macmillan, 2015), 62.
21. On the art of reading photographs for bodily tension, see Campt, *Listening to Images*, particularly chapter 2, "Striking Poses in a Tense Grammar."
22. A beautiful early daguerreotype portrait that Hermann Krone took of himself and his wife shows her sitting on his lap in their wedding attire. This shows that such gestures and emotional expressions were not unimaginable in the period, even if they were unusual. The evidence suggests that most of the couples photographed by Wehnert-Beckmann were married. The inventory of Wehnert-Beckmann's photographs housed at the City Museum of Leipzig provide the family names of sitters, often without an indication of who was in the photograph—for example, "Brockhaus." In some cases, the inventory marks whether a woman was married or unmarried, but nothing comparable exists in the inventory for men. Nonetheless, the fact that so many portraits bear only one family name suggests that these were often family portraits.

Bibliography

Abu-Lughod, Lila, and Catherine A. Lutz, eds. *Language and the Politics of Emotion.* Cambridge, UK: Cambridge University Press, 1990.
Barthes, Roland. *Camera Lucida: Reflections on Photography.* New York: Hill and Wang, 1981.

Batchen, Geoffrey. *Forget Me Not: Photography and Remembrance*. New York: Princeton Architectural Press, 2004.

Campt, Tina. *Image Matters: Archive, Photography, and the African Diaspora in Europe*. Durham, NC: Duke University Press, 2012.

—— *Listening to Images*. Durham, NC: Duke University Press, 2017.

Caviness, Madeline H., and Charles G. Nelson. *Women and Jews in Medieval German Law: The Sachsenspiegel Books*. Turnhout, Belgium: Brepolis Press, forthcoming.

Downes, Stephanie, Sally Holloway, and Sarah Randles, eds. *Feeling Things: Objects and Emotions Through History*. Oxford: Oxford University Press, 2018.

Harris, Oliver T. J., and Tim Fohr Sørensen. "Rethinking Emotion and Material Culture." *Archaeological Dialogues* 17 (2010): 145–63.

Harvey, Elizabeth, and Maiken Umbach, eds. Special Issue: "Photography and Twentieth-Century German History." *Central European History* 48 (2015): 287–99.

Martin, Anton. *Handbuch der gesammten Photographie*, 4th ed. Wien: Carl Gerold und Sohn, 1854.

Ramsbrock, Annelie. *The Science of Beauty: Culture and Cosmetics in Modern Germany, 1750–1930*. Translated by David Burnett. New York: Palgrave MacMillan, 2015.

Scheer, Monique. "Are Emotions a Kind of Practice (And Is That What Makes Them Have a History)? A Bourdieuian Approach to Understanding Emotion." *History and Theory* 51, no. 2 (2012): 193–220.

Schmidt, Christian Friedrich. *Handbuch der Photographie*, 2nd ed. Weimar: B. F. Voigt, 1858.

Starl, Timm. "Fortschrit und Phantasma: Zur Entstehung der photographischen Bildwelt." In *Silber und Salz: Zur Frühzeit der Photographie im deutschen Sprachraum*, edited by Bodo von Dewitz and Reinhard Matz, 80–87. Heidelberg: Edition Bras and Cologne: Agfa Foto-Historama, 1989.

Tucker, Jennifer, ed. Special Issue: "Photography and Historical Interpretation." *History and Theory* 48 (2009).

Voigt, Jochen. *A German Lady: Bertha Wehnert-Beckmann, Leben und Werk einer Fotographiepionieren*. Chemnitz: Edition Mobilis, 2014.

Voigt, Jochen, and Christoph Kaufmann. *Der gefrorene Augenblick: Daguerreotypie in Sachsen 1839–1860: Inkunabeln der Photographie in sächsischen Sammlungen: gemeinsamer Bestandskatalog "Daguerreotypie."* Chemnitz: Edition Mobilis, 2004.

von Dewitz, Bodo, and Reinhard Matz. *Silber und Salz: zur Frühzeit der Photographie im deutschen Sprachraum, 1839–1860*. Cologne: Edition Braus, 1989.

Wexler, Laura. "Seeing Sentiment: Photography, Race, and the Innocent Eye." In *The Familial Gaze*, edited by Marianne Hirsch, 52–93. Hanover: University Press of New England, 1999.

CHAPTER 12

The Emotional Language of Flowers

UTE FREVERT

Statistics tell us that the average German currently spends more than one hundred Euros per year on flowers and flowerpots. A fifth of this sum usually goes into bouquets bought for Mother's Day, and a growing percentage for Valentine's Day.[1] The national flower industry is thriving, and so are florists, who buy from both national and international markets. Florists also invented the slogan "say it with flowers" (*Lasst Blumen sprechen*), which an online idiomatic dictionary translates into "express your feelings by giving flowers" (*Bringt eure Gefühle zum Ausdruck, indem ihr Blumen schenkt*).[2] The slogan is communicated through various media: postcards, gift cards, and, increasingly, the Internet. Numerous websites inform inexperienced consumers about which emotions should be expressed through which and how many flowers. Color plays an important role and can make all the difference.[3]

Flowers seem to "speak" an emotional language, or, to be more precise, are supposed to and forced to "speak" it. Emotions are embodied, represented, and expressed by roses and daffodils, violets and chrysanthemums, lilies and carnations. Compared with all other goods, flowers appear to convey emotional messages in the most direct manner, and when used as gifts, they define a specific, emotion-based relationship between giver and receiver. Even beyond gift cultures, they are said to communicate feelings, moods, and sentiments, as articles of fashion, as decorative objects in private and public spaces, or as ornaments in paintings.[4]

To apply Clifford Geertz's terms, flowers might thus be theorized as symbols that "give meaning, that is, objective conceptual form" to emotions. They can do this in two ways: by offering a model *of* reality and "shaping themselves to it," and/or by constituting a model *for* reality, which entails shaping "real" emotions to be like or as flowers.[5] The chapter predominantly focuses on the first aspect (i.e., on flowers as symbols of emotions). But it also invites an exploration of the manner in which flowers have themselves molded and modeled emotions in given contexts—by privileging certain emotions over others, or by highlighting positive feelings in political actions that might otherwise have raised negative emotions and violent reactions. In this regard, flowers can themselves exercise agency: they mobilize emotions in social relationships, and thus actively influence or even transform those relations.

Such transformative power can be studied on several levels: in private, intimate relations as well as in politics or at the workplace. Starting around 1800 in Europe, flowers were increasingly used to emotionalize people's interactions and communication. In an age that dramatically changed how individuals conceived of themselves and their relations with others, flowers served as a gift or an accessory of positive emotional value. Emotions, so to speak, became visible, tradable, and negotiable through the language of flowers that, for these very purposes, invited and enabled a multitude of social practices. Some of them will be analyzed in this chapter. It first focuses on the role flowers played in political communication, as party emblems or gifts sending emotional messages from giver to receiver, adorning the latter with a warm humane glow. Flowers thus served to emotionalize and personalize politics in the modern era of mass political participation. Second, flowers also intensified emotional communication in the private sphere, among friends and lovers. They were supposed to communicate a set of positive feelings, and they did so in a language that had to be taught and learned. Consequently, special genre and advice books proliferated during the nineteenth and twentieth centuries. At the same time, the production and consumption of flowers grew at an exponential rate that was further fostered by the invention and commodification of highly emotionalized holidays, like Mother's Day or St. Valentine's Day. The latter point, thirdly, to the gendered structure of flower-centered practices. In most cases, men bought and gave flowers to women, not the other way around. This was facilitated by the common assumption that women bore a certain resemblance to flowers, and vice versa. As much as the modern age worked toward drawing clear lines of distinction between men and women, masculinity and femininity, it also enlisted flowers to both confirm and romanticize the distinction.

Political Flower Power

On 19 July 2017, Prince William and his wife Kate, the Duchess of Cambridge, arrived in the German capital for an official visit. Many Berliners gathered in front of the Brandenburg Gate to catch a glimpse of the royal couple or even secure a handshake. Women in particular were smitten by the Duchess and expertly commented on what she was wearing: a coatdress that looked both "serious" and "feminine." In addition to its elegant style, its color caught everyone's attention: a fabulous blue, neither dark nor light—"*kornblumenblau*" (cornflower blue), as Christin "from Potsdam" expertly observed.[6]

Her observation was undoubtedly correct. The dress was indeed the color of the cornflower. But probably neither Christin nor any other person gathering in Berlin's center that day was aware of the political symbolism. Cornflowers had acquired a particular emotional significance in late nineteenth-century Germany. They were widely known as the first German Emperor's favorite flower, and citizens hurried to send him cornflower gifts on every occasion. Starting in the 1870s, the cornflower was regarded as the *Kaiserblume*, the emblematic flower of the new Empire, and, as Eva Giloi has shown, a veritable cult emerged that even outlasted Wilhelm I.[7] Nowadays, this cult seems to be largely forgotten—with the exception, perhaps, of some protocol experts in the British Foreign Office. Considering that the Duchess of Cambridge chooses her outfits very carefully so as to include references to national styles and traditions, it is not altogether improbable that politics was in the background of her cornflower blue coatdress choice. This choice might have been meant to convey a message of sympathy: "Look, we (the British) know about your (the Germans') history, and we appreciate your traditions and pay them respect." With Brexit looming, such a message could hardly be ignored by those who grasped its meaning.

Around 1900, the cornflower conveyed other messages. Tied to the often-recounted story of the young Prussian Prince Wilhelm consoling his mother Luise in the bitter times of Napoleonic conquest, it signified vulnerability as much as a child's love and trust. As a wildflower blossoming in fields and meadows, it symbolized modesty rather than regal magnificence.[8] The 1806 narrative served to remind the Emperor and his loyal citizens of the humiliation Prussia suffered at the hands of France, and of the seemingly ongoing threat posed by the neighboring country. In this perspective, the blue cornflower represented national perseverance and ultimate victory against all odds. As such, it was held in high esteem during the Imperial era. Veterans' associations used it in their efforts to raise funds, and welfare organizations staged so-called *Kornblumentage* (cornflower days) in order to collect donations for social purposes.[9]

The practice of attaching sentimental value to flowers and instrumentalizing this attributed significance for political ends was not a Prussian–German invention. Napoleon I, Luise's counterpart and enemy, had created a similar tradition for himself. During his lifetime, he became known as "Père la Violette" (Papa Violet), with narratives weaving private issues (Napoleon's love affair with Josephine de Beauharnais and her passion for violets) into political visions of regaining power and imperial regalia after the defeat in 1813. Even after he was finally exiled in St. Helena, his followers chose to wear violets on their lapels as a symbol of loyalty and a sign of mutual recognition.[10]

Attributing political symbolism to flowers actually stemmed from a long tradition. Since ancient times, lilies had adorned royal coats of arms and palatial spaces. The modern era not only challenged the rule of kings and queens, opening up politics to ordinary citizens, but also added sentiment to symbolism. For French aristocrats in danger of being decapitated under the guillotine, red carnations became symbols of passionate resistance.[11] After the Bourbons returned to the throne in 1814, white (or silver) lilies reappeared on the political stage and were the emblem of the royalist camp that took vicious revenge on Napoleon's henchmen.[12]

The red carnation was also adopted as a party flower, but in altogether different settings. From 1890 onward, men and women who supported the socialist movement and its struggle against capitalist exploitation wore red carnations. As recommended by the International Socialist Workers Congress in Paris in 1889, May 1st was chosen to mark the worldwide campaign for the eight-hour working day. In Germany, where the socialist movement was legally constrained and politically suppressed until 1890, no public rallies or red flags were allowed. Instead, supporters chose to wear red carnations, thus starting a tradition that continues to the present day.[13] In the GDR, everyone participating in May Day celebrations wore a red carnation on their lapel. Even after the demise of state socialism, every year, left-wing politicians and citizens gather in early January to adorn the graves of communist leaders like Rosa Luxemburg, Karl Liebknecht, Wilhelm Pieck, Walter Ulbricht, and others, in continuation of a GDR propaganda event.[14]

The red carnation, however, was also the favorite flower of Emperor Wilhelm II, clearly without any reference to socialism. Accordingly, shops and department stores used to display patriotism by decorating their windows with carnation garlands wound around the imperial bust.[15] Loyal citizens sent flowers for the Emperor's birthday or other festivities, thus forming an intimate bond with the royal family. This tradition had become popular with Wilhelm I and his famous cornflowers, but faded after the forced abdication of the Hohenzollern in 1918, only to be resumed under National Socialism. Adolf Hitler was again flooded with flower bouquets, sent or given mostly by female admirers. Children, too, decorated their handwritten letters to the Führer with flowers, privileging the alpine edelweiss, which was supposed to be his favorite and interpreted as plain and unpretentious.[16] Nevertheless, the song "*Hitlers Lieblingsblume ist das Edelweiß*" was banned in 1939 as "national kitsch."[17]

Flowers thus conveyed different messages when used as a means of political communication. Whereas citizens chose them to demonstrate their emotional attachment and approval, politicians and heads of state liked to be photographed with bouquets that showcased their popularity and legitimacy, while, at the same time, testifying to their humane character. With flowers in their hands, even mass killers like Hitler or Stalin looked peaceful, benevolent, and friendly.[18]

The kind of flowers did not seem to really matter. In most European countries, roses were held in high regard, as personal as well as political gifts. The Second Socialist International also adopted them as a political emblem. In West Germany, Social Democrats used both red carnations and red roses as party flowers. In 1986, the British Labour Party replaced the red flag with the red rose as their logo, thus paying tribute to England's national flower. For different reasons, the French Parti Socialiste had adopted the red rose in 1969. In the same year, the West German artist Joseph Beuys exhibited a *Revolutionsklavier* at the Düsseldorf Academy of Arts; the revolutionary piano was strewn with more than two hundred red flowers, both carnations and roses. Three years later, at the fifth Kassel Documenta exhibition of contemporary art, Beuys took a red rose to explain the relation between evolution and revolution: although the blossoming flower signified revolutionary change, it was likewise the product of organic development.[19]

The party that Beuys eventually helped to found did not choose the red rose as a symbol, opting instead for the yellow sunflower. Even before various local and regional initiatives merged to formally establish the Green Party in 1980, sunflowers appeared on flyers, brochures, and election posters. They symbolized the Greens' emphasis on nature and ecology, and they sent a message of optimism, hope, and grassroots enthusiasm.[20] When twenty-eight newly elected party members entered the federal parliament in 1983, they carried with them sick fir trees in order to raise awareness of dying forest syndrome. But they also brought sunflowers, signaling their positive commitment to ecological improvement and social change. Despite several visual adjustments in recent years, the sunflower continues to serve as the Green Party's main logo. Even without consulting online or offline lexica on the language of flowers, its emotional meaning is easily decoded as representing joy, human warmth, and cheerfulness.

Codes of Knowledge

The fact that the Green Party chose a flower as an emblem of its political goals and program might have seemed quasi-"natural." In general, however, there was no obvious reason why parties should adopt flowers for their logos, and most parties actually did not.[21] On the other hand, flowers had long since been discovered and put to use as multivariant symbols. Starting in the early nineteenth century, European authors drafted elaborate "languages of flowers" that connected type and color to specific meanings and messages. According to the booklet *Vollständige Blumensprache* (*Complete Language of Flowers*) published in 1850, the sunflower symbolized distant, unfulfilled love and reverence; red carnations represented lovesickness; while red roses were associated with eternal, passionate love.[22]

In alphabetical order, the booklet listed about seven hundred different flowers with their associated symbolism. Other publications of a similar kind were equally comprehensive, referencing far more species than an ordinary flower garden or florist's shop contained. This indicated the lists' artificial character and undoubtedly reduced their practical usage. Flowers' meanings seem to have been invented and attributed at random, and no man or woman could possibly remember their origin. In all probability, the knowledge transmitted through such guides was hardly ever practiced in daily life.[23]

Still, these guides did exist, and were indeed quite successful in European and North American book markets. The French started the hype and set the tone, with other countries following suit. Popular French books were often quite literally adapted by British or German authors. In a similar fashion, German texts quickly appeared in French and English translations. Readers, predominantly female, across the channel and on each bank of the River Rhine seemed equally eager to read about flowers and what they had to tell, and publishers were keen to make this information available.

To explain the obsession with the language of flowers, it helps to examine the contexts in which such language was "spoken." The 1850 booklet declared explicitly that it was dedicated to "love and friendship," and not, for this matter, to politics. Flowers were to "speak" predominantly in intimate relations between lovers, friends, parents, and children, and literary texts, poems, and novels presented adequate models to emulate.[24] As a late nineteenth-century author recommended, his book should be used as a present intended for lovers only: "Both parts can then interpret the sent or given flowers and their meaning according to what the sender wanted to say. In the gentlest way, wishes, explanations, thoughts and feelings are thus to be mutually exchanged, without letting any stranger know and interfere."[25]

This promise implicitly referred to the popular narrative about the genre's allegedly Asian origin. From the very start, authors had drawn upon the so-called Selam tradition as communicated by European travelers from the Ottoman Empire. Selam, the secret language of flowers, was said to be spoken between a male lover and the woman he courted behind the closed walls of the harem. Although scholars had cast serious doubt on its actual practicality, the legend's popularity persisted, since it both eroticized the code and gave it an exotic twist.[26] Endowed with such pedigree, flowers were the best means to communicate finely nuanced messages of affection, longing, hope, gratitude, and devotion. In less intimate relations, they might mean something else, as meanings did not necessarily travel from one domain to the other. Flowers offered by an employer to a long-standing employee bore a different meaning from the flowers that a suitor gave to his potential mother-in-law.

In each and every relationship, however, flowers were thought to communicate feelings. As such, they became highly praised and valued during the age of sensibility and romanticism that marked the late eighteenth and early nineteenth centuries. Since feelings were deemed to be crucial markers of a person's character and individuality, they came to be regarded as important tools for communication. It was considered a major challenge to cultivate one's feelings in a way that rendered them readable by others, above all among the educated middle classes, whose emotional culture aimed to distinguish them from both the aristocracy and the common people. In this context, flowers were discovered as a means to both facilitate and complicate emotional communication. They could send discreet messages that were otherwise difficult to convey through words and sentences. Potentially, every feeling, with all its nuances, could be expressed by a certain flower—hence the extensive lists mentioned in many guide books and lexica. In actual fact, however, the sheer number could not but overwhelm and baffle those who were intent on learning the art of giving and receiving flowers for sentimental reasons.

But even though nineteenth century books on flowers were of limited practical value, they sold very well and went through numerous editions. In fact, they were popular as the perfect gift for Christmas or the New Year, and were designed, as an American author suggested in 1854, "as a Table Book for the Parlor, of a sentimental character, to diversify the monotony of a long winter evening."[27] To own such a book signaled a family's or a person's cultivation and civility, marking them as members of a certain social class and culture.

At the same time, however, the books' message was not altogether irrelevant in real life. A part of their content was used in the manner books and advice manuals that proliferated throughout the nineteenth and early twentieth centuries. In such condensed version, the language of flowers indeed managed to influence people's behavior and mode of communication. While earlier manuals, above all the famous *Knigge* of 1788, did not mention this language, later ones did. In the 1870s, Franz Ebhardt's *Der gute Ton in allen Lebenslagen* (*Appropriate Behavior in all Circumstances*) included a chapter about flowers, which were introduced as "signs" and "symbols" for "what lives in our heart and shies away from being openly expressed and addressed." Giving credit to the French and their elaborate expertise, the author confirmed that the language of flowers and colors was also well understood in Germany. Peonies, for example, were known as the flowers to express love without words, while violets represented grace, lilies innocence, and daisies truth and modesty. Ebhardt's list was manageable and easy to grasp and remember. Equally clear was the advice he gave, especially to young women: red flowers were a taboo since they expressed "fiery passion," which was by tradition men's territory. Young ladies in France, he warned, would never wear red carnations, poppies, or roses since those flowers were hardly compatible with the female sex and its "gentle dignity."[28] At the most, ladies could claim a light rosy red for themselves—which, since the 1920s, has become the typical female color for baby clothes as well as toys, bed linen, and room decorations.[29]

Gendered Practices

Colors were thus used as a marker of the difference between men and women, most conspicuously in wedding clothes, which, starting in Queen Victoria's era, were white (the color of purity) for the bride and black (the color of respectability) for the groom. Linked to flowers, colors became even more significant in their symbolism. A bouquet of red roses meant something completely different than white or yellow roses. Such meanings were particularly crucial in interactions between men and women. It was here that the language of flowers had the greatest significance. Relevant manuals offered detailed advice to young men on how to use it properly, avoiding mistakes that might ruin a relationship before it had the chance to blossom. In addition to choosing the appropriate flowers and colors, men had to ensure that flowers were nicely arranged in sophisticated bouquets. It was unacceptable to offer a potted flower to a young woman, although such gifts were popular among female friends. A man's gift should only draw short-term attention; anything else would immodestly imply that he claimed a longer presence in the life of his beloved.[30]

Flowers were not only given (usually by men) and received (by women) as a token of affection and adoration. They were also worn by both genders. Fashion dictated that women adorn dresses and hats with flowers, fresh as well as synthetic. Men wore flowers on the lapels of their coats or suits. The custom of the Social Democrats in 1890 to wear a red carnation as a sign of protest and solidarity was thus in tune with current fashion. A lucrative industry and trade developed after French Huguenots introduced the production of artificial flowers in Germany in the late eighteenth century.[31] Mainly women were employed in cottage industries for very low wages to craft flowers from silk or paper that looked as beautiful as freshly cut flowers but lasted much longer.[32] Women also sold flowers as shop assistants in the burgeoning florist shops, or as volunteers during the so-called *Blumentage* (flower days) that became widely popular in the early twentieth century. Organized mainly by middle-class women with the help of high-level institutions, the "fair sex," and especially its younger members, sold white daisies and blue cornflowers to local citizens; the money earned went into social welfare projects, particularly for children. Everyone was addressed, men and women of all social classes. "In the service of giving love," the flower was supposed to form a "bond between all circles," gracing "the frock-coat and the tennis clothing, the officer's uniform and the worker's hat, the elegant ladies' suit and the dress of the cleaning woman."[33]

Women thus figured prominently as producers, sellers, and consumers of flowers, albeit not as the main buyers.[34] Up to this day, it is usually men that give flowers to women, not the reverse. Men rarely receive flowers (or sweets and perfumes, which are also typically feminine gifts). On more formal occasions, however, men as politicians or CEOs or colleagues are more and more often congratulated with a bouquet (which is then quickly handed over to their wives or female partners). In the era of Wilhelm I, gender roles were far more rigid, as the aging Emperor jokingly confirmed. At the sight of the many birthday bouquets he received from far and wide, he remarked: "It isn't right; it doesn't suit an old man like me at all—yes, if I were a pretty young woman or a little girl that would be different!"[35] More than age, gender mattered when it came to flowers, although royals obviously were exempted.

There was another exception, and it concerned the manliest of all men: soldiers. When German troops were mobilized in August 1914, men in military uniforms, conscripted or volunteering, were trimmed with flowers when they departed for the battlefront. Women who gathered at train stations made sure that no defender of home and hearth left without a flower. Even after the defeat in 1918, they welcomed back with garlands those who had survived the carnage. Flowers here were a symbol of life and gratitude; even critical citizens like Käthe Kollwitz, who had come to oppose the war, did not hesitate to honor those who had fought in it (among them her two sons).[36] Unlike Britain, however, in Germany there was no particular flower dedicated to the memory of those who had fallen on the field of honor. The red poppy, still worn by British citizens during Remembrance Week in early November, is not a custom encountered in France or Germany.[37]

Women giving flowers to departing or returning soldiers seemed, at first sight, to turn the traditional order upside down. At closer examination, however, the gender system remained intact. Men, as the common narrative had it, went to war in order to protect women and children; women had to reward them with even greater love, submission, and devotedness. Flowers in the hands of women thus symbolized an intimate promise: "When you come back, you will find a grateful wife or yearning bride welcoming you to her bed." The close connection between women and flowers that stemmed from a century-old tradition thus persisted.

Such connections had been addressed with particular zeal by female and male authors alike since the late eighteenth century. In 1802, the young German romantic poet Novalis, alias of Friedrich von Hardenberg, had his hero Heinrich von Ofterdingen dream of a blue flower, symbolizing his longing for a loving woman. Three decades earlier, in her poem "To a Lady, with some painted Flowers," the prominent English author Anna Laetitia Barbauld compared women to flowers: "Flowers sweet, and gay, and delicate like you; Emblems of innocence, and beauty too." The analogy was not meant to embarrass the lady or make her "blush": "Your best, your sweetest empire is—to please."³⁸

The analogy, however, did make some women blush—Mary Wollstonecraft vigorously rejected it since, in her opinion, virtue "must be acquired by *rough toils*, and useful struggles with worldly *cares*." She remarked with contempt that to reduce women to sweet and delicate flowerlike creatures was what "the men tell us," whereas women should know better.³⁹ Yet, mainstream attitudes favored Barbauld and countless other writers who repeated the same message over and over again. As a magazine stated in 1848, women and flowers shared a "natural sympathy: women are themselves flowers, gently, diligently and lovingly cultivated so that they can bring joy to their future owners through beauty and grace."⁴⁰

Capitalizing on the analogy, from the early twentieth century onward, florists started to market flowers more aggressively. The slogan "say it with flowers" ("*Laßt Blumen sprechen*") was used, implying that flowers should, above all, speak of love.⁴¹ Moreover, commercial associations started to popularize the so-called Mother's Day. Invented in the United States before World War I, it gained the support of conservative and religious groups as well as welfare associations during the Weimar Republic, and was widely celebrated around 1930. The perfect gift for mothers was, unsurprisingly, flowers—in all shapes, kinds, and colors, but with a single message: love and gratitude.⁴² During the era of National Socialism, Mother's Day was transformed into a political propaganda event and officially staged, with particular honors given to mothers of large families. After World War II, the GDR, in unison with other socialist countries, instead chose to celebrate International Women's Day in early March—with different ideological messages, but also with loads of flowers, mostly red carnations.⁴³ Starting in the early 1990s, florists again took the initiative and heavily campaigned to popularize St. Valentine's Day in Germany (and continental Europe). Lufthansa's proud announcement that in 2013 the carrier transported one thousand tons of roses from Nairobi, Bogota, and Quito to Frankfurt in order to be sold on February 14 offers a clue as to how successful and lucrative the business with flowers turned out to be. Again, love paved the commercial way, and lovers eagerly picked up the offer to express their passionate and deeply felt emotions through flowers. More precisely, men are still usually the ones who buy and give flowers to women as a token of their affection.⁴⁴

The profound gendering of most practices and interactions involving flowers was not beyond criticism. Like Mary Wollstonecraft, who had found the analogy between flowers and women demeaning, feminists in the 1970s opposed Mother's Day and its flowery ornamentation as camouflaging women's discrimination in society and politics. The International Women's Day attracted similar criticism, even though it was originally initiated by women demanding female suffrage. Around 1900, socialists in many European countries and the United States had started to campaign for social and political rights. Rose Schneiderman, a textile worker and trade union organizer from New York, set the tone in 1912: "What the woman who labors wants is the right to live, not simply exist.... The worker must have bread, but she must have roses, too." Addressing "women of privilege," she claimed that "even the humblest worker" had a right to "the sun and music and art," and she willfully chose the rose to symbolize the difference between sheer existence and true life.[45] Furthermore, she deliberately claimed the rose for female workers, thus invoking the popular trope about women's love of flowers.

Schneiderman's quote about bread and roses was quickly popularized in poems and songs, and the feminist movement later adopted it as a major slogan. The 1960s, however, also witnessed a movement to break down gender divisions, at least when it came to flowers. In 1967, Scott McKenzie landed a global hit with his song "San Francisco" and its first line: "If you're going to San Francisco, be sure to wear some flowers in your hair." This appealed to women and men alike, and was received enthusiastically by a generation that set out to replace war (Vietnam) with peace, sexual constraints with freedom, and gender hierarchy with equality. Flowers again proved of symbolic value as the "hippies" wished to "blossom freely like flowers" so that "the world will be saved by this now free generation."[46] But flowers were not just used to adorn one's hair and clothes. Following the prompt of poet Allen Ginsberg in 1965, flowers were also given to policemen and soldiers. "Flower power" was supposed to send a peaceful, cheerful, and nonviolent message of antiwar protest, as in October 1967, during the March on the Pentagon, when a young man placed carnations into the rifle barrels of military policemen—a scene immortalized in an iconic photograph.[47] Seven years later, the scene was repeated in Lisbon, with a young Portuguese woman handing a red carnation to a rebellious soldier; soon after, red carnations flooded Lisbon, and the military revolt was baptized the *"revolução dos cravos"* ("The Carnation Revolution").[48]

Conclusion

Starting in the late eighteenth century, flowers became strongly associated with emotions. Poems, novels, lexicons, paintings, picture books, and advice manuals all emphasized this relationship in great detail and high ingenuity. Addressed, above all, to lovers, they marketed and popularized an emotional language of flowers that was well received in middle-class circles, particularly among women. Flowers thereby became powerful symbols of femininity and gentility. With the untiring assistance of business-minded florists, these symbols reached more and more households, especially on Mother's Day, celebrated since the 1920s, and Valentine's Day, popularized, in Germany, in the 1990s. Flowers have thus sustained their deeply gendered meanings, although men also occasionally receive flowers as a token of professional or political recognition.

This was facilitated by flowers acquiring political symbolism. Within socialist movements, red carnations or roses were used and worn by men (and, later, by women, too) as symbols of solidarity and the struggle for progress. A hundred years later, the ecological movement adopted the sunflower as its logo. A decade earlier, activists had boldly proclaimed flower power to be the antidote to the destructive power of war and military intervention. Flowers here symbolized nonviolence, individual and political freedom, and, as in the Bread & Roses campaigns, the power of aesthetics to beautify human life and existence.

Throughout the modern period, flowers have thus served as material representations of emotions, imbuing the latter with color, shape, and smell. At the same time, they have helped to bring emotions to the fore, giving them a loud and audible voice. Their agency does not stop with representation: they are also utilized to promote emotions in private and public communication. Gaining prominence during the Age of Sensibility and Romanticism, flowers have outlived those eras and cultures, stabilizing emotions as a crucial mode of social interaction in both intimate and more formalized relationships. When, in the early twentieth century, florists embarked on an aggressive and highly successful marketing campaign, they cleverly capitalized on the symbolism of flowers. They became a mass commodity, their status as vessels of emotions bolstered by advertising ingenuity.[49]

Different people have expressed their emotions through flowers in distinct social contexts: individuals who either were or wanted to be in a special relationship with one another; members of a community that shared certain political goals and values; citizens sending flowers to politicians, statesmen, and stateswomen as gifts of personal allegiance and dedication; or friends, neighbors, and colleagues giving them as tokens of respect, gratitude, and appreciation. Contexts and practices are crucial in order for the emotional language of flowers to function and flourish. Removed from these contexts, meanings shift and symbolic references collapse.

As an overall trend, however, the ever extensive, diverse use of flowers in private and public communication since around 1800 testifies to a growing emotionalization that took hold in European and other westernized societies. The emotional language of flowers became part of an elaborate code to highlight, address, and share various kinds of feelings: love, above all, and attachment, as well as longing, grief, sorrow, and solidarity. Negative feelings, such as anger, rage, envy, or jealousy, were implicitly left out and tabooed. In certain cases, as in the flower power movement, flowers could even deliberately be employed to highlight positive feelings in political actions that might otherwise have raised negative emotions and violent reactions.

At the same time, earlier attempts to formalize and thus restrict the emotional coding of flowers have not been successful. In contemporary Western culture and society, people tend to use flowers at their own gusto. While red roses still symbolize deep and passionate love, red carnations have all but lost their political relevance, except for a limited number of citizens and events. The pluralization of lifestyles and the dissolution of political milieus all contributed to the language of flowers becoming less fixed and more polysemic and individualized. Even the more recent interest in reformalizing social relationships and rites of passage has not succeeded in bringing back a mandatory flower alphabet, grammar, and syntax. People still use flowers to communicate feelings, but they increasingly do so free from prescribed rules.

Ute Frevert is Director at the Max Planck Institute for Human Development in Berlin. From 2003 to 2007, she was professor of German history at Yale University, and prior to that, she taught History at the Universities of Konstanz, Bielefeld, and the Free University in Berlin. She is the author of numerous books, including *Emotions in History—Lost and Found* (2011); *A Nation in Barracks: Modern Germany, Military Conscription and Civil Society* (2004); *Men of Honour: A Social and Cultural History of the Duel* (1995); and *Women in German History: From Bourgeois Emancipation to Sexual Liberation* (1988).

Notes

1. "Entwicklung und Trends im Blumen- und Pflanzenmarkt 2015/2016," *Beschaffungsdienst GaLaBau*, accessed 5 August 2017, http://www.soll-galabau.de/aktuelle-news/ansicht-aktuelles/datum/2015/11/11/entwicklung-und-trends-im-blumen-und-pflanzenmarkt-2015-2016.html.
2. Karin Hausen, "'... durch die Blume gesprochen': Naturaneignung und Symbolvermarktung," in *Fahrrad, Auto, Fernsehschrank: Zur Kulturgeschichte der Alltagsdinge*, ed. Wolfgang Ruppert (Frankfurt: Fischer, 1993), 52–78, 223–25, esp. 69–70; accessed 5 August 2017, https://www.redensarten-index.de/suche.php?such begriff=~~Lasst%20Blumen%20sprechen!&bool=relevanz&suchspalte[]=rart_ou, Redensartenindex.
3. See, among many others, Pflanzenfee, "Lasst Blumen sprechen—wir sagen Ihnen, was es bedeutet!," accessed 5 August 2017, https://www.pflanzenfee.de/info/ratgeber/lasst-blumen-sprechen-wir-sagen-ihnen-was-es-bedeutet.
4. See, as a global overview, Jack Goody, *The Culture of Flowers* (Cambridge, UK: Cambridge University Press, 1993). As for Japan and its infatuation with cherry blossoms, see Emiko Ohnuki-Tierney, *Flowers That Kill: Communicative Opacity in*

Political Spaces (Stanford: Stanford University Press, 2015), 25–56. On paintings, see Andreas Honegger, *Die Blumen der Frauen: Blumensymbolik in Gemälden aus 7 Jahrhunderten* (Munich: Sandmann, 2011).
5. Clifford Geertz, *The Interpretation of Cultures* (New York: Basic Books, 1973), 93.
6. "Berlin macht königsblau." *Der Tagesspiegel*, 20 July 2017: 9.
7. Eva Giloi, *Monarchy, Myth, and Material Culture in Germany 1750–1950* (Cambridge, UK: Cambridge University Press, 2011), 161–66.
8. Giloi, *Monarchy*, 163. The cornflower story about Wilhelm and Luise comes in different versions: in some versions, Wilhelm consoles his mother; in other versions, Luise comforts her son (see, for example, Emmy Giehrl, "Kornblumen," *Deutsche Revue über das gesamte nationale Leben der Gegenwart* 22, no. 1 [1897]: 121–23).
9. Eva Schöck-Quinteros, "Blumentage im Deutschen Reich: Zwischen bürgerlicher Wohltätigkeit und Klassenkampf," *Ariadne* 39 (2001): 44–51. See also Siegfried Becker, "Kornblumen: Zur politischen und kulturellen Symbolik in den Nationalitätenkonflikten Österreich-Ungarns," *Hessische Blätter für Volks- und Kulturforschung* 34 (1998): 69–114.
10. Karl Gottlieb Bretschneider, *Der vierjährige Krieg der Verbündeten mit Napoleon Bonaparte in Rußland, Teutschland, Italien und Frankreich in den Jahren 1812 bis 1815*, vol. 2 (Annaberg: Freyer, 1816), 434; Karl Reimer, "Parteiblumen," *Innsbrucker Nachrichten*, 3 May 1900: 1–2. Napoleon III continued his uncle's tradition.
11. Gabriele Tergit (alias Elise Reifenberg), *Kleine Geschichte der Blumen* (Berlin: Ullstein, 1981), 116.
12. Reimer, "Parteiblumen," mentions the Order of the (Silver) Lily under Louis XVIII; it was obviously given to so many followers of the royalist cause that it eventually came to figure as a party flower.
13. Gottfried Korff, "Seht die Zeichen, die euch gelten: Fünf Bemerkungen zur Symbolgeschichte des 1. Mai," in *100 Jahre Zukunft. Zur Geschichte des 1. Mai*, ed. Inge Marßolek (Frankfurt: Büchergilde Gutenberg, 1990), 15–39; for Austria, see Brigitte Lehmann, "Ehrwürdige Rote Nelke," in *Die ersten 100 Jahre: Österreichische Sozialdemokratie 1888–1988*, ed. Helene Maimann (Vienna: Brandstätter, 1988), 102–5.
14. Zentralfriedhof Friedrichsfelde, "Die Gedenkstätte der Sozialisten," accessed 5 August 2017, http://sozialistenfriedhof.de/gedenkstaettesoziali.html. As I witnessed in 2010, carnations (which were quickly sold out in nearby florist shops) were distributed quite unevenly to the graves of socialist heroes: the grave with the most flowers was that of Rosa Luxemburg, while Walter Ulbricht's grave had the fewest.
15. Dirk Reinhardt, *Von der Reklame zum Marketing: Geschichte der Wirtschaftswerbung in Deutschland* (Berlin: Akademie-Verlag, 1993), 416. According to the popular writer Elsbeth Ebertin (born in 1880), though, Wilhelm II's favorite flowers were tea roses and mignonettes: *Die Lieblingsblumen der deutschen Kaiser und des Führers Adolf Hitler* (Weinsberg: Dr. Brot & Feierabend, 1935), 5.
16. See the compilation of letters (often accompanied by flowers) in Bundesarchiv Berlin, NS 51, No. 63–77; Ebertin, *Die Lieblingsblumen*, 7.
17. Hans-Jörg Koch, *Das Wunschkonzert im NS-Rundfunk* (Cologne: Böhlau, 2003), 366.
18. See the propaganda photos reprinted in Ohnuki-Tierney, *Flowers That Kill*, 71–74 (Stalin), 74–78 (Hitler); Joachim Fest and Heinrich Hoffmann, *Hitler—Gesichter eines Diktators: Eine Bilddokumentation*, 2nd ed. (Munich: Herbig, 1993), 58–59, 98–99.

19. Götz Adriani, Winfried Konnertz, and Karin Thomas, *Joseph Beuys* (Cologne: DuMont, 1994), 128.
20. Roland Vogt, "Auf der Suche nach dem Salzkorn—Symbolnutzung bei der Friedensbewegung und bei den Grünen," *Forschungsjournal Neue soziale Bewegungen* 1 (1988): 36–42; Gudrun Silberzahn-Jandt, "Die Sonnenblume und der Müll," *Hessische Blätter für Volks- und Kulturforschung* 34 (1998): 115–26, here 120–22. The sunflower also referred to the image of the laughing sun that, since 1975 and starting in Denmark, has become the long-standing emblem of the international antinuclear movement.
21. With the exception of Sweden, where most parties use flower symbols.
22. *Vollständige Blumensprache, der Liebe und Freundschaft gewidmet, oder Bedeutung der Pflanzen und Blumen nach occidentalischer Art* (Warburg: Schilp, 1850), 29, 33, 37.
23. M. Unterbeck, *Neueste vollständige Blumen-, Fächer- und Briefmarkensprache* (Stuttgart: Schwabacher'sche Verlagsbuchhandlung, n.d.—possibly from the 1870s or 1880s), 9–68 (with a list from "Adlerkraut" to "Zittergras"), claimed that the language of flowers was "by now well-known and popular" (4), which was probably correct considering the number of books sold in many copies. This, however, did not mean that the language was actually spoken and used in everyday communication.
24. Anna Ananieva, "Getrocknete Blumen: Literarische Figurationen sentimentaler Erinnerungspraktiken zwischen modischer Chiffre und intimem Souvenir in Révéroni Saint-Cyrs 'Sabina d'Herfeld,'" in *Die Sachen der Aufklärung*, ed. Frauke Berndt and Daniel Fulda (Hamburg: Meiner, 2012), 389–401; Anna Ananieva and Christiane Holm, "Phänomenologie des Intimen: Die Neuformulierung des Andenkens seit der Empfindsamkeit," in *Der Souvenir: Erinnerung in Dingen von der Reliquie zum Andenken* (Cologne: Wienand, 2006), 156–87.
25. Unterbeck, *Neueste vollständige Blumen-, Fächer- und Briefmarkensprache*. 4.
26. Beverly Seaton, *The Language of Flowers: A History* (Charlottesville: University Press of Virginia, 1995), 61–65; Clemens Alexander Wimmer, "Bücher über Blumensprache," *Zandera* 13 (1998): 15–25.
27. Quoted in Seaton, *Language of Flowers*, 19.
28. Franz Ebhardt, *Der gute Ton in allen Lebenslagen: Ein Handbuch für den Verkehr in der Familie, in der Gesellschaft und im öffentlichen Leben*, 3rd ed. (Berlin: Ebhardt, 1878), 220–25. The book's 12th edition of 1892 added the information that the cornflower, known as an "emblem of trust and steadfastness," had turned from "Kaiserblume to Volksblume" as Wilhelm I's predilection was mirrored by his loyal subjects (191–92).
29. Eva Heller, *Wie Farben wirken: Farbpsychologie—Farbsymbolik—Kreative Farbgestaltung* (Reinbek: Rowohlt, 1989), 118. Traditionally, however, light blue was used to dress girls, while young boys were dressed in pink (just as red was predominantly taken to be a "male" color and blue a "female" one) (56).
30. Ebhardt, *Der gute Ton*, 220, 226–27.
31. Alfred Meiche, *Die Anfänge der Kunstblumenindustrie in Dresden, Leipzig, Berlin und Sebnitz* (Dresden: Meinhold, 1908).
32. Regarding work conditions, see the 1908 and 1911 minutes of congresses organized by the Zentralverband der in der Blumen-, Blätter-, Palmen- und Putzfederfabrikation beschäftigten Arbeiter und Arbeiterinnen Deutschlands, in *Quelleneditionen zur Geschichte der deutschen Arbeiterbewegung, Projekt 2: Proletarische Frauenbewegung* (Wildberg: Belzer, 1998).

33. Quoted in Schöck-Quinteros, "Blumentage," 46–47 (from the *Casseler Tageblatt*, 14 August 1910).
34. It is unclear when exactly women started to buy flowers for themselves in order to decorate their homes. Victorian interiors showed little evidence of cut flowers (although vases were ubiquitous), while potted plants prevailed. See Judith Flanders, *Inside the Victorian Home: A Portrait of Domestic Life in Victorian England* (New York: W. W. Norton, 2004), 177, 180, 196.
35. Quoted in Giloi, *Monarchy*, 162.
36. Käthe Kollwitz, *Die Tagebücher*, ed. Jutta Bohnke-Kollwitz (Berlin: Siedler, 1989), 844, 384, 389.
37. Jennifer Iles, "In Remembrance: The Flanders Poppy," *Mortality* 13 (2008): 201–21. France adopted blue cornflowers as emblems of remembrance, albeit for a shorter time and with less popularity.
38. Anna Laetitia Barbauld, "To a Lady, With some painted FLOWERS," accessed 8 August 2017, https://en.wikisource.org/wiki/Poems_(Barbauld)/To_a_Lady,_with_painted_Flowers.
39. G. J. Barker-Benfield, *The Culture of Sensibility: Sex and Society in Eighteenth-Century Britain* (Chicago: University of Chicago Press, 1992), 265.
40. *Neubert's Deutsches Magazin für Garten- und Blumenkunde* 1 (1848): 148, quoted in Hausen, "'…durch die Blume," 224.
41. See the commercial ad inviting florists to decorate their shop windows with a pretty sign ("Laßt Blumen sprechen") and a heart-shaped garland of flowers (Hausen, "'…durch die Blume,'" 69).
42. Hausen, "'…durch die Blume,'" 74–76; Karin Hausen, "Mothers, Sons, and the Sale of Symbols and Goods: The 'German Mother's Day' 1923–1933," in *Interest and Emotion*, ed. Hans Medick and David Warren Sabean (Cambridge, UK: Cambridge University Press, 1984), 371–413; Irmgard Weyrather, *Mutterkreuz und Muttertag: Der Kult um die "deutsche Mutter" im Nationalsozialismus* (Frankfurt: Fischer, 1993).
43. Temma Kaplan, "On the Socialist Origins of International Women's Day," *Feminist Studies* 11 (1985): 163–71; Gudrun Hamacher, ed., *Internationaler Frauentag: Tag der Frauen seit 75 Jahren* (Frankfurt: Vorstand d. IG Metall, 1985).
44. Lufthansa, "1000 Tonnes of Roses on Board," accessed 10 August 2017, https://lufthansa-cargo.com/-/lhc-press-media-details-2013-page4-6-wc.
45. Sarah Eisenstein, *Give Us Bread but Give Us Roses: Working Women's Consciousness in the United States, 1890 to the First World War* (London: Routledge, 1983), 32.
46. Bennett M. Berger, "Hippie Morality—More Old than New," *Trans-action* 5 (1967): 20. See Allen Ginsberg, "Demonstration as Spectacle or Example, As Communication, or How to Make a March/Spectacle," in *The Portable Sixties Reader*, ed. Ann Charters (London: Penguin, 2002), 208–12.
47. Worcester Art Museum, "Kennedy to Kent State: Images of a Generation," accessed 10 August 2017, http://worcesterartmuseum.org/exhibitions/kennedy-to-kent-state/2011-135.htmlhttp://worcesterartmuseum.org/exhibitions/kennedy-to-kent-state/2011-135.html.
48. Kenneth Maxwell, "Portugal: 'The Revolution of the Carnations,' 1974–75," in *Civil Resistance and Power Politics: The Experience of Non-violent Action from Gandhi to the Present*, ed. Adam Roberts and Timothy Garton Ash (Oxford: Oxford University Press, 2009), 144–61.

49. As to the commodification of emotions, see Eva Illouz, *Consuming the Romantic Utopia: Love and the Cultural Contradictions of Capitalism* (Berkeley: University of California Press, 1997); and Eva Illouz, ed., *Emotions as Commodities: Capitalism, Consumption and Authenticity* (London: Routledge, 2017).

Bibliography

Adriani, Götz, Winfried Konnertz, and Karin Thomas. *Joseph Beuys*. Cologne: DuMont, 1994.

Ananieva, Anna. "Getrocknete Blumen: Literarische Figurationen sentimentaler Erinnerungspraktiken zwischen modischer Chiffre und intimem Souvenir in Révéroni Saint-Cyrs 'Sabina d'Herfeld.'" In *Die Sachen der Aufklärung*, edited by Frauke Berndt and Daniel Fulda, 389–401. Hamburg: Meiner, 2012.

Ananieva, Anna, and Christiane Holm. "Phänomenologie des Intimen: Die Neuformulierung des Andenkens seit der Empfindsamkeit." In *Der Souvenir: Erinnerung in Dingen von der Reliquie zum Andenken*, 156–87. Cologne: Wienand, 2006.

Barbauld, Anna Laetitia. "To a Lady, With some painted FLOWERS." Accessed 8 August 2017. https://en.wikisource.org/wiki/Poems_(Barbauld)/To_a_Lady,_with_painted_Flowers.

Barker-Benfield, G. J. *The Culture of Sensibility: Sex and Society in Eighteenth-Century Britain*. Chicago: University of Chicago Press, 1992.

Becker, Siegfried. "Kornblumen: Zur politischen und kulturellen Symbolik in den Nationalitätenkonflikten Österreich-Ungarns." *Hessische Blätter für Volks- und Kulturforschung* 34 (1998): 69–114.

Berger, Bennett M. "Hippie Morality—More Old than New." *Trans-action* 5 (1967): 19–27.

"Berlin macht königsblau." *Der Tagesspiegel*, 20 July 2017: 9.

Bretschneider, Karl Gottlieb. *Der vierjährige Krieg der Verbündeten mit Napoleon Bonaparte in Rußland, Teutschland, Italien und Frankreich in den Jahren 1812 bis 1815*, vol. 2. Annaberg: Freyer, 1816.

Ebertin, Elsbeth. *Die Lieblingsblumen der deutschen Kaiser und des Führers Adolf Hitler*. Weinsberg: Dr. Brot & Feierabend, 1935.

Ebhardt, Franz. *Der gute Ton in allen Lebenslagen: Ein Handbuch für den Verkehr in der Familie, in der Gesellschaft und im öffentlichen Leben*, 3rd. ed. Berlin: Ebhardt, 1878.

Eisenstein, Sarah. *Give Us Bread but Give Us Roses: Working Women's Consciousness in the United States, 1890 to the First World War*. London: Routledge, 1983.

"Entwicklung und Trends im Blumen- und Pflanzenmarkt 2015/2016." *Beschaffungsdienst GaLaBau*. Accessed 5 August 2017. http://www.soll-galabau.de/aktuelle-news/ansicht-aktuelles/datum/2015/11/11/entwicklung-und-trends-im-blumen-und-pflanzenmarkt-2015-2016.html.

Fest, Joachim, and Heinrich Hoffmann. *Hitler—Gesichter eines Diktators: Eine Bilddokumentation*, 2nd ed. Munich: Herbig, 1993.
Flanders, Judith. *Inside the Victorian Home: A Portrait of Domestic Life in Victorian England.* New York: W. W. Norton, 2004.
Geertz, Clifford. *The Interpretation of Cultures.* New York: Basic Books, 1973.
Giehrl, Emmy. "Kornblumen." *Deutsche Revue über das gesamte nationale Leben der Gegenwart* 22, no. 1 (1897): 121–23.
Giloi, Eva. *Monarchy, Myth, and Material Culture in Germany 1750–1950.* Cambridge, UK: Cambridge University Press, 2011.
Ginsberg, Allen. "Demonstration as Spectacle or Example, As Communication, or How to Make a March/Spectacle." In *The Portable Sixties Reader*, edited by Ann Charters, 208–12. London: Penguin, 2002.
Goody, Jack. *The Culture of Flowers.* Cambridge, UK: Cambridge University Press, 1993.
Hamacher, Gudrun, ed. *Internationaler Frauentag: Tag der Frauen seit 75 Jahren.* Frankfurt: Vorstand d. IG Metall, 1985.
Hausen, Karin. "'... durch die Blume gesprochen': Naturaneignung und Symbolvermarktung." In *Fahrrad, Auto, Fernsehschrank: Zur Kulturgeschichte der Alltagsdinge*, edited by Wolfgang Ruppert, 52–78, 223–25. Frankfurt: Fischer, 1993.
——— "Mothers, Sons, and the Sale of Symbols and Goods: The 'German Mother's Day' 1923–1933." In *Interest and Emotion*, edited by Hans Medick and David Warren Sabean, 371–413. Cambridge, UK: Cambridge University Press, 1984.
Heller, Eva. *Wie Farben wirken: Farbpsychologie—Farbsymbolik—Kreative Farbgestaltung.* Reinbek: Rowohlt, 1989.
Honegger, Andreas. *Die Blumen der Frauen: Blumensymbolik in Gemälden aus 7 Jahrhunderten.* Munich: Sandmann, 2011.
Iles, Jennifer. "In Remembrance: The Flanders Poppy." *Mortality* 13 (2008): 201–21.
Illouz, Eva. *Consuming the Romantic Utopia: Love and the Cultural Contradictions of Capitalism.* Berkeley: University of California Press, 1997.
——— ed. *Emotions as Commodities: Capitalism, Consumption and Authenticity.* London: Routledge, 2017.
Kaplan, Temma. "On the Socialist Origins of International Women's Day." *Feminist Studies* 11 (1985): 163–71.
Koch, Hans-Jörg. *Das Wunschkonzert im NS-Rundfunk.* Cologne: Böhlau, 2003.
Kollwitz, Käthe. *Die Tagebücher*, edited by Jutta Bohnke-Kollwitz. Berlin: Siedler, 1989.
Korff, Gottfried. "Seht die Zeichen, die euch gelten: Fünf Bemerkungen zur Symbolgeschichte des 1. Mai." In *100 Jahre Zukunft: Zur Geschichte des 1. Mai*, edited by Inge Marßolek, 15–39. Frankfurt: Büchergilde Gutenberg, 1990.
Lehmann, Brigitte. "Ehrwürdige Rote Nelke." In *Die ersten 100 Jahre: Österreichische Sozialdemokratie 1888–1988*, edited by Helene Maimann, 102–5. Vienna: Brandstätter, 1988.

Lufthansa. "1000 Tonnes of Roses on Board." Accessed 10 August 2017. https://lufthansa-cargo.com/-/lhc-press-media-details-2013-page4-6-wc.

Maxwell, Kenneth. "Portugal: 'The Revolution of the Carnations,' 1974–75." In *Civil Resistance and Power Politics: The Experience of Non-violent Action from Gandhi to the Present*, edited by Adam Roberts and Timothy Garton Ash, 144–61. Oxford: Oxford University Press, 2009.

Meiche, Alfred. *Die Anfänge der Kunstblumenindustrie in Dresden, Leipzig, Berlin und Sebnitz*. Dresden: Meinhold, 1908.

Ohnuki-Tierney, Emiko. *Flowers That Kill: Communicative Opacity in Political Spaces*. Stanford: Stanford University Press, 2015.

Pflanzenfee. "Lasst Blumen sprechen—wir sagen Ihnen, was es bedeutet!" Accessed 5 August 2017. https://www.pflanzenfee.de/info/ratgeber/lasst-blumen-sprechen-wir-sagen-ihnen-was-es-bedeutet.

Quelleneditionen zur Geschichte der deutschen Arbeiterbewegung, Projekt 2: Proletarische Frauenbewegung. Wildberg: Belzer, 1998.

Redensartenindex. Accessed 5 August 2017. https://www.redensarten-index.de/suche.php?suchbegriff=~~Lasstpercent20Blumenpercent20sprechen!&bool=relevanz&suchspalte[]=rart_ou.

Reimer, Karl. "Parteiblumen." *Innsbrucker Nachrichten*, 3 May 1900: 1–2.

Reinhardt, Dirk. *Von der Reklame zum Marketing: Geschichte der Wirtschaftswerbung in Deutschland*. Berlin: Akademie-Verlag, 1993.

"Rote Nelken im Schnee für Rosa und Karl: Tausende gedenken Liebknecht und Luxemburg." *Berlin Online*. Accessed 5 August 2017. https://www.berlinonline.de/friedrichshain/nachrichten/4717578-4015997-rote-nelken-im-schnee-fuer-rosa-und-karl.html.

Schöck-Quinteros, Eva. "Blumentage im Deutschen Reich: Zwischen bürgerlicher Wohltätigkeit und Klassenkampf." *Ariadne* 39 (2001): 44–51.

Seaton, Beverly. *The Language of Flowers: A History*. Charlottesville: University Press of Virginia, 1995.

Silberzahn-Jandt, Gudrun. "Die Sonnenblume und der Müll." *Hessische Blätter für Volks- und Kulturforschung* 34 (1998): 115–26.

Tergit, Gabriele (alias Elise Reifenberg). *Kleine Geschichte der Blumen*. Berlin: Ullstein, 1981.

Unterbeck, M. *Neueste vollständige Blumen-, Fächer- und Briefmarkensprache*. Stuttgart: Schwabacher'sche Verlagsbuchhandlung, n.d.

Vogt, Roland. "Auf der Suche nach dem Salzkorn—Symbolnutzung bei der Friedensbewegung und bei den Grünen." *Forschungsjournal Neue soziale Bewegungen* 1 (1988): 36–42.

Vollständige Blumensprache, der Liebe und Freundschaft gewidmet, oder Bedeutung der Pflanzen und Blumen nach occidentalischer Art. Warburg: Schilp, 1850.

Weyrather, Irmgard. *Mutterkreuz und Muttertag: Der Kult um die "deutsche Mutter" im Nationalsozialismus*. Frankfurt: Fischer, 1993.

Wimmer, Clemens Alexander. "Bücher über Blumensprache." *Zandera* 13 (1998): 15–25.
Worcester Art Museum. "Kennedy to Kent State: Images of a Generation." Accessed 10 August 2017. http://worcesterartmuseum.org/exhibitions/kennedy-to-kent-state/2011-135.html.
Zentralfriedhof Friedrichsfelde. "Die Gedenkstätte der Sozialisten." Accessed 5 August 2017. http://sozialistenfriedhof.de/gedenkstaettesoziali.html.

CHAPTER 13

Banners and Flags, Mottoes, *Lieder*
German Choral Societies and Material Culture, 1871–1918

RUTH DEWHURST

For three days in early August 1874, members of the German Choral Association (*Deutsche Sängerbund*) assembled in Munich for the second national choral festival.[1] Singers representing 385 cities gathered on the first day at the train station, then collected their banners and proceeded to the *Rathaus*. After official greetings, they paraded their banners around the hall and heard some speeches before retiring for the night. The second day was filled with song—the choirs singing separately and together fifteen works, including motets and chorales, but primarily *Lieder*. The third day was set aside for a sightseeing trip to Starnberger See.[2] The member choruses of the German Choral Association (DSB) were made up exclusively of men. It was the largest choral organization in the world in the late nineteenth century and included members from any country where German was spoken; but the members were above all concerned about nurturing German national identity and believed this could be done through singing together.[3] I argue that one lens through which to analyze this is what Barbara Rosenwein has termed "emotional communities," or groups of people who "adhere to the same norms of emotional expression."[4] Equally pertinent is musicologist Christopher Small's concept of "musicking," meaning that every act involved in a musical performance establishes a "set of relationships."[5] Emotional communities were created and nurtured from these relationships, as we can observe in the local, regional, and national choruses that fostered national pride during the *Kaiserreich*. I depart from Rosenwein's exclusive adherence to textual analysis to draw attention to ways architectural spaces and objects elicited enthusiasm, joy, excitement, or national pride.

Music is a nonrepresentational art form, so German choral societies created tangible objects to portray connections to a musical past and their current identities. In what ways did choral members attach emotions to the objects they fashioned, and how did the spaces in which they moved and performed reinforce these emotions? I find the methodology suggested by archeologists Oliver Harris and Tim Flohr Sørensen useful. They developed a vocabulary of overlapping concepts that offer a means to decode the emotions generated by choral festivals and to analyze how "things that are handled, and spaces that are moved through" both reify and generate emotions.[6] The men claimed: "We in the North as well as the South, the East as well as the West have the same melodic expression—the German Lied! . . . The entire German Volk sing. . . . Song is the revelation of the German genius . . . in which we find the Germanic essence."[7] Singing, objects, and settings combined to create emotional connections across the geographic spaces of the new German nation and beyond. These can be excavated not only through texts, but equally and concurrently by means of material culture.

Harris and Sørensen offer the following terminology, which they have left purposefully inclusive rather than reductive. Emotion is not only the act of being moved, of physically moving through a space and experiencing joy or sorrow, but also generating social bonds. Affective fields are networks through which emotions are generated. The German Choral Association was at the center of a network of choral associations. The smallest town's twenty-voice men's choir formed the outermost strand of this web. These tiny choirs joined together in regional associations centered in larger cities like Nuremberg or Leipzig, and these in turn belonged to the DSB. The board of directors decided what types of music to privilege over others, established guidelines for how festivals should function, and set standards for the quality of musical performances.[8] Attunement is "the practice of attending to the material world and its emotional qualities."[9] Not only the participants in a choral festival, but also the parade route observer or audience member would attune to the meanings of the costumes/attire of the choir members, the banners they carried, and the common objects surrounding the entire event—song books, greenery and wreaths used to festoon the streets and performance halls, musical instruments, and more. Finally, they define atmosphere as a physical space in which people and things interact and generate emotions. The atmosphere generated by a choral performance transformed the Munich *Rathaus* from a space of everyday business to a national celebration.[10] These terms were developed to facilitate archeological research at prehistoric sites. Harris and Sørensen were interested in utilizing physical remains, both buildings and objects, in order to incorporate emotions into interpretations where there were no written records. I find their terminology apt for examining the material objects of nineteenth- and twentieth-century German music festivals, and I have the advantage of a set of texts that allow me to read what the participants said about the objects.

The German Choral Association (DSB) published a newspaper that spans the time period I am examining here.[11] It first appeared bimonthly, then once a week from the 1890s until September 1914, when war conditions constrained it once again to a bimonthly publication. It existed primarily to inform the various choral associations and music clubs about each other and to promote German music culture. There were long lists of member choruses and their activities and records of anniversary celebrations, regional festivals, and choral events across the German-speaking lands. The national festivals that I want to examine here were held on a regular basis: Munich (1874), Hamburg (1882), Vienna (1890), Stuttgart (1896), Graz (1902), Breslau (1907), and Nuremberg (1912).[12] Not every festival recorded exact numbers of participants, but in Graz and Breslau, they needed to plan and build enormous festival halls in order to host the thousands of participants, and in Nuremberg, the choirs had to be divided into two massive groups. Besides the historical data that can be gleaned from these newspapers, *Die Sängerhalle* is itself an object of material culture. The image that makes up the masthead of the paper in 1870 is saturated with historical referents that provide an artistically interpreted summary of pre-1870 German history.

The entire masthead image evokes a romantic woodland scene. Rods or tree branches, vines, and leaves frame an image foregrounded by the newspaper's title (*Die Sängerhalle*). Above the title is a ribbon with three words: *Freiheit, Friede, Fröhlichkeit* (Freedom, Peace, Cheerfulness). The largest image under the paper's title is a harp and the rest of the images are situated on either side or under this harp: a ribbon with the name Walter Vogelweide flows along the bottom of the harp; groups of cherubs grace either side of the harp either holding lutes or a chalice—often used as a trophy; a castle appears in the distance on the left side; under the harp four names are highlighted on yet another flowing ribbon: Arndt, Uhland, Zelter, and Kreutzer. This masthead offers an opportunity to prove archeologist Chris Gosden's claim that "emotions are materially constituted and material culture is emotionally constituted."[13]

The artist who created the image for the masthead highlighted and condensed the emotionally charged national events of the early nineteenth century into personal names and slogans. Germans reading *Die Sängerhalle* in the late nineteenth century understood the images and allusions and assigned emotional valence to them. Early nineteenth-century Romanticism was evoked through the naturalistic framing of branches, vines, and leaves as well as the medieval evocations of a castle, a Minnesinger (Walter Vogelweide), the harp and lute instruments, and unearthly cherubs.[14] The early Romantics were also the pioneers of a "national" culture encapsulated in the names Arndt, Uhland, Zelter, and Kreutzer. Ludwig Uhland (1787–1862) was a poet and a student of German folklore whose *Vaterländische Gedichte* (1815) was part of a corpus of early nationalistic songs. Conradin Kreutzer (1780–1849) was a composer who, among other things, wrote part-songs for men's voices—a very popular genre in the nineteenth century and the lifeblood of the DSB.

Carl Friedrich Zelter founded the Berlin *Liedertafeln* in 1808 (the first amateur men's chorus) and directed the Berlin *Singakademie* from 1817 to 1832. All other amateur choruses grew out of his work in Berlin. Finally, Ernst Moritz Arndt (1769–1860) was closely associated with the Napoleonic Wars of Liberation because of his role as propagandist—writing patriotic songs was part of this job. His "*Was ist des deutschen Vaterland*" ("What Is the German Fatherland?") served as an unofficial German national anthem throughout the nineteenth century. Germans looking at this masthead did not need an explanation of who these people were—they instantly associated them with the early nineteenth century Wars of Liberation (1813–15), early attempts at German unification, and German song. The slogan at the top of the image—*Freiheit, Friede, Frölichkeit*—was a shorthand version of the one adopted by *Burschenschaften* students who fought in the Wars of Liberation.[15]

The slogans, names, and images encapsulated the spirit of the early Romantics and their efforts to unify the German nation—a *Volk* they envisioned with roots in a medieval past and liberated from French cultural and political dominance. The drawing is unsigned, but the artist carefully chose the historic figures, the musical instruments, and the landscape because of their patriotic impact and historical allusions. The young men who formed the core group of anti-Napoleon patriots were often the original members of the early choral associations, the representatives in Frankfurt in 1848, and the founders of the DSB in 1867. The masthead of the newspaper not only articulated their deep-seated pride in the past and German unity but also resonated powerfully like a synchronized musical-patriotic-historical heartbeat with members of late nineteenth-century/early twentieth-century choruses who may have been sons and grandsons of the earlier patriots.[16]

With this affective imagery as a background, we can more closely analyze the elements of a late nineteenth-, early twentieth-century DSB festival. I will begin with the train station. The terminology of Harris and Sørensen and the overlapping nature of their concepts work well here. The small Bavarian town of Feuchtwangen, whose choral association was typical of most German towns, had only two men who traveled to the 1890 national festival in Vienna, but they joined a growing crowd of singers. Organizers of the festival sent out notices well in advance about train schedules, and members from Bavaria convened in Munich.[17] The train stations, and the trains, are spaces with a specific atmosphere—they immediately conjure up travel, specific noises, smells, and sensations. People congregated, recognized one another (or met for the first time), and interacted for the purpose of participating in a shared experience—first travelling, but more importantly participating in the choral festival. As they began the long train ride across Germany and Austria, the landscape changed, villages and towns appeared and disappeared, the train stopped and started again, and the passengers interacted with one another as well as the physical space of the train. The atmosphere on the train was enhanced both by the singers' shared experience of going to Vienna to participate in a festival, but also by moving through the same landscape seated on the same train. Certainly, an emotion generated by the train was anticipation as the passengers interacted with one another and as they moved toward Vienna. Their sense of excitement rose—perhaps the kind of nervous excitement one experiences before a big event whose outcome is not entirely clear, or the nerves related to train travel—but the presence of other people going through the same experience enhanced the anticipation and mitigated fear or fatigue.

When the singers arrived in Vienna, the train station momentarily took center stage as crowds of singers swarmed into that space.[18] There was an appointed time for the general arrival, and formal greetings followed. The two prime events of every choral festival, whether it was a local, regional, or national festival, were the parade of banners and the musical performances with combined choirs. As the singers moved out of the train station, they moved to the parade route. The station was the site of anticipation and joyful greetings, and it was also the staging ground for collecting the banners that each individual chorus and regional association had carefully transported; people and banners began moving into the city proper. In the 15 August 1907 edition of *Die Sängerhalle*, there was a description of the crowd: The Austrian banner carrier wore a feather in his beret, a white velvet coat, and gauntlets. The Hamburgers were especially "elegant," as they had chosen not only to wear uniform hats but also a uniform style of dress. The writer goes on to describe the colorful attire of the Chemnitz singers, those from Schweidnitzer, Leipzig, and a group from Bavaria.[19] The individuality of the costumes and the banners demonstrate an interesting feature of emotional communities. Each chorus chose objects that set them apart, but the collective affective field demonstrates that these objects were common and unifying objects—each group wore hats or carried banners, and the entire crowd, participants and observers, was attuned to the individual and collective meanings. The reporter went on to proclaim: "It is perfectly clear that such a genuine patriotic festival, such a glorious revelation of the idyllic powers of the German Volk, resembles a mighty spring, from which all the participants draw. And this is not only for themselves but also for those left behind in their homeland. . . . What an immense unifying power this festival has!"[20] Here, the language of the observer enhances what we might presume about the emotions embodied in those along the parade route. The experience was glorious (*herrlich*) and swelled up like a mighty spring from which all could drink—thirst serving as a sensory word for the emotion of longing or yearning. The physical objects were attached to the emotions of pride in a local place and a communal place.

Banners were not new to choral societies in the 1870s, but the parades in which choral members marched together from the train station to the festival hall and then hung the banners on the walls was formally prescribed by the governing board of the DSB shortly before the founding of the *Kaiserreich*. The memorial book (*Gedenkbuch*) of the first national festival in Dresden (1865) offers a vivid image of a parade of a thousand banners and flags as a "procession of Germanism" and a "living heartbeat of Germany."[21] Singers moving out of the train station and walking in groups down the parade route were surrounded by fellow musicians from all over Germany waving their identifying flags and banners. A photograph from the 1912 newspaper shows how tightly packed the streets were—marchers in the middle and observers pressing in on both sides. Strung across the street from buildings on either side were garlands of greenery.[22] Thinking about the connection between emotions and material objects is intensified by comparing the above description with the experience of walking down the same street when it was deserted. The street itself is there and the buildings, but it is difficult to imagine that the emotions engendered by the parade—exhilaration, pride, companionship, love, patriotism—would exist. In the same way, a nineteenth-century choral banner displayed in a museum, discovered in an attic, or abandoned in a garbage dump would not evoke the same emotions of joy and pride that it did for the participants in Dresden, Vienna, or Nuremberg. The specific place and the crowds of people with a common interest and purpose, together with the objects they wore or carried, generated the emotions. When the processing singers and observers arrived at the festival hall, the banners were arrayed around the walls along with more wreaths and garlands. The banners, with their images of Minnesingers, harps, regional colors, and the names of member associations, were a visual reminder of the common roots of the German people. But as another contributor to *Die Sängerhalle* reminded its readers, it was through song that faith in (German) unity was planted in the breasts of the *Volk*, and through song, the fruit would ripen.[23]

Singers are accustomed to attending, or being attuned, to each other's voices, intonations, facial expressions, and movements—these are essential features of practicing and performing choral music. In order to sing together, members of a chorus attune their voices and breathing to one another—and at least for the duration of the performance, they experience the collective joy or pathos of the song. The repertoire of songs (or *Lieder*) was one of the most emotionally and historically weighted aspects of the choral movement and perhaps the most defining feature of what it meant to be German. Mottoes and banners had the power to evoke historic memories, but the *Lied* unearthed the very essence of being German. Johann Gottfried Herder (1744–1803) developed the concept that music and language have common roots and that language is the defining feature of a nation.[24] In conjunction with Johann Wolfgang von Goethe (1749–1832), he espoused joining German verse with German music. Herder coined the term *Volkslied* (the song of the people) and claimed, "The language, sound, and content of the old songs shape the way a people thinks, thereby leaving its mark on the nation."[25] The *Lied* is considered a purely German genre, and in the *Constitution* of the *Fränkische Sängerbund*, the stated purpose of their association was to cultivate the German *Lied* and thereby refine and improve the traditions of the *Volk* and facilitate the German "mind" (*Sinn*).[26]

The model for German music festivals was the Lower Rhine Music Festival, which first took place in 1818 and continued with few exceptions until 1958. These were considered to be "national festivals" even in the early years, but they did not consist primarily of choral music.[27] The programs of the DSB festivals are replete with *Lieder*, and songs were frequently published in *Die Sängerhalle*. In the 1870s and 1880s, there were constant complaints about choruses who were not prepared to sing difficult songs; but by the 1890s, *Die Sängerhalle* included performance notes to prepare singers. I will use one example that illustrates several things: the emergent role of choral directors in German music culture, the increase in numbers of people participating in national festivals, and the emotions entwined with a piece of music. At the Breslau festival in 1907, the assembled choruses performed "Bonifacius," composed by Heinrich Zöllner and directed by Gustav Wohlgemuth. Boniface brought Christianity to the German lands in the eighth century and was considered a mediating figure between Catholics and Protestants in the late nineteenth century.[28] Wohlgemuth communicated some ideas about how to perform the piece in the 21 March 1907 edition of *Die Sängerhalle*. He mentioned tempo and dynamics, but dwelt particularly on how to sing the minor key passages of the song: "The principal thing . . . is the solemn mood, the re-cultivation of the mental passion which every single singer is to convey."[29] Here, we see the conductor anticipating the space where the musical piece would be performed, the accompanying affective field, and the atmosphere. It was important to Wohlgemuth that the singers conveyed the "solemn mood" of the piece to the audience, and he believed it was within their mental powers to do this. As we have seen with the parade crowds, the observers participated in the emotions generated by the participants and objects. In the festival performances, the members of the audience shared the space occupied by the singers (festooned with banners and garlands) and were invited to attenuate with the mood of the singers—to share in the solemn mood of this particular piece of music. It was Wohlgemuth's job to constantly communicate with the singers by his actions and facial expressions.[30] Conductors took over the role of masterminding orchestral and choral works in the late-nineteenth century, thus attuning the singers with their own ideas about interpreting the music. In turn, they transformed the atmosphere of the space by mediating between the performers and the audience. We do not know where the next national festival would have taken place; World War I created a disruption, but not a break, in choral performances.

The records of the Feuchtwangen *Musik- und Chorverein* end abruptly in mid-July of 1914, and national festivals were cancelled. However, it is still possible to trace the role of music throughout the war years. The *Deutsche Sängerbundeszeitung*, as the paper was now known, gave sources for music on the home front during the war, and military papers linked the home front to the war fronts. Between September 1914 and November 1918, about 110 military field newspapers appeared, and they are valuable as material culture as much as for the written content. There are numerous references to previous wars with the French, Germany's medieval heritage, the Reformation, and beloved poets. These themes encouraged artists to create rich visual images—*Heimat* and Christmas scenes, fortresses, mothers and children, and musical references like Wagner's *Valkyries*. The German government understood which cultural elements most resonated with the *Volk* and consciously encouraged those. No explanations accompany the artwork, and every German felt pleasure, satisfaction, or comfort when he/she opened the *Kriegszeit: Künstflugblätter* to see a drawing of a large rooster flapping its wings in panic or a well-known fortress overlooking the Rhine.[31]

The mastheads of military newspapers feature the same kind of images choral societies fostered—a castle atop a grassy knoll, or a stereotypical German village—rooftops, church steeple, and a fortress surrounded by fields of crops and hills. One "viewed" this scene from the window of a stone castle with gargoyles and a heraldic crest.[32] The familiar images and symbols on the newspaper mastheads served as a type of propaganda, but the papers were also filled with references to poetry, *Lieder*, and the patriotic songs of the nineteenth-century. There was a sense of communal comfort. The war might be raging on the Eastern and Western Fronts, but the soldiers were protecting the homeland. On the home front, singers put less emphasis on festivals and more on "artistic" individual concerts. A report from the *Bonner Männergesangverein* from 9 January 1915 is representative of many other cities and towns. Seventy of their members had gone to war; the association collected Christmas packages for those at the Front; they offered regular performance at the Bonn military hospital and raised money for the Red Cross.[33] The atmosphere of the concert hall was now more serious and reflected the sorrow and worry of those whose loved ones were at the Front or in a hospital.

The affective field of a frontline trench represented a complementary but more acute anxiety or fear. Some soldiers chose to alleviate the grimness of warfare by reverting to the companionability of music. The *Seventh Army Newspaper* as well as the *Badener Lazarett Paper* referenced organized choirs and choir practice. The list of songs sung in their concerts mirrored the repertoire of the prewar years—*Heimat-* or *Soldatenlieder*, as well as classic choral works. On the Western Front, the Seventh Army chorus went on tour in 1916, presenting nineteen concerts in fifteen days—30,000 soldiers attended.

The journalist who recorded this ascribed courage and endurance to the soldiers and claimed that the music brought a tender comfort to them.[34] Singing was no longer merely an occasion for a festival weekend; it became the entire nation's expression of endurance in the midst of sorrow and national solidarity.

In the Leipzig City History Museum, there is a large banner created for a nineteenth-century women's chorus. A female figure is prominently displayed. Dressed in a flowing blue Grecian robe, she holds an immense harp. A placard accompanying the banner explains to the modern museum visitor that banners symbolized group unity and flourished from the founding of the German Reich in 1871, and they were also "proudly" paraded on important occasions in front of the members of the extensive German network of clubs and associations. "Today, these flags are witnesses of a lost culture of celebration."[35] It was a culture that put music at the center of bourgeois community, but the setting was the treasured objects and ceremonies that fostered pride in the nation, love for fellow Germans, and joy in celebration.

When I began working on this chapter, I searched the Internet for images of "banners," hoping to find nineteenth-century choral banners. In the process, I came across a twenty-first century banner that demonstrates, at least in part, that the nineteenth-century "culture of celebration" is not lost—it has merely shifted to different affective fields and spaces, but with similar material objects. The banner was for the Liverpool Football Club, and it suggests connections between modern sporting events and those of nineteenth-century music festivals. Behavioral scientist Andrei S. Markovits and political scientist Lars Rensmann claim that sports "shape and stabilize social and . . . political identities, . . . mobilize collective emotions . . . and create community."[36] A soccer match in Europe can generate powerful emotions evoked by team colors, banners, scarves, chants, and especially song. There are whole communities of fans who follow their team from one location to another—bound together in spaces where they attune to one another's enthusiasm, create an atmosphere of camaraderie, and even comfort one another in suffering (defeat). Markovits and Rensmann make a powerful argument for sports as binding cultural, social, and political forces with the power to overcome long-held prejudices as sports heroes become international figures and a team like Liverpool is cheered on by fans across the globe. They trace this phenomenon to nineteenth-century British imperialism, but I suggest that German festival culture (and the power of singing) plays a role, as well.[37] Bodies and things are essential to how emotions present themselves in any cultural setting. The space of a concert hall or sports stadium, parades and banners, mottoes or team chants are features of different emotional communities, but enable us to analyze emotions as more than a solitary, individual experience. It is the relationships created by the spaces and objects that both elicit emotions and generate the material objects that bind the participants.

Ruth L. Dewhurst is a PhD candidate in modern German cultural history, studying under the direction of Professor Joe Perry at Georgia State University. Her master's thesis *The Legacy of Luther: National Identity and State-Building in Early Nineteenth-Century Germany*, and her dissertation are a further exploration of Luther's contribution to music and the role of music in creating a common national culture. As an interdisciplinary study, it explores ways choral music fostered emotional communities during the Kaiserreich and is entitled *Unison and Harmony, Dissonance and Dissolution: The Role of Choral Societies in Expressing Germany Identity and Community, 1870–1918*.

Notes

1. The first national festival was held in 1865 in Dresden in *anticipation* of the unification of Germany.
2. 3 September 1874, *Die Sängerhalle: Allgemeine deutsche Gesangvereins-Zeitung für das In- und Ausland*, Z128.12, 126–36, Leipziger Stadtbibliothek, Leipzig, Germany.
3. Friedhelm Brusniak, *Das grosse Buch des fränkischen Sängerbundes*, vol. 1 (Munich: Schwingenstein Verlag, 1991), 8.
4. Barbara H. Rosenwein, *Emotional Communities in the Early Middle Ages* (Ithaca: Cornell University Press, 2006); and Barbara H. Rosenwein, "Problems and Methods in the History of Emotions: Passions in Context," *Journal of the History and Philosophy of Emotions* 1, no. 1 (2010): 1–32.
5. Christopher Small, *Musicking: The Meanings of Performing and Listening* (Middletown, CT: Wesleyan University Press, 1998), 13.
6. Oliver J. T. Harris and Tim Flohr Sørensen, "Rethinking Emotion and Material Culture," *Archaeological Dialogues* 17, no. 2 (2010): 145–63.
7. 3 September 1874, *Die Sängerhalle*, Z128.47, 128.
8. Constitution of the Franconian Choral Association, 23. Mai 1908, B 71 1.1.2 (90.5), 71, Archiv der Stiftung Dokumentations- und Forschungszentrum des Deutschen Chorwesens, Bestand Gesang- und Musikverein Feuchtwangen, Germany. Hereafter denoted ZFC-Archiv.
9. Harris and Sørensen, "Rethinking Emotion," 151.
10. Harris and Sørensen, "Rethinking Emotion," 149–52.
11. *Die Sängerhalle*, 1870–1918, Z128.70–Z129.12.
12. The locations chosen for these festivals demonstrate one of the guiding principles of the DSB. The organizers believed in a concept of German-ness that included all German speakers. There were participants from Hungary, Romania, Switzerland, and the United States. It is also significant that the first festival after unification was held in Munich—southern Germans had resisted unification with the Protestant north. The Vienna location was chosen specifically as a means of patching up differences after the Austro-Prussian War and the Austrian city of Graz was also chosen to host. After reading dozens of these newspapers, I maintain that the leadership of the DSB seemed to be cheerfully indifferent to regional or religious differences, emphasizing instead German unity through language and song.

13. Harris and Sørensen rest their theory of emotions and material culture on this contention from C. Gosden, "What Do Objects Want?" *Journal of Archaeological Method and Theory* 12 (2005): 193–211. This image was the masthead from 1870 to 1886. The name of the paper changed in 1912 to *Deutsche Sängerbundeszeitung*.
14. Walter von der Vogelweide was the greatest German lyric poet of the Middle Ages.
15. Thomas Nipperdey, *Germany from Napoleon to Bismarck, 1800–1866*, trans. Daniel Nolan (Princeton: Princeton University Press, 1996), 243–47.
16. Presumably, German women had similar sentiments, but I use the terms "men," "sons," and "grandsons" because the DSB was exclusively male.
17. ZFC-Archiv B 71 1.1.2 (90.5), 59.
18. Wolfgang Schivelbusch, *The Railway Journey: The Industrialization of Time and Space in the 19th Century* (Berkeley: University of California Press, 1986).
19. 15 August 1907, *Die Sängerhalle*, Z128.47, 604.
20. 15 August 1907, *Die Sängerhalle*, Z128.47, 604.
21. Quoted by Brusniak, *Das grosse Buch*, 132.
22. Photograph from newspaper, 10 July 1912, *Die Sängerhalle*, Z129.4, 556.
23. 25 July 1907, *Die Sängerhalle*, Z128.47, 585.
24. Johann Gottfried Herder, *Against Pure Reason: Writings on Religion, Language, and History*, trans. and ed. Marcia Bunge (Minneapolis: Fortress Press, 1993), 101–6.
25. "An Sprache, Ton und Inhalt sind sie Denkart des Stamms oder gleichsam selbst Stamm und Mark der Nation," Johann Gottlieb Herder, "Alte Volkslieder," in *Sämmtliche Werke*, vol. 25. (Berlin: Weidmannsche Buchhandlung, 1885), 8. The English translation is from Philip V. Bohlman, *Song Loves the Masses: Herder on Music and Nationalism* (Oakland: University of California Press, 2017), 50.
26. ZFC-Arch B 71 1.1.2 (90.5), 71. Collections of *Lieder* were divided into topics. The songbooks of the DSB divided them into the categories of *Leben, Liebe, Lust,* and *Leid* (life, love, joy, and sorrow). Well-known composers, like Brahms, often composed a set of three or four *Lieder* around a single theme.
27. Cecelia Hopkins Porter, "The New Public and the Reordering of the Musical Establishment: The Lower Rhine Music Festivals, 1818–67," *19th-Century Music* 3, no. 3 (1980): 211–24.
28. Barbara Eichner, *History in Mighty Sounds: Musical Constructions of German National Identity 1848–1914* (Rochester: The Boydell Press, 2012), 169 ff.
29. 21 March 1907, *Die Sängerhalle*, Z128.47, 201–2.
30. Small, *Musicking*, 68–69.
31. 1 July 1915, *Kriegszeit: Künstlerflugbläter*, http://digi.ub.uni-heidelberg.de/diglit/feldztgkrzeit1914bis1916.
32. 19 December 1917, *Aus Sundgau und Wasgenwald: Feldzeitung der Armeeabteilung B*, http://digi.ub.uni-heidelberg.de/diglit/sundgau_wasgenwald.
33. 9 January 1915, *Deutsche Sängerbundeszeitung*, Z129.7, 3.
34. 5 October 1916, *Kriegszeitung der 7. Armee* 5, http://digi.ub.uni-heidelberg.de/diglit/feldztgkr7armee1916/0313, and http://digi.ub.uni-heidelberg.de/diglit/feldztgbadlaz.1916bis1918/0001.
35. Choral banner "Gew. v. d. Damen d. Vereins," Stadtgeschichtliches Museum Leipzig, Leipzig, Germany

36. Andrei S. Markovits and Lars Rensmann, *Gaming the World: How Sports Are Reshaping Global Politics and Culture* (Princeton: Princeton University Press, 2010), 3.
37. Markovits and Rensmann, *Gaming*, 3, 72.

Bibliography

Archival Sources

Archiv der Stiftung Dokumentations- und Forschungszentrum des Deutschen Chorwesens, Bestand Gesang- und Musikverein Feuchtwangen, Bestandssignatur B 71. Feuchtwangen, Germany.
Aus Sundgau und Wasgenwald: Feldzeitung der Armeeabteilung B. http://digi.ub.uni-heidelberg.de/diglit/sundgau_wasgenwald.
Die Sängerhalle: Allgemeine deutsche Gesangvereins-Zeitung für das In- und Ausland. Z128.70–Z129.12. Leipziger Stadtbibliothek. Leipzig, Germany.
Kriegszeit: Künstlerflugblätter. http://digi.ub.uni-heidelbereg.de/diglit/feldztgkrzeit 1914bis1916.
Kriegszeitung der 7. Armee. http://digi.ub.uni-heidelberg.de/diglit/feldztgkr7armee.

Literature

Bohlman, Philip V. *Song Loves the Masses: Herder on Music and Nationalism.* Oakland: University of California Press, 2017.
Brusniak, Friedhelm. *Das grosse Buch des fränkischen Sängerbundes.* Vol. 1. Munich: Schwingenstein Verlag, 1991.
Eichner, Barbara. *History in Mighty Sounds: Musical Constructions of German National Identity 1848–1914.* Rochester: The Boydell Press, 2012.
Gosden, C. "What Do Objects Want?" *Journal of Archaeological Method and Theory* 12 (2005): 193–211.
Harris, Oliver J. T., and Tim Flohr Sørensen. "Rethinking Emotion and Material Culture." *Archeological Dialogues* 17, no. 2 (2010): 145–63.
Herder, Johann Gottfried. *Against Pure Reason: Writings on Religion, Language, and History.* Translated and edited by Marcia Bunge. Minneapolis: Fortress Press, 1993.
———. "Alte Volkslieder." In *Sämmtliche Werke.* Vol. 25, 1–50. Berlin: Weidmannsche Buchhandlung, 1885.
Levitan, Daniel J. *This Is Your Brain on Music: The Science of a Human Obsession.* New York: Dutton, 2006.
Markovits, Andrei S., and Lars Rensmann. *Gaming the World: How Sports Are Reshaping Global Politics and Culture.* Princeton: Princeton University Press, 2010.

Nipperdey, Thomas. *Germany from Napoleon to Bismarck, 1800–1866.* Translated by Daniel Nolan. Princeton: Princeton University Press, 1996.

Porter, Cecelia Hopkins. "The New Public and the Reordering of the Musical Establishment: The Lower Rhine Music Festivals 1818–67." *19th-Century Music* 3, no. 3 (1980): 211–24.

Rosenwein, Barbara H. *Emotional Communities in the Early Middle Ages.* Ithaca: Cornell University Press, 2006.

——— "Problems and Methods in the History of Emotions: Passions in Context." *Journal of the History and Philosophy of Emotions* 1, no. 1 (2010): 1–32.

Schivelbusch, Wolfgang. *The Railway Journey: The Industrialization of Time and Space in the 19th Century.* Berkeley: University of California Press, 1986.

Small, Christopher. *Musicking: The Meanings of Performing and Listening.* Middletown, CT: Wesleyan University Press, 1998.

CHAPTER 14

Corporeality, Materiality, and Unnamed Emotions in Rilke's *Dinggedichte*

LORNA MARTENS

Rilke's poems in his *Neue Gedichte* (New poems, 1907) and *Neue Gedichte anderer Teil* (New poems: the other part, 1908) are often called "Dinggedichte" (thing poems). As critics have pointed out, not all of the poems in the two volumes are about things. Yet some of the most famous among them do focus on things, broadly construed: art objects, animals, plants, architectural structures, places, and even an occasional everyday object. In these poems about things, Rilke sets about capturing the response that the object triggers in a human being. Corporeal as well as mental, this response corresponds to scientific definitions as well as to popular notions of "emotion." For example, the neurobiologist Antonio Damasio defines the perception of something that is triggered by a stimulus and viscerally felt as "feelings of emotion." Damasio writes in his 2010 book *Self Comes to Mind*:

> The world of emotions is largely one of actions carried out in our bodies, from facial expressions and postures to changes in viscera and internal milieu. Feelings of emotion, on the other hand, are composite *perceptions* of what happens in our body and mind when we are emoting. . . . Seen from a neural perspective, the emotion-feeling cycle begins in the brain, with the perception and appraisal of a stimulus potentially capable of causing an emotion and the subsequent triggering of an emotion. . . . Feelings of emotion are composite perceptions of (1) a particular state the body, during actual or simulated emotion, and (2) a state of altered cognitive resources and a deployment of certain mental scripts. In our minds, these perceptions are connected to the object that caused them.[1]

Damasio distinguishes between "emotion," a word he reserves for the bodily response, and "feelings of emotion," his term for the mental experience or "composite perceptions." He thereby departs from everyday usage. Ordinarily, we mean by "emotion" what he calls "feelings of emotion"—the mental experience. Here, I shall follow common usage: I will call "emotion" what he calls "feelings of emotion." Terminology aside, Damasio's view that three components play a role in emotion—a stimulus, a corporeal response, and "feelings of emotion"—is highly relevant to Rilke. A corresponding sequence underlies Rilke's representations of human emotions in his "Dinggedichte": a thing (the stimulus) triggers a bodily response and a mental experience.

This fundamental correspondence between Damasio's account of emotion and the "emotion scenarios" in the *Neue Gedichte* will serve as point of departure from which to explore Rilke's practice in this poetry. Damasio gives a classic neuroscientific account of what an emotion involves. A concept of emotion that predicates a stimulus, a corporeal response, and a mental experience is very well established in neuroscientific circles.[2] On other issues, however, neuroscientists disagree. A closer look at one current issue in neuroscientific emotion theory—the role of language—will help situate the way Rilke figures the interaction between the object (the thing) and the human subject in his "Dinggedichte."

Damasio does not tie feelings of emotion to words. He argues that we have preverbal feelings. He asserts that it is a proven fact that the brain maps the body continuously and that much of the information does not enter the conscious mind.[3] He hypothesizes that a first, subcortical mapping generates "primordial feelings," which we are conscious of in the form of images, not words. "Core consciousness," according to Damasio, does not require words. He believes that many species have core consciousness.[4]

In complete contrast, Joseph Ledoux in his most recent book *Anxious* (2015) and Lisa Feldman Barrett in her 2017 book *How Emotions Are Made* want to understand emotion as something that exists only when consciously grasped. For Ledoux, the only reliable test of emotion is self-report: the ability to talk about it.[5] Barrett, who aims to demolish the "basic emotion theory" that Damasio and others subscribe to, accords an even larger role to language. In her theory of "constructed emotion," an emotion is one's brain's "*creation* of what your bodily sensations mean"[6] —a creation that relies heavily on preexisting, culturally transmitted "emotion concepts," for which "emotion words" serve as a convenient shorthand. If we think we are experiencing distinct, discrete emotions, it is because language tells us we are. Thus for Barrett, language plays a crucial role in the very genesis of emotions: words make emotions. "Constructed emotion theory," according to Barrett, implies that we have more control over our emotions than "classic emotion theory."

This neuroscientific argument over the role of words in emotions will remind literary scholars of the all-too-familiar battles over the respective claims to primacy of language and thought that were long fought without resolution. In this debate, Rilke would have confidently sided with Damasio. An outstanding feature of his representation of emotions in the *Neue Gedichte* poems is that he does not name them. Given that poems are verbal artifacts, it would have been easy enough for him to have used "emotion words." But in fact, Rilke avoids triggering "emotion concepts" in the reader by using ready-made labels like "joy," even when he has precisely that emotion in mind. Moreover, he often invokes unusual, idiosyncratic emotions that have no names. It follows that he would not have agreed with Barrett's "cognition-and-words-first" theory of emotions. In Rilke's poems, emotions—emotions that have a distinct corporeal and mental profile—arise spontaneously and wordlessly out of a person's encounter with an object. Conveying them in verbal form ultimately becomes a challenge for poetry.

Given the historical context in which he wrote, it is not at all surprising that Rilke signals the significance of the effect of objects by representing it as visceral rather than cognitive. At the end of the nineteenth century, "consciousness" stood in low repute. Starting with Dostoevsky's Underground Man, overconscious antiheroes who could not feel, empathize, or love appeared regularly in fiction. Thinkers from different disciplines at the *Jahrhundertwende*, such as Max Müller, George Romanes, and Freud, aligned language with rational thought. Of course, a lot of experience, including emotional experience, counted as not rational, and such experience was thought to elude expression in language. The famous "language crisis" of the *Jahrhundertwende* immortalized in Hofmannsthal's *Ein Brief* (1902) went so far as to denigrate language as not only incapable of grasping anything real or important—where the real and important was often emotional experience—but also likely to interpose itself between ourselves and things and prevent us from having natural, unmediated experiences. The "confusions" of Musil's Törless, for example, consist of Törless's sense that an unbridgeable gap separates rational thought and language from irrational experiences and involve his vain attempts to grasp sexual and other feelings in words.[7] For Rilke, rational thought and verbalizability lag behind significant experiences and creative moments, as illustrated by the sequence of events in his poem "Eingang" (Entrance, 1900): first the human subject, who is universalized as "you," perceives (sees) what is outside his "house," then he performs the magical and creative act of moving a tree to the horizon "with his eyes," and only thereafter gets around to "understanding the meaning" of what he has just done, whereupon his eyes release the tree.

A major difference between Rilke and all the neuroscientists is that Rilke twists the lens to focus on the object. At the center of neuroscientific concerns are the body and the mind—not the stimulus. Contemporary neuroscientists are interested in the legibility of types of emotions in the body, the connections between the bodily responses and "feelings" (the way emotions become conscious), the definition of consciousness itself, and the role of cognition in emotion. It is a matter of indifference to them whether fear is triggered by a bear or a wolf. Rilke's focus, in contrast, is the object in all its specificity. He highlights the object's mystique and power by showing how it provokes an emotional response in the subject.

Rilke believed in and deeply respected the psychological power of objects.[8] In *A Sense of Things* (2003) Bill Brown posits a distinctively modernist relationship to things, namely an object fetishism that opposes and resists commodity fetishism. According to Brown, modernist object fetishism is

> part of the modernist's effort to arrest commodity-fetishism-as-usual: that is, an effort to interrupt the habit of granting material objects a value and power of their own, divorced from, and failing to disclose, the human power and social interaction that brought those objects into being. ... The modernist's fetishized thing—excised from the world of consumer culture, isolated, refocused, doted upon, however momentarily—is meant to be saved from the fate of the mass-produced object ... the humiliation of homogeneity ... and ... the tyranny of use.[9]

Modernists also, according to Brown, imagine the work of art as seeking "to attain the status of a thing."[10] Rilke is not among Brown's examples, which he takes primarily from American art and literature, yet Rilke perfectly exemplifies his contentions. Rilke had a lifelong love affair with things. The things Rilke worshiped were not commodities, which he hated, but things that carried a freight of human significance—things that had absorbed human thought, imagination, and care and therefore have a concentrated power to move and instruct us. Rilke's convictions about the importance and power of things prefigure Walter Benjamin's theory of the "auratic" object. "To perceive the aura of an object," Benjamin writes, "means to invest it with the ability to look at us in return."[11] Long before Benjamin wrote these words, Rilke accorded things the ability to look back at us. In a letter to Clara Rilke of 8 March 1907, he writes that things can serve as repositories of inner process and cause us momentarily to become aware of what was going on inside us.[12] Elsewhere he calls things "vessels" (*Gefäße*) filled with human significance.[13] In the postwar period, he complained that the age of the thing-as-vessel was fast receding. He lamented that in the present day, hardly any such things are left, for empty, American things (commodities!) were supplanting them.[14] Moreover, Rilke's "Dingedichte" themselves were the literary result of his fascination with Auguste Rodin's ability to "make things." Rilke, who went to Paris in 1902 to study and write a monograph on Rodin, resolved to emulate the sculptor in his own art by "making things"—not out of stone, but out of words.

In keeping with these ideas, in the poems from the *Neue Gedichte* discussed below, the object affects the subject viscerally. In the typical "emotion scenario" in these poems, an encounter with an object provokes a response in a subject, which, it is strongly suggested, is a mental event (an "emotion"), but which is not named and in fact sometimes has no name, but is principally figured in corporeal signs, whether these are actual, metaphoric, or implied. The physical effect of the object on the subject leads the reader to interpret the encounter as an emotional one. Thus the reader (not the subject of the emotion) "reads" the physical signs together with the context and imagines what the subject must be feeling—that is, deduces the impact of the object on the subject. Rilke frequently addresses his poems to a universalizing "du," which encourages this imagining.

I shall discuss four emotions provoked by objects in the *Neue Gedichte*. The most familiar of these is nostalgia, an emotion that is frequently evoked in *Jahrhundertwende* literature. In Rilke's "Das Karussell" (The merry-go-round), the merry-go-round provokes the "basic emotion" of happiness in the children but the mixed emotion of nostalgia in the spectator.[15] A second is the emotion elicited by confinement in a closed space. Rilke alludes to an oppressive sense of having no space and no exit often enough in his writing for it to be considered autobiographical in origin. As he projects this feeling onto the pacing captive panther in "Der Panther" (The panther), one might call it depression; but in "Der Gefangene II" (The prisoner II), it is something else that has no name: confinement causes the mind to fester like a sick body and churn ceaselessly in a kind of perpetual craziness. Third, Rilke shows how certain spaces and material objects are capable of provoking a response that could be described as a "change your life imperative": a special emotion that we surely do not experience every day, but that in Rilke's description starts with a physical effect. Such a conversion experience is described in "Archaïscher Torso Apollos" (Archaic torso of Apollo) and "Die Fensterrose" (The rose window). Literary representations of epiphanies often come tagged with a corporeal response. In *A Portrait of the Artist as a Young Man*, for example, James Joyce describes Stephen Dedalus's response to his most famous epiphany thus: "His cheeks were aflame; his body was aglow; his hands were trembling."[16] In the two poems under discussion, Rilke rebalances the epiphany trope so as to stress the power of the object over the beholder—not just an individual beholder, but everyone, "you." Fourth, in several "Dinggedichte," mirrors signal an awakening of the imagination, a shift into hypothetical or counterfactual daydreaming. This sparking of the imagination, seen in "Venezianischer Morgen" (Venetian morning), "Dame vor dem Spiegel" (Lady before the mirror), and "Die Flamingos" (The flamingos), is accompanied by a corporeal change in the form of a "Rausch," a high, tinged by erotic arousal.

First, nostalgia.

Das Karussell

Jardin du Luxembourg

Mit einem Dach und seinem Schatten dreht

sich eine kleine Weile der Bestand
von bunten Pferden, alle aus dem Land,
das lange zögert, eh es untergeht.

> Zwar manche sind an Wagen angespannt,
> doch alle haben Mut in ihren Mienen;
> ein böser roter Löwe geht mit ihnen
> und dann und wann ein weißer Elefant.
>
> Sogar ein Hirsch ist da, ganz wie im Wald,
> nur daß er einen Sattel trägt und drüber
> ein kleines blaues Mädchen aufgeschnallt.
>
> Und auf dem Löwen reitet weiß ein Junge
> und hält sich mit der kleinen heißen Hand,
> dieweil der Löwe Zähne zeigt und Zunge.
>
> Und dann und wann ein weißer Elefant.
>
> Und auf den Pferden kommen sie vorüber,
> auch Mädchen, helle, diesem Pferdesprunge
> fast schon entwachsen; mitten in dem Schwunge
> schauen sie auf, irgendwohin, herüber—
>
> Und dann und wann ein weißer Elefant.
>
> Und das geht hin und eilt sich, daß es endet,
> und kreist und dreht sich nur und hat kein Ziel.
> Ein Rot, ein Grün, ein Grau vorbeigesendet,
> ein kleines kaum begonnenes Profil—.
> Und manchesmal ein Lächeln, hergewendet,
> ein seliges, das blendet und verschwendet
> an dieses atemlose blinde Spiel . . .

Translation:

THE MERRY-GO-ROUND

Jardin du Luxembourg

With a roof and its shadow the stock of colored horses turns for a short while, all of them from the land that hesitates for a long time before it vanishes. Some, to be sure, are hitched to carriages, but all of them have courage in their mien; an angry red lion goes with them and now and then a white elephant. Even a stag is there, just like in the woods, except he wears a saddle and on it a little blue girl buckled up. And on the lion a boy rides, white, and holds on with his little hot hand, while the lion shows its teeth and tongue. And now and then a white elephant. And on the horses they come by, also girls, bright, who have almost outgrown this horses' leap; in the middle of a jump they look up, somewhere, over here— And now and then a white elephant. And it goes on and hurries to its end and just circles and turns and has no goal. A red, a green, a gray sent by, a little scarcely begun profile—. And sometimes a smile, turned this way, a joyous one, that blinds and spends itself in this breathless blind game . . .[17]

"Das Karussell" shows how an object, a merry-go-round, provokes two different emotions in the child riders and the adult spectator. The speaker is an adult observer watching the twirling merry-go-round from a position outside it, as indicated by the words *herüber* (over here) and *hergewendet* (turned this way). This observer speaks in sophisticated adult language in the first four lines and in the last two stanzas of the poem (not counting the refrain). He muses about the merry-go-round, which, he intimates, symbolizes childhood (it comes from a land that hesitates for a long time before it disappears) and a child's sense of time (it turns and turns with no goal). Beginning with l.9, however, the diction becomes childish, suggesting that the observer loses himself imaginatively in the children's experience. The small children's emotion is legible in Rilke's description of their bodies. He gives straightforward corporeal indicators of their absorption, joy, and excitement. Their posture testifies to their absorption in the activity of riding on the animals' backs while the merry-go-round turns. One sees an immature profile, indicating that its owner looks straight ahead, as though he or she were focused on riding and undistracted by other people or the surroundings. Sometimes one catches a blissful smile turned toward the spectators, a classic expression of joy. A little boy's hand is hot, testifying to excitement. The speaker then takes note of some older girls who are almost too big to ride. Their posture is different: they look up, and sometimes they look out beyond the circling carousel. They are, therefore, not wholly caught up in the game, but aware of the world outside the merry-go-round, which distracts them from it. These half-grown girls are transitional figures; they represent a state of mind different from that of the small children yet also not that of the adult spectator who is wholly outside the charmed circle. As the adult spectator disengages himself from his identification with the children, returns to his musings, and pronounces the small children's breathless but blind happiness "dazzling," his emotion can be identified as nostalgia. He relives the happiness of the past while realizing that he has lost it.

Second, Rilke wrote two "Dinggedichte" about the emotion provoked by captivity with no prospect of freedom. The object is a cage or prison. The emotion could be described as a desperation so protracted that the prisoner loses hope. Rilke's most famous poem about this subject is "Der Panther." The caged panther's movements, his tired pacing in a circle, betray his state of mind. But an intriguing application of the same idea to a human subject is found in "Der Gefangene," part II.

DER GEFANGENE

II

Denk dir, das was jetzt Himmel ist und Wind,
Luft deinem Mund und deinem Auge Helle,

das würde Stein bis um die kleine Stelle
an der dein Herz und deine Hände sind.

Und was jetzt in dir morgen heißt und: dann
und: späterhin und nächstes Jahr und weiter—
das würde wund in dir und voller Eiter
und schwäre nur und bräche nicht mehr an.

Und das was war, das wäre irre und
raste in dir herum, den lieben Mund
der niemals lachte, schäumend von Gelächter.

Und das was Gott war, wäre nur dein Wächter
und stopfte boshaft in das letzte Loch
ein schmutziges Auge. Und du lebtest doch.

Translation:

THE PRISONER II

Imagine that what's now sky and wind, air for your mouth and brightness for your eye, turns into stone, but for the little place where your heart and your hands are. And what in you now means tomorrow, and then, and later, and next year, and so forth, turns into a sore in you and just festers and no longer opens up. And that which was goes crazy and rages around in you, your dear mouth that never laughed foaming with laughter. And what was God is now just your warden and maliciously stuffs a dirty eye into the last hole. And still you live.

In *Ewald Tragy*, *Das Stundenbuch* (The book of hours), and *Die Aufzeichnungen des Malte Laurids Brigge* (The notebooks of Malte Laurids Brigge), Rilke described his own experiences of claustrophobia, in which he imagined he was being crushed by stone. It was a close step to imagining the state of mind of a prisoner held in permanent captivity. In "Der Gefangene," part II, he asks the reader to imagine that the expanse and variety of the natural world are replaced by stone. Stone, he asks you to imagine, surrounds you and confines you in a small space. By consequence, your mental energy, which would have found its outlet in imagining the future, is bottled up and festers, while your memories, now useless, turn against your mind the way an autoimmune disease turns against the body. This last idea resonates with contemporary memory theory, which holds that the faculty of memory exists because it is adaptive—or in other words, human beings have memory because memories help them predict what will likely happen in the future. More recently it has been shown that persons with memory disorders have trouble imagining the future.[18] In this poem Rilke reaches for a physical analogy in order to get at the quality of the emotion. Thus, the confined body provokes an emotion that he describes in terms of a pus-filled wound and that expresses itself physically in foaming, involuntary laughter.

Third, Rilke evokes the "change your life" imperative, the experience of conversion, in two poems. The objects in question are a statue and a stained glass window respectively, and the viewer's emotional response is evoked through metaphors of the body. Rilke proposes that all of a sudden, something—some encounter with a material object—compels you to change your life. The way he describes the experience, it is not cognitive, not based in gradual reflection leading to insight, but emotional, physical, sudden, and overwhelming. The more famous of the two poems is "Archaïscher Torso Apollos."

ARCHAÏSCHER TORSO APOLLOS

Wir kannten nicht sein unerhörtes Haupt,
darin die Augenäpfel reiften. Aber
sein Torso glüht noch wie ein Kandelaber,
in dem sein Schauen, nur zurückgeschraubt,

sich hält und glänzt. Sonst könnte nicht der Bug
der Brust dich blenden, und im leisen Drehen
der Lenden könnte nicht ein Lächeln gehen
zu jener Mitte, die die Zeugung trug.

Sonst stünde dieser Stein enstellt und kurz
unter der Schultern durchsichtigem Sturz
und flimmerte nicht so wie Raubtierfelle;

und brächte nicht aus allen seinen Rändern
aus wie ein Stern: denn da ist keine Stelle,
die dich nicht sieht. Du mußt dein Leben ändern.

A literal translation of this poem presents particular difficulties on account of Rilke's puns. Alternative possibilities are given in parentheses.

Translation:

ARCHAIC TORSO OF APOLLO

We did not know his astonishing (or: unheard) head, in which the eye-apples ripened. But his torso still glows like a candelabra, in which his gaze, just turned down, persists and shines. Otherwise his chest's curve could not blind you, and in the slight turn of his loins a smile could not go toward the mid-point that supported procreation. Otherwise this stone would stand deformed and short under the shoulders' translucent [gas lamp] chimney (or: transparent ledge) and would not flicker like the coats of beasts of prey; and would not burst out of all its borders like a star: for there is no place there that does not see you. You must change your life.

Blinded by the star-like radiance of the statue that appears to see the viewer, the viewer registers an imperative: you must change your life. The trope of being blinded by light to signal revelation is conventional: since Plato's "Allegory of the Cave," truth has been likened to a blinding light, while in the Bible, Paul's conversion is initiated by a "light from heaven."[19] Rilke mixes the classical and biblical traditions and ascribes a conversion-compelling blinding light to the sun god Apollo, or rather to his statue. Moreover, this statue is headless and interestingly truncated in such a way that attention is drawn to the figure's Dionysian characteristics. What is so compelling about this statue? Wherein does its power lie? Is it that it unites Nietzsche's two divergent *Kunsttriebe*, the Apollonian and the Dionysian? Rilke's innovation is to ascribe the light that blinds and compels conversion to a work of art. In so doing, he inverts the relation of art to truth that Goethe allegorizes in "Zueignung" (Dedication) in which Truth appears as a woman in a blinding light ("ein Glanz umgab mich, und ich stand geblendet" [a radiance surrounded me, and I stood blinded]), then hands Poetry to the poet in the form of a mitigating veil ("Empfange hier ... der Dichtung Schleier aus der Hand der Wahrheit" [Receive here the veil of Poetry from the hand of Truth]).[20]

In "Die Fensterrose," a similar encounter with an object compels religious faith in the medieval churchgoer:

DIE FENSTERROSE

Da drin: das träge Treten ihrer Tatzen
macht eine Stille, die dich fast verwirrt;
und wie dann plötzlich eine von den Katzen
den Blick an ihr, der hin und wieder irrt,

gewaltsam in ihr großes Auge nimmt,—
den Blick, der, wie von eines Wirbels Kreis
ergriffen, eine kleine Weile schwimmt
und dann versinkt und nichts mehr von sich weiß,

wenn dieses Auge, welches scheinbar ruht,
sich auftut und zusammenschlägt mit Tosen
und ihn hineinreißt bis ins rote Blut—:

So griffen einstmals aus dem Dunkelsein
der Kathedralen große Fensterrosen
ein Herz und rissen es in Gott hinein.

Translation:

THE ROSE WINDOW

In there: the sluggish kneading of their paws creates a stillness that almost confuses you; and how then, suddenly, one of the cats violently takes your glance at her, which strays here and there, into her great eye—the glance that, as if seized by a whirlpool's circle, floats for a short while and then sinks and no longer knows anything of itself, when this eye, which seemingly rests, opens up and slams shut with a roaring and drags it in, right into the red blood—: thus, once upon a time, the great rose windows seized a heart out of the cathedrals' darkness and dragged it into God.

This object is the rose window, located high above the entry door—an immense spot of luminescent color in the dark interior of the cathedral. Rilke likens the effect of the rose window on the churchgoer, even the modern one, to that of a cat fixing its prey and to a whirlpool sucking in an object. Thus, the rose window is hypnotic, and the effect is violent. The emotional effect on the viewer is described in terms of a conventional metaphor of the body—the heart—for feeling: the heart is seized and torn away, appropriated for God.

Fourth, Rilke devotes several poems to an emotion that he, as a supremely imaginative poet, must often have experienced: what it feels like to imagine. He figures it as an exciting, intoxicating, even erotic activity. The material object involved here is the mirror. Rilke often uses the mirror to signal that fantasy and creativity are at play. He was fascinated by mirrors and reflecting surfaces generally, often wrote about them, and obviously gave careful thought to the properties that made them so magical. A mirror creates an illusory reality and also an alternative reality, since even a flat, clear mirror does not give a true image, but a laterally inverted one. Curved mirrors, broken mirrors, and dull mirrors give back a distorted image of the real. Moreover, a mirror creates the illusion of doubling space. In addition, a mirror allows one to see one's own face—although when one looks at it in a mirror, one's face assumes a special expression. Finally, mirrors are an ancient topos for art.

In the *Neue Gedichte*, Rilke frequently mentions mirrors or creates mirror effects. In "Quai du Rosaire" and "Spätherbst in Venedig" (Late autumn in Venice), he uses mirroring as a device to contrast a European city that in his day had dwindled to a relic of its onetime self with its former importance and power. He confronts the real with its imaginative remembrance. Thus in "Quai du Rosaire," an image of Bruges appears in the water that is claimed to be "more real," more awake, than the quiet present-day town, while in "Spätherbst in Venedig," Rilke contrasts the lazy tourist trap of his own day with energetic medieval Venice, which he resurrects in the second half of the sonnet by mirroring and inverting the features of the present-day city point by point. Excitement rises here with the turn from the real to the imagined. Two further mirror poems, "Venezianischer Morgen" and "Dame vor dem Spiegel," involve women looking at their reflection in the mirror. In each case, the confrontation with the mirror initiates a brief state of narcissistically tinged altered consciousness in which the woman acquires a sense of identity by seeing her image. "Venezianischer Morgen" is a sonnet about Venice in the early morning when the light touches the water, a moment that Rilke chooses to represent as erotic: Venice, personified as a noblewoman, is likened to a nymph who receives Zeus. Insouciant and unpressured, the beautiful city comes to consciousness and self-awareness by seeing multiple reflections of herself in the water. Finally awake and apparently in a good mood, she pursues her self-admiration by raising San Giorgio Maggiore like a hand mirror and smiling languidly into it. In "Dame vor dem Spiegel" a woman likewise looks into a mirror, and with more agency than personified Venice:

Dame vor dem Spiegel

Wie in einem Schlaftrunk Spezerein
löst sie leise in dem flüssigklaren
Spiegel ihr ermüdetes Gebaren;
und sie tut ihr Lächeln ganz hinein.

Und sie wartet, dass die Flüssigkeit
davon steigt; dann gießt sie ihre Haare
in den Spiegel und, die wunderbare
Schulter hebend aus dem Abendkleid,

trinkt sie still aus ihrem Bild. Sie trinkt,
was ein Liebender im Taumel tränke,
prüfend, voller Mißtraun; und sie winkt

erst der Zofe, wenn sie auf dem Grunde
ihres Spiegels Lichter findet, Schränke
und das Trübe einer späten Stunde.

Translation:

Lady Before the Mirror

Like spices in a sleeping potion she quietly dissolves her tired demeanor in the liquid-clear mirror; and she puts her smile completely in. And she waits for the liquid to rise from it; then she pours her hair into the mirror and, lifting her splendid shoulder out of her evening dress, she silently drinks from her image. She drinks what a lover would drink in delirium, testingly, full of mistrust; and she only beckons her maid when at the bottom of her mirror she finds lights, closets, and the murk of a late hour.

The woman here wants to change her tired appearance and transform herself into a beauty. Echoing the conflation of memory and anticipation seen in "Der Gefangene," Rilke leaves unclear whether she is preparing for a party or recovering from one before going to bed: her actions could be read either way. What is important is that she brews a magic potion out of her initial appearance and the mirror—Rilke's analogy is to dropping dry spices into a sleeping potion—then brushes her hair into the mirror (one can imagine her bending her neck forward and brushing it up from behind)—strikes the pose of lifting one shoulder out of her evening dress—and finally drinks out of her image. Like the personification of Venice, she acquires identity from her image. Unlike a lover, who would drink the identical beverage in a frenzy, she sips her appearance critically, studying herself, yet apparently fully absorbed in herself in this ritualized dialectic with the mirror, aware of nothing but herself. The outcome of her interaction with the mirror is apparently satisfactory, since at length she is collected enough so that she can disengage her full attention from her appearance. She becomes aware of the world around her (the things behind her in the room that she sees in the mirror). The allusion to the lover, the woman's beauty, and the notion of ingesting one's own appearance in the form of a mind-altering drink all suggest an erotic—narcissistic—dimension to this remake in front of the mirror. The woman simultaneously works on her appearance and experiences changes in her mental state as she passes from tiredness through self-scrutiny and reassured self-identification to composure.

In "Die Flamingos" finally, a complicated tour de force of a poem, Rilke suggests to the reader through the activities of the titular flamingos an autoerotic scenario involving a girlfriend and her voyeuristic lover.

Die Flamingos

Jardin de Plantes, Paris

In Spiegelbildern wie von Fragonard
ist doch von ihrem Weiß und ihrer Röte
nicht mehr gegeben, als dir einer böte,
wenn er von seiner Freundin sagt: sie war

noch sanft von Schlaf. Denn steigen sie ins Grüne
und stehn, auf rosa Stielen leicht gedreht,
beisammen, blühend, wie in einem Beet,
verführen sie verführender als Phryne

sich selber; bis sie ihres Auges Bleiche
hinhalsend bergen in der eignen Weiche,
in welcher Schwarz und Fruchtrot sich versteckt.

Auf einmal kreischt ein Neid durch die Volière;
sie aber haben sich erstaunt gestreckt
und schreiten einzeln ins Imaginäre.

Translation:

The Flamingos

Jardin des Plantes, Paris

In mirror images like Fragonard's, though, no more of their white and redness is given than someone might offer you if he said about his girlfriend: she was still soft with sleep. For if they climb into the greenery and stand, slightly turned on pink stems, together, blooming, as if in a bed, they seduce themselves more seductively than Phryne, until, thrusting with their necks, they hide the pallor of their eyes in their own softness, in which black and fruit-red lie hidden. Suddenly an envy screeches through the aviary. But they have stretched out in astonishment and stride singly into the imaginary.

The name "Fragonard," a rococo artist famous for his sly erotic paintings such as "The Swing," where a voyeur is positioned so as to look up a woman's skirts, as well as other more explicit paintings of half-naked women in bed, is dropped early. The man who says, in a counterfactual conditional, that his girlfriend was still soft from sleep, also arouses the reader's suspicions. But overtly, the poem is about flamingos. To this day, the flamingos in the venerable Jardin des Plantes are kept in a grassy area enclosing a pond that is close to a large volière. The flamingos in question must be thought of as pink flamingos, such as those in the Camargue, whose red and black markings become visible only when their wings are spread. In Rilke's scenario, the flamingos are at first in their pond. One sees only their pink outside, which is also reflected in the water. "Spiegelbilder," a word that has long puzzled critics because Fragonard did not paint mirror images, alludes in my view to the counter-proofs for which Fragonard was famous and which are sometimes pink. Rilke calls them "Spiegelbilder," mirror images (which they indeed are) instead of using their technical name, in my opinion, in order to invoke the magical word "Spiegel" (mirror) and also to suggest the mirrored images of the flamingos in their pond. If, then, Rilke continues, the flamingos walk onto their lawn, they stand about like flowers in a bed (erotically suggestive vocabulary in German as in English), eventually engaging in self-penetration as they curl their long necks and stick their beaks down into the more vividly colored portions of their anatomy. This activity is interrupted by the envious squawking of the birds in the volière, whereupon the flamingos stalk into "the imaginary." Literally, one can imagine that they retreat to the mirroring pond; but figuratively, they reveal themselves to be figments of the imagination, erotic fantasies spun by an overstimulated human mind. The reader, turned into a voyeur like the lover and the volière birds, is seduced into figuring out the poem as though it were a Fragonard painting and readily reads the birds as an anamorphosis for a human erotic scene.

Emotions in literature are an enticing area of study, but there is a considerable gap between the scientific studies on emotion and the emotions that are most intriguingly evoked in literary works. The emotions that Rilke describes in the *Neue Gedichte* would probably be disqualified by the neuroscientists with whose theories his representations are most consistent as not meeting their stringent criteria. Classic neuroscientific theory, such as that of Damasio and others, works with lists of emotions—lists that, admittedly, have a fair degree of variation. This is because the scientists are interested in emotions that are "robust": universal, observable, testable, and thus productive for analysis. By these criteria, not many emotions pass muster. The poet, in contrast, is interested in capturing elusive states of mind that are not necessarily generalizable to the entire human race. It is noteworthy, however, that such "poetic emotions" also prove to have corporeal and material dimensions. In the *Neue Gedichte*, Rilke foregrounds the material stimulus for the emotion by investing certain things—whether spaces, art objects, animals, plants, or everyday objects—with specific emotional powers over the person who interacts with them. The conceptual—cognitive and linguistic—substructure of emotion hypothesized by Barrett, which suggests that we have considerable control of our emotions, remains foreign to Rilke, who is intent on showing the object's power over the human subject.

Lorna Martens is Professor of German and Comparative Literature at the University of Virginia. Her research centers on comparative literature of the eighteenth to twentieth centuries, modern German and Austrian literature, women's studies, GDR literature, poetry, narrative and narrative theory, and cognitive approaches to literature. Her books include *The Promise of Memory: Childhood Recollection and Its Objects in Literary Modernism* (Cambridge, MA: Harvard University Press, 2011); *The Promised Land? Feminist Writing in the German Democratic Republic* (Albany: State University of New York Press, 2001); *Shadow Lines: Austrian Literature from Freud to Kafka* (Lincoln: University of Nebraska Press, 1996); and *The Diary Novel* (Cambridge, UK: Cambridge University Press, 1985).

Notes

1. Antonio Damasio, *Self Comes to Mind* (New York: Pantheon Books, 2010), 109, 111, 116.
2. For example, Joseph Ledoux, *The Emotional Brain* (New York: Simon & Schuster, 1996), 267–68 (see, too, his historical account in chapter 3); Jaak Panksepp and Lucy Biven, *The Archaeology of Mind* (New York: Norton, 2012), 2.

3. Damasio, *Self Comes to Mind*, chapter 4.
4. Panksepp and Biven, *Archaeology of Mind*, 14, argue likewise: "Clinical observation suggests that neither cognitive ability nor the ability to think in words is a necessary precondition for affective consciousness."
5. Joseph Ledoux, *Anxious* (New York: Viking, 2015), 149–50.
6. Lisa Feldman Barrett, *How Emotions Are Made* (Boston: Houghton Mifflin Harcourt, 2017), 30.
7. For more detail, see Lorna Martens, *Shadow Lines: Austrian Literature from Freud to Kafka* (Lincoln: University of Nebraska Press, 1996).
8. For the importance of things for Rilke, see Lorna Martens, *The Promise of Memory* (Cambridge, MA: Harvard University Press, 2011), 23–136. Rilke's contemporary Marcel Proust and subsequently Walter Benjamin similarly elevated objects to privileged repositories of human significance. Proust theorized that things hold a key to memory: they have the power to magically resurrect the forgotten past in a beholder who fortuitously reencounters them. Benjamin gives things along with places a comparable power to evoke memories. For more detail about Proust and Benjamin, see Martens, *Promise of Memory*.
9. Bill Brown, *A Sense of Things: The Object Matter of American Literature* (Chicago: University of Chicago Press, 2003), 8.
10. Brown, *Sense of Things*, 3.
11. Walter Benjamin, *Illuminations*, ed. and Introduction by Hannah Arendt, trans. Harry Zohn (New York: Schocken, 1969), 188.
12. Rainer Maria Rilke, *Briefe in zwei Bänden*, vol. 1: 1896–1919, ed. Horst Nalewski (Frankfurt am Main: Insel, 1991), 247.
13. For example, in his letter of 13 November 1925 to Witold Hulewicz, in Rainer Maria Rilke, *Briefe*, ed. Karl Altheim (Frankfurt am Main: Insel, 1987), III: 898–99.
14. Letter to Hulewicz, Rilke, *Briefe*, III: 899.
15. Even the anti-basic emotions theorist Barrett concedes: "'Happy' might be the closest thing we have to a universal emotion category with a universal expression," Barrett, *How Emotions Are Made*, 51.
16. James Joyce, *A Portrait of the Artist as a Young Man* (N.L.: CreateSpace Independent Publishing Platform, 2017), 148.
17. The literal prose translations of Rilke's poems here are mine. For poetic translations, see Rainer Maria Rilke, *New Poems*, trans. Edward Snow (New York: North Point Press, 1984), and Rainer Maria Rilke, *New Poems: The Other Part*, trans. Edward Snow (New York: North Point Press, 1987).
18. Sinéad L. Mullally and Eleanor A. Maguire, "Memory, Imagination, and Predicting the Future: A Common Brain Mechanism?" *The Neuroscientist* 20 (June 2014): 220–34.
19. Acts 9:3.
20. Johann Wolfgang von Goethe, *Gedichte* (Munich: Beck, 1988), 150, 152.

Bibliography

Barrett, Lisa Feldman. *How Emotions Are Made*. Boston: Houghton Mifflin Harcourt, 2017.
Benjamin, Walter. *Illuminations*, edited and with Introduction by Hannah Arendt. Translated by Harry Zohn. New York: Schocken, 1969.
Brown, Bill. *A Sense of Things: The Object Matter of American Literature*. Chicago: University of Chicago Press, 2003.
Damasio, Antonio. *Self Comes to Mind*. New York: Pantheon Books, 2010.
Goethe, Johann Wolfgang von. *Gedichte*. Munich: Beck, 1988.
Joyce, James. *A Portrait of the Artist as a Young Man*. N.L.: CreateSpace Independent Publishing Platform, 2017.
Ledoux, Joseph. *Anxious*. New York: Viking, 2015.
——— *The Emotional Brain*. New York: Simon & Schuster, 1996.
Martens, Lorna. *The Promise of Memory*. Cambridge, MA: Harvard University Press, 2011.
——— *Shadow Lines: Austrian Literature from Freud to Kafka*. Lincoln: University of Nebraska Press, 1996.
Mullally, Sinéad L., and Eleanor A. Maguire. "Memory, Imagination, and Predicting the Future: A Common Brain Mechanism?" *The Neuroscientist* 20 (June 2014): 220–34.
Panksepp, Jaak, and Lucy Biven. *The Archaeology of Mind*. New York: Norton, 2012.
Rilke, Rainer Maria. *Briefe*, edited by Karl Altheim. Frankfurt am Main: Insel, 1987.
——— *Briefe in zwei Bänden*. Vol. 1: 1896–1919, edited by Horst Nalewski. Frankfurt am Main: Insel, 1991.
——— *Neue Gedichte und der Neuen Gedichte anderer Teil*. Frankfurt am Main: Insel, 1991.

CHAPTER 15

Inscribing Grief
Private Practices of Bereavement in Wartime Germany

ERIKA QUINN

> I am sitting on the kitchen bench next to the pretty lamp you bought in Berlin, which brings me enjoyment every day. Each piece in the room has its own history—we gathered them all with a lot of love. And each piece speaks of you, each picture, each book, every little knick-knack—you, my dearest! ... Dearest, all of your most recent photos are so happy and joyful; I always have to look at them. And then I have to cry. Your dear letters, all of which I have carefully saved, are also of great value. I am so glad that I still have the long letter from you that you wrote the day before you went missing.
> —Vera Conrad, diary[1]

Excerpted from a diary kept by Vera Conrad from 1939 to 1948, the quotation above reveals the materiality of emotional experience and expression. While previous thought about emotions has insisted on a separation of mind and body, current work in the field suggests that the two are interconnected. Indeed, emotions are "embodied ... and tied to our engagements with material things."[2] Emotions are situated in objects and within the space in which they are located. As Sara Ahmed observes, "Emotions are both about objects, which they hence shape, and are also shaped by contact with objects."[3] Objects exercise power on humans as we interact with them in that they can make us respond to them in a myriad of emotional responses, from frustration to joy to sadness. Conrad's emotions developed through and manifested in her experiences with objects and in space. For example, the kitchen bench, a comfortable, intimate, yet familial space was a site where Conrad did much of her writing because she felt safe and calm there. It evoked time spent in the kitchen together with her husband. Her mention of the "pretty lamp" and "every little knick-knack" speaks to how objects acquire significance as bearers of emotional memory for their owners. Contact with objects can bring to mind past events, feelings, or sensations associated with the objects. As historian Pierre

Nora observes, memory, an "organic process of remembering the past ... is rooted in the concrete: in space, gesture, image, and object."[4] Conrad felt strongly attached to the objects she and her husband had gathered: "I always have to look at them. And then I have to cry."[5] The objects were reminders of a past reality in which her husband was safe and brought her gifts.

The "little book," as Conrad called it, was originally intended as a baby book for the couple's first child, a gift from her mother-in-law. The Conrads were married in 1937 and lived with his parents on their sizable farm in Saxony-Anhalt. Born in 1906 and 1912, respectively, Joachim and Vera had fairly advanced educations: he had completed the *Abitur* and a few years of university, and she attended a girls' secondary school where she intended to take the *Abitur* before family circumstances drew her back home prematurely. They expected their first child with joy, and Vera's diary entries recorded their courtship and early years together. With the December 1943 entry quoted above, however, the diary's function and audience shifted radically—from a celebratory and commemorative document intended for her son to a "letter diary"[6] for her husband that she began when she was notified that Joachim was missing in action on the Eastern Front. The frequency of entries increased after that letter arrived; and in particularly stressful times, Conrad wrote several times a week.

The diary became a totemic object for its author as well as her children; the meaning Vera invested in the little book over time imbued it with sacrality.[7] The diary embodied Vera's ongoing relationship with her husband Joachim; the powerful emotions created and impressed in the book—love, fear, and grief—"stuck" (Ahmed) to the author and others who came in contact with the diary. Not only was the book itself imbued with emotion; it revealed other objects and spaces as emotional repositories. It was in dynamic relationship with the author, a kind of feedback loop as she enacted her emotions in it and had them reanimated by revisiting her prior entries.

Historians of modern Europe have recently been examining emotions as another approach to help us understand the people and societies of the past.[8] Yet in this new work, historians overlook some key insights from cultural studies and the social sciences. While historians have adopted insights about how emotions "work" from anthropology, they often do so through a discursive focus on language. I echo Michael Roper's dismay that linguistic analysis neglects "a sense of the material, the practices of everyday life, . . . [and] human experience formed through emotional relationships with others."[9] Because written words serve as our bread and butter, historians often overlook other kinds of historical evidence and limit ourselves to a discursive study of written documents. However, the past cannot simply be captured in language or words; emotions surely can transcend discourse. As the editors of this volume point out, bodily experience can serve as an alternative to language as a way in to investigating emotions. While historians may be bound to examining textual artifacts from the past, we can read them for clues of the embodied, material, and spatial elements of emotional experience. Like other essays in this volume, my project investigates the relational character of emotions.

Sara Ahmed's work in affect theory and Monique Scheer's use of practice theory based on Pierre Bourdieu's work offer insights into the transmission of emotions between people and/or objects, reminding readers that humans share an embodied state that shapes and constrains emotional experience and expression. Ahmed emphasizes the relational interconnectivity of humans. She asserts that emotions are transmissible via physical contact; our skin is an important definer of individuality as well as a receiver for "impressions" from others. Contact between physical objects, or affective contact between living beings, leaves behind "sticky" impressions. That stickiness can transfer to other objects or affective relationships.[10] The weakness of affect theory is that it tends to universalize and ahistoricize emotions, which are at least to some extent culturally constructed, as many historians of emotion consistently argue.[11] Working with Bourdieuian sociology, Scheer suggests that emotions are a kind of practice, both limited by the fact of our physicality and malleable because they are culturally and socially embedded. As she points out, writing or talking about feelings is "always bound up in a bodily practice."[12] Scheer's claim that "we *have* emotions and we *manifest* emotions"[13] underlines the experiential and performative sides of emotions. The verbs "have" and "manifest" indicate one interconnected process rather than two. This activity, understood by Scheer as "emotional practice," is constituted by "habits, rituals, and everyday pastimes that aid us in achieving a certain emotional state. This includes the striving for a desired feeling as well as modifying of the one that is not desirable . . . . These practices are very often . . . carried out together with other people, artifacts, aesthetic arrangements, and technologies."[14] Applying practice theory aids in moving beyond discursive analysis; it "encourages us to read textual sources for traces of observable action."[15]

My particular research interest—grief—lends itself to these approaches that emphasize embodiment and practice. Mourning is an individual's psychological response to loss and its expression or communication[16] that entails negotiating and renegotiating the meaning of the loss over time, as opposed to the Freudian approach of completely giving up the lost object. Ahmed and other affect theorists emphasize that the perceived separateness and distinction between people is an illusion; she asserts: "We pick up bits and pieces of each other as the effect of nearness or proximity."[17] We are intertwined with other people and the impressions they leave on us. Given this reality of connection, maintaining attachments to the dead can enable the construction of new meanings rather than blocking new forms of attachment, as posited in early psychotherapy.[18] The lost loved one is not abandoned, but transfigured from an external to an internal relationship with the bereaved.

Women have long been associated with grief and mourning in the West.[19] The emotional work of bereavement was often performed by women, often with the aid of the ritualized use of objects. Literature scholars Beth Tobin and Maureen Goggin point out that "memorial culture created, shared, and used by women, particularly in the nineteenth century, includes memorial samplers, postmortem photographs, mourning stationery, and condolence calls."[20] In rural settings like the Conrads', mourning was quite prescriptive, dictating clothing, practices, and even familiar phrases with which to console the bereaved.[21] Practices such as the engagement of a *Leichenfrau* (laying-out woman) to prepare the corpse for the funeral persisted into Vera's time.[22] In this rural world, "material objects were not only representations of needs but also guides through life, to a certain extent a catalogue of collective memories, bringing before people's eyes the prospect of how life would proceed and how it would eventually come to an end."[23] Bridal dresses and funeral dresses, embellished with the same trimmings, were hung side-by-side in the same cabinet with baby clothes: death and mourning were a predictable part of life expected by all, and observed with traditional practices.

Some had expressed discontent and frustration with the constraints of mourning practice before the war: industrialization and the rise of consumer culture likely fueled these perceptions. In the countryside, traditional practices slowly disappeared as large numbers of young people left the countryside for the cities. World War I provided the material and emotional conditions for the break to become quite pronounced: the strict mourning practices of the late nineteenth-century largely disappeared by the end of the war. Mourners became uncertain about mourning practices that had largely become impractical or undesirable.[24] This uncertainty led to the creation of new practices in some cases and a clinging to tradition in others.[25] For example, soldiers killed in action whose bodies were not recovered were buried in "book tombs," which were any form of "writing, whether in the form of fiction, testimony, poem or book or remembrance" created by the bereaved.[26] Official state-sponsored war commemoration became the dominant public form of mourning, while private forms became more individualized. World War II intensified and accelerated these shifts. After that conflict, especially in Germany, it was more difficult to give death meaning, to construct private biographies and public forms of commemoration, than after World War I.[27] The emotional response was much different too; there were few debates about commemoration after World War II as had raged after World War I.[28] The mass death from both world wars and concomitant unease with existing or state-sponsored public commemorations indicates that mourners often made their own rituals, frequently involving objects.

Objects possess a power "to recall the presence of the missing dead;" in outlasting their owners, objects can "convey a sense of permanence in the face of loss."[29] Objects that possess this power and ability, fashion historian Juliet Ash argues, are "memory-objects."[30] These items could serve as emotional replacements for the actual body or presence of the deceased or missing person, and become symbolic representations of the ongoing relationship between the living and the dead. Such objects exercise agency in that they "can become subjects as they take on new roles in different spaces," as Tobin and Goggin note.[31] While Ash focuses on the deceased person's clothing, Conrad's diary took on a new role, as opposed to the wedding ring Joachim Conrad left behind when he left for the front, or photographs of him that fixed his existence in the past.[32] The letter-diary, I argue, became a form of ongoing conversation that allowed Conrad to contain her emotions to a greater degree than less dynamic objects would have allowed. Objects, in this case the letter-diary, aid in the externalization and expression of emotions. The "little book" helped Conrad contain and frame her emotions as well as create desired emotional states.

The diary was kept in circumstances that made open, public expression of grief potentially dangerous. The National Socialists aimed for a "revolution of feeling," as Nicholas Stargardt observes.[33] Seeking to supplant the myriad of emotional communities that people inhabited and moved between and with a single "emotional communit[y],"[34] in which people's emotions and their expression were aligned to support the regime, the National Socialists created a street theater of marching boots and uniforms, parades, flags, and rallies. Whether one truly supported the Nazi program or not, to get along, one needed to appear to fit in by participating. Singing folk songs, waving flags, and using the Hitler salute were all physical gestures and activities that signaled belonging to the people's community (*Volksgemeinschaft*) and support of the regime. The regime's emotional demands on the population were not limited to the enthusiastic support exhibited in parades and rallies. It also required a new kind of emotional cultivation. Borrowing to an extent from experiences in World War I, the Nazis promoted a cult of the fallen soldier.[35] This cult was related to the primary emotional virtue for the Nazis, that of "hardness," which had emerged as an antidote to nervousness and vulnerability in the early twentieth century.[36] Leaning heavily on his flawed understanding of Nietzsche's "superman" concept, Hitler saw Christian values such as compassion, turning the other cheek, and loving enemies as friends as weaknesses that threatened the German race. He wanted Germans to overcome what he perceived as emotional or moral weaknesses, like compassion and fear.[37] In the cult, battlefield deaths were celebrated as "heroic deaths," or sacrifices for the Fatherland. Widows and other mourners were to participate proudly and silently in public funeral rites, and to willingly sacrifice their loved ones to the Fatherland without complaint.[38] This kind of emotional stance was difficult for many women to maintain, making alternative expressions of grief all the more important.

Despite its relentless focus on public life and its ruthless suppression of interiority, the Nazi regime actually encouraged the population to keep diaries. Germany had a highly literate culture, and writing was a valued activity, understood as a form of self-expression and self-cultivation, particularly among the middle classes. Like the practice of sending troops into battle with inexpensive cameras in order to document their victories, diary keeping was meant to serve posterity in recording the glorious events and experiences of the Third Reich.[39] Although the Nazi regime discouraged individualism and hoped that diaries would reflect collective heroic values, older traditions of writing and reading persisted. Many women did indeed pick up pen and paper; they most often began writing when the war began to personally impact them, often in 1943 when significant bombing raids terrorized German civilian life.[40] Other women turned to diary keeping when the mail stopped or, as in Vera Conrad's case, when their husbands were declared missing.

Diaries can serve as important psychological and emotional tools for their authors. In unusual and crisis-ridden times, they can become key coping mechanisms. The "healing power of speaking and writing" can be employed in order to make sense of traumatic events, loss, or a conflict of core values.[41] While most authors intend for their writings to remain private, they nonetheless may have an audience beyond themselves, or alternately, "serve as a form of conversation or correspondence between the writer's selves."[42] In Conrad's era, more women were able to keep diaries because literacy had spread, and a practice previously restricted to the elite became more democratic.[43] Diary keeping also built on practices developed in World War I like the creation of "book tombs."

Conrad kept the diary to achieve several outcomes. Not only was she recording events so that her husband could catch up on them when he returned; she also used the diary as an important form of maintaining a relationship with him. In conducting the diary as a sort of conversation, she could imagine his responses and pour out her emotions to him via the "little book." She wrote familiarly: "I just have to talk (*plaudern*) with you again."[44] In a small way, this practice filled the gap left behind by the end of his letters in November 1943. Thus, the letter-diary became an emotional confidante, a safe place to express and create her feelings of pain, fear, and sadness.

Other women continued to write to their husbands at the front, which I see as a much different practice. For example, Clara Aßman in Berlin stopped receiving letters from her husband in August 1943.[45] During the next year, she continued to write to him, telling him about the dreams she had of him, bombing attacks, and their sons. She wrote, "If only I knew if you received any letters."[46] Her situation was very similar to Conrad's, but she chose to address it differently. The letters have a conversational tone, but are much briefer, perhaps because of paper shortages or Aßman's relatively poor education compared to Conrad's. The letters, however, were not something Aßman could retain and revisit like the letter-diary. Her letters were sent into a void that made a two-way conversation with her husband much more difficult for her to imagine. The letter-diary also literally frames emotions as experiences that can be opened and shut, or fixed and carried around. In this way, I suggest, the letter-diary had a way of containing and perhaps taming some of the desperate anxiety felt by women seeking news of their missing husbands.

Scholars have frequently claimed that twentieth-century war presented an upheaval in mourning practices and a crisis of meaning because of the unprecedented manner and numbers of deaths. Some say that these experiences left the bereaved without language to express themselves,[47] while others state, "individuals generally tackled the emotional and practical issues they faced, rather than bearing witness to them on paper."[48] Ego documents from the war era contradict these assertions. Conrad's diary uses quite simple and very repetitive language to express her grief. Like other waiting wives, she repeats the phrases "if only I had some sign of life," "when you come home," and "where are you?" Building on Suzanne zur Nieden's observations about the conversational quality of diaries, I suggest that rather than lacking language, Conrad and other writers reiterated their emotions to themselves when they engaged in conversation with their grieving selves. In Conrad's case, that self was put away from consciousness as much as possible when she was working, managing employees or apprentices, spending time with her children, or engaging in other everyday activities; she moved between the emotional communities of everyday village life and National Socialist prescriptions of hardness. The time she set aside for herself to write in her diary, however, was the time to enact and recreate her grief and to confide emotions or thoughts she wanted to keep private. The diary was a repository charged with emotion: her grief, fear, and hope left impressions in the letter-diary. In attempting to continue the relationship with her missing husband, she in fact constructed it through the diary text by naming and performing her emotions.[49] As Ahmed observes, discourse has a power to produce effects through reiteration.[50]

The performative and expressive components of emotions are clearly illustrated by the theme of "hope" as expressed in the letter-diary. In her first entry after she was notified of Joachim's missing status, Conrad wrote, "Dearest, you are alive, I can feel it! If only we could be among the happy ones who had gotten a sign of life from their loved ones! But for us there is still hope, and I will not give it up."[51] Two months later, she asked, "And where are you, how are you doing? It is so unspeakably torturous to think [of your death], but I still remain hopeful after all that you will come home and we will begin a new life, or continue the old one."[52] One month later, she asserted that things were very difficult, "but I will not give up hope that we will be together again. That gives me strength and the courage to keep going."[53] In May, that "but" became even more important as it contradicted Conrad's present reality. "But I always have the thought and the hope that you will come back and everything will be good again."[54] Half a year later, she insisted, "I cannot give up hope. I hope and believe that you will come back!"[55] This cycle of assertions of hope acquired a desperate sense in which Conrad attempted to shift her emotional state from despair to hope. She was trying to write herself into feeling the hope that she continually emphasized.

The diary enabled Conrad to process her probable loss and reevaluate her possible future even while hoping for Joachim's eventual return. Conrad's loss of her husband didn't fit her own projected biography: the disruptive news of his missing status meant that their shared future was much more difficult to imagine. As someone attempting to cope with an unimagined, unwelcome intrusion in her life, she knew only that "something happened"; until she produced a new story, she couldn't say what precisely had happened. The letter-diary was a manifestation of her attempt to manage the crisis of meaning by continuing an important relationship and starting a new meaningful narrative about it.[56] The emotional practice of writing served other women in a similar fashion. One woman kept a diary as a form of conversation with her missing husband and wrote him poems at night. Another began to use a notebook her children had given her for Christmas as a "kind of diary," which would, for her, "replace the letters which I can no longer write to you. I want to tell you in it what I would have otherwise written in my letters and so it ought to be a kind of bridge to the time when you are with us again."[57]

The letter-diary itself is hard bound in a roughly woven, cream-colored fabric; and as a physical artifact, it retains traces of Conrad's emotional states. Keeping a diary is a physical act: the pressure of the pen leaves an impression on the paper that can then be read. As literature scholar Elspeth Probyn points out, "Writing is a corporeal activity . . . [that] . . . affects bodies. Writing takes its toll on the body that writes and the bodies that read or listen."[58] Conrad mostly wrote in "the German handwriting" using fountain pen. Later on in the diary, she shifted to the Roman script used by English speakers, and often resorted to pencil. When serious bombing raids began and she snatched any time she had to write, her handwriting became larger and looser. The physical act of writing could be soothing, as when Conrad curled up on the kitchen bench and lost herself thinking about better or future times; but it could also be exhausting, as well as a means of confronting the author with grim realities—the act of committing words to paper made the events described more real and permanent.[59] Another way in which the diary was both relief and burden was the fact that Conrad allowed herself to be afraid, doubtful, pessimistic, and in pain—emotional expressions she did not allow her public self.

As in the quotation that began this piece, Conrad often mentioned writing while seated on the kitchen bench near the "memory-objects" dear to her, or seated on the bed near Joachim's photo. The kitchen—often the center of the home and the hearth, and a place of nourishment—and the bedroom—an intimate space of shared time together—were safe spaces associated with positive emotions. By choosing these rooms to write in, Conrad engaged in "emotional practice,"[60] reenacting, or attempting to, special shared moments—putting her body in proximity to his imagined presence. The ritualized sense of settling in for a talk is emphasized by her descriptions of herself as "curled up" on the kitchen bench, or "in bed." As she frequently stated, she could not imagine him at the front, nor what he was going through, but she could generate a concrete image and physical sensation in her memory and bodily memory in spaces they inhabited together. For example, "I sit comfortably on the bench near the stove, hold the book on my knees and warm my back. And you, dearest? Every night when I go to bed, in the soft down bed, I think about you and where you might be housed!"[61] The comfort she gained from the warmth and emotional association with her husband sparked anxiety about his circumstances. In another instance, Conrad indicated, "Today I'm writing in bed."[62]

As the letter-diary amassed more entries, it attested through its increasing volume and the impressions of ink on paper to the passing of time. Filling the last page was always a sad moment for Conrad, as she dreaded starting a new book. Yet the volume and physicality of the books made them meaningful artifacts of their marriage, a testament to its existence. "Dearest! I've gotten to the last page of my little book. I started it so gladly and happily and now I have to close it with such a heavy heart."[63] The filled book and need for another were tangible reminders of Joachim's continued absence. In 1946, she wrote, "Now I really have to start writing in the third book already.... I had so hoped that you would come soon and we could experience everything together."[64]

These documents from the war were precious to many German families. One father had written faithfully to his eleven-year-old daughter while he was at the front. When his unit faced capture in Romania, he was in possession of her letters to him, which he buried under a tree. In the 1950s, he returned to the spot in Romania to retrieve them, so dear were they to him.[65] Scholars have noted the haunting presence of "millions" of boxes of photographs and papers from

> all the former belligerent nations. While these boxes preserve mementoes of lives and places that were loved, they also contain the evidence of ... irretrievable loss. These boxes are not shrines at which one could mourn, however, ... they seem to be postwar reproductions of Pandora's box, the opening of which might unleash unspeakable horror or unbearable sadness.[66]

Vera Conrad's diary is so "sticky" even now that until recently, her son, Joachim, had not read it in entirety: it was too "painful." His wife, Friede, had read it during nights when she couldn't sleep. Although Joachim was not aware of that, it was "not a secret," she assured me. Vera Conrad kept the diary in a special metal box, along with her bankbook and other important documents. While Joachim doubts that she ever reread it, when she left her house in the fall to overwinter with him and Friede, the diary always came with her.[67] It was a holy object. Now, Joachim has read it in the transcribed form I mailed him, attesting to the impression left by his mother's physical presence, personality, and pain.[68] Conrad's diary was a relic and totemic object for her. In it, she rehearsed and revisited emotions recorded through the pressure of her fingers on the pen, impressing the paper with incontrovertible evidence of her strong emotions. It had served as her private vehicle for mourning.

While Conrad attempted to adhere to commemorative practices developed during World War I to mourn her husband in a public fashion, these failed. Mourning one's dead, fallen in what the East German regime deemed a criminal, fascist war, was suppressed under East German regime. Conrad's attempt to have a commemorative plaque naming the dead of World War II hung alongside the one from World War I in the local Lutheran church was blocked by authorities. In addition to keeping her diary, Conrad also participated in Lutheran religious life—an activity frowned upon by the regime. For Conrad and many other East Germans, the private sphere served as an "outpost of individuality, potential dissent, and alternative identity-formation."[69] Like millions of mourners across Europe, Conrad's bereavement found its most important expression between the diary's pages for reasons imposed by the state, the difficulty of finding meaning in her loss, and her own emotional needs.

Erika Quinn is Professor of History at Eureka College. Her research interests lie in Central European cultural history, focusing on questions of subjectivity formation and the history of emotions. Her book, *Franz Liszt: A Story of Central European Subjectivity*, was published by Brill in 2014. She has also published articles on twentieth-century German war widows in the *Journal of First World War Studies* and elsewhere. Her current book project is based on a bereaved German woman's diary from 1939–48.

Notes

1. December 1943, Nr. 2910, Walter Kempowski-Archiv, Akademie der Künste, Berlin; complete diary in private collection. All translations mine unless otherwise noted. Names were changed to respect the family's desire for privacy.

2. Oliver J. T. Harris and Tim Flohr Sørensen, "Rethinking Emotion and Material Culture," *Archaeological Dialogues* 17 (2010): 145.
3. Sara Ahmed, *The Cultural Politics of Emotion* (New York: Routledge, 2004), 7.
4. Pierre Nora, *Realms of Memory: The Construction of the French Past*, vol. 1 of *Conflicts and Divisions* (New York: Columbia University Press, 1996), 3.
5. December 1943, Walter Kempowski-Archiv.
6. Sabine Grenz, "Feldpostbriefe, die nie vesandt wurden: Das Brieftagebuch der Ursel H.—Konstruktion einer Beziehung," in *Schreiben im Krieg, Schreiben vom Krieg: Feldpost im Zeitalter der Weltkriege*, ed. Veit Didczuneit, Jens Ebert, and Thomas Jander (Essen: Klartext, 2011), 256.
7. Nora, *Realms of Memory*, 3.
8. Richard Bessel, "Hatred After War: Emotion and the Postwar History of East Germany," *History and Memory* 17 1/2 (2005): 195–216; Frank Biess, "Feelings in the Aftermath: Toward a History of Postwar Emotions," in *Histories of the Aftermath: The Legacies of the Second World War in Europe*, ed. Frank Biess and Robert G. Moeller (New York: Berghahn Books, 2010), 30–48; William C. Rosenberg, "Reading Soldiers' Moods: Russian Military Censorship and the Configuration of Feeling in World War I," *American Historical Review* 119 (June 2014): 714–40.
9. Michael Roper, "Slipping out of View: Subjectivity and Emotion in Gender History," *History Workshop Journal* 59 (Spring 2005): 62.
10. Ahmed, *Cultural Politics*, 91.
11. See Hester Vaizey, *Surviving Hitler's War: Family Life in Germany, 1939–48* (Basingstoke: Palgrave Macmillan, 2010); Mark D. Steinberg and Valeria Sobol, eds., *Interpreting Emotions in Russia and Eastern Europe* (Dekalb, IL: Northern Illinois University Press, 2011); Barbara H. Rosenwein, "Worrying about Emotions in History," *American Historical Review* 107 (June 2002): 821–45; Ute Frevert, "Angst vor Gefühlen? Die Geschichtsmächtigkeit von Emotionen im 20. Jahrhundert," in *Perspektiven der Gesellschaftsgeschichte*, ed. Paul Nolte, Manfred Hettling, Frank-Michael Kuhlemann, and Hans-Walter Schmuhl (Munich: C. H. Beck, 2000), 95–111.
12. Monique Scheer, "Are Emotions a Kind of Practice (and What Is It That Makes Them Have a History)? A Bourdieuian Approach to Understanding Emotion," *History and Theory* 51, no. 2 (May 2012): 212.
13. Scheer, "Are Emotions," 195, emphasis in original.
14. Scheer, "Are Emotions," 209.
15. Scheer, "Are Emotions," 218.
16. Jeffrey Kauffmann, "Mourning," in *Encyclopedia of Death and Dying*, ed. Glennys Howarth and Oliver Leaman (New York: Routledge, 2001), 311.
17. Ahmed, *Cultural Politics*, 160.
18. Ahmed, *Cultural Politics*, 169; Judith Butler, *Precarious Life: The Powers of Mourning and Violence* (New York: Verso, 2004), 21.
19. See Beth Ann Bassein, *Women and Death: Linkages in Western Thought and Literature* (Westport, CT: Greenwood Press, 1984); Nigel Barley, *Grave Matters: A Lively History of Death around the World* (New York: Henry Holt & Co., 1997); Marjo Buitelaar, "Widows' Worlds," in *Between Poverty and the Pyre: Moments in the History of Widowhood*, ed. Jan Bremmer and Lourens van den Bosch (London: Routledge, 1994), 1–18.

20. Beth Fowkes Tobin and Maureen Daly Goggin, "Connecting Women and Death: An Introduction," in *Women and the Material Culture of Death*, ed. Beth Fowkes Tobin and Maureen Daly Goggin (Burlington, VT: Ashgate, 2013), 3.
21. Rudolf Reichardt, *Geburt, Hochzeit und Tod im deutschen Volksbrauch und Volksglauben* (Jena: H. Costenoble, 1913), 166–67.
22. 30 April 1944, Walter Kempowski-Archiv.
23. Utz Jeggle, "The Rules of the Village: On the Cultural History of the Peasant World in the Last 150 Years," in *The German Peasantry: Conflict and Community in Rural Society from the Eighteenth to the Twentieth Centuries*, ed. Richard J. Evans and W. R. Lee (London: Croom Helm, 1986), 275.
24. Irene Guenther, *Nazi Chic? Fashioning Women in the Third Reich* (New York: Berg, 2004), 30–31.
25. Jay Winter, *Sites of Memory, Sites of Mourning: The Great War in European Cultural History* (Cambridge, UK: Cambridge University Press, 1995).
26. Luc Capdevila and Danièle Voldman, *War Dead: Western Societies and the Casualties of War*, trans. Richard Veasey (Edinburgh: Edinburgh University Press, 2006), 126.
27. Richard Bessel and Dirk Schumann, "Introduction: Violence, Normality, and the Construction of Postwar Europe," in *Life after Death: Approaches to a Cultural and Social History of Europe during the 1940s and 1950s*, ed. Richard Bessel and Dirk Schumann (Cambridge, UK: Cambridge University Press, 2003), 2.
28. Monica Black, *Death in Berlin: From Weimar to Divided Germany* (Cambridge, UK: Cambridge University Press, 2010), 10.
29. Tobin and Goggin, "Connecting Women and Death," 1. See also Elizabeth Hallam and Jenny Hockey, *Death, Memory, and Material Culture* (New York: Berg, 2001).
30. Juliet Ash, "Memory and Objects," in *The Gendered Object*, ed. Pat Kirkham (Manchester: Manchester University Press, 1996), 219.
31. Tobin and Goggin, "Connecting Women and Death," 2.
32. Jenny Edkins, *Missing: Persons and Politics* (Ithaca: Cornell University Press, 2011), 1.
33. Nicholas Stargardt, *The German War: A Nation Under Arms, 1939–1945* (New York: Basic Books, 2015), 12.
34. Rosenwein, "Worrying about Emotions," 842.
35. See also George Mosse, *Fallen Soldiers: Reshaping the Memory of the World Wars* (New York: Oxford University Press, 1990); Jay W. Baird, *To Die for Germany: Heroes in the Nazi Pantheon* (Bloomington: Indiana University Press, 1990).
36. Joachim Radkau, *Das Zeitalter der Nervosität: Deutschland zwischen Bismarck und Hitler* (München: Carl Hanser Verlag, 1998), 357.
37. Peter Fritzsche, *Life and Death in the Third Reich* (Cambridge, MA: Harvard University Press, 2008), 3.
38. Sabine Behrenbeck, *Der Kult um die toten Helden: Nationalsozialistische Mythen, Riten, und Symbole 1923 bis 1945* (Vierow bei Greifswald: S-H Verlag, 1996), 514–16.
39. Fritzsche, *Life and Death*, 66.
40. Susanne zur Nieden, *Alltag in Ausnahmezustand: Frauentagebücher im zerstörten Deutschland 1943 bis 1945* (Berlin: Orlanda Frauenverlag, 1993), 9, 16, 73.
41. zur Nieden, *Alltag in Ausnahmezustand*, 17; see also Vaizey, *Surviving Hitler's War*, 13.
42. zur Nieden, *Alltag in Ausnahmezustand*, 28, 32, 41–42.

43. Janosch Steuwer and Rüdiger Graf, "Selbstkonstitution und Welterzeugung in Tagebüchern des 20. Jahrhunderts," in *Selbstreflexionen und Weltdeutungen: Tagebücher in der Geschichte und der Geschichtsschreibung des 20. Jahrhunderts*, ed. Janosch Steuwer and Rüdiger Graf (Göttingen: Wallstein Verlag, 2015), 10–11, 14.
44. 16 January 1944, Walter Kempowski-Archiv.
45. Museumsstiftung Post und Telekommunikation (MPT), 3.2002.0215 AK 2.
46. MPT, 21 November 1943.
47. Stéphane Audoin-Rouzeau and Annette Becker, *14–18 Understanding the Great War*, trans. Catherine Temerson (New York: Hill and Wang, 2002), 176.
48. Vaizey, *Surviving Hitler's War*, 10.
49. Grenz, "Feldpostbriefe," 255–57.
50. Ahmed, *Cultural Politics*, 92.
51. December 1943, Walter Kempowski-Archiv.
52. 18 February 1944, Walter Kempowski-Archiv.
53. 22 March 1944, Walter Kempowski-Archiv.
54. 27 May 1944, Walter Kempowski-Archiv.
55. 1 January 1945, Walter Kempowski-Archiv.
56. Edkins, *Missing*, xiv.
57. Stargardt, *German War*, 340–41.
58. Elspeth Probyn, "Writing Shame," in *The Affect Theory Reader*, ed. Melissa Gregg and Gregory J. Seigworth (Durham, NC: Duke University Press, 2010), 76.
59. zur Nieden, *Alltag in Ausnahmezustand*, 52.
60. Scheer, "Are Emotions."
61. 12 November 1944, Walter Kempowski-Archiv.
62. 14 September 1944, Walter Kempowski-Archiv.
63. 27 May 1944, Walter Kempowski-Archiv.
64. 27 May 1946, Walter Kempowski-Archiv.
65. Nicholas Stargardt, *Witnesses of War: Children's Lives under the Nazis* (New York: Alfred A. Knopf, 2006), 155.
66. Elizabeth Domansky, "A Lost War: World War II in Postwar German Memory," in *Thinking about the Holocaust After Half a Century*, ed. Alvin H. Rosenfeld (Bloomington: Indiana University Press, 1997), 237.
67. Interview with Joachim Conrad, Ostrau, Germany, 7 July 2015.
68. Interview with Joachim Conrad.
69. Paul Betts, *Within Walls: Private Life in the German Democratic Republic* (Oxford: Oxford University Press, 2010), 6.

Bibliography

Ahmed, Sara. *The Cultural Politics of Emotion*. New York: Routledge, 2004.
Ash, Juliet. "Memory and Objects." In *The Gendered Object*, edited by Pat Kirkham, 219–24. Manchester: Manchester University Press, 1996.
Audoin-Rouzeau, Stéphane, and Annette Becker. *14–18 Understanding the Great War*. Translated by Catherine Temerson. New York: Hill and Wang, 2002.

Baird, Jay W. *To Die for Germany: Heroes in the Nazi Pantheon*. Bloomington: Indiana University Press, 1990.
Barley, Nigel. *Grave Matters: A Lively History of Death around the World*. New York: Henry Holt & Co., 1997.
Bassein, Beth Ann. *Women and Death: Linkages in Western Thought and Literature*. Westport, CT: Greenwood Press, 1984.
Behrenbeck, Sabine. *Der Kult um die toten Helden: Nationalsozialistische Mythen, Riten, und Symbole 1923 bis 1945*. Vierow bei Greifswald: S-H Verlag, 1996.
Bessel, Richard. "Hatred After War: Emotion and the Postwar History of East Germany." *History and Memory* 17 1/2 (2005): 195–216.
Bessel, Richard, and Dirk Schumann. "Introduction: Violence, Normality, and the Construction of Postwar Europe." In *Life after Death: Approaches to a Cultural and Social History of Europe during the 1940s and 1950s*, edited by Richard Bessel and Dirk Schumann, 1–14. Cambridge, UK: Cambridge University Press, 2003.
Betts, Paul. *Within Walls: Private Life in the German Democratic Republic*. Oxford: Oxford University Press, 2010.
Biess, Frank. "Feelings in the Aftermath: Toward a History of Postwar Emotions." In *Histories of the Aftermath: The Legacies of the Second World War in Europe*, edited by Frank Biess and Robert G. Moeller, 30–48. New York: Berghahn Books, 2010.
Black, Monica. *Death in Berlin: From Weimar to Divided Germany*. Cambridge, UK: Cambridge University Press, 2010.
Buitelaar, Marjo. "Widows' Worlds." In *Between Poverty and the Pyre: Moments in the History of Widowhood*, edited by Jan Bremmer and Lourens van den Bosch, 1–18. London: Routledge, 1994.
Butler, Judith. *Precarious Life: The Powers of Mourning and Violence*. New York: Verso, 2004.
Capdevila, Luc, and Danièle Voldman. *War Dead: Western Societies and the Casualties of War*. Translated by Richard Veasey. Edinburgh: Edinburgh University Press, 2006.
Conrad, Joachim. Interview: Ostrau, Germany, 7 July 2015.
Domansky, Elizabeth. "A Lost War: World War II in Postwar German Memory." In *Thinking about the Holocaust After Half a Century*, edited by Alvin H. Rosenfeld, 233–72. Bloomington: Indiana University Press, 1997.
Edkins, Jenny. *Missing: Persons and Politics*. Ithaca: Cornell University Press, 2011.
Frevert, Ute. "Angst vor Gefühlen? Die Geschichtsmächtigkeit von Emotionen im 20. Jahrhundert." In *Perspektiven der Gesellschaftsgeschichte*, edited by Paul Nolte, Manfred Hettling, Frank-Michael Kuhlemann, and Hans-Walter Schmuhl, 95–111. Munich: C. H. Beck, 2000.
Fritzsche, Peter. *Life and Death in the Third Reich*. Cambridge, MA: Harvard University Press, 2008.
Grenz, Sabine. "Feldpostbriefe, die nie versandt wurden: Das Brieftagebuch der Ursel H.—Konstruktion einer Beziehung." In *Schreiben im Krieg, Schreiben vom Krieg:*

Feldpost im Zeitalter der Weltkriege, edited by Veit Didczuneit, Jens Ebert, and Thomas Jander, 253–62. Essen: Klartext, 2011.

Guenther, Irene. *Nazi Chic? Fashioning Women in the Third Reich*. New York: Berg, 2004.

Hallam, Elizabeth, and Jenny Hockey. *Death, Memory, and Material Culture*. New York: Berg, 2001.

Harris, Oliver J. T. and Tim Flohr Sørensen. "Rethinking Emotion and Material Culture." *Archaeological Dialogues* 17 (2010): 145–63.

Jeggle, Utz. "The Rules of the Village: On the Cultural History of the Peasant World in the Last 150 Years." In *The German Peasantry: Conflict and Community in Rural Society from the Eighteenth to the Twentieth Centuries*, edited Richard J. Evans and W. R. Lee, 265–89. London: Croom Helm, 1986.

Kauffman, Jeffrey. "Mourning." In *Encyclopedia of Death and Dying*, edited by Glennys Howarth and Oliver Leaman, 311–14. New York: Routledge, 2001.

Mosse, George. *Fallen Soldiers: Reshaping the Memory of the World Wars*. New York: Oxford University Press, 1990.

Nora, Pierre. *Realms of Memory: The Construction of the French Past*. Vol. 1 of *Conflicts and Divisions*. New York: Columbia University Press, 1996.

Probyn, Elspeth. "Writing Shame." In *The Affect Theory Reader*, edited Melissa Gregg and Gregory J. Seigworth, 71–90. Durham, NC: Duke University Press, 2010.

Radkau, Joachim. *Das Zeitalter der Nervosität: Deutschland zwischen Bismarck und Hitler*. München: Carl Hanser Verlag, 1998.

Reichardt, Rudolf. *Geburt, Hochzeit und Tod im deutschen Volksbrauch und Volksglauben*. Jena: H. Costenoble, 1913.

Roper, Michael. "Slipping out of View: Subjectivity and Emotion in Gender History." *History Workshop Journal* 59 (Spring 2005): 57–72.

Rosenberg, William C. "Reading Soldiers' Moods: Russian Military Censorship and the Configuration of Feeling in World War I." *American Historical Review* 119 (June 2014): 714–40.

Rosenwein, Barbara H. "Worrying about Emotions in History." *American Historical Review* 107 (June 2002): 821–45.

Scheer, Monique. "Are Emotions a Kind of Practice (and What Is It That Makes Them Have a History)? A Bourdieuian Approach to Understanding Emotion." *History and Theory* 51, no. 2 (May 2012): 193–220.

Stargardt, Nicholas. *The German War: A Nation Under Arms, 1939–1945*. New York: Basic Books, 2015.

———. *Witnesses of War: Children's Lives under the Nazis*. New York: Alfred A. Knopf, 2006.

Steinberg, Mark D., and Valeria Sobol, eds. *Interpreting Emotions in Russia and Eastern Europe*. Dekalb, IL: Northern Illinois University Press, 2011.

Steuwer, Janosch, and Rüdiger Graf. "Selbstkonstitution und Welterzeugung in Tagebüchern des 20. Jahrhunderts." In *Selbstreflexionen und Weltdeutungen: Tagebücher in der Geschichte und der Geschichtsschreibung des 20. Jahrhunderts,*

edited by Janosch Steuwer and Rüdiger Graf, 7–26. Göttingen: Wallstein Verlag, 2015.
Tobin, Beth Fowkes, and Maureen Daly Goggin. "Connecting Women and Death: An Introduction." In *Women and the Material Culture of Death*, edited by Beth Fowkes Tobin and Maureen Daly Goggins, 1–12. Burlington, VT: Ashgate, 2013.
Vaizey, Hester. *Surviving Hitler's War: Family Life in Germany, 1939–48*. Basingstoke: Palgrave Macmillan, 2010.
Winter, Jay. *Sites of Memory, Sites of Mourning: The Great War in European Cultural History*. Cambridge, UK: Cambridge University Press, 1995.
Zur Nieden, Susanne. *Alltag in Ausnahmezustand: Frauentagebücher im zerstörten Deutschland 1943 bis 1945*. Berlin: Orlanda Frauenverlag, 1993.

INDEX

affect (*Affekt*), 2, 4, 7–8, 14n6, 17n42, 17n43, 17n44, 17n45, 25–35, 37n8, 52, 91n1, 149, 151, 254
Sara Ahmed on, 9, 254–5
affection, 173, 187, 195, 207, 209, 211
affectionate, 194, 195–6
affectation, 133
affective, 9, 13, 25–6, 28–35, 52, 53, 55, 63–4, 67, 69, 70–1, 96, 149, 189, 191, 194–5, 198, 250n4, 254
  Capitalism
  contagion, 136
  field, 158, 160, 223, 226, 228–30
  imagery, 225
  potential, 2
  practices, 96, 102, 104–5, 190
affectivity, 7
agitprop, 78–80, 83, 88–91, 92n7, 93n22
  communist, 9, 13, 77–80, 88
agitation, 78–9, 84–5, 90
  as an emotion, 158
agitator, 77, 79, 80, 83, 92n10
  Agitator (1931), 81
  Agitator/Volksredner (1920), 84
  Agitator/ Otto Rühle spricht (1920), 80, 81
Ahmed, Sara, 149, 252–4, 258
Angst. See under fear
animal, 9, 173–4
  animal magnetism, 9, 25–33, 35, 36n2, 37n8, 38n18, 50
anti-Semitism, 9–10, 13, 100–2, 104, 108n24
  practices of, 9, 96, 105
anxiety, 63–4, 67–8, 71, 103, 116, 122, 131, 147, 229, 258, 260
Appadurai, Arjun, 142
Arndt, Ernst Moritz, 225
attunement (*Befindlichkeit*), 7, 160, 223

Ausdrucksbewegung (expressive movement), 9, 63–5, 67, 69
Ausdruckstanz (expressionist dance), 85
avant-garde, 70, 80, 88

Baden Baden, 156, 159
Bad Homburg, 143, 145
Bakhtin, Mikhail, 122–3
balneology, 160, 162
banners, 4, 12, 222–3, 225–8, 230
Barrett, Lisa Feldman, 97, 100, 236, 249, 250n15
Bayreuth, 47
Becher, Johannes, 89
Befindlichkeit. See under attunement
behavior, 119, 123, 173, 175, 208
  Verhalten, Haltung, 78–9
Benjamin, Walter, 155, 238, 250n8
  Arcades Project, 151–2
bereavement, 12, 255, 261
Berlin, 47–52, 55, 84–5, 257
Beuys, Josef, 206
Bildungsroman, 128
Blanc, Louis and François, 143, 145
Bloch, Ernst, 80
bodiliness, 2, 4, 9
body
  affective body, 70
  and behavior, 1, 133, 136
  and class, 77–80, 85, 198
  and kinetics, 9, 62–64, 66–67, 69–71
  and physiological connections, 25, 28, 30
  and psychological connections, 25, 98
Bourdieu, Pierre, 78, 91n3
Brandstetter, Gabriele, 70, 88
Brecht, Bertolt, 78–9, 89
Breslau, 224, 228
Brockhaus, Rudolf, 189, 199n7, 200n22
Brown, Bill, 4, 15n11, 142, 238

Brunnenschriften (spa literature), 156, 158
Bürgertum (bourgeoisie, burghers), 52, 90, 187, 190
Butler, Judith, 99, 107n14

calmness (*Ruhe*), 44, 156, 158, 161
Campe, Joachim Heinrich, 133, 173
Campe, Rüdiger, 1, 14n6, 127
Campt, Tina, 190, 199n8
Carlsbad, 156, 158–61, 164n17
casino, 10–1, 143–152, 157, 169–70
   and emotions, 145–8, 150
cheerfulness (*Heiterkeit*), 156–160, 158, 160–1, 206, 224
choral societies, 12–13, 222–6, 239
cognitive phenomena, 65, 97, 100, 130, 132, 136, 142, 171, 235, 237, 243, 249
collective emotions, 101, 105, 226–7, 230
color, 202–4, 206, 209, 213, 245
   blue, 89, 204, 209–10, 216n29, 217n37, 230, 240
   brown, 83
   green, 84, 240
   red, 206–14, 216n29, 240, 245, 248
   yellow, 206, 209
commodification, 10–2, 116, 123, 142, 162, 203, 218n49
commodity, 4, 10, 142, 155, 161, 162n3, 213,
   commodity fetishism, 3, 238
Communism, 78, 83
Communist, 9, 13, 78–80, 81–6, 88–9, 91, 205
   agitprop, 9, 79–80, 88
   Communist Party of Germany (KPD), 9, 77–80, 83, 88–91, 93n22
   habitus, 9, 77–9, 84, 86, 91
communitarian culture (*Gemeinschaftskultur*), 9, 77, 79, 84
community. *See* emotional communities
corporeality, 6, 8, 44, 66, 96
   and emotions, 1, 5, 123, 235–249
curiosity, 67, 172, 175

Damasio, Antonio, 235–6, 249
daguerreotype, 11–3, 187, 189, 192, 194, 199n6, 200n22

Deleuze, Gilles, 8, 46, 50
diary, 12, 117, 252–3, 256–61, 261n1
dietetics, 157–8, 160, 163n12
Dilthey, Wilhelm, 3, 6–7, 16n30, 17n34, 97
disgust, 29, 63–4, 68, 70–1, 135
Dix, Otto, 81
Dostoyevsky, Fyodor, 147
   The Gambler, 146–7
Dresden, 51, 81, 227, 231n1
Dudow, Slatan, 89
   Kuhle Wampe, 89

ecological conception of emotions. *See under* emotions
education, 11–2, 83, 90, 123, 127, 131, 172–7, 179–80, 253, 258
   and objects, 171, 178
Einfühlungsästhetik (empathy aesthetics), 5–6
Eisler, Hans, 89
embodiment, 8, 63, 66, 73n24, 78, 80, 90–1
embodied ideology, 27, 35, 62–3, 66, 71, 78, 80, 88, 91, 142
embodied practices, 2, 6, 27, 77, 117, 122, 198, 198
embodied sensation, 27, 29, 31, 35, 37n8, 86, 116
emotions
   authenticity of, 25, 133, 189, 191, 200n17
   and banners, 4, 12, 222–30
   body and, 4, 8–9, 12, 15n16, 27, 29–30, 43–46, 50, 55, 63–7, 69, 70–1, 78, 80, 83, 85, 88, 96–100, 103–104, 115, 117, 123, 133, 135–6, 143, 146, 157, 191, 194–8, 235–7, 239, 242, 252
   and children, 28, 102–3, 171, 172, 174–8, 180, 195, 239, 241
   and class, 3–5, 9, 15n15, 77–78, 80, 85, 88–91, 97, 123, 194, 198, 208–9, 212
   clothing and, 121, 127, 131–2, 188, 190, 192, 194–5, 198, 200n22, 204, 209, 223, 226, 246–7, 255
   and codes, 66, 78, 99, 104, 206–9
   commodity and, 3–4, 10, 155–6, 161, 213, 238
   communication of, 11–2, 46, 135, 203, 205, 208, 213, 254
   constructed view of, 97, 236, 254, 258

ecological conception of, 97
education of, 172–4
embodiment of, 4, 6, 8–9, 25–6, 32, 63, 70, 77, 78, 88, 191, 202, 226, 252–4, 254
emotional style, 11, 13, 99, 187, 189
as enactive emotions, 66–7, 73n26
vs. feelings of emotion, 235–7
and flowers, 4, 11–3, 48, 190, 202–21, 248
and furniture, 119, 125n18, 128–9, 144–5, 146–8, 150–1, 195, 210, 248, 260
and gambling, 142–54
and hermeneutics, 3, 5
history of, 4, 7–8, 15n14, 45, 54, 78, 90, 143, 187,
and jewelry, 11, 192, 194, 256
in literary studies, 2, 5, 7–8
and masthead, 222–30, 232n13
materiality of, 1, 3–8, 15n15, 41, 43, 45–6, 50–1, 55, 57n20, 66, 71, 96, 116, 122, 128, 131, 143, 146, 149–50, 155, 174, 178, 190–1, 194, 198, 213, 223–4, 227, 230, 232n13, 235–49, 252–5
material interests and, 3–4, 8, 10–1, 155–62, 162n2, 162n3
and messages, 69, 202–8, 211–2
and music, 58n44, 158, 160–1, 222–3, 227–30
and New Materialism, 97
and objects, 1, 3–4, 6, 9, 11–2, 16n30, 25–6, 28–31, 35, 37n8, 142–3, 146, 149–51, 155–6, 161, 162n2, 171, 173–8, 180, 191–194, 198, 202, 222–3, 226–8, 230, 237–9, 243, 249, 252–6, 260
and photography, 11, 187, 190
as practice, 103, 116–7, 123, 129, 132, 134–5, 137n5, 151, 190–1, 204, 213, 223, 252––61
and politics, 77–9, 90, 97, 99, 103–4, 137, 203–7, 211
and representation, 7–8, 71, 96, 194, 213, 236, 249
and rhetorics, 2–3, 5, 7, 14n6, 80, 115,
and sales talk, 10–1, 155–62, 162n4

somatization of, 15n16, 66, 98
and songs, 2, 80, 89, 132, 176–8, 212, 224–5, 227–9, 256
and space, 1–3, 8, 10–1, 63, 67–8, 71, 100–5, 116–22, 125n15, 158, 162n2, 187, 189, 191–4, 202, 222–3, 225, 228, 230, 239, 242, 249, 252–3, 256, 260
stickiness of, 254, 261
and things (*see under* objects)
use value of, 155–6
words, 1–2, 4, 14n5, 15n16, 97, 100, 103, 135, 175, 208, 226, 235–7, 250n4, 253,
writing and, 252
emotional communities, 2, 55, 90, 93, 104, 222, 226, 230, 256, 258
emotional contagion, 9, 49–50, 136
emotional expectations, 156, 158–61, 162n4
emotional gravitation, 42, 46, 50–1, 64–5
emotional regimes, 9, 79, 90, 131–2, 147
emotional register, 78, 85, 190
emotional repository, 258
emotional style, 11, 13, 187
emotionology. *See under* emotional expectations
empathy, 5–6, 10, 70, 128, 132–6, 137n5, 178
empathy aesthetics. See under *Einfühlungsästhetik*
Empfindsamkeit. See under sentimentalism
enthusiasm, 12, 41–3, 129, 138n20, 206, 222, 230
Erfurt, 101–2, 106n4,
excitement, 10–1, 48, 147, 156, 159–62, 222, 226, 241
expressionist dance. See under *Ausdruckstanz*
expressions, 188, 189, 194, 198, 223, 230, 237, 257
of emotions, 189, 194, 197–8, 200n22, 222, 241, 250n15, 252, 254, 256–7
expressive movement. See under *Ausdrucksbewegung*
exteriority, 7, 10, 12, 128

face, 42, 62, 64, 67–8, 83, 95, 99, 196, 245, 256
facial expression, 2, 6, 9, 14n9, 48, 64, 80, 88, 122, 189, 227–8, 235

family, 9, 13, 26, 33, 35, 62–3, 89, 95,
  100–3, 117, 119, 121, 131, 173, 176,
  179–80, 190, 195–6, 199n7, 200n22,
  205, 253
fear, 7, 9–10, 63, 66, 68–71, 101–2, 105,
  131, 146, 226, 229, 237, 253, 256–8
  Angst, 7, 63–4, 68
  Furcht, 7, 63
feeling, 2, 4–9, 17n43, 29, 31, 64, 70, 78, 85,
  95, 97–100, 103, 105, 116, 129, 131–2,
  142, 144, 146, 151–2, 174, 176, 191,
  198, 208, 235, 239, 245, 254, 256, 259
  intensification of, 6, 10, 161
feelings, 2, 10, 12, 15n16, 17n44, 26, 32, 64,
  69, 74n30, 97, 99–104, 134, 136, 152,
  156, 171, 175, 191, 202–3, 207–8,
  213–4, 235, 237, 252, 254, 257
  preverbal feelings, 236
Felixmüller, Conrad, 77, 80–1
Feuchtwangen, 225, 229
Fiedler, Konrad, 65–7
Finland, 47, 51, 54
flags, 12, 205–6, 222–30, 256
flowers, 202–21
  and agency, 213
  carnations, 202, 205–208, 211–14,
    215n14
  and emotions. See under emotions
  and gender, 203, 209–13
  lilies, 202, 205, 208
  roses, 202, 206–209, 211–14, 215n15. See
    also under love
fragmentation, 64
Francke, August Herrmann, 3
Frevert, Ute, Somatization of emotions, 66,
  98, 15n16
friends, 10, 33, 95, 101–03, 117–120, 127,
  145–47, 195–97, 203, 207–09, 213, 256
friendship. See under friends
Fröbel, Friedrich, 171–2, 177–80
Furcht. See under fear

Gambler's Luck (*Spielerglück*), 144
gambling, 10, 12, 142–154. See also under
  casino
  and body, 146
  and emotional contexts, 146
  and emotional distress, 146
  and emotions (see under emotions)
  and France, 143
  and Germany, 143
  and Illegalization, 143
  and moral danger, 144
  and Rhineland, 143
  games, 143, 145, 150, 160, 177–78
  roulette, 143, 146–47, 150–51, 153n29
gaming, 143, 145–48, 151
  and passions, 144–45, 147
German Democratic Republic, 205, 211
Gebärde. See under movements
Geertz, Clifford, 202
Gefühl, 129, 173, 202
Gemeinschaftskultur (communitarian culture),
  9, 77, 79, 84
Gemütsbewegung (movement of temper),
  64–65, 67
gender, 9–11, 13, 15, 15n15, 26, 35, 77,
  85–88, 90–91, 99, 116, 119–20, 176,
  179, 203, 209–13, 227
German Choral Association (*Der Deutsche
  Sängerbund*), 222–23
German workers' movement, 79, 83, 89
gesture, 11, 13, 16, 18–19, 212, 22n9, 44, 48,
  55, 62–71, 79–80, 88–89, 97, 117, 133,
  187–88, 191–92, 194–98, 200n22,
  253, 256
Gilman, Sander, 83
Giloi, Eva, 204
Gmelin, Eberhard, 26, 28–34
Goethe, Johann Wolfgang von, 127, 133–34,
  136, 227, 244
Goethe, *Die Leiden des jungen Werthers*,
  133–34, 136
goose pimples (*Gänsehaut*), 9, 96–101, 103,
  106n9, 98, 107n13
Gotha, 95, 100–102, 106n4
Green Party, 206
grief, 115, 160, 213, 253, 258
Guattari, Félix, 46, 50
Guimps, Roger, 176

habitus, 9, 77–80, 84–86, 88–89, 91
hands, 67–69, 71, 83, 90, 120, 178, 180, 187,
  192–94, 198

Hanslick, Eduard, 42
happiness, 115, 159, 239, 241
 and gambling, 144, 159
Hardenberg, Friedrich von, 210
hardness (emotional), 79, 256, 258
Harris, Oliver, 158, 223, 225
Haug, Wolfgang Fritz, 155
Heidegger, Martin, 7, 142
Heine, Heinrich, 42, 47, 49, 50–54
Heiterkeit. See under cheerfulness
Herder, Johann Gottfried, 127, 227
hermeneutics, 3, 5
hippies, 212
Hitler, Adolf, 205–06, 256
Hlawaczek, Eduard, 158
hope, 101, 206–07, 258–60
Hoffmann, E.T.A., 44–46
Husserl, Edmund, 7

Innerlichkeit (interiority), 1, 8, 28, 117, 127
International Women's Day, 211
interoceptive processes, 100

joy, 10, 12, 63, 66, 133, 160, 178, 206, 211,
 222–23, 227, 230, 237, 241, 252–53

Kaiserreich, 222, 227
Kampfkultur, militant culture, 77, 79, 91
Kant, Immanuel, 172–73, 177
Kate, the Duchess of Cambridge, 203–204
Kindergarten, 171, 177–79
Kissingen spa, 156, 160–61
Klassenstandpunkt (class standpoint), 77–78
Klopstock, Friedrich Gottlieb, 127
Kollwitz, Käthe, 210
Kosstrin, Hannah, 78
Kreutzer, Conradin, 224
Krone, Hermann, 187, 200n22
Kuhle Wampe, film, 89

laughter, 10, 13, 100, 102, 115–23, 124n1,
 124n2
 and the civilizing process, 124
Ledoux, Joseph, 236
Leipzig, 51, 199n3, 200n22, 223, 226, 230
Lesewut (passion for reading), 136
Leys, Ruth, 27

linguistic turn, 4, 15n14, 142
Liszt, Franz, 9–10, 41–53
Lisztomania, 42, 47–50, 53–55
lived experience, 3, 6–7
living presence, 3, 12, 155
Locke, John, 172–73, 175
Löffler, Petra, 70
London, 42, 52
love, 49, 54, 68, 132–33, 174–78, 204,
 206–08, 209, 212–14
 and education
 and flowers, 204, 206–08, 209, 212–14
 and maternality, 11, 171, 173–74
Luther, Martin, 1, 10, 128

machine, 44, 50, 53, 146–48, 151
magic, 53, 159, 246
magnetism. *See under* animal magnetism
Marcard, Heinrich Matthias, 157
Marienbad spa, 156, 159
Marxist theory, 13, 78, 80, 90, 91n1
Massumi, Brian, 8, 17n44, 27, 52
material culture, 3–4, 6–8, 97, 171, 223–24,
 229
materiality, 1, 3–6, 8, 41, 43, 45–46, 50, 55,
 66, 71, 96, 102, 104, 116, 122, 129,
 150, 155, 194, 198, 252
maternality, 177, 178. *See also* love
May Day, 205
Medick, Hans, 3–4
memory, 116–117, 147, 192, 194, 197, 210,
 227, 242, 246, 250n8, 252–53, 255
 and bodies, 9, 63, 68, 95–97, 100–104,
 260
 and objects, 197, 255–56, 260
Menke, Karl Theodor, 158
Merleau-Ponty, Maurice, 68
Mesmer, Franz Anton, 8, 25, 27, 32, 35,
 36n2
Mesmerism, 27, 37n17, 50
Mihaly, Jo, 77, 85–8
militant culture. *See under Kampfkultur*
money and emotion, 4, 144, 146, 148–152
Monte Carlo, 143–5, 153n29
moods (*Stimmungen*), 7, 33, 83, 131, 158,
 202, 228
Moritz, Karl Philipp, 127–141

Mother's Day, 202–3, 211–2
mourning, 63, 254–5, 258, 261
  and East Germany, 261
movement (*Gebärde*), 6, 64–5, 67, 69–70, 116, 227
movement of temper. See under *Gemütsbewegung*

Napoleonic Wars, 171–2, 204, 225
nation, 77, 90, 176, 223, 227–8
national pride, 12, 222, 225–6, 230
National Socialists and emotions, 103, 108n24, 109n36, 256–258
nerves, 2, 28, 30–4, 38n24, 65, 99, 226
Neue Sachlichkeit. See under New Objectivity
neurology, 1–2
neuroscience and emotions, 2, 8, 235–7, 249
New Materialism. See under material culture
New Objectivity (*Neue Sachlichkeit*), 81

objects
  and aura, 238
  and effects, 238–39
  and sacred, 49, 269
  and totem, 12, 253, 261
  See also memory

Paganini, Niccolò, 42–4, 47, 50–2, 55, 56n6, 56n12, 56n13
Paris, 25, 43–4, 49, 52, 155, 161, 205, 238, 247–8
passion/s. See under emotions
Pathosformel (pathos formula), 3, 14n9, 70, 88,
performativity, 79, 84, 88, 128, 254, 258
Pestalozzi, Johann Heinrich, 11, 171–186
phenomenology, 7, 16n33, 29, 68
Philanthropists, 172–3, 176
photographs, 4, 11–2, 85, 88, 187–201, 255–6, 270
photography, 11, 64, 187–201,
physical exercises, 83
physical gestures, 62, 65, 79, 256,
physical phenomena, 5, 10, 30, 43–4, 46, 49, 64–6, 70, 73n17, 79, 97–8, 100, 117–8, 121, 127, 155, 191, 195, 223, 260
physiology, body, 98, 117, 156

Pietism, 128, 131–132
playthings, 11, 178
political attitudes, 79
political critique, 79
political stance, 83
politics and emotions, 77, 90, 99, 137
posture, 78, 80, 83, 187, 188–190, 194–196, 198, 235, 241
Potsdam, 204
power, 1, 8, 10, 26, 31, 33, 35, 42, 50, 51, 53, 55, 77, 78, 80, 97, 104, 105, 115, 117, 144, 149, 150, 151, 171, 174, 192, 203, 204, 212, 213, 226, 227, 237–239, 244, 249, 252, 256, 257, 258
Practice Theory, 129, 191–192, 254
  and anti-Semitism, 9–10, 96, 102, 104, 105
preverbal feelings. See under feelings
Prince William, 203–204
proletariat, 83
proletarian, 80, 85, 88, 89, 91
psychology, 2, 3, 17fn44, 66, 78, 83, 127, 128, 129, 138fn14, 143, 151
  body, 2, 3, 143
  money, 151
Pyrmont spa, 156–159, 163n7, 163n10

Queen Victoria, 209
Querner, Curt, 77, 81, 83, 85
Querner, Agitator (1931), 81
Quietism, 131–132

Rabelais, Francois, 116–117, 122–123
rapport, 25, 31–32, 34, 38n33
Reichardt, Herr (case of), 26, 28–31, 32–34, 35, 37fn14
Reinisch, Marion, 85
religion, 1, 70, 99, 122, 128, 130, 131, 132, 176, 178
  Pietism, 128, 131–132
  Quietism, 131–132
Rhineland, 10, 143
Rilke, Rainer Maria, 9, 12, 62–63, 64, 66, 67–69, 70, 74fn30, 74fn31, 235–239, 241–249
  Die Aufzeichnungen des Malte Laurids Brigge (The Notebooks of Malte Laurids Brigge), 9, 62–63, 64, 66,

Index ~ 275

67–69, 70, 74fn30, 74fn31, 235–239, 241–249
Rodin, Auguste, 64, 68, 238
Rosenwein, Barbara, 2, 14fn5, 93fn23, 98, 104, 107fn14, 109fn34, 112, 123, 125fn32, 126, 222
Das Rote Sprachrohr, Red Megaphone, journal, 77, 88, 89
Rousseau, Jean Jacques, 16fn23, 18, 127, 172–173, 176
  Émile, 172
Ruhe. See under calmness
Rühle, Otto, 80, 81

Sabean, David, 3–4
Sala, George, 145–146
Scheer, Monique, 4, 100, 104, 116, 117, 129, 137fn1, 191, 187, 254
Schelling, Friedrich Wilhelm Joseph, 177
Schreiber, Hippolyt, 159, 164fn18, 164fn24
senses, 30, 31, 32, 98, 100, 146, 150, 172, 173, 178
sentiment, 2, 17fn43, 90, 136, 150, 200fn10, 202, 204, 205, 232fn16
sentimentalism (*Empfindsamkeit*), 89, 127, 132–133, '135–136, 139fn30, 204, 208
  critique of, 132–133
  and theatrical gestures, 133
serenity (*Heiterkeit*), 10, 11, 156, 158, 159, 160, 161
shame, 10, 126, 128–132, 134–135, 137, 155
Silberman, Marc, 79
Simmel, Georg, 128, 142, 143, 148–149
  on *blasé attitude*, 148
  on gambling, 148, 150
  Philosophy of Money, 148–149, 151
  on sociability, 143
singing, 89, 176, 222–223, 230, 256
six nonnatural things, 157, 158, 160
Smith, Adam, 132, 135–136, 137fn5
  and concept of sympathy, 132, 135–136, 137fn5
social, 1, 2, 3, 9–12, 26, 43, 50, 55, 62–64, 69, 70, 77, 79, 83, 89–91, 96, 97, 100, 115–117, 118–119, 120–122, 127–128, 129–130, 131–132, 134–135, 136, 142, 143, 149, 150, 157, 160, 173, 178–180, 190, 192, 194, 197, 198, 203, 204, 205, 206, 208, 209, 212–214, 223, 230, 238, 253, 254
  movements, 77, 89–91, 205
  structures, 79, 104
solemn, 158, 228
songs, 12, 80, 89, 132, 176, 177, 178, 212, 224, 225, 227–228, 229, 256
Sørensen, Tim Flohr, 16fn21, 158, 162fn2, 181fn2, 183fn44, 223, 225, 232fn13
Soviet Union, 78, 73, 83
  and behaviorist psychology, 78
space, 1–3, 8, 10, 11, 25, 31, 63, 66–68, 70–71, 72fn12, 79–80, 102, 105, 116–119, 120–122, 124fn15, 149–150, 158, 161, 162fn2, 187–194, 198, 202, 205, 222–223, 225–226, 228, 230, 239, 242, 245, 251–253, 256, 260
  and casino, 149–150
  and spa, 161
space, everyday sites for anti-Semitism, 102, 105
space, sites for laughter, 10, 116–119, 120–122, 124fn15
spas, as material objects, spa guides, spa literature (*Brunnenschriften*), 10, 154–162
SPD, Social Democratic Party of Germany, 9, 77, 79, 88, 89, 206, 209
speech, 2, 80, 173, 222
Spielerglück (Gambler's Luck), 144
sports, 161, 230
steadfastness/steadiness (as opposed to adaptability), 79, 216fn28
storytelling, 62–64, 71
Strasbourg, 44–45, 119, 120
Suvin, Darko, 78–79
Sympathie, 32
sympathy, 32–33, 132, 135–136, 137fn5, 177, 178, 204, 211
sympathy, Adam Smith, 132, 135–136, 137fn5

Toller, Ernst, 85
toys, 11, 177, 178, 209

theory of the auratic object, 238
things, 2, 4–6, 8, 11, 25, 32, 49, 52, 64, 71–72, 104, 133, 142–143, 148–149, 152, 155, 157, 160, 171, 174, 178, 191, 194, 223, 230, 235, 237–238, 247, 250fn8, 252
thingliness, 2, 8
thing theory, 142, 191
touch, 6, 31, 3–34, 38fn18, 50, 63, 66, 159, 174–175, 190–192, 194–196, 198, 245

Uhland, Ludwig, 224

Valentine's Day, 202, 203, 211, 213
Vallentin, Maxim, 88–89, 94
Vienna, 25, 44, 49, 224, 225–227, 231n12
Vischer, Friedrich Theodor, 5, 6
visual history testimonies, 96, 97, 101
Voltaire, 42

Wangenheim, Gustav von, 89
Warburg, Aby, 3, 14fn9, 70, 88
Wehnert-Beckmann, Bertha, 187, 189, 192–193, 195, 196–198, 199n3, 199n7, 200n22
Weidt, Jean, 77, 85–86, 88, 92n15
Weimar Republic
Wiesbaden, 143, 146, 164n17
Wilhelm I, 204, 205, 210, 216fn28
Wohlgemuth, Gustav, 228
Wollstonecraft, Mary, 173, 211
working class, 4, 77, 80, 83, 85, 88–90
World War I, 99–100, 101, 211, 228, 255–257, 261
    mourning and commemoration, 211, 228, 255–257, 261
Wundt, Wilhelm, 64–65, 66, 73n16, 73n17
    and affect, 64–65

Zeller, Magnus, 75, 84
Zelter, Carl Friedrich, 224–225

www.ingramcontent.com/pod-product-compliance
Lightning Source LLC
Chambersburg PA
CBHW072047110526
44590CB00018B/3071